BOOKS THAT CHANGED
THE WORLD

BOOKS THAT CHANGED THE WORLD

SECOND EDITION

ROBERT B. DOWNS

American Library Association

Chicago 1978

Library of Congress Cataloging in Publication Data

Downs, Robert Bingham, 1903-
    Books that changed the world.

    Bibliography: p.
    1. Civilization, Occidental—Addresses, essays, lectures. 2. Books and reading—Addresses, essays, lectures. 3. Literature—History and criticism—Addresses, essays, lectures. I. Title.

CB245.D67   1978   001.3   78-13371

ISBN 0-8389-0270-7

Copyright © 1956, 1961, 1964, 1970, 1978 by the American Library Association

Printed in the United States of America

CONTENTS

Contents

PREFACE

Chapters in the present work relating to pre-Renaissance writers have been carried over, in revised and modified form, from my *Famous Books Ancient and Medieval*, originally published by Barnes & Noble in 1964. The chapters dealing with Mary Wollstonecraft, Andreas Vesalius, and Edward Jenner appeared originally in *Molders of the Modern Mind* (Barnes & Noble, 1961). The chapter on Rachel Carson's *Silent Spring* is reprinted by permission of the Macmillan Company from *Books That Changed America* (1970). The remaining titles are retained from the first edition of *Books That Changed the World* (American Library Association and New American Library, 1956).

Two longtime associates prepared the manuscript for publication: Clarabelle Gunning and Deloris Holiman. Their assistance was indispensable, as it has often been in the past.

IDEAS IN THE FLOW OF CIVILIZATION

The scope of the first edition of *Books That Changed the World* was limited to a four-hundred-year period, the sixteenth century to the twentieth. Obviously the roots of modern civilization precede that era by thousands of years, and a true understanding of our own culture must be based upon knowledge of the ancient and medieval world.

The thesis of the present work is that certain books have exerted a profound influence on history, culture, civilization, and scientific thought throughout recorded time. The principal aim, therefore, has been to discover and to analyze two categories of writings: first, those that were direct, immediate instruments in determining the course of events, and second, works that have molded the minds over centuries of time, slower in their effect than the first, but sometimes penetrating more deeply. In every historical era, we find overwhelming evidences of the power of the written word, without which a high state of civilization and culture is inconceivable in any time or place.

The beginnings of history are lost in the mists of antiquity. Although in part the earliest stages can be painfully and laboriously reconstructed by the sciences of paleontology and archeology, much, in the nature of things, is irretrievably lost. Not until the evolution of writing—the pictograph, hieroglyph, ideogram, and, ultimately, the alphabet—did adequate records of the race begin to emerge. Even these records, however, present serious dilemmas, including the difficulty of deciphering ancient inscriptions and the partial or complete disappearance, by human design or natural attrition, of many chronicles of the past. For the first several millennia of recorded history, far more has vanished than has been preserved.

Nevertheless, through artifacts and monuments, cuneiform and hieroglypic writings on stone, clay, and papyrus, historians have been able to put together in reasonably accurate and authentic fashion a picture of Sumerian, Babylonian, Egyptian, Hittite, Phoenician, Assyrian, and other civilizations stretching back into remote time, probably no less than seven thousand years. Furthermore, every great culture of the ancient world is intimately and inextricably related to the rest, due to the migrations of peoples, military conquests, trade and similar economic factors, and the widespread dissemination of the written word.

In writing ancient history, the fashion formerly prevailing of dividing the whole era into two neat packages, Greek and Roman, is passé. There is, instead, general recognition that every civilization has deep roots in the past, that none existed in a vacuum, and that for full understanding the history of the ancient age must be studied as a unit. As presently defined, the scope of ancient history covers the entire spectrum from the rise of the earliest civilizations in the Near, Middle, and Far East to the collapse of the Roman Empire in the West, early in the Christian Era.

On the other hand, though conceding that the remarkable Greek and Roman peaks hardly sprang full-grown without antecedents as did Athena from the brow of Zeus, one must recognize that the literary productivity of Athens and that of Rome are unparalleled among peoples of the classical period. There is nothing elsewhere remotely comparable in extent, variety, and significance to the writings that poured out of these two dynamic centers of antiquity at their height.

For this reason primarily, Western civilization has been formed by the merger of the two mighty currents, the Greek and the Roman. Numerous subsidiary streams have flowed into the great river, but their contributions are secondary to those of the Hellenic and Latin worlds. It is, in fact, a virtual impossibility to discover a modern philosophical concept, a social or political theory, a literary form, or a scientific idea not foreshadowed and often fully developed in the writings, first of the Greeks, and subsequently of Roman authors who emulated them.

An exception is the field of religion. The predominant religions of modern times—Judaism, Christianity, Islam, Buddhism, Confucianism, Hinduism—owe little to the mythologies and superstitions of Greece and Rome. To the first three the Babylonian tributary was important. There is, for example, a close resemblance between Babylonian stories of the creation and those narrated in the first chapter of Genesis, and some other parts of the Babylonian mythology are incorporated in the great literatures of the Christian world. From the Egyptian Book of the

Dead, one of the oldest written works extant, comes an advanced code for ethical conduct, in its essentials later embodied in the principal religions of the West. Many of the laws formulated by Hammurabi found their way into the Mosaic and other ancient codes of law.

The Greek people first began to play an important part in world affairs about the seventh century B.C. The period during which Athens achieved a supreme place in the intellectual history of the world was amazingly brief. From Hesiod in the eighth century B.C., the first clearly identifiable Greek author, to Archimedes in the third century, scarcely five hundred years elapsed. The supreme interlude, the golden age in which virtually all the notable names of Athenian literature, philosophy, history, art, and science are concentrated, is even shorter, spanning the years from the birth of Aeschylus (525 B.C.) to the death of Aristotle (322 B.C.).

Insofar as surviving examples can testify, the literature of Greece was in a high state of perfection from its birth. In the mid-ninth century B.C., Homer, thoroughly immersed in the epic traditions of his people, added his own poetic genius and produced two of the world's literary masterpieces, the *Iliad* and the *Odyssey*. When and where Homer lived the ancients did not know; according to one theory he was two men, a century apart in time. In any event, Homer's epic creations, centering on the Trojan War, established for all time the greatness of Greek literature.

Thus begins an incomparable parade of poets, dramatists, and storytellers: Hesiod, Aesop, Aeschylus, Pindar, Sophocles, Euripides, Aristophanes, and Menander; of such statesmen as Solon and Pericles; of the historians Herodotus, Thucydides, Xenophon, and Polybius; of the master orators Demosthenes and Isocrates; of men of science Hippocrates, Theophrastus, Euclid, and Archimedes; and finally two supreme geniuses whose minds encompassed all knowledge, Plato and Aristotle. Modern thinkers, striking out alone on what they believe are untrodden paths, are rendered humble by the discovery, sooner or later, that some ancient Greek has preceded them on the same journey.

The fall of Athens in 404 B.C., at the end of the long-drawn-out Peloponnesian War, and the disastrous Sicilian expedition, followed by an extended period of military adventures on various fronts, left the Athenians in an exhausted state from which they failed to recover. The spirit of the Classic Age could never be recaptured. The great days of Attic tragedy and comedy were over, and the new literature of oratory, history, and philosophy was profoundly different. It was during this era, the fourth century B.C., however, that Plato and Aristotle attained the most superlative triumphs of Greek thought. Also notable were the advances in science and mathematics in the fourth and third centuries accomplished by Euclid, Archimedes, Theophrastus, and their contemporaries.

The torch dropped by the Greeks was picked up by the Romans, whose culture was in many respects derivative, but whose own peculiar genius made contributions of permanent significance in political science, law, military tactics, history and biography, belles lettres, and science. Rome accomplished successfully what the Greeks had failed to do; she united the ancient world into one vast empire, in which peoples of all races and nations could live and prosper side by side with their Roman conquerors.

Greek influences pervaded numerous aspects of Roman civilization. The models for the two leading Roman playwrights, Plautus and Terence, were the Greek comedies of Menander; Cicero's orations, philosophical treatises, and writings on political theory drew heavily on Demosthenes, Plato, and Aristotle; Julius Caesar learned primary lessons of military tactics from Xenophon's *Anabasis;* Vergil's *Aeneid* was inspired by Homer's *Odyssey,* Horace's odes by Pindar; the Roman historians emulated Herodotus and Thucydides; Galen admitted his indebtedness to Hippocrates in laying the foundation of medical science down to the sixteenth century; and Pliny the Elder's *Natural History* relied extensively upon Aristotle's *History of Animals.*

Rome's law was more authentically Roman than her literature, and in this area she made one of her most enduring contributions to the Western world. The Roman jurists became acquainted with various systems of foreign law from the time of Hammurabi onward. Gradually, the Roman law itself took on a universal character, and its systematization and codification under Justinian in the sixth century A.D. established its place as a permanent landmark in legal history and practice.

Historical writing in Rome was heavily slanted toward the biographical. Plutarch, a Greek who lived and taught for some years in Rome, helped to set the style with his *Parallel Lives of*

Greeks and Romans. Adding to the many graphic portraits of Romans, famous and infamous, are Sallust, Livy, Tacitus, and Suetonius. They fixed for us our images of the emperors Nero, Claudius, Augustus, Caligula, Tiberius, and Domitian.

When did the classical civilization end and the Middle Ages begin? The date has long been a matter of dispute among historians. The time is popularly held to coincide with the decline and fall of the Roman Empire, but that event cannot be precisely dated. Actually, an age of transition, lasting for centuries, makes timing a purely arbitrary matter.

The one salient factor that distinguished the ancient from the medieval world was the coming of Christianity. Whether Christianity was the prime cause of Rome's fall, as Gibbon charges, is debatable; unquestionably other elements were involved. But nothing was ever the same again after the emergence of the new faith. Several centuries, however, elapsed before Christianity had firmly rooted itself in the West.

Whether the medieval centuries deserve the epithet "the Dark Ages" has also divided scholarly opinion. Even Gibbon's hostility is tempered, for he concedes that "the authority of the priests operated in the darker ages as a salutary antidote: they prevented the total extinction of letters, mitigated the fierceness of the times, sheltered the poor and defenceless, and preserved or revived the peace and order of civil society." Throughout the Middle Ages, the Church was nearly the sole custodian of such classical learning and literature as survived the assaults of the barbarians. Monasticism was the one refuge of scholars who desired to escape from the chaotic world around them. Books were preserved for the exclusive use of the clergy. Elsewhere mass illiteracy prevailed. Except for the efforts of the Church and its institutions, there would have been no remnants of classical learning for the Renaissance scholars of the fifteenth and sixteenth centuries to have revived.

Among literary immortals a few names stand out: Dante Alighieri, Francesco Petrarch, Giovanni Boccaccio, and Geoffrey Chaucer. In government and political science, John of Salisbury's *The Statesman's Book*, in defense of the divine right of kings, exerted a far-reaching influence, though of far more permanent significance was the great charter of English liberties, the Magna Carta. Another secular work, Marco Polo's *Travels*, opened a wide new world to provincial-minded Europe.

Until recently, historians regarded the period of the Renaissance as the first chapter of modern history, marking the rebirth of humanism and a revolt against the authoritarianism, aesceticism, and submergence of the individual characteristic of the medieval era. As research on the preceding millennium has proceeded, however, the break between the Middle Ages and the Renaissance has appeared less decisive. Scholars now generally recognize that the great intellectual and cultural flowering of Europe starting in the mid-fifteenth century did not spring forth full-grown, but was a natural evolution from the late Middle Ages.

Nevertheless, the amazing growth in cultural progress during the era known as the Renaissance represents in many of its aspects a new day in the life of the Western world. Nowhere are the changes better exemplified than in the field of book production. Before Gutenberg's invention of movable type in Germany, dated approximately 1450, books were handwritten. Forty-five copyists working for two years under Cosimo de Medici are reported to have produced only two hundred volumes. In striking contrast to the painfully slow, inaccurate manuscript method, during the first half-century after the invention of printing there appeared in Europe approximately ten million books, comprising forty thousand titles, with hundreds of printers busily turning out new works. The accelerated multiplication of books made possible an equally rapid spread of knowledge. Without printing, the wide dissemination of Greek, Latin, and other classical writings so closely identified with the Renaissance would have been impossible.

The intellectual awakening, accompanied by the rise of universities and remarkable developments in art and architecture, produced an unsettling of traditional beliefs, a questioning of religious institutions, and, on occasion, a reversion to almost pure paganism. The road was being paved for the cataclysm of the Protestant Reformation and momentous succeeding events.

Sir Thomas More's *Utopia* reflects the early sixteenth-century preoccupation with geographical discovery. Like Erasmus, More opposed the abuses and superstitions prevailing among the contemporary clergy, though he, too, feared the disruptive effects of religious controversy. More, like Erasmus a great humanist, presented the utopian ideal: a perfect society in which men might be happy, tolerant, and well adjusted throughout their earthly existence.

Four years before Luther nailed his ninety-five theses to the door of the Wittenberg church, Machiavelli had written, "Whoever examines the principles upon which that religion [Christianity] is founded, and sees how widely different from these principles its present practice and application are, will judge that her ruin or chastisement is near at hand." A generation later, Roman Catholicism had lost half of Europe to the Protestant Reformation.

The underlying causes of the Reformation were complex, and historians have differed in their interpretations. Some have pictured it as a revolt against medieval tyranny and superstition. Political forces unquestionably played a major role, as the emerging nations of Europe inevitably clashed with the secular powers of the Church. In effect, the economic and political interests of the Church as an international state collided with those of the new national states. The chief appeal of Luther's *Address to the Christian Nobility of the German Nation*, it may be noted, stemmed from his arguments supporting the independence of civil power.

The rising tide of nationalism in the sixteenth and seventeenth centuries inspired numerous other political theorists, notably Niccolò Machiavelli in Italy, Jean Bodin in France, Hugo Grotius in Holland, and Thomas Hobbes and John Locke in England. Each of these five eminent political philosophers has, in turn, provided the stimulus for a large library of critical comment.

Sinister connotations, probably undeserved, have grown up around the name of Machiavelli. His *The Prince* was a brutally realistic portrayal of the cruel, corrupt politics of the Renaissance, especially as practiced in Italy. The realities did not coincide with Machiavelli's personal convictions and ideals, for he believed in republican government; the people, he thought, could more safely be entrusted with power than a dictator or oligarchy. In writing *The Prince*, Machiavelli was motivated entirely by his passionate devotion to the city-state of Florence and by his ultimate dream of a unified Italy—realized several centuries later by Mazzini and Cavour.

Hobbes reinforced his arguments for absolutism by means of the social contract theory, a prime premise among political scientists up to the French Revolution. As Hobbes interpreted the theory, all civil authority, resting originally in the people, had been bestowed by them on the ruler in order that he might perform certain necessary functions. The only reservation made by Hobbes in his *Leviathan* to the dictum that the individual owes complete, unquestioned obedience to the sovereign applied to the contingency of the state's becoming so disorderly that life was made insecure, in which event the individual would have the right to protect his own life and security in any way possible.

The apologists for monarchical absolutists did not go unchallenged. John Milton's *Areopagitica* presented the basic arguments for freedom of expression. Later, Locke's *Two Treatises of Civil Government* justified the Revolution of 1688 in England and provided arguments in the eighteenth century for the American and French revolutions. Locke not only refuted the doctrine of absolute monarchy but also believed that government is responsible both to the people and to the moral law of Nature.

The Renaissance was essentially a revival of the humanities. In educated circles the natural sciences were largely ignored or scorned. The Reformation was marked by a still more direct and aggressive hostility to the scientific spirit. Poets and painters far outnumbered great scientific names between 1500 and 1690. Nevertheless, the resurrection of classical learning represented by the Renaissance and the questioning of established beliefs inevitably accompanying the Reformation created an intellectual climate favorable to science. The works of Archimedes, Aristarchus, Hippocrates, Galen, Euclid, Ptolemy, and other ancients enabled early modern scientists to take up where like-minded men had left off centuries before. The new advance of science ignored national boundaries. Of the five geniuses who laid the foundations for modern astronomy, Copernicus was a Pole, Brahe a Dane, Kepler a German, Galileo an Italian, and Newton an Englishman.

By common agreement, modern science dates its birth from the publication of Copernicus' epochal *Concerning the Revolutions of the Heavenly Spheres,* in which the earth and the planets were conceived as revolving around the sun. The disturbing effect of the theory upon man's faith and philosophy can scarcely be overestimated. In the same year (1543) was published Vesalius' *The Structure of the Human Body,* equally revolutionary in its field and likewise indicative of a new spirit in scientific investigation. There followed in succession Brahe's accumulation of an immense body of astronomical data, systematically collected over a period of years; Kepler's formulation of three laws of the solar system, based upon Brahe's observations; Galileo's invention of the telescope and fundamental discoveries in dynamics and mechanics; and the work of the most universal genius of all, Sir Isaac Newton's mathematical proof of the discovery and establishment of the physical law by which the whole universe is governed.

In other branches of scientific effort, Sir William Gilbert was describing and experimenting with magnets and magnetism; William Harvey was establishing modern experimental medicine through his discovery of the circulation of the blood; Robert Boyle's laboratory experiments were beginning to separate medieval alchemy from modern chemistry; and Robert Hooke and Anton van Leeuwenhoek were carrying on pioneer research in microscopy. Two other thinkers, Francis Bacon in England and René Descartes in France, were making theoretical rather than practical contributions to science through their emphasis on scientific method and research. Bacon's enthusiasm for planned experimentation and his proposal for a cooperative research institute had immense influence in bringing about the establishment of scientific societies and of scientific research as a recognized profession. Descartes' great historical achievement was his teaching that, through proper and systematic use of intelligence, divorced from myth, magic, and superstition, human beings could penetrate the most hidden secrets of the universe.

Thus did the Renaissance, the Reformation, and the rise of modern science set the stage for the century of Enlightenment and Reason to follow.

The Enlightenment, sometimes referred to as the Age of Reason—corresponding roughly to the eighteenth century in Europe, was a natural culmination of the Renaissance and of the scientific revolution. Opposition to theological modes of thought among the intellectual classes had become almost universal. Beginning about 1650, educated persons were dominated by two concepts: first, the remarkable advances in science had convinced them that all Nature could be reduced to a series of mathematical laws; and, second, they concluded that human beings, possessing an infallible method of acquiring truth, could achieve infinite progress through reason.

The additional necessity for tolerance was recognized by John Locke. From his point of view, it was no part of a government's function to save souls. Instead, its purpose was secular only, to preserve rights. A church he considered "a free and voluntary society." The true faith was most likely to prevail wherever toleration of all beliefs was an accepted principle.

Scientific progress vastly increased the faith of the men of the Enlightenment in Nature and reason. Notably, Newton's perfection of the calculus and his mathematical formulation of a "system of the world," showing the relationship of the planets to the laws of gravity, appeared to his contemporaries to explain, or at least to point the way to an explanation of, all natural phenomena. Instead of a dark, malevolent power to be feared and placated, as in earlier eras, Nature was considered a benign concept in the Enlightenment. The working of the universe was seen to be orderly and simple. If the same principles operative in Nature could be applied to human affairs, humankind's happiness would be assured. Such "unnatural" social phenomena as class distinctions, special privileges of clergy and royalty, and the distressing contrast between the rich and the poor would disappear.

The understanding of Nature and of its bearing on human behavior, according to the Enlightenment, could be achieved through Reason, represented in its purest form by the science of mathematics. Reason enabled men and women to differentiate between "natural" and "unnatural" human institutions and thus to eliminate error, injustice, and superstitions. A dominant theme running throughout the Enlightenment, consequently, was the desire to extend to individuals and society the methods and laws of the natural scientists. Reason, if logically followed, it was believed, was opposed to tradition, authority, and revelation. Voltaire called it "the light of common sense."

Growing out of their unlimited confidence in the omnipotence of controlled Nature and science was the somewhat naive faith in progress universally held by the *philosophes* of the Enlightenment. With no distrust of human nature or of machine technology, there was an almost mystical trust in the future, and solutions were believed imminent for all the great political and social problems inherited from the past.

Inevitably the new concepts of science and reason began to be applied to theories of government. The medieval notion of the divine right of kings could not bear close scrutiny in the atmosphere created by science. Existing governments, therefore, could only be defended if they met the tests of Nature and Reason.

In England, a solution was found in constitutional reform,

whereby, in the Bill of Rights of 1689, the Parliament assumed the powers of the monarch, though without abolishing the monarchy as an institution. The chief apologist and philosopher of the movement, John Locke, proclaimed in his second *Treatise on Civil Government*, published the next year, the "social contract" or natural rights theory of government. In essence, the theory held that governments are based on contract and that whenever a tyrannical ruler infringes upon the natural and inalienable rights of his people, revolution is the appropriate remedy.

Revolution, in its most violent form, was required to achieve reform in France, whose Bourbon kings, like the Hapsburg, "never learned anything nor forgot anything." Four names stand out among the writers whose theories provided the philosophical foundation for one of the most far-reaching upheavals in history: Montesquieu, Rousseau, Voltaire, and Diderot.

A theorist who exerted far more direct and profound influence on the character of the French Revolution was Jean Jacques Rousseau. His *The Social Contract* preached two radically new doctrines: the sovereignty of the people and the sacredness of the General Will. A social and political structure built upon the will of a majority of the people, he held, would insure equality, freedom, and harmony for all. The concept of government based on majority decisions has, of course, enormous historical significance because of its subsequent adoption throughout the world, even though usually with constitutional restrictions.

A contrast to Rousseau, the idol of the masses, was Voltaire, the darling of the intellectuals. Even in his own lifetime, Voltaire became a legend, a symbol of the struggle for freedom of thought. Three years in England, observing the British constitutional form of government in operation, strengthened his conviction of the importance of intellectual freedom and made him a propagandist for reason. A prolific output of plays, poems, satires, and articles won for Voltaire the spiritual leadership of the Enlightenment. By open attacks on religious superstition and political tyranny, he contributed immensely to undermining the old regime in France. From the eighteenth century to the present day, Voltaire has loomed as a heroic figure in the endless fight for civil liberty and toleration.

While lacking the color and fire of their French contemporaries, eighteenth-century observers of the social scene elsewhere were also composing works destined to leave permanent impressions on the modern mind. William Blackstone's *Commentaries on the Laws of England* presented the first systematic and definitive compilation of British statutes and common law principles, a work which has remained for over two centuries one of the legal world's primary sources. A few years later, Adam Smith's *The Wealth of Nations* appeared, influencing generations of economists and laying the foundation for the faith in natural liberty and in a laissez faire system of economics which became England's guiding creed. In America, Thomas Paine's *Common Sense*, Thomas Jefferson's *A Summary View of the Rights of British America*, and the *Declaration of Independence* were igniting revolutionary fires.

In summary, the philosophers and thinkers of the Enlightenment hardly foresaw or wished for a revolution, but their caustic criticism of existing conditions and their urgent insistence upon social betterment were undoubtedly instrumental in creating revolutionary sentiment. Their hopes and dreams were only partially realized by reforms that grew out of the French Revolution. Nevertheless, the ferment of the Enlightenment left a permanent imprint upon the Western world. Among peoples everywhere, the desire for national independence, for constitutional government, and for personal liberty had been firmly implanted. In the New World, especially, liberal ideas were free to develop with few restrictions. The Age of Reason may be justly said to have reawakened faith in the destiny of man.

The thinkers of the Enlightenment prepared the ground for the French Revolution. Absolute monarchy and the special privileges enjoyed by the clergy and the nobility were their prime targets. By action of the relatively moderate National Assembly from 1789 to 1791, the king's powers were strictly circumscribed and all privileges of an economic and political nature were abolished.

The lasting consequences of the French Revolution were many. Still under the spell of the Enlightenment, the whole fabric of law, economics, politics, education, religion, and society in general underwent basic modification in France, with shock waves felt throughout Europe and America. The results of the Revolution may be summarized under three headings:

1. *The ending of feudalism, accompanied by the rising dominance of the middle class.* Such vestiges of the past had vanished as privileged groups, inequality before the law, and oppressive religious intolerance.

2. *The principle of majority rule.* Solidly established now was Rousseau's doctrine of the sovereignty of the people and the rule of the majority, leading logically as it developed to the concept of universal suffrage.

3. *Nationalism.* Originally, the Enlightenment had advocated an international brotherhood. Opposition to the Revolution among other European powers, however, brought an almost hysterical upsurge of nationalism in France. The Napoleonic wars stimulated similar sentiment among the nations opposing the French armies. Thus was immensely strengthened one of the most powerful forces affecting world history of the past two centuries.

The period following the French Revolution is sometimes referred to as the bourgeois century. The middle class was riding the crest of the wave, and the culture, economics, and government of the age reflected the values of that class. Even Karl Marx, bitterly opposed to bourgeois civilization, had to pay grudging tribute to its accomplishments. In the *Communist Manifesto* of 1848, he and Friedrich Engels conceded that "the bourgeoisie, during its rule of scarce one hundred years, has created more massive and more colossal productive forces than have all preceding generations together."

The new middle-class capitalists and manufacturers took readily to Adam Smith's laissez-faire doctrines, determined to follow policies of extreme individualism and to resist governmental control or regulation. Their opposition to any form of labor organization was equally vigorous. Free competition and the law of supply and demand, it was argued, would result in the highest wages industry could afford. Under this system, each person would struggle for what he or she wanted and receive as much as was merited. The end result would be "the greatest good for the greatest number." The state's sole functions should be to maintain peace, enforce contracts, and protect individuals in their property rights.

Further justification for industrial practices was found in Thomas Malthus' population theories. Europe's population had doubled in a short term of years, a fact which led Malthus to conclude that human beings multiply at a geometrical rate, while the food supply could be increased only in arithmetical progression. Consequently, wage increases and charity were mistakes, and the constant threat of starvation was essential to keep the world's population in balance. The Malthusian theory has had a prolonged influence upon economic, political, and social thought, as lively today as when first set forth 180 years ago.

In other areas, the esthetic sensibilities of the art critic John Ruskin were offended by the ugliness and overstandardization of nineteenth-century culture. The inequality of man and the misery of the masses were favorite themes of other influential writers. The long fight for the emancipation of women from medieval servitude was measurably advanced by Mary Wollstonecraft's polemic, *Vindication of the Rights of Women.*

Political and social experimentation likewise proceeded apace in America. The process of hammering out a national constitution, described by Hamilton, Madison, and Jay in *The Federalist,* had been successfully completed. Forty-seven years later, its operation and that of the American political system were brilliantly analyzed by a young and perceptive Frenchman, Alexis de Tocqueville, in his *Democracy in America.*

But there was a cancer at the heart of the new republic—the institution of human slavery. Attempts to deal with the issue at the time the United States Constitution was written had failed. Controversy over slavery mounted steadily in the first half of the nineteenth century. In his *Resistance to Civil Government,* Henry David Thoreau offered a drastic proposal—civil disobedience and refusal to pay taxes—as a means of forcing an end to the evil. Shortly afterward, Harriet Beecher Stowe's *Uncle Tom's Cabin* ignited a fuse that could lead to but one thing: civil war.

The march of scientific progress continued uninterrupted throughout the period. Astronomy had dominated the thinking of scientists in the sixteenth and seventeenth centuries, and the eighteenth was outstanding for pioneer investigations in chemistry. Important beginnings had also been made earlier in biological research, notably by Vesalius, Harvey, Leeuwenhoek, Linnaeus, Buffon, Cuvier, Lamarck, and others. But it is the nineteenth century that may properly be entitled the Age of Biology, especially if the term is interpreted broadly to include medicine. A field closely related to biology in many of its aspects, geology, also came of age and firmly established itself as a major science.

Among the distinguished biologists of the nineteenth century, Charles Darwin unquestionably ranks first. For several generations a long line of workers had been developing the idea for which Darwin is most celebrated, the theory of organic evolution. It was Darwin's masterly achievement to bring the mass of facts and theories derived from studies by himself and others into a coherent whole. Seeking an explanation of why some species survive and others perish, Darwin formulated the principle of natural selection, theorizing that those that were best adapted to live in their particular natural environment would survive and perpetuate themselves. Evolution occurred chiefly, it was held, through minute variations among individuals.

Though Darwin conceded that man is evolution's major triumph, the theory still made man a descendant from lower forms and a member of the animal kingdom. Inevitably, therefore, the Darwinian hypothesis was an object of bitter theological attack, on the grounds that it contradicted the Bible and degraded man. Nevertheless, with the enthusiastic support of such aggressive and able advocates as Thomas Huxley and Herbert Spencer, the general concept of evolutionary progress rapidly invaded all fields of thought.

Medical science was also making phenomenal advances. After the work of William Harvey in the seventeenth century, the next great landmarks were Edward Jenner's discovery, in 1796, of vaccination as a preventive of smallpox, and Louis Pasteur's development of the germ theory in the mid-nineteenth century. Subsequently, the British surgeon Joseph Lister applied Pasteur's bacterial discoveries to antiseptic surgery, with remarkable success, and Robert Koch in Germany used them as a basis for pioneer researches in preventive medicine.

Numerous forces and movements have reshaped the world since 1750, and any attempt to summarize them necessarily tends toward oversimplification. There would be general agreement, however, on several factors as most characteristic and influential for the period here under consideration. First, the Industrial Revolution transformed the economic and social system. Second, liberal ideas spread, accompanied by a trend toward greater democracy and universal education. Third, a spirit of nationalism pervaded the Western world, with almost incalculable consequences, good and bad. Fourth, there occurred a reaction from the extreme individualism of the Enlightenment and of the revolutionary era, but at the same time there was a growth of social consciousness. Finally, continued faith in the idea of progress led to constant stress on scientific research and on the practical applications of science to human affairs. By the end of the era, virtually all the elements that were to mold the twentieth century were present, at least in embryo form.

The tempo of change in the past one hundred years has constantly accelerated. Unquestionably, the principal factor in the rate at which the modern world has been transformed is the growth of science and technology. It is startling to realize that since 1870 there have come into existence such commonplaces of contemporary life as the electric light, the telephone, the automobile, the airplane, wireless telegraphy, radio broadcasting, moving pictures, and television.

The ominous aspect of this transformation is that man has perfected weapons potentially capable, within the space of a few hours, of wiping all human life from the earth. Due to the march of technology, supersonic planes, flying at several times the speed of sound and only recently regarded as the ultimate in military aircraft, are already obsolete. The atomic bombs which in 1945 virtually erased two Japanese cities from the map have been replaced by infinitely more devastating intercontinental ballistic missiles armed with hydrogen warheads.

The anxieties of the nineteenth century were as nothing contrasted to those of the twentieth. Two world wars, by far the most catastrophic in history, decimated populations and devastated immense areas. Half the world's peoples came under the absolute control of totalitarian governments, powerful, ruthless, and unscrupulous. Individualism, in which eighteenth- and early-nineteenth-century philosophers had placed unlimited faith, began to lose ground to collectivism, while idealism was abandoned for materialism. Even in democracies, big government, big business, and big labor reduced the individual to relative insignificance.

Another badly battered concept, cherished by liberals of the preceding age, was that of harmony between individuals and their countries. An extraordinary diversity of thought militated against genuine unity. The situation is well illustrated by a comparison of the doctrines of the three most popular and influential social philosophers of the nineteenth century: Auguste Comte, Herbert Spencer, and Karl Marx. Each advocated a social program radically at variance with the others. Comte was dedicated to the enlightened despotism of the older order; Spencer preached a businessman's individualism, a return to laissez-faire notions; and Marx was fanatically convinced that salvation could be gained only through industrial socialism.

As industrialization spread to more nations, business crises and depressions became frequent, and industrial competition raised both internal and international problems. Conflicts between employers and labor, recurring poverty and unemployment, trade wars, and the worldwide scramble for the control of raw materials were some of the earmarks of the times. The key dilemma was distribution; modern science had made possible the production of sufficient material things to feed and clothe the earth's inhabitants, but how could the wealth be effectively disseminated?

Karl Marx's *Das Kapital* maintained that these economic problems could be solved only by the abolition of the capitalist system. While approving science and technology, Marx condemned private ownership of the means of production as unjust, wasteful, and inefficient. He saw all history as basically a struggle between economic groups. An era of bourgeois capitalistic domination over a proletariat of wage earners would be ended, according to Marx, by a workers' revolution and the establishment of a collective or communist state. In his judgment, the proletarian revolution would occur first in the most highly industrialized nations, such as England and Germany, while Russia was least ripe for revolt, a prediction of course not borne out by subsequent events.

The spread of Marxism to Russia, China, and other vast areas, bringing an estimated one billion people under its sway, has posed urgent problems for the modern world. Actually, the present-day Soviet Union fulfills few of Marx's ideas and ideals for communism, though its leaders continue to pay lip service to Marxian dogma. Since the successful Bolshevist revolution of 1917, Russia has been shaped primarily by Lenin, Stalin, and most recently by Khrushchev. Of the three, Lenin easily rates first as party dialectician and theorist. In his *The State and Revolution* Lenin sets forth his views on the relationship of the proletarian revolution to the state, on the forthcoming Russian revolution, on the dictatorship of the proletariat, and on what would happen in communist society after the bourgeois states had been overthrown. *The State and Revolution* is one of the fundamental works in the body of Marxist ideology, but Lenin's greatest service to Marxism was as organizer of a successful revolution in a backward country.

Throughout the nineteenth and well into the twentieth century there was slowly developed a radically different philosophy of government, one which would, with the possible exception of communism, ultimately offer the most dangerous challenge to the continued existence of democracy. Known in later stages as fascism, its dark antecedents can be traced far back in political thought. The absolutism preached by Thomas Hobbes in the *Leviathan* is believed by some political scientists to have provided inspiration for twentieth-century Fascist and Communist totalitarians, and a number of dictators have boasted of their spiritual descent from Niccolò Machiavelli. More directly, especially in Germany, ideological bases for fascism were laid by such nineteenth-century philosophers as Johann Fichte, Georg Hegel, and Friedrich Nietzsche. Fichte's identification of the individual with the state, his support of national absolute sovereignty and self-sufficiency, and his inflated ideas of the importance of German culture justify including his name among the intellectual forebears of Nazism. Likewise, Hegel's political theory, as elaborated in *The Philosophy of Right*, contains all the essential ingredients of fascism: racialism, nationalism, the leadership principle, government by authority rather than consent, and the worship of power.

The quintessence of the Fascist dream—subsequently translated into a nightmare for the rest of the world—was Adolf Hitler's *Mein Kampf*. In this work, Hitler plainly revealed his intentions several years before he came to power in Germany and more than a decade prior to the beginning of World War II. The threats were ignored, partly because the book was available in unexpurgated form only in the German language and partly because of the prevailing atmosphere of appeasement, wishful thinking, and peace at any price.

An Englishman provided inspiration for Hitler's soaring ambitions. The writings of Sir Halford Mackinder, "father of geopolitics," as interpreted by Karl Haushofer, convinced Hitler that the vast expansion which he visualized for Germany should take place principally at the expense of Russia. Also appealing to Hitler was the idea of a widely spaced population, for "military-geographical" reasons, because it would be less vulnerable to an enemy—a prime feature of Mackinder's thesis in *The Geographical Pivot of History*.

Like Napoleon, Hitler fancied himself a great military commander. Though reportedly an avid reader of Karl von Clausewitz's *On War*, he failed to heed Clausewitz's warning to avoid Napoleon's fatal error in attempting a midwinter invasion of Russia. Hitler's obsession with submarine warfare and maritime might was doubtless a carryover from the theories of Admiral Mahan, whose *Influence of Sea Power upon History* had convinced pre–World War I statesmen that "whoever rules the waves rules the world."

In the public mind, the name that best represents the scientific revolution of the first half of the twentieth century is that of Albert Einstein. Less spectacular, but of profound significance for the human race, were the investigations of certain psychologists—Havelock Ellis, Sigmund Freud, and Ivan Petrovitch Pavlov—all trained originally in medicine.

Pavlov's most noteworthy contribution was the idea of conditioned reflexes, demonstrated through years of experiments on canine subjects. Symptoms like human neurosis, or even psychosis, could be produced in the laboratory animals by certain kinds of frustrations which induced mental confusion. Social scientists are in general agreement that the concept of conditioned reflexes developed by Pavlov goes far toward explaining habit formation in human beings and apparently irrational behavior of people under given sets of conditions.

Sigmund Freud has been characterized as one of the most complex figures in the intellectual history of the West, the subject of innumerable controversies. Whether supported or rejected, however, Freud has continued to exert a powerful influence not only on psychology and psychiatry, but on twentieth-century art, literature, biographical writing, and religious thought. In the medical field, the impact of his teachings has been felt particularly in the treatment of psychoneurotic personality disorders and in the coordination of information about psychological and bodily functions known as psychosomatic medicine.

It has not been feasible to discuss in detail in this book the varied works chosen. The original edition of *Books That Changed the World* included only sixteen titles—ten in the social sciences and six in the sciences. That number has been more than doubled here, if two or more books treated in one chapter are counted, and could easily be doubled again. At most, they are short summaries of the works, with some attempt at evaluation.

The critical problem in an undertaking like the present one is selection. Certain titles come readily to everyone's mind, after which individual choices vary widely. A majority are eliminated by application of the number-one criterion: the book must have had a great and continuing impact on human thought and action for a major segment of the world. When exposed to this acid test, only a small proportion survives.

It is of interest to note and to compare previous attempts to name the books of greatest influence. One such list was prepared for *Publishers Weekly* in 1935 by Edward Weeks, John Dewey, and Charles A. Beard. Each selected twenty-five books issued since 1885 which, in his opinion, had been most influential. The poll resulted in a final list of fifty titles, only four of which were unanimous choices, while twenty-nine titles received but a single vote.

A similar approach was used by Malcolm Cowley and Bernard Smith a few years later (1939) in their *Books That Changed Our Minds*. On the basis of a poll of American educators, historians, critics, lecturers, and publicists, a dozen titles came to the top as having had most weight, in the opinion of the group, in shaping the contemporary American mind, but a total of 134 different books were recommended by the various individuals consulted. Of the top dozen, Weeks, Dewey, and Beard had seen fit to include only four.

Another essay toward determining the most influential books was made by an English writer, Horace Shipp, in his *Books That Moved the World* (1945). Without any restrictions as to time, or place, or subjects, Shipp settled upon ten titles, starting with the Bible and including works by Plato, St. Augustine, Dante, Shakespeare, Bunyan, Milton, Darwin, and Marx.

Eric F. Goldman, writing in *Saturday Review* in 1953, on "Books That Changed America," looked for books that had had "a substantial role in changing America during a particular period," books which, appearing "at some critical juncture, caught a latent trend and by catching it with just the right nuance, whirled it ahead." Goldman came out with thirteen titles: Paine's *Common Sense*, *The Federalist*, Stowe's *Uncle Tom's*

Cabin, Spencer's *Study of Sociology*, George's *Progress and Poverty*, Sheldon's *In His Steps*, Freud's *Interpretation of Dreams*, Beard's *Economic Interpretation of the Constitution*, Keynes' *Economic Consequences of the Peace*, Dewey's *Human Nature and Conduct*, Lewis' *Babbitt*, Steffens' *Autobiography*, and Willkie's *One World*.

In 1964, again in *Saturday Review*, Rochelle Girson polled twenty-seven historians, economists, social scientists, and others to ascertain "what books during the preceding four decades had most significantly altered the direction of our society," and also ended with a list of thirteen titles.

Clearly, a unanimous verdict is difficult to achieve on any given book, and selection must remain personal and subjective. The important consideration, however, is that the fact of influence be widely recognized, although it may differ in kind from one work to another, and vary with the time, prevailing conditions, or field of concern. A legitimate question to ask is whether a specific book had an impact because the period was ripe for it. Would the work have been equally significant in another era, or could it even have been written at any other date? The evidence seems to show that, in most instances, the time produced the book, though it might remain historically meaningful long afterward.

Limiting examples to recent centuries, Machiavelli's *The Prince* was written for the express purpose of freeing his beloved Italy from foreign oppression. England was ready for a vast expansion of her commercial and industrial economy when Adam Smith was writing his *Wealth of Nations*. Thomas Paine's *Common Sense* triggered the American Revolution, already primed for explosion; and Harriet Beecher Stowe's *Uncle Tom's Cabin* did likewise for the Civil War. Except for dreadful conditions prevailing in European industry, especially the English factory system, in the mid-nineteenth century, Karl Marx would have lacked ammunition for *Das Kapital*. Inauguration of a naval race among world powers after 1890 was inspired by Admiral Mahan's *Influence of Sea Power upon History*, but the pressure for expansion and imperialistic adventure already existed. Adolf Hitler might well have remained an unknown Austrian house painter except for the chaos in Germany following World War I.

On the other hand, like slow fuses, there are books which did not make their full impact until years after their initial publication. Adam Smith and Karl Marx, to illustrate, were dead when the importance of their books was perceived. Thoreau had been gone half a century when his doctrine of civil disobedience was applied by Mahatma Gandhi in India and South Africa; and nearly a century when his ideas were applied by Martin Luther King and others to the antisegregation movement in the United States. Not until the rise of the German school of geopoliticians under Haushofer's direction did Mackinder's theories, formulated several decades earlier, receive the notice they deserved.

Also a recurring question in the back of one's mind, while pondering the select roll, is this: how can influence be measured? As has been said, in each case the aim has been to choose books whose effects can be judged in terms of concrete results or actions. That is, they must have demonstrated a direct connection with certain courses of events. Frequently, a book has attempted to find a solution to problems in a limited field at some particular period. Dealing as they do, therefore, with timely and topical matters, such books inevitably tend to date more rapidly than the great works of religion, philosophy, or literature.

A well-nigh infallible index to the extent of influence is the strength of contemporary sentiment, pro and con. If a book stirs up violent opposition and equally partisan feeling in support of its point of view, the probabilities are that it has deeply affected the thinking of the people. Official censorship and other efforts at suppression also are indicative of its reception. Insight into these attitudes is provided by such sources as contemporary newspapers, controversial pamphlets, accounts of historians, and biographical studies. The crucial test is whether or not the theories, programs, or ideas advocated eventually win acceptance, cross international borders, are translated into other languages, cause disciples, imitators, and rivals to rise, and are gradually incorporated into the thoughts and lives of peoples and nations.

A curious manifestation of fame is the creation of adjectives and nouns drawn from an individual's name to describe a particular concept or pattern of thought. Thus there have been added to everyday vocabulary such terms as Machiavellian, Copernican, Malthusian, Newtonian, Freudian, Darwinism, Marxism, and Hitlerism, each connoting a definite set of ideas, and attesting to the fame or infamy—depending upon the point of view—of its prototype.

In view of the extreme difficulty of reading many influential books, this question may reasonably be asked: How could these works exert influence on any except a narrow band of specialists? Certainly few laymen could comprehend and follow with ease the original Latin texts of Copernicus, Harvey, and Newton, or Einstein's theories in any language. Only the trained social scientist will be able to appreciate fully the often tortuous reasoning of an Adam Smith, a Malthus, or a Marx, while a biological background enriches the understanding of a Harvey, Darwin, or Freud. The answer to the question is that the mass of people obtain ideas secondhand, predigested, by way of a filtering-down process, through popularizations in book form, magazines and newspapers, classroom lessons, public lectures, and, more recently, radio, television, and motion pictures. Influence, accordingly, has resulted from interpretation by experts. Oftentimes, applications to daily living are made without the conscious knowledge of people generally, as, for example, in the mechanistic discoveries of Newton, or with Einstein's theories in relation to nuclear fission and atomic energy.

As one reviews the selected books chronologically, one is struck by the continuity of knowledge, the connecting threads which tie them together. Truly, as Robert Hutchins phrased it, there is in progress here "The Great Conversation." Copernicus received inspiration from the ancient Greek philosophers. Newton, in turn, "stood on the shoulders of giants," Copernicus, Galileo, Kepler, and others. Without them, an Einstein's work might never have come into existence. Darwin freely acknowledged his debt to a host of preceding biologists, geographers, and geologists, on whose work he built in developing the theory of the origin of species. The experimental laboratory approach to science, as opposed to the strictly philosophical, may be said to have begun with Copernicus and to have been practiced by all his great successors, including Harvey, Newton, Vesalius, Jenner, Darwin, and Freud.

The passion for freedom, conceivably an age-old concern, is exemplified by the stirring pleas of Machiavelli, Adam Smith, Paine, Thoreau, and Stowe. Karl Marx drew heavily on classical English economists, especially Adam Smith, Malthus, and Ricardo, and tried to pattern his work on Darwin's. Mahan's *Influence of Sea Power upon History* was essentially a secondary work, utilizing as sources the writings of earlier naval, military, and general historians. While not accepting some of Mahan's conclusions, Mackinder and later geopoliticians found his ideas provocative and stimulating. Consciously or unconsciously, Hitler's *Mein Kampf* derived much from Machiavelli, Darwin, Marx, Mahan, Mackinder, and Freud.

Another criterion in the selection of seminal works is the definition of a book. What is a book? Should it be judged by size alone? Strictly defined, Paine's *Common Sense*, Thoreau's *Civil Disobedience*, Mackinder's *Geographic Pivot of History*, and the original statement of Einstein's *Special Theory of Relativity* are no more than pamphlets. The last three, in fact, first appeared as periodical articles. What a contrast these offer to heavy tomes like the *Principia Mathematica*, *The Wealth of Nations*, later editions of Malthus on population, *Das Kapital*, and *Mein Kampf*. Voltaire is quoted as having said that the big books are never the ones to set a nation on fire: "It is always the little books, packed with emotions, aflame with passion, that do the business." For the present list, size is virtually without significance.

A related consideration is the length of time spent in writing. The record, apparently, was established by Copernicus, whose *De Revolutionibus* was more than thirty years in the making, though the author was certainly not continuously engaged in its production. Who would be willing to say that the Copernican treatise is a more profound work than Newton's *Principia Mathematica*, which was completed in an eighteen-month period? By a curious coincidence, Adam Smith's *Wealth of Nations*, Darwin's *Origin of Species*, and Marx's *Das Kapital* were each seventeen years in the writing. At the other end of the scale, Machiavelli's *The Prince* was turned out in six months, and Paine's *Common Sense* in perhaps three or four months.

The wide variations in writing periods may be attributed to several factors. Individual personalities account for some of the differences. Scientists like Copernicus, Newton, Harvey, and Darwin refused to rush into print until their findings had been thoroughly verified and subjected to stringent tests. Even after the most careful checking, they hesitated to publish, because of fear of controversy, potential censorship, their desire for absolute perfection, possible criticism by fellow scientists, dislike of publicity, or like reasons. The economic treatises of Smith and Marx involved the time-consuming assembling of an enormous mass of data, and extensive revisions. On the other hand, such impetuous fellows as Machiavelli, young Malthus, Paine, and Thoreau had urgent messages to deliver without delay.

A majority of the selected authors are known principally for a single book. With few exceptions, the fame of each rests upon one title and all else is forgotten. Harvey, Newton, Smith, Malthus, Marx, Stowe, Mahan, and Einstein wrote other books—in some cases were prolific authors—but who save a few specialists could name them? Paine, Thoreau, Darwin, and Freud are exceptions to the rule, for their fertile pens produced other books that are in some ways as celebrated as those here listed.

By way of summary, certain characteristics shared by many of the authors stand out. Omitting the scientists in the group, for whom these comments are less pertinent, the books printed since 1500 were written by nonconformists, radicals, fanatics, revolutionists, and agitators. Often, they are badly written books, lacking in literary style. The secret of their success, to repeat, was that the times were ready for them. The books carried messages, frequently of a highly emotional nature, appealing to millions of people. Sometimes the influence was beneficent and sometimes evil; clearly, books can be forces for both good and bad. The intention here, in any case, is not to measure moral values, but instead to demonstrate that books are dynamic and powerful instruments, tools, or weapons.

1

THE BOOK OF BOOKS

The Bible

Out of the ancient, immemorial wisdom of the East, the Hebrew prophets developed the concept of one God, a national deity but one supreme over all creation, the source and being of moral perfection and of absolute justice. The great body of religious literature known as the Bible which grew up around this mono-theistic faith was in process of formation for about twelve hundred years.

The Bible as it has come down to modern times is composed of history, legend, biography, genealogies, ethics, law, proverbial wisdom, sermons, prophesy, lyric poetry, hymns, and theology. It is not simply a book but a collection of books. Much of it is of unknown origin and of uncertain date. A critical study of the Bible is rendered more complex by the revisions and accretions of later centuries to the original writings. Nevertheless, a har-monious theme pervades and dominates the vast work from the first book, Genesis, to the last, Revelations.

The Bible comprises two major divisions. The Old Testament (thirty-nine books in the King James Version) was written originally almost entirely in Hebrew, with a little Aramaic, from the eleventh to the second centuries B.C. It represents the na-tional religious literature of the people of Israel, with additions from the period after Israel had ceased to be an independent nation. The New Testament (twenty-seven books in the King James Version) was written in Greek from about A.D. 40 to 150. It contains the earliest documents extant on the life, teaching, crucifixion, and resurrection of Jesus; the witness of the apostles; and the establishment of the Christian Church.

The diversity and richness of the Bible as literature, especially the Old Testament, are unparalleled. An important element in the earlier books is folklore used to illustrate religious beliefs and moral truths. Thus, the story of the Creation emphasizes keeping the Sabbath ("God blessed the seventh day, and sanctified it"); the Garden of Eden story demonstrates the severe punishment suffered by those who violate Jehovah's commandments; and the story of the Flood offers a graphic account of obedience rewarded.

Other short stories, historical and fictional, are scattered profusely through both the Old and New Testaments. Noteworthy in the Old Testament are such narratives as Isaac's marriage, the Joseph stories, David and Jonathan, Jonah and the whale, Job, and Ruth, while in the New are the parables and miracles.

In another literary form, poetry, the Bible is unsurpassed. Entire books—Psalms, Proverbs, Lamentations, Song of Solomon, and most of Job—are poetical compositions; and poetry, songs, and prayers are abundant elsewhere. The essay as a literary type is represented in Ecclesiastes, Hebrews, Peter, John, and the Epistles of Paul.

History and biography in both the Old and New Testaments are characterized by vivid portrayal of incident and the impression of strong personalities. Modern standards of historiography are, of course, lacking; the purposes, instead, were to select facts and traditions to support deeply felt religious doctrines, and to illustrate what the writers considered to be eternal truths.

Taken as a whole, then, the Bible is an assemblage of literature of immense variety by numerous authors, composed over more than a millennium. The blending of the thought, emotion, experience, and imagination of a great race and the interweaving of literature and religion place the Bible in a unique position among the world's books for the richness of its artistic and spiritual values.

Old Testament

The first five books of the Old Testament (Genesis, Exodus, Leviticus, Numbers, and Deuteronomy) are known collectively as the Pentateuch, or Five Books of Moses. The authorship was traditionally ascribed to Moses, though the work is now generally recognized as a composite document based in part on oral traditions first written down from about the eleventh to the sixth centuries B.C. The Pentateuch begins with narratives describing the Creation and the primeval history of the world, after which it turns specifically to tracing the fortunes of the children of Israel from the call of Abraham to the death of Moses. In the mass of heterogeneous materials are mythological poems, tribal sagas, genealogies, historical legends, liturgical hymns, secular songs, aphorisms and fables, legal decisions, ritual and moral precepts, civil and criminal codes.

Although the books of the Pentateuch are not history in the modern sense, when combined with recent archeological discoveries they provide a reliable general picture of early civilization. Genesis tells of the beginnings of history, and the lives of the patriarchs, Abraham, Isaac, Jacob and his sons, down to the migration of the Israelites into Egypt, where they became enslaved. Exodus tells of the deliverance from Egypt and subsequent journeyings in the wilderness. Leviticus, "pertaining to the Levites," relates to laws ordained while the Israelites were encamped at Sinai. Numbers begins with a description of a census of the Israelite tribes and continues with an account of the forty years of wandering as far as the border of Canaan. Deuteronomy contains four farewell addresses of Moses, culminating in a passionate appeal for love toward God as the motive of all true religion and virtue; the book closes with the death of Moses in the land of Moab. A leading Biblical scholar, Samuel R. Driver, notes: "The influence of Deuteronomy upon subsequent books of the Old Testament is very perceptible. Upon its promulgation it speedily became the book which both gave the religious ideals of the age and moulded the phraseology in which these ideals were expressed."

In the Pentateuch the Mosaic Code is set forth. Hence arose the Jewish custom of referring to the entire section as the Torah, or Law. The earliest nucleus is the Book of the Covenant in Exodus, which contains very ancient laws, including the Decalogue, or Ten Commandments. The Holiness Code, or ceremonial code, is incorporated in Leviticus. Additional laws are found in Numbers. Deuteronomy reviews the law and stresses the development of its humanitarian features. The Ten Commandments and related laws are foundations of Judeo-Christian morality, and their substance has been woven into the fabric of Western jurisprudence.

The second principal division of the Old Testament made by

the Hebrews is the Prophets, a total of twenty-two books, separated by the Jewish canon into the Former Prophets (Joshua,
Judges, Samuel, and Kings—classified as historical books in
Christian Bibles), and the Latter Prophets (Isaiah, Jeremiah,
Ezekiel, and twelve Minor Prophets). The Israelite prophets were
a unique group of men, without parallel in earlier or later history.
They were devoted, fearless reformers, delivering their oracles in
poetry and prose. In their utterances we find fiery, inspired words
which did much to shape the course of events around them. As
a whole, the prophetical books attempt to trace the history of
the Hebrew nation from the time of the entrance into the land
of Canaan to that of the Babylonian captivity, a period of some
six hundred years.

The theme running through Joshua, Judges, Samuel, and Kings
is the rise and fall of Israel; the conquest of Canaan by Joshua;
victories over surrounding tribes; the twelve tribes that made up
the nation coming into possession of the Promised Land of the
Covenant; the rise of the monarchy under Saul, David, and
Solomon; the schism into the separate kingdoms of Israel and
Judah after the death of Solomon; the destruction of Jerusalem
by Nebuchadnezzar and the deportation of the people to Babylon, about 586 B.C. Among the memorable actors in the great
drama are Samson, Samuel, Saul, David, and the prophet Elijah.

Of the Latter Prophets, the book of Isaiah (divided by some
scholars into two or three sections by different authors) is most
celebrated, in part because of its Messianic and Suffering Servant
passages, interpreted by Christians as prophesying Jesus Christ.
Other great Old Testament prophets were Amos, who called for
social justice; Hosea, who stressed God's love; Jeremiah, who
proclaimed a new personal covenant between God and man; and
Ezekiel, who emphasized individual responsibility. Essentially the
prophets were "spokesmen for God," rising to supreme heights
during crises in the national history, deeply concerned with the
deteriorating morality of their people, and continually preaching
to them the ideals of human duty and of religious truth. Often
in exalted poetical form and with the use of striking symbols,
they emphasize the relation of man to God, urge repentance for
sin, praise justice and integrity, appeal for mercy and philanthropy, express indignation against the oppression of the weak,
and promise future rewards to the righteous.

The remaining books of the Old Testament, classified in the
Hebrew Scriptures as the Writings, are miscellaneous in nature,

but include some of the most beautiful and beloved poetry, stories, and accumulated wisdom of the race. The poetic books proper all belong to this section of the Hebrew Bible. Of these, the best-known is Psalms, a collection of sacred lyrics ranging in date from perhaps as early as the tenth to as late as the fourth century B.C. The psalmists sing the praises of God the Creator, grieve for national guilt and ordeals, rejoice over salvation, and express deep faith in the ultimate triumph of God's rule. The moods range from jubilation to despair; penitence and resignation, tenderness and beauty, hope and confidence, thankfulness and adoration are all poured forth in verse that has inspired many great poets and musicians of later ages.

Philosophers of all succeeding eras have pondered the problems posed by the Book of Job. Although a man of God, Job is suddenly visited by a series of calamities: he loses his possessions, family, and health. Why have these disasters happened to a good man? Is he being punished for sins of which he is unaware? Thus we are led into an examination of the problem of evil and the meaning of true religion. Through his ordeal, Job learns to abandon pride and to trust in his Creator, who finally restores him to health and prosperity.

More of the "Wisdom-Literature" of the Hebrews is found in Proverbs and Ecclesiastes. The Book of Proverbs, traditionally ascribed to Solomon but doubtless produced by a long succession of wise men, discusses the nature of wisdom as a guide to the right conduct of the individual, and follows with a collection of maxims, moral judgments, and short sayings. Ecclesiastes is a moralizing book, deeply pessimistic in tone, lamenting the evil times, the futility of human endeavor, and the inability of man to remedy injustices.

Properly classifiable as literature are several short books of the Writings. The Song of Solomon (or Song of Songs) is exquisite poetry, a collection of love poems of great beauty. A Biblical authority, Aubrey Johnson, believes that "the inclusion of these charming but obviously sensuous lyrics in the sacred literature of Judaism must be explained by the fact that they came to be used in certain pious circles as an allegory of the love which the heavenly King bore toward his chosen people." Two dramatic short stories are Esther, an account of a Jewish queen who risks her life to save her people; and Ruth, an idyllic romance in which the foreign-born heroine, a Moabite girl, marries into a Jewish family and becomes an ancestress of King David. Lamentations consists of five elegies on the fall of Jerusalem. Daniel, partly in prose and partly in poetry, describes experiences and visions of its hero; the narrative is famous for the episodes of the Fiery Furnace and the Lions' Den.

Also grouped with the Writings are books of a historical character (I and II Chronicles, Ezra, and Nehemiah), carrying on the story of Judah and of the Jerusalem community after exile. Chronicles covers much the same ground as the Pentateuch and the books of the Former Prophets, including genealogies of patriarchs, kings, priests, and others, and the history of David, Solomon, and the kings of Judah to the captivity. Ezra deals with the return from the Babylonian exile and rebuilding the Temple. Nehemiah continues the history of the exiles' return, the rebuilding of Jerusalem and other cities, and efforts to restore national purity and morale.

In addition to the foregoing version of the Old Testament, the Roman Catholic Bible includes certain works, referred to collectively as the Apocrypha, which are omitted from the Jewish and commonly from the Protestant Scriptures. These pieces of late Jewish literature include Tobit, a tale of two Jewish families whose adversities end happily in their union by marriage; Judith, a religious romance, involving feminine heroism in time of war; Baruch, a religious interpretation of the destruction of Jerusalem by the Romans (A.D. 70) and a message of hope to distressed Jews; Wisdom and Ecclesiasticus, books of proverbs; and Maccabees, a chronicle of the revolt of the Jewish people against Hellenistic oppression, from about 168 to 135 B.C. As a group, the Apocryphal books shed considerable light on a crucial period of Jewish history from about 200 B.C. to A.D. 100.

New Testament

The force which created Christianity was of course the life and person of Jesus, around whom the New Testament was created. The formation of the Gospel began with the utterances of Jesus; there ensued a brief period of oral transmission and of the rise of traditions. The witnesses of the risen Christ spread in a few years from Palestine to the larger cities of the Roman Empire. From memory, they repeated the sayings of Jesus; told the story of his life, death, and resurrection; and discussed the meaning of his teachings.

The earliest of the traditions to be put into writing was the

Gospel of Mark, about A.D. 65. The shortest Gospel, it is written in simple, straightforward narrative style. Mark begins his account with the baptism of Jesus, making no reference to his miraculous conception and birth or to his childhood and youth. The book in general consists of miscellaneous short sayings and scattered incidents relating to Jesus' Galilean ministry. A detailed account of the imprisonment and execution of John the Baptist is given. Mark ends abruptly, saying little about the resurrection of Jesus or of his subsequent appearances.

Two other so-called Synoptic Gospels, those of Matthew and Luke (c. A.D. 75–85), possess a number of common elements: for example, each tells of Jesus' miraculous conception, and of the miracle of driving out an unclean spirit during Jesus' visit to Capernaum. Only Matthew, however, relates the story of the wise men coming to see the babe Jesus, and only Luke includes the story of the shepherds, the miracle of raising the Nain widow's son, and the Ascension. Matthew adds to Mark's account long passages on Jesus' teaching and works, parables, and discourse. Luke "the beloved physician," traditionally identified as a Gentile, writes as a historian. The portrait of Jesus which he presents is broadly humane: the friend of all men, the perfect example of a life, and the lover and savior of mankind.

Of a different character from the three Synoptic Gospels is the Gospel of John, dating about A.D. 100. This work has played a basic part in the history of the Church and of Christian theology. It exalts the nature of Christ, Son of God and Son of Man: "the Word was made flesh, and dwelt among us." John conceives Jesus as the embodiment of divine light, life, and love. He formulates the leading doctrines of Christianity in such fashion as to make them acceptable to the gentile world. "It is probably true to say," observes William Sanday, "that no other primitive Christian writing had so marked an effect on all later attempts to systematize the Christian creed."

According to the traditional arrangement of the New Testament, the four Gospels are followed by the Acts of the Apostles (c. A.D. 85), ascribed to Luke as a sequel to his Gospel. Acts is a historical account of the period between about A.D. 30 and 65, telling the story of the early Church in Jerusalem; the preaching of Peter, Stephen, and Philip; the conversion of Saul of Tarsus; and the expansion of Christianity throughout Asia Minor and Greece toward Rome.

The Gospels in their present form were not the earliest New

Testament writings. They are antedated by the letters of Paul, issued between about A.D. 50 and 65. The Epistle to the Romans heads Paul's great series of messages to the churches. Others were addressed to the Corinthians, Galatians, Ephesians, Philippians, Colossians, and Thessalonians. There are also personal letters, two to Timothy and one each to Titus and Philemon. (There is some question as to whether all of these letters were actually written by Paul, but all embody his teachings.)

The conversion of Saul of Tarsus to become the Apostle Paul marks the first major turning point in the history of Christianity. Paul was, next to Jesus, the greatest personality in the early history of the Christian movement. He gave the new religion a system of theology, raising its intellectual level above other contemporary religions; devised a sound administrative organization; supplied leadership and far-sighted strategy; and brought harmony, unity, and effective cooperation to a faction-ridden body. Under the guiding hand of this genius, Christianity began its development as a world force.

Paul was a master letter-writer. His Epistles communicate the spirit of a great evangelist and teacher; at the same time, they are practical, human approaches to the problems of Christian conduct and belief. The Thessalonian letters, written from Corinth during Paul's second missionary journey, about A.D. 50, exhort the new converts to wait patiently, in holy conduct and brotherly love, for the Second Coming of Christ. Galatians, called the Magna Carta of Christianity, was probably written in Antioch about A.D. 52. It sets forth the supremacy of the Christian Gospel over the Mosaic law, and the doctrine of death to old claims and rebirth in Christ. The Corinthian letters, written about three years later from Ephesus and Macedonia during Paul's third missionary journey, advise the Corinthians on community matters; warn against immorality and factions; and show that love is the greatest spiritual gift. In his Epistle to the Romans, written from Corinth about A.D. 55, Paul summarizes his whole philosophy of the Christian life, including spiritual regeneration, fellowship with Christ, moral freedom, and personal immortality.

Revelations, the last book of the Bible, differs in style and content from the other books of the New Testament. It is a work filled with splendid apocalyptic visions, resembling those of Daniel in the Old Testament. The purpose of the book appears to have been to encourage and to comfort Christian believers at a time of hardship and persecution. Written near the end of the first century, it gave dramatic and positive assurance that Christ would soon return to establish his kingdom on earth, whereupon the faithful would be rewarded and the wicked punished.

The Bible has exercised a more profound and continuous influence upon Western civilization than has any other literary work. To consider only one phase, Biblical language, style, and content pervade the writings of countless poets, dramatists, and other authors. The jurisprudence and customs of the West have been shaped by the legal and ethical precepts of the Bible. Even more fundamental, its deep insights into the motives of human nature and conduct, the tragedy of man's earthly destiny, and the search "for a better country, that is, an heavenly" have throughout the centuries directed human faith, thought, behavior, and endeavor.

Two principal versions of the Bible in English translation exist: the King James and the Douay. In 1611 a group of scholars appointed by James I of England completed the Authorized or King James Bible, based mainly on earlier English Bibles. The King James, which became the standard Bible for English-speaking Protestants, is widely esteemed for its eloquence and superlative use of language. The Douay version, a translation of the Latin Vulgate, was completed in 1609 by a group of English Catholic priests exiled in France. This work subsequently became the accepted Bible of English-speaking Catholics.

During the past century, in recognition of new archeological discoveries and scholarly textual studies, better knowledge of ancient languages and access to older manuscripts, a number of revised translations of the Bible into English has appeared. Their rendition in modern language is often a radical departure from traditional versions. For that reason, conservative readers often feel that modern translations lack the dignity and grandeur of the King James version.

The Bible is the most widely distributed of all books. Christian missionaries have translated it into all important languages and many minor tongues. The whole Bible has been translated into no less than 210 languages and dialects, the New Testament into 271, and parts of the Bible into more than 2,000. Bible societies have distributed the Bible into virtually every corner of the globe.

2

EPIC POET

Homer: Iliad, Odyssey

The Homeric poems may be compared to the goddess Athena, who sprang full-grown from the brow of Zeus. The two great epics, the *Iliad* and the *Odyssey*, together contain about twenty-eight thousand lines. The earliest literary creations, some thirty centuries old, that have survived to our own day, they constitute the primary source from which all later European literature derives. Preceding their appearance and for hundreds of years following, there is nothing remotely resembling these amazing achievements in their well-rounded perfection, maturity, completeness, and length.

The era during which the Greek epics evolved was violent and disorganized; old civilizations, such as the Egyptian and Cretan, were collapsing, while more virile races were developing new cultures. As the barbaric tribes in their wanderings came into conflict with established peoples, they took over their cities, settled down to a civilized life, and began to create a literature of their own. This was evidently the pattern followed by the ancient Greeks.

In the *Iliad* and the *Odyssey*, Homer drew upon a vast repertoire of poems and legends transmitted orally by memory over an indefinite period of time. Homer's predecessors, professional troubadours, improvised and recited poetry of an epic nature at public festivals and in the houses of nobles. Authentic records exist of bards who memorized as many as eighty thousand verses. Originally these lays—the beginning of literature—were short poems, dealing with single exploits, chanting of tribal gods and brave heroes.

36

After the passage of some centuries, perhaps about 850 B.C., an Ionian poet identified as Homer took the scattered stories, hitherto known only through oral traditions, and by giving them order and integrated style, form, and vision, produced the epic cycles known as the *Iliad* and the *Odyssey*. These great popular poems were distillations of the culture of a whole people, due in the first place to many authors, but in their finished form probably the work of a single great literary genius. Into these first epics of the Western world was woven a mass of histories, legends, mythologies, genealogies, ideals of character, manners, and modes of life—the epitome of Greek civilization as it had slowly matured.

Of Homer himself nothing is known. He used the Greek language, but it was not the classical Attic Greek of a later era, being earlier in form and incorporating many words from other dialects. A lively controversy has raged for generations among scholars on the questions: "Who was Homer?" and "Was there a Homer?" After a minute examination of the texts, certain critics have suggested that there may have been two Homers, one the author of the *Iliad*, the other of the *Odyssey*. Modern commentators are in general agreement with the Greek scholar L. A. Post, who concludes that the important consideration is: "We have the *Iliad* and the *Odyssey;* their artistic unity forbids us to suppose that they had more than one author each. . . . It is easier to believe in one genius called Homer, as the Greeks did, than in two." Not improbably, as some interpreters have suggested, the *Iliad* was the poem of Homer's maturity and the *Odyssey* the poem of his old age. It may seem less strange that Homer cannot be positively identified as the writer of the *Iliad* and the *Odyssey* when it is recalled that we cannot prove beyond dispute the authorship of the Shakespearean plays—written a mere three-and-a-half centuries ago.

The text of Homer, fortunately, is well established. According to ancient evidence, an attempt at a complete and accurate version of the epics, based on the recitations of professional declaimers of the Homeric poems, was made under Peisistratus of Athens around the year 600 B.C. In the second century B.C., Aristarchus, librarian of the great Alexandrian library, with the assistance of other scholars, undertook to establish an authoritative text. Though the oldest surviving manuscripts are much later, the poems have come to us entire, and it is not necessary to depend principally upon fragments, as is so frequently the case with ancient authors.

The *Iliad* (the story of *Ilios*, or Troy) is an epic of war: the heroic events of the Trojan War, fought and won by the Greek-speaking peoples about 1200 B.C. The *Odyssey* begins at the conclusion of the war and relates the adventures of Odysseus, one of the Greek leaders, returning to Ithaca after the fall of Troy. The time element in each poem is relatively brief. The Trojan War lasted ten years, but the *Iliad* covers only about six weeks of it, focusing upon a single major episode, while in the *Odyssey* we meet Odysseus six months before the end of his ten years of travel.

Examples of divine interference are numerous in both the *Iliad* and the *Odyssey*. The gods of the Homeric world have all the foibles, frailties, idiosyncrasies, and desires of human beings. They love and hate, are jealous and quarrelsome, and indulge their baser appetites much as men do. But strong, beautiful, and immortal, they are above man's law. Because they are deeply interested in human affairs, the gods cannot refrain from intervening to shape events as they wish them to occur.

Homer's moral ideals, apart from the actions of the gods, are clearly revealed. First is justice: punishment for murder, humiliation of the proud, and chastisement for perjurers. Second is manliness, which may be defined as both physical and moral courage. Subordinate to this virtue are a sense of honor, dignity, self-respect, and humility.

Iliad

The essential plot of the *Iliad*, as told by Homer, begins with a visit by Paris, son of Priam, king of Troy, to the palace of Menelaus, king of Sparta. Paris abuses hospitality by persuading Menelaus' wife Helen, the most beautiful woman in the world, to abandon her husband and return with him to Troy. Revenge is demanded by the injured husband, his relatives, and friends. Under the leadership of Agamemnon, king of Mycenae and brother of Menelaus, the princes of Greece assemble a fleet of more than a thousand ships, manned by fighters, and set sail for Troy. For nine years after landing, the Greek forces besiege the city, keeping the Trojans on the defensive, but are unable to win final victory.

As the *Iliad* begins, the monotony of camp life and desultory periods of actual fighting are beginning to affect the morale of the Greek soldiers, though they are still loyal to Agamemnon and ready to carry on the war until Troy is destroyed. An exception is Achilles, leader of the Myrmidon tribe and the most powerful Greek fighting man, who has long been dissatisfied with Agamemnon's conduct of the war. A quarrel between Archilles and Agamemnon in the first book of the *Iliad* sets the stage for all subsequent action.

The break between the two leaders is caused by Agamemnon's selfish, stupid behavior. The beautiful daughter of a priest of Apollo is captured and awarded to Agamemnon as a prize of honor. A plea from her father that he be permitted to ransom her is rudely rejected by Agamemnon. In retaliation, Apollo visits a plague on the Greek camp and many die. The king finally yields and returns the daughter, but to salve his pride demands that there be surrendered to him a fair captive named Briseis, who had fallen to Achilles' lot. Achilles indignantly refuses to be defrauded of what belongs to him, makes a speech insulting Agamemnon, and swears that he will remain in his tent until his honor has been satisfied.

The withdrawal of their greatest fighter and his troops is disastrous for the Greek army, which suffers several severe defeats at the hands of the Trojans, led by Hector, bravest of the sons of Priam. Without Achilles, the most valorous of the Greek heroes are unable to withstand the Trojans. The Greek ships are about to be set afire, and the Greek forces driven into the sea.

At this point, Patroclus, Achilles' dearest friend and comrade, begs Achilles to lend him his armor and to allow him to lead the rest of the Myrmidons to the rescue of the hard-pressed Greeks. Achilles consents, and in the ensuing battle Patroclus is killed by Hector, who strips his body of Achilles' armor. News of Patroclus' death is brought to Achilles, who is wild with grief at the loss of his friend and feels a deep sense of personal guilt for having sent him to his doom. The event arouses in Achilles a tempest of fury and rage for vengeance against Hector and the Trojans. Hector must be killed for the death of Patroclus.

Achilles strides into battle and for a long sequence we see the incomparable warrior in action, wreaking dreadful carnage on his foes. The Trojans in great numbers fall before his savage attack. At first, Hector flees with the remnants of the Trojan army, but finally he has the courage to remain outside the city walls and to face the mortal enemy of his people. The single combat between Achilles and Hector is the climax of the *Iliad*. Achilles strikes down his foe and carries the body to the Greek camp as a trophy. But yielding to the supplications of Hector's father, Priam, he restores the body and Hector is buried by the Trojan people with honors to a hero who gave his life for his people.

Mythological Background for the Interval between the Iliad and the Odyssey

A short while later, Achilles himself is slain by Paris with the aid of Apollo, and Paris is then killed, but Troy does not submit. The Greeks build a great hollow wooden horse, in which some of the chiefs conceal themselves, and the rest of the Greek forces pretend to sail away. The wooden horse is drawn by the Trojans inside the city walls as an offering to the gods. At night, the Greek ships return, the gates are opened by the chiefs out of the horse, most of the defenders are killed, and the kingdom of Troy is annihilated.

As the Greeks set out on their homeward voyage, a storm arises, wrecking a large part of the fleet. Menelaus and Helen are driven to Egypt and wander eight years before finding their way back to Greece. Agamemnon returns safely, but is slain by his cousin, his faithless wife's paramour. The long and eventful homeward journey of another of the Greek heroes, Odysseus, is recounted in the *Odyssey*.

Odyssey

The *Odyssey* has been described as a kind of novel, the first in world literature. It is a work full of romance, magic, and adventure. The central theme is the remarkable experiences, temptations, and dangers encountered by Odysseus as he makes his way back to Ithaca after the Trojan War. Ten years before, he had bidden farewell to his young wife Penelope and his infant son Telemachus. Because he had offended the god Poseidon, another decade was to elapse before he would be reunited with them.

In the *Odyssey*, Homer uses the literary device of the narrative flashback. Six months before Odysseus is destined to end his adventures, the hero himself tells the tale of his woes and wanderings. Thus, he has been away from home nearly twenty years when the story opens.

When Odysseus does not return to Ithaca with the other Greek leaders, rumors of his death are spread, and Penelope is urged to take another husband. With the rightful sovereign absent, the prince but a boy, and the queen a beautiful and wealthy woman, confusion and disorganization are rife. The princes of the country and of the neighboring islands move into the palace, demanding that Penelope make her choice of one of them. Under the excuse of wooing the queen, they eat, drink, and carouse, devouring the substance of Odysseus; Penelope and her young son cannot control them. But Penelope has faith that Odysseus is still alive and will return, and therefore uses her wits to delay an answer to the persistent suitors, while Telemachus slips away to go in search of his father.

Meanwhile, Odysseus, thinking only of a speedy return, has his ship driven by a tempest into the western sea, toward Sicily, Sardinia, and northwest Africa, a place considered by the Greeks to be a fearsome region filled with fantastic perils and monsters. While in this region, Odysseus has many adventures, with the lotus-eaters, who subsist on a plant which makes seamen forget their homeland; with the Cyclops, one-eyed giants who eat men raw; with the king of the winds, who can stuff tempests into a leather bag; with the goddess Circe, who changes men into lions, wolves, swine, and other animals; with the Sirens, fairy bird-women who attract men by their irresistible voices and then devour them; with Scylla, a kind of devil-fish whose long tentacles reach out to grab sailors from the decks of their ship; with Charybdis, a maelstrom that sucks everything down to the sea bottom; and with other terrifying marvels, including even a visit to Hades. Odysseus alone of his crew survives these multiple hazards and ordeals.

Odysseus is finally shipwrecked on a solitary island, where he lives for seven years with a beautiful fairy woman, Calypso, never ceasing, however, to long for his home and family. Through the intervention of Athena, Calypso unwillingly agrees to Odysseus' departure. After a shipwreck and sundry other dramatic incidents, he lands on the Ithacan coast. Athena brings Telemachus back from his travels to meet his father. Clad as a beggar, Odysseus goes to his own house, but does not immediately reveal himself to his wife. During the night he strips the hall of all weapons, to disarm his enemies. With the coming of morning, the suitors are back, more arrogant and insolent than ever. Odysseus, still in the guise of a beggar, enters a contest with them to shoot his own great bow and arrow. He bends the bow when no one else has the immense strength required. Before the suitors are aware of what is happening, Odysseus turns his deadly arrows on them and slaughters them all at the banquet tables. The story ends with a banquet celebrating the happiness of Odysseus, Penelope, and Telemachus in being reunited.

A notable aspect of Homer's genius, both in the *Iliad* and the *Odyssey*, is the creation of character. Despite the great number of actors in the two dramas, each individual is carefully delineated. Brave soldiers, for example, are courageous in different fashions, each according to his temperament. Achilles is impetuous, hotheaded, quick to anger, violent in action, fearless. The courage of Hector is more rational, derived from a victory over his own nature and a discipline that he has imposed upon himself. Homer perceived that men are complexes of emotions, motives, and reason. Human nature in all of its extremes is revealed in his meticulously drawn portraits.

Though epics of primitive society, the *Iliad* and the *Odyssey* are also rich in memorable characterizations of women. The combination of freedom, dignity, and respect enjoyed by women of the Homeric age is far removed from the Eastern harem tradition. Penelope is perhaps the highest and purest of Homer's heroines, remaining true and steadfast to her long-missing husband, resisting all pressures and temptations. Appealing and beautiful, too, is Andromache, the wife of Hector. Helen is a tragic character, a helpless victim of Aphrodite, who forces her to flee with Paris, even though she despises him. Her beauty is her fatality, a destructive flame received from heaven—a curse as much as a gift.

The epics of Homer are generally acknowledged to be the highest literary achievements of Hellenic culture. Homer's supremacy as a poet was recognized by Greeks and Romans alike for a thousand years, until the Dark Ages brought a temporary eclipse in his popularity. It was not uncommon accomplishment for a Greek boy to commit both the *Iliad* and the *Odyssey* to memory. In the schools of the ancient Greek world, Homer was regarded as the one great authority in Greek religion, history, and patriotism. Aside from formal education, all literary artists throughout the Greek world were influenced directly or indirectly by Homeric poetry. It may also be said that every European literary epic poem since Homer's time has drawn inspiration and form from him, notably Apollonius of Rhodes' *Argonautica*, Vergil's *Aeneid*, Dante's *Divine Comedy*, and Milton's *Paradise Lost*. The *Iliad* and the *Odyssey* together are the gates through which we enter the literature of Western civilization.

3

FAMED FABULIST

Aesop: Fables

Aesop, whose name is attached to the greatest and most popular of all collections of fables, is as shadowy a figure as Homer. Even his existence has frequently been doubted, but a substantial body of tradition supports the belief that such a personage once lived, probably in the sixth century B.C. Herodotus mentions Aesop as having flourished about 550 B.C.; Socrates, in 399 B.C., passed his last days in prison turning the Aesopic fables into verse; Aristotle's *Rhetoric* tells the fable "The Fox and the Hedgehog"; Demosthenes used "The Wolves and the Sheep" to persuade the Athenians not to betray him into Philip's power; and Aristophanes and Plato, among others, ascribed to Aesop the fables that they related.

Whether the work of one man or of various hands, Aesop-type fables antedated Aesop by ages, fading back into the prehistoric past. Primitive man, intimately acquainted with the habits of wild beasts, inevitably built a lore around, say, the wily fox, the timid deer, and the noble lion, attributing to them human passions, motives, feelings, and even speech. With variations the fables are found in the oldest Chinese literature; inscribed on Sumerian and Babylonian clay tablets; in an Egyptian papyrus of about 1200 B.C. (the fable of the lion and the mouse); the Jataka stories and the *Hitopadesa of India*, drawn largely from the Sanskrit *Panchatantra*, the oldest monument of Hindu literature. The early portions of the Old Testament also contain moralizing plant and beast tales, e.g., the fable of the trees and the bramble (Judges 9:8–15). The Oriental or Eastern origin of the fable is revealed by the introduction of such animals as the

44

ape, panther, and peacock. In Hellenic literature the first appearance of an Aesopic fable is in Hesiod's *Works and Days*, about the eighth century B.C.

A legendary life of Aesop is held by scholars to be entirely apocryphal. According to a romantic biography, composed long after his time, Aesop was a slave born in Phrygia, Asia Minor. Traditionally, he was exceedingly homely: dwarfish, potbellied, with swarthy skin, pointed head, snub nose, bandy legs, short arms, and squint eyes. Further, he was mute until the goddess Isis conferred the power of speech upon him for a good deed he had performed. His keen wit and ingenuity in tight situations, however, matched those of some of his animal characters.

For example, it is related that when Aesop was going to Ephesus with other slaves, the burdens they had to carry were distributed. Because Aesop chose a large basket of bread, twice as heavy as any of the other loads, he was called a fool by his fellow-slaves. But the bread was used to feed the slaves and before evening Aesop had nothing to carry except an empty basket. Another anecdote demonstrates his use of fable in dealing with a practical problem. During the reign of the tyrant Pisistratus in Athens, Aesop visited the city. To dissuade the rebellious citizens from revolution, Aesop related the fable "The Frogs Asking for a King," with the obvious moral that the Athenians conceivably would be in a worse state if they exchanged rulers.

The way in which Aesop met his end is as generally accepted or rejected as other traditions associated with him. He is said to have won the favor of King Croesus of Lydia, who sent him to Delphi with a gift of money for its citizens; in a dispute with the Delphians, Aesop was slain by being thrown from a precipice. About two hundred years after his death, a statue of Aesop, the work of Lysippus, was erected at Athens, placed in front of the statues of the Seven Sages.

No word of writing by Aesop is known to exist. Why, then, in view of the fable's ancient antecedents, the possibility that Aesop was a wholly mythical person, and no manuscript of his survives, is Aesop's name virtually synonymous with the word fable? Aesop, or someone like him, was the first to collect, retell in concise, easy-to-remember style, and disseminate widely for moral instruction previously existing fables, doubtless adding a number of his own. Thus Aesop and the fable became so closely identified with each other as to be inseparable. Passed on orally from person to person, from generation to generation, all Aesop-type stories eventually were assumed to be derived from Aesop.

The transmission route for the Aesopic fables is reasonably definite. The Athenian statesman and orator Demetrius Phalerus in 320 B.C. gathered and published the fables in ten books, for the use of orators; the text is lost, but fragments of a Greek papyrus scroll of the first century A.D. may be a copy. Also belonging to the first century is a versified Latin rendition of some of the fables done by the freedman Phaedrus. Another important version, an iambic rendering into Greek, was made in the third century by Babrius, a Roman and tutor of the son of Emperor Alexander Severus. About A.D. 400, Avianus turned forty-two fables into Latin elegiac verse, all based on stories taken from Babrius. The Avianus version was widely read throughout the Middle Ages and is the chief source for modern renderings.

Typically, the Aesopic fable is brief, simple, and direct; the language clear and unpretentious, apparently artless. It is dramatically effective, though, in bringing out a witty, emotional, or didactic point. To serve his practical purpose—the teaching of a moral lesson—the fabulist incorporates folklore, tradition, superstition, and sophistry. Frequently he does violence to the facts of natural history, quite aside from the literary device of having dumb animals or inanimate cities, trees, mountains, rocks, and rivers talking to one another.

The moral significance gives the fable unity and makes of it a work of art. To insure against the point's being missed or lost, it is always spelled out, in a kind of Q.E.D. statement, as the fable's conclusion, often in the form of a proverb. Nevertheless, as the Aesop editor and translator Lloyd W. Daly observes, in his *Aesop Without Morals*: "Far from being highly moral stories, the fables are not always even conducive to moralizing . . . the vast majority of the tales . . . serve as examples, usually horrible, of human behavior." They embody both the wisdom and the cynicism of mankind, dissecting human rather than animal nature. Satire is therefore a common element in the fables. Cunning, trickery, and other devious methods are rewarded, while the honest and well-meaning, but stupid, individual may suffer disaster for his ineptness and lack of guile. Thus Aesop is essentially a satirist who inclines toward a cynical view of human character. It is ironical that, although the fables were meant for adults, like Swift's *Gulliver's Travels*, they are now read chiefly by children. Daly, in his comprehensive, unexpurgated translation, specifically states that this version "is not intended for the edification of the young."

It has been objected that Aesop took unfair advantage of the animals and unjustly libeled them in attributing human behavior to innocent beasts. At least three rationales have been suggested. First, from the standpoint of primeval man, with whom the fable originated, animals were almost brothers, and there seemed nothing incongruous in giving them human characteristics. Second, as civilization advanced, men would have resented and found unpalatable being depicted as hypocritical, weak, dishonest, and sly—all traits clearly implied in the Aesopic fables. Finally, and closely related to the second point, the fable flourishes under tyranny and dictatorship; subtle satire voiced by animals is tolerated by the despot who would ruthlessly suppress direct criticism.

The influence of Aesop's fables on popular thought and formal literature has been far-reaching. Innumerable Aesopic expressions and moral teachings have become common currency. Note, for example, "fishing in muddy waters," "out of the frying pan into the fire," "the goose that laid the golden eggs," "the dog in the manger," "the boy who cried wolf," "the hare and the tortoise," "the wolf in sheep's clothing," "the fox and the sour grapes," "the ass in the lion's skin," "the bundle of sticks."

Literary figures who have emulated, paraphrased, or have been inspired by Aesop are numerous. The great beast-epic known as the "History of Reynard the Fox," dating from about the tenth century A.D., consists of independent episodes of a fabulous nature woven together. Among other medieval specimens are Geoffrey Chaucer's "The Nun's Priest's Tale" and John Lydgate's tale of "The Churl and the Bird." Of modern fabulists, the most renowned is the seventeenth-century French author Jean de La Fontaine. La Fontaine's first fables were based mainly on Aesop as told by Phaedrus; later, he was considerably influenced by Persian and Indian examples. In England, Sir Roger L'Estrange in the seventeenth century wrote satirical bestiaries as vehicles for his political opinions, and the verse fables, also often political satires, of John Gay were popular in the eighteenth century. Subsequently, Gotthold Lessing in Germany, Leo Tolstoy and

Ivan Krylov in Russia, and Joel Chandler Harris (Uncle Remus) in the United States were some of the eminent writers who utilized fable motifs in short stories. Twentieth-century English and American authors have also followed the form effectively in such creations as Rudyard Kipling's *Jungle Book*, George Orwell's *Animal Farm*, and James Thurber's *Fables for Our Time*.

Aesopic fables and their predecessors represent the earliest stage of literary art. Apparently they possess an irresistible appeal for man at every cultural level from the savage to the savant. The secret of their charm lies in their simplicity, directness, native shrewdness, and a curious combination of naïveté and sophistication. In a sense, the fables are the essence, a kind or distillation, of the universal experience and age-old wisdom of the race.

4

JUDGE OF NATURE AND MANKIND

Plato: Symposium, Apology, Crito, Phaedo, Republic, Statesman, Laws, Timaeus

The true philosopher, as Plato described him, is "a spectator of all time and all existence . . . a gentle and noble nature" who "desires all truth," and who "seeks to be like God as far as that is possible for man." In these few brief phrases, Plato was unconsciously drawing a perfect representation of his own nature and personality.

Plato, a native Athenian of noble ancestry, appears to have absorbed all the culture of his time. His thorough acquaintance with classical Greek literature is attested by the frequency and aptness with which he quotes it.

Two major influences in Plato's youth and early manhood shaped his political, philosophical, and ethical ideas and ideals for the remainder of his career. The first was the historical era to which he belonged, and the second was his friendship with Socrates. The period of the Peloponnesian War was almost coterminous with the first twenty-three years of Plato's life. The war ended in 404 B.C. with the surrender of Athens and occupation of the city by the Spartans, followed by serious economic problems, rapid political changes, and popular unrest among the Athenians.

Nevertheless, Athens continued to be the center of a vast intellectual ferment, doubtless provoked and inspired by a diffusion of ideas and wide differences of opinion among the citizens. A dominant personality was the philosopher Socrates, who bequeathed not one line of writing to posterity, but whose thoughts, as recorded and interpreted by Plato, have left a profound impress upon all succeeding generations.

Plato was about twenty when he met Socrates, and he became his ardent disciple for the remaining seven or eight years of the sage's life. Socrates was a strange, uncouth figure (ridiculed by the comic writers, such as Aristophanes), wandering about the city barefoot and poor, said to be neglectful of his wife and children and given to endless argumentation. As described by G. W. Botsford in his *History of Greece*, "With his enormously large bald head, protruding eyes, flat nose, and thick lips, he resembled the satyr masks displayed in the shop windows at Athens; big-bodied and bandy-legged, he stalked like a pelican through the streets." Yet the magic of the master teacher's words affected all hearers. Feigning ignorance, Socrates did not profess to know or teach anything. Instead he induced everyone who approached him to give an account of his soul and to defend his views and opinions in the light of reason. His technique invariably was to ask a series of searching questions—queries that explored men's innermost thoughts, stimulated the mental processes of the young men by whom he was constantly surrounded, and exposed the pretensions of pompous citizens who claimed superior knowledge.

Despite the fact that Socrates appears as a leading character in virtually everything written by Plato, he himself left no clearly defined body of doctrine or system of philosophy. He was eternally in quest of precise definitions. Paul Shorey, a classical scholar who has analyzed Plato's works in detail, concludes that the only philosophical dogmas definitely attributable to Socrates "are the principles that no man willingly does wrong, that virtue is knowledge, and that all wrongdoing and error are ignorance, to which we may possibly add that it is better to suffer injustice than to inflict it." The permanent significance of Socrates, Shorey observes, is as "a personality, a method, an inspiration, a moral and religious ideal."

After the execution of Socrates, who had been falsely accused of atheism and of corrupting the morals of the young, Plato left Athens for a prolonged period of travel in Greece, Egypt, Italy, and Sicily. At the age of forty, according to tradition, he returned to Athens, and there established his famous Academy, a more or less formal school of philosophy and science, destined to continue in existence for nearly nine hundred years. Plato himself was associated with the school for some forty years. His aim was to make philosophers and perhaps statesmen of the students, to give them a love of knowledge and of wisdom, to teach them the principles of education, ethics, and politics. In these lofty purposes the institution failed. Edith Hamilton notes that "no great and good leaders came of it, no philosopher-king to banish injustice and establish good government on earth."

Plato's most celebrated contribution to philosophy, dominating his thought on every subject, recurring throughout his writings, and presumably taught in the Academy, was the theory of Ideas. He held that the objects seen with our eyes are, like shadows, only appearances. Behind the object is an Idea. For example, we may see horses, varied in form and certain to vanish from the earth. The Idea of the horse, though it cannot be seen or touched, is indestructible and eternal. Therefore, while the material world around us is subject to corruption and death, the world of Ideas is incorruptible, ageless, and real. Ideas can be classified and arranged in order of importance; the supreme Idea is the Idea of Good. Real knowledge, Plato teaches, can be built only upon the foundation of immaterial ideas. The theory of Ideas, from which was derived the concept of universals, dominated medieval thought. George Sarton points out: "The Platonic point of view allured poets and metaphysicians, who fancied that it made divine knowledge possible; unfortunately, it made the more earthbound scientific knowledge impossible."

A distinguishing feature of all Plato's writings, except for the *Apology* (Socrates' speech to an Athenian jury) and a few minor pieces of dubious origin, is their dialogue form. This characteristic format enabled Plato to present naturally and logically various sides of a question, frequently without revealing his own opinion. While the dialogues are diverse in subject matter and treatment, two dominant themes pervade them: a passion for human improvement and an abiding faith in the power and supremacy of the mind.

It is remarkable that, unlike those of nearly all other writers of ancient times, the works of Plato have survived virtually intact—attesting to the high esteem in which they have been held in succeeding centuries. Shorey states that "our text of Plato is one of the best and purest that have come down to us from antiquity." The total corpus of his writings includes the *Apology* and twenty-five to twenty-eight dialogues (the genuineness of several are doubted). The exact chronology of various titles is uncertain and has long been the subject of scholarly controversy. The Socratic dialogues, written when Plato was completely under the influence of Socrates, are generally assumed to have come first and to have been followed by the educational and philosophical dialogues. Works relating to political science and science are products of Plato's middle years and old age. Selected for discussion here are writings representative of these several categories and of widest general significance.

Symposium

The *Symposium* is generally regarded as Plato's artistic masterpiece. A noted classical scholar, Gilbert Murray, suggests that it would not be difficult to uphold the claim "that the *Symposium* was absolutely the highest work of prose fiction ever composed, most perfect in power, beauty, imaginative truth." The theme is love in all of its aspects. The influence of the *Symposium* on philosophy, poetry, and human behavior has been immense.

As the stage is set, Socrates and several of his convivial friends are gathered around a banquet table. The place is Athens, and the time 416 B.C. Participants in the brilliant and witty dialogue include the host Agathon, a successful playwright; Aristophanes, comic poet supreme; Eryximachus, the physician; Pausanias, Aristodemus, Phaedrus, Alcibiades, and finally Socrates himself. Each guest in turn discourses on love from his individual viewpoint, praising every manifestation of Eros, the god of love, from the sheerly physical to the completely abstract. Love is treated with a keen realization of its universal importance and with deep insights.

Phaedrus, the first speaker, delivers an encomium on love in general. Only men and women in love, he declares, will consent to die for others. Further, love overcomes the base in man and teaches high thoughts and honorable deeds. Love, he concludes, "is the most venerable and valuable of the gods and has sovereign power to provide all virtue and happiness for men whether living or departed."

Pausanias distinguishes two types of love, the heavenly and the earthly; followers of the latter are lovers of the body, not of the soul. The nobler love reveals itself, for example, in the friendship of man and youth. Only the higher love of soul and character is enduring. Pausanias concludes that love in itself is neither good nor evil.

When the turn comes for the physician Eryximachus, he, too, agrees that there are two loves, but he maintains that one is good and should be fostered, while the other is bad and ought to be suppressed. He sees love or desire as a physiological and cosmic force of attraction and repulsion, to be found in all living things. The two loves represent wholesome and unwholesome appetites, healthy and unhealthy desires, which must be harmonized and reconciled by making the higher master over the lower.

Aristophanes' contribution to the theme is to relate the myth of an original human being, a man-woman, with two heads, four arms, four legs, and other parts to match, spherical in shape. For being insolent toward the gods, this strange creature was punished by being split in two, resulting in the creation of man in his present form, with two arms, two legs, and one head. In all succeeding ages, love has been a quest for the divided half of ourselves and a yearning for an impossibly complete reunion.

Two speakers remain: Agathon and Socrates. Love, says Agathon, brings like and like together, and he imagines a primeval chaos ended by the rule of love. Love has many characteristics: it is soft, because it lives in men's hearts; it is temperate, because temperance is superior to pleasure, and love is master over pleasure; it is just, for everyone is willing to do anything for love; it is brave, for not even the god of war can resist it; it is wise, for it makes everyone a poet; it is lord of gods and men; it turns away hostility, inspires courtesy, and brings men together in happy communion; it produces gentleness, and kindness; it smiles upon the good, is desired by the unfortunate, and is bestowed upon the happy. Love, also, continues Agathon, is "father of luxury, tenderness, elegance, grace, desire and yearning; regardless of the good; regardless of the bad"; in all matters, the fairest and best leader whom all men should follow, singing its praises as love casts its spell on the minds of gods and men alike.

Socrates begins by doubting that love is everything claimed by Agathon's eloquent encomium. Love is the pursuit of the beautiful, he believes, a desire for what we do not possess. The true philosophy of love, Socrates claims to have learned from the prophetess Diotima, who explained to him that love is neither a god nor a demon, but an intermediary and interpreter between gods and men. Love is the child of Plenty (the son of Discretion) and of Poverty, conceived on the day of Aphrodite's birth. Hence he has the conflicting qualities of the two parents. Elaborating further, Socrates says:

Love is always poor, and anything but tender and fair, and he is rough and squalid and he has no shoes nor a house to dwell in. On the very earth exposed he lies under the open heaven, in the streets or at the doors of houses taking his rest, and like his mother, he is always in distress. Like his father, too, whom he also partly resembles, he is always plotting against the fair and the good. He is bold, enterprising, strong, a mighty hunter, always weaving some intrigue or other, keen in the pursuit of wisdom, fertile in resources; a philosopher at all times, terrible as an enchanter, sorcerer, sophist. He is by nature neither mortal nor immortal, but alive and flourishing at one moment when he is in plenty, and dead at another moment; and again alive by reason of his father's nature. But that which is always flowing in is always plotting against the fair and the good. He is bold, enterprising, And further, he is a mean between ignorance and knowledge. Wisdom is a most beautiful thing, and love is of the beautiful, and therefore love is also a philosopher or lover of wisdom. And being a lover of wisdom, he is a mean between wise and ignorant. And of this too his birth is because his father is wealthy and wise and his mother, poor and foolish.

Love should be identified as the lover, Socrates maintains, rather than as the beloved. Love desires reproduction of the beautiful and is repelled by ugliness; it is a yearning for the immortality and permanence denied to mortals, manifested in the begetting of children and in the desire of statesmen and poets for fame. A still higher stage of love is reached when the passion for the beautiful, beginning as devotion to one beautiful person, becomes generalized in love of universal, absolute beauty—the love of all bodily beauty rising to the love of beautiful souls, thoughts, laws, institutions, and finally to a contemplation of the infinite sea of the beautiful, removed from earthly embodiments.

Life and Death of Socrates: Apology, Crito, Phaedo

Socrates was indicted in 399 B.C. before an Athenian criminal tribunal, for not believing in the Greek gods and for corrupting young men. When his trial began, the Peloponnesian War had been over for five years; the Athenian empire was in ruins; and Athens was split into factions and beset with internal troubles. Observing that ancient religious beliefs were discredited and established political principles were being questioned, the conservative-minded sought a scapegoat. Their suspicions began to center on Socrates, who they determined should be compelled to stand trial as a public nuisance.

The indictment was brought by an obscure young poet, Meletus, who was prompted by more influential and powerful figures in the background. Meletus' accusation read: "Socrates commits a crime by not believing in the gods of the city, and by introducing other new divinities. He also commits a crime by corrupting the youth. Penalty, Death." A jury of 501 persons was drawn by lot to hear the case. After the prosecutors, who claimed to be moved solely by patriotism and not by malice, had presented their evidence, Socrates rose to reply. His speeches and those of his friends fill the first twenty-four chapters of the *Apology.*

In his *apologia pro vita sua,* Socrates explains his life and motives and states that he acted as he did at the command of the gods. He has made enemies, he concedes, by proving men ignorant when they thought themselves wise, exposing their pretense of knowledge. His life has been one of unselfish dedication to the state; therefore, rather than being angry with him, the Athenians should thank the gods for sending him to stir them from their lethargy and for turning their minds toward the true realities, virtue and justice. As a public benefactor, Socrates concludes that he should be supported by the state.

Despite his eloquent plea, the jurors find Socrates guilty, though by a close vote, and death is decreed. Thus the trial ends, but Socrates addresses some last words to those who have condemned him. He rebukes them for their crime, warning them that they cannot silence the voices of criticism by putting men to death. He bids his friends be of good cheer. No harm can befall a good man in life or in death. Death is either an eternal and dreamless sleep or a journey to another and a better world. In either case, it is not an evil but a good. "Whether life or death be better is known only to God."

According to a narrowly legalistic interpretation, Socrates' accusers had a case. As George Bernard Shaw ironically remarks,

"One of the famous feats of the Athenian Democracy was to execute Socrates for using his superior brains to expose its follies." Socrates was introducing a new spiritual and intellectual era; he asserted that the individual conscience should be supreme over man-made laws; he insisted upon the public value of free discussion in the pursuit of truth; and he taught youth to place reason and inward conviction above authority—all of which teachings were correctly seen by conservatives as subversive of the status quo. Though Socrates was indicted and condemned as an offender against religion and morality, the predominant motive of his accusers was indubitably political.

The scene of the *Crito* is laid in prison, where Socrates' friend Crito arrives in early morning while Socrates is still asleep. The prime purpose of the dialogue seems to be to establish Socrates' complete integrity and patriotism. Crito implores him to escape and save himself. It will be easy and there are many places where he may go. Further, by escaping, Socrates will avoid loss of personal reputation or injury to his children. These arguments Socrates rejects. One should not return evil for evil, he declares, and he will be wronging the state if he breaks the law and escapes. Hence, though he has been unjustly condemned, he will give up his life, because he is an obedient citizen, unwilling to flout the authority of the state. If he disregards and dishonors the laws of his own country, he will be regarded as the enemy of the law everywhere.

The political teachings of the *Crito* are a faithful representation of Socrates' views. To him, to break the laws is to strike at the root of all society and to leave the state that he has hitherto accepted and loved simply to save his own life would be cowardly. Further, Socrates absolves the state from guilt for what is to be in effect a judicial murder. His acquittal of the state is in effect both a condemnation of his judges and a counteraccusation of high treason against individuals. Clearly, since the state is innocent, the guilt rests with the judges and accusers, who have misinterpreted and misapplied the law.

Another important consideration for Socrates, in refusing to accept Crito's offer to aid his escape, is his age. He is now old and has finished his mission. It is a propitious time to die, and his death in this manner will insure his fame and future influence.

The *Phaedo* reports the last hours of Socrates in prison before his execution, as told by Phaedo, who has been with him, to

Echecrates. Some friends have come to be with Socrates at the end. The conversation turns naturally to death, and the *Phaedo* is essentially an inspiring discourse on the immortality of the soul.

Socrates conceives death to be merely the separation of body and soul. The true philosopher does not fear death, because in afterlife, he will be cared for by the gods, surrounded by the best of companions, and released from the body, which is a constant hindrance to the contemplation of justice, beauty, goodness, and other eternal ideas. Those who fear death love their bodies or wealth or honor above wisdom.

When one of his auditors questions the future existence of the soul, Socrates advances the doctrine of opposites: death succeeds life and therefore life must succeed death. Also supporting this belief is the doctrine that knowledge is derived from recollection: all our knowledge is a remembrance of what we have known at some previous time, presumably before we were born. Our souls, accordingly, must have existed before they entered our bodies. The pure soul goes to live with the gods in a place that is glorious, pure, and invisible. On the other hand, the impure soul remains earthbound until it enters the body of a congenial lower animal (e.g., the sensual soul goes into the body of an ass, and the unjust or tyrannical soul into the body of a wolf).

Another friend asks whether the soul is independent of generation and corruption. Socrates answers that life is the opposite of death, and that life is inseparable from the soul. The soul, being immortal and therefore indestructible, will not admit death, and survives unharmed the death of the body.

Socrates then describes the soul's journey to the other world and its life there. He introduces the myth of the earth as a globe balanced in space with many mansions for the soul above the area now occupied by man. All souls will be judged, and suitable rewards and punishments await them. The man who has devoted himself to his soul rather than to his body will find a place of wondrous beauty prepared for him in the hereafter.

The *Phaedo* concludes with Socrates' final preparations and death: a bath, to save the women the trouble of washing a corpse; a brief interview with his wife and children; last injunctions to his friends; and then draining the cup of poison brought by the executioner. "Such was the end," Phaedo tells Echecrates, "of our friend, who was, as we may say, of all those of his time whom we have known, the best and wisest and most righteous man."

A reading of this trilogy—the *Apology, Crito,* and *Phaedo*—must leave one profoundly impressed with Socrates' sincerity, high principles, and burning faith. Edwin A. Quain aptly observes: "The basic concepts involved in the structure of morality—death, immortality, duty, the sanctity of law, and its inevitable retribution—these are the contents of the gospel according to Socrates."

Republic, Statesman, and *Laws*

The political philosophy of Plato is contained in three treatises dealing primarily with affairs of state: the *Republic,* the *Statesman,* and the *Laws.* The *Republic,* written in Plato's middle age, sets forth his ideals; the *Statesman,* written later, states some ideas more precisely; and the *Laws,* Plato's largest book, composed in his old age, aims to adapt in practical fashion his political dreams to human nature. In these, as in most of his other writings, Plato employs his characteristic dialogic method of presentation. The framework is a supposed discussion between Socrates and several friends, a group typical of such people as Plato may have met in the Athens of his day.

Of all Platonic writings, the *Republic* is most renowned, widely read, and influential. Though usually described as a utopia, the commonwealth depicted by Plato does not purport to be the kingdom of heaven. Reform of Greek society—not the millennium—is the aim. Realistically, it is proposed to take human nature as we find it and make the best of it. Plato conceived the Greek city-state as the highest known form of society, but one obviously suffering from serious internal weaknesses. Consequently, the problem to which Plato addressed himself was: What changes should be made in the organization of the city-state to eliminate strife and factionalism, provide the greatest good for all its inhabitants, and achieve a stable order?

An English scholar, F. R. Hoare, points out that *Republic* is not an accurate translation of the Greek title of Plato's masterpiece and that the work has nothing to do with republicanism. As used by Plato, Hoare suggests, the Greek word means "balanced constitutional government," or perhaps "constitutional regime."

The troubled era in which Plato lived was a major element in shaping his political ideas. He had observed the disastrous consequences of the Peloponnesian War; witnessed the utter defeat of Athens and the downfall of democracy; seen crimes committed by both mobs and aristocrats; had the extremely painful personal experience of losing his revered teacher Socrates through a death sentence and being himself forced to leave the city by an intolerant government; and noted the calamitous consequences of political chaos. Thus, the motivations behind the *Republic* appear to have been despair and frustration.

Instead of a government buffeted constantly by the winds of change and chance, undertaking opportunistically to improvise short-range solutions to unforeseen emergencies—simply "muddling through"—Plato conceived that rigorous scientific thinking, reason, and critical analysis could be applied to political and social issues. From intense meditation and examination, men could build a state free of corruption and changeless in form. The product of Plato's imagination bears a far closer resemblance to the austere, disciplined, tightly regimented government of Sparta than to the intellectual, artistic, freedom- and luxury-loving Athenian society.

Plato's basic doctrine in the *Republic* is that men vary widely in abilities, mental capacities, and temperaments. The first step in the organization of the state, therefore, is a broad classification of human types, to be followed by a division of functions in the community. Roughly stated, there are the producers on the one hand and those who direct and protect the commonwealth on the other. Plato's state has three classes. At the top are the Guardians, who constitute the governing class; in the middle, their auxiliaries, a citizen army responsible for enforcing the Guardians' orders and for fighting the commonwealth's wars against other states (Plato's ideal state, it should be noted, does not abolish war); and at the bottom the artisans, the industrial and agricultural workers, including about 80 per cent of the population.

There are no great differences between the two highest classes in Plato's hierarchy, and as the auxiliaries or soldiers become older and wiser, while less fit for military duty, they may join the ruling aristocracy. Between the rulers and the masses, however, there is an unbridgeable gap. Nature, Plato is convinced, has created some men to rule and others to be ruled. The mass of the people are to receive a common education, including gymnastic and music training, but in Plato's view it is pointless to go further, since a large proportion of them are mentally incompetent to profit from advanced education.

Chief attention is concentrated by the *Republic* on the governing elite, who are to be morally and intellectually superior. In Plato's view expressed here, a strong government demands a governing class possessing a high degree of wisdom, who will control the desires of the common herd, knowing what is best for all the people. Plato's ideal is a well-trained administrative and political class dedicated to public service, oblivious to financial gain or even personal happiness.

Exceptionally able persons qualified to be rulers and true guardians of the welfare of all are few in number, says Plato. They are lovers of wisdom and philosophy; strong of character, temperate, and unselfish; contemptuous of rich living; and eager to do only what is in the best interests of the state.

Plato deals at length with the selection and training of the Guardians. They must, first of all, be supermen in physique, mind, and character. The body of Guardians will be chosen by a small number of true philosophers, who will recognize the qualities essential to the ruling class. Both the Guardians and the auxiliaries are required to undergo a long course of mathematics (arithmetic, geometry, and astronomy), harmonics, and gymnastics. Music is included because of the Greek belief that it has certain specific effects on character and the emotions. Also, as Lowes Dickinson remarks, "We have to remind ourselves that the term [music] in Greek was far more comprehensive than it is with us, and included all moral, aesthetic, and intellectual culture." The successful candidates for guardianship also devote five years to the study of philosophy.

Thus the training of Guardians and auxiliaries is to be well-rounded—mentally, morally, physically—and rigorous in all its phases, beginning from childhood. As to specific aspects of the curriculum, the music should be simple and severe; nursery stories derogatory to great men or to the gods must be excluded; Homer and other poets are to be banned, because they often represent the weaknesses of the gods and overdramatize the emotions.

After the rulers are selected, trained, and installed in office, Plato realizes that they might be tempted by their great power to become avaricious at the expense of the state. To preserve their virtue and to insure undivided devotion to the state, Plato proposes to protect them against disrupting and corrupting influences, especially financial greed and sexual excesses. Therefore, the Guardians are to be forbidden to hold property beyond a few incidentals or to have families.

In effect, the governing elite in Plato's *Republic* lives under a communistic regime. Its members are required to share their goods, houses, and meals. No one has a home which others may not freely enter; all living is in common, and everyone takes his meals at public tables, military fashion. Communism applies not only to property but to women and children. No man may claim a woman as his own; all ruling-class citizens are brothers; the children belong to the community, and their family is the state. Thereby, "in every one he meets the citizen will think he has a brother or sister, or father or mother, or son or daughter, or grandchild or grandparent." Plato's reasoning is that normal family life, marriage and parenthood, absorb too much of a man's energy and interest, which are better reserved for the state.

These arrangements do not imply debauchery or promiscuity. Since the most intellectual and spiritual individuals are to be chosen for the governing hierarchy, celebacy is not to be practiced; propagation of Guardians will enrich the race. The children of the Guardians are to be bred according to strict eugenic principles and brought up in state nurseries and schools. Parents and children will be unknown to each other. The best families will create as many children as the state needs, no more.

Plato never married nor possessed a family and could therefore view matrimony and the family as an institution objectively and theoretically, though hardly realistically.

Plato's concept of the role of women in his ideal society is enlightened. He would exercise as much care in selecting women of suitable temperament and ability for the Guardian class as in choosing men, and would assure their proper education. The only radical difference recognized between men and women is childbearing, and women, he asserts, vary as widely in their aptitudes and abilities as do men. Because the Guardian women are freed from the task of rearing children and maintaining a family, they are able to share equally with the men the duties of governing the state. Woman suffrage would also prevail for the two upper classes.

Plato's ideal commonwealth would thus be ruled by a gifted class of men and women who have sacrificed property and material comforts, who procreate in the best interests of the state, who subordinate passion and individuality to the spirit and to reason.

It should be stressed that the Platonic scheme of marital and birth control applies solely to the governing class. The peasants, artisans, and tradesmen would be left to their old institutions, including marriage, family life, and private property. The lower classes, it is assumed, are in no need of superior morality and therefore may indulge their appetites as much as they please—provided they remain obedient, well-behaved members of the community.

One of the less savory aspects of Plato's *Republic* is its insistence upon censorship, with the Guardians serving as censors. Only music that would stimulate vigor and virtue is to be permitted. Belles lettres, including most poetry, are accepted only in part, after suitable expurgations, and the Greek classics must not be given to youth until censored. Plato finds the influence of poetry wholly bad except for hymns to the gods and praise of great men. In short, poetry, art, and music are to be subordinated to political needs.

The role of religion in Plato's ideal state is basic. All citizens are to be compelled to believe in the gods on pain of death or imprisonment, because lack of piety undermines the strength of the state. A severe critic, John Bagnell Bury, in his *History of the Freedom of Thought* notes: "But the point of interest in Plato's attitude is that he did not care much whether a religion was true, but only whether it was morally useful; he was prepared to promote morality by edifying fables; and he condemned the popular mythology not because it was false, but because it did not make for righteousness."

Would the general populace accept the system of government to be imposed upon it in Plato's commonwealth? To make the scheme palatable, the people are to be persuaded, through "beneficent falsehoods," that the Guardians are endowed with a kind of divine power and are a chosen people. One of the characters in the *Republic* asks, "Is such an order of things possible, and how, if at all?" Socrates is quoted as replying, "Until philosophers are kings or the kings and princes of this world have the spirit and power of philosophy, and political greatness and wisdom meet in one, and those common natures who pursue either to the exclusion of the other are compelled to stand aside, cities will never have rest from their evils—no, nor the human race, as I believe, and then only will this our State have a possibility of life and behold the light of day."

Plato saw that a perfect state would be constantly imperiled by reaction and potential disintegration. He describes four stages on the downward path. When the rulers seek personal power and honor, the ideal republic will be superseded by a timocracy, a government dominated by men of ambition. In time, timocracy is transformed into oligarchy or plutocracy, where riches and power are concentrated in the hands of a few great families or individuals, and the masses live in poverty. Eventually there is revolution, the oligarchs are overthrown, and the people rule—a democracy. But the people are incapable of self-government, and a period of moral laxity, lawlessness, anarchy, mob rule, and demagoguery ends in a tyranny or despotism—the lowest form of the state.

Platonic politics takes as a fundamental premise the absolute supremacy of the state. Though the ideal state is to be governed by philosophers, there is scarcely any freedom allowed in any human activity, and intellectual freedom, in particular, is ruthlessly suppressed. The welfare of the state is all-important, and only the state is enduring. Individuals come and go in quick succession, and they must, if necessary, be sacrificed to the state. For these reasons, Plato has been called "the greatest exponent of totalitarianism." Bertrand Russell has remarked on the close resemblances between the Republic of Plato and the Bolshevik regime in the Soviet Union during the latter's early years:

The Communist Party corresponds to the Guardians; the soldiers have about the same status in both; there is in Russia an attempt to deal with family life more or less as Plato suggested. I suppose it may be assumed that every teacher of Plato throughout the world abhors Bolshevism, and that every Bolshevik regards Plato as an antiquated *bourgeois*. Nevertheless, the parallel is extraordinarily exact between Plato's Republic and the régime which the better Bolsheviks are endeavouring to create.

Francis M. Cornford of Cambridge University rises to Plato's defense, suggesting that "the philosophies which severally inspire the two systems are almost diametrically opposed; and I am inclined to think that . . . Plato would have repudiated dialectical materialism founded on a false analysis of human nature." A close student of the *Republic* is forced to the conclusion, however, that Plato distrusted the masses and rejected all democratic concepts. "It is paradoxical," says George Sarton, "that the writer who hated individualism was canonized as a master of humanism," to which Marie Louise Berneri, in her *Journey Through Utopia*, adds that the *Republic* "has been chiefly admired by men whose principles were completely opposed to those of Plato."

Subsequent to writing the *Republic*, Plato was provided with an opportunity to inaugurate the aristocracy of his dreams under the patronage of Dionysius II of Syracuse. In the year 367 B.C., Plato was invited by Dionysius the Younger, ruler of Syracuse, capital of Sicily, to come and turn his kingdom into a utopia. Plato accepted, but the experiment was a fiasco, ending in a bitter quarrel, and, according to one tradition, on his way home Plato was captured and sold into slavery until ransomed by a friend.

It was, then, in a spirit of complete disillusionment, late in life, that Plato wrote his two final political treatises, the *Statesman* and the *Laws*.

In the *Statesman*, a young Socrates and his friends compare forms of government, and discourse on the qualities necessary for a perfect ruler. Originally, it is theorized, God ruled over men and cared for them. For unknown reasons, the perfect state came to an end, to be succeeded by the various types of government now to be found in the world. Some of these are superior to others. In preferred order they are: monarchy, aristocracy, democracy (subdivided into the lawful and the mob-directed), oligarchy, and tyranny. "But are any of these governments worthy of the name?" it is asked. "Is not government a science, and are we to suppose that scientific government is secured by the rulers being many or few, rich or poor, or by the rule being compulsory or voluntary?"

Only under an ideal ruler, trained, experienced, and unrestricted by law, it is concluded, can true political science be achieved. Such a monarch must be learned, wise, impartial, upright, diligent, able, and masterful—resembling closely the divine power who once ruled over mankind. Present forms of government are tolerated because "men despair of the true king ever appearing among them; if he were to appear they would joyfully hand over to him the reins of government." Humanity would be restored to paradise with his coming, and all imperfect forms of government swept away.

Socrates does not appear in the *Laws*, but the dialogue is carried on by other characters. Plato's apparent aim is to design a complete system of laws for the government of a state. W. W. Willoughby, in his *The Political Theories of the Ancient World*, offers the following critical estimate of the work:

In a tedious way specific laws are laid down for the regulation of the most trivial of human actions and interests. Unfortunately, moreover, these legislative minutiae are given in no coherent order, and are without any very evident attempt to apportion the amount of discussion according to their relative degrees of importance. Particular laws are taken up at random, apparently as they happen to occur to the mind; sometimes they are preceded by elaborate introductions, but at other times, and more often, are brought up and dismissed without comment.

A significant indication of changes in Plato's political theories, to be seen in the *Laws*, is abandonment of the more unrealistic doctrines of communism contained in the *Republic*. Community property is replaced by an equal division of land, with regulations to prevent future concentration of ownership. Inheritance laws would make illegal the building up of large estates, and the use of money is banned, as is the charging of interest.

Also discarded by the *Laws* is the community of wives and children, and marriage is permitted, though under strict state control and supervision. The behavior of married couples would be regulated by a state official during the first ten years—a period to be devoted to the bearing of children for the state. Until the age of seven, children remain with their parents, after which they would become wards of the state and be educated according to the principles stated in the *Republic*. Women would receive the same education as men, though would not be relieved of domestic duties.

Two classes of citizens are provided for by the *Laws*: freemen, similar to the Guardians in the *Republic*, who would devote themselves entirely to public affairs; and industrial workers to carry on the community's economic activities. Buying or selling for profit is forbidden. Government would be administered by a popularly elected assembly and executive council, though with provisions to maintain control in the hands of the wealthier classes. Finally, a supreme tribunal of censorship would be established to review all legislation and to maintain unchanged the fundamental character of the state. The *Laws* manifest Plato's innate conservatism and deep aversion to innovations in political science.

Timaeus

The *Timaeus* is generally regarded as Plato's most important scientific treatise. One commentator (R. G. Bury, Plato editor and translator) declares that "the literary genius displayed in the style and diction of its central Myth has compelled the admiration of the artistic reader." A historian of science (George Sarton), on the other hand, damns it as "a monument of unwisdom and recklessness." The diametrically opposing views reflect the attitudes of literary scholars and of men of science generally.

Ostensibly, the *Timaeus* is a sequel to the *Republic*, and it summarizes portions of the latter work in a prefatory chapter. The central myth referred to by Bury is the creation of the universe. Predominant throughout is the thought that the universe is a product and revelation of intelligent design and beneficent purpose. Plato's dialogue is voiced by Timaeus, a Pythagorean philosopher, who proceeds to expound a theory of the whole universe, from the motions of the heavens to human physiology. A poetic analogy is drawn between the human body (a microcosm) and the universe or universal body (the macrocosm).

In the introduction of the *Timaeus* is the famous story of Atlantis, as told by Solon, the wisest of the Seven Wise Men. Atlantis was a mythical island in the western sea, inhabited by a barbarian people defeated in a glorious war by the ancient Athenians nine thousand years earlier, after which Atlantis sank into the sea. These prehistoric Athenians are assumed to have been citizens of Socrates' ideal state.

The remaining five-sixths of the *Timaeus* is Plato's discourse on creative evolution, his "hymn of the universe," the making of the Soul of the World. As in Genesis, we are asked to imagine a point before time began and "the earth was without form and void." A vaguely visioned chaos is transformed, step by step, by the World-Artificer, a supreme artisan, into a cosmos, a fully harmonious structure. The World-Artificer is not, strictly speaking, a creator, but one who brings order and system out of a previously existing confused state of primordial matter. From certain elements of Platonic logic, psychology, and metaphysics, and the harmonic ratios of the Greek scales, a soul of the universe is created and placed in the body of the world to regulate eternally the movements of the sun, moon, planets, and stars. Along with the heavens, the days and nights, the months and years—that is, time—come into being.

Plato's description of the process of creation is written in obscure, mystical language, a mixture of mathematics and myth, which philosophers have been trying to interpret for the past two thousand years. His intention, apparently, was to explain the heavenly bodies, their periods and revolutions. Thus, the World-Soul combines a "Circle of the Same," referring to the fixed stars, and "Circles of the Other," meaning the seven planets. Seven kinds of motion are distinguished, with the Soul as the originator of all movement. The highest type of motion is the uniform revolution of a sphere revolving on its own axis and in the same spot. The "Body of the Universe," says Timaeus, is compounded of the four elements—fire, air, water, and earth.

This is the framework in which Plato places an accumulation of facts, ideas, and fanciful notions. Patently, it is a conglomeration of myths, allegories, and symbols. One of Plato's chief purposes in studying the cosmos was, R. G. Bury believes, "as a help to the knowledge of law and order, measure and symmetry, uniformity and regularity, harmony and rhythm; and to the application of these to the art of life." By learning to keep in step with the rhythm of the cosmos and in tune with the celestial harmonies, men may discover a pattern for their own souls and emotions.

Projecting his theories to physiology and the human body, Plato concludes that the World-Artificer sowed a divine seed in man and endowed him with an immortal soul but then, so that he might be also mortal, allowed the lesser gods to fashion his body and implant in his chest a mortal soul. The body is constituted from the four elements and disease is caused by the disarrangement of the elements, leading to a lack of balance in the four qualities (hot, cold, moist, and dry) and the four temperaments (blood, phlegm, black bile, and yellow bile).

Plato's science is for the most part fantastic, bearing little resemblance to modern scientific discoveries. He emphatically rejects the practice of experimentation as impious or as a base mechanical art, although he prizes mathematics, and his philosophy is colored with mathematical ideas, derived chiefly from his Pythagorean friends. Only pure mathematics is to be tolerated; Plato in fact so disliked practical applications that he condemned the use of instruments except perhaps the ruler and the compass. Mathematics, Plato says in the *Republic*, "is to be pursued for the sake of knowledge and not for huckstering."

Another deleterious effect of Plato's cosmic concepts is pointed out by Sarton, who notes: "The astrologic nonsense that has done so much harm to the Western world and is still poisoning weak-minded people today was derived from the *Timaios*, and Plato's astrology was itself an offshoot of the Babylonian one."

The influence of *Timaeus* upon later times was immense, second probably only to Aristotle's *Physics*. Its exotic hypotheses were accepted as scientific truth, and its errors and superstitions perpetuated from century to century. Paul Shorey observes that "the Middle Age found in the *Timaeus* the Trinity, the cross of Christ, and the Holy Ghost (World-Soul)." A great seventeenth-century astronomer, Johannes Kepler, embraced without question the Platonic idea of universal harmony in the cosmic order. But neither Plato nor Aristotle should be overly blamed for seeking to find truth, or for the later misuse of their unproven guesses. Of Plato, R. G. Bury's fair judgment is that "we must give him the credit of making a brave effort, in the *Timaeus*, to master and set down the best that was then known about the world of Nature and of Man."

5

UNIVERSAL MAN

**Aristotle: Organon, History of Animals, Physics,
On the Heavens, Meteorologics, Mechanics, Ethics,
Politics, Rhetoric, Poetics**

Aristotle, pupil of Plato and tutor of Alexander the Great, was the first universal man in the breadth of his interests. Proceeding on the conviction that unity and order prevail in the universe, "The Philosopher," as the ancients entitled him, set out to inventory and describe every imaginable aspect of learning: logic, mechanics, physics, astronomy, meterology, botany, zoology, psychology, ethics, economics, politics, metaphysics, and literature. The encyclopedic writings ascribed to him, estimated in excess of four hundred titles, encompass virtually all the existing knowledge of his time. A comprehensive view, based on facts, was essential, Aristotle believed, before any rational explanation of the cosmic order could be attempted.

Though the hazards of time and fortune have caused the loss of many Aristotelian works, those which have survived reveal a mind of prodigious erudition and versatility. Extant writings ascribed to Aristotle include six treatises on various aspects of logic, twenty-six in the natural sciences, four on ethics and morals, three on art and poetry, one each on metaphysics, history, and politics, and four on miscellaneous subjects. His learning ranged over every field of direct concern to ancient Greek civilization, and to each he brought a masterly touch.

For more than a thousand years after his own time, Aristotle was the supreme authority in all intellectual matters. On logic, mechanics, metaphysics, physics, physiology, astronomy, ethics, art, poetry, economics, and politics, his words were deemed irrefutable. To doubt them was little short of blasphemy and heresy.

Organon

Logic, the art and method of correct thinking, was created by
Aristotle virtually single-handed in a series of trailblazing
treatises known collectively as the *Organon* or *Instrument*—the
science of science. Six titles are included in this wide-ranging
compilation: the *Categories, On Interpretation, Prior Analytics,
Posterior Analytics, Topics*, and *Sophistic Elenchi*. Aristotle did
not originally conceive these volumes as divisions of a single
work, but the combination was made at an early date by some
of his followers. In their totality they possess considerable unity,
each pertaining to a separate aspect of the major theme, logic.

In the *Categories*, Aristotle deals with ten predicates—i.e.,
qualities, attributes, or properties. These are substance, quantity,
quality, relation, place, time, position, condition, action, and
passion.* The categories represent what may be stated in words,
answering questions one might ask in trying to learn the character of an object. The primary category is substance, the basis
of all the other predicates. Substance is divided into primary
substance (e.g., a particular man or animal) and secondary substances (the species and genera in which primary substances are
included). There follows a comparison of the characteristics of
substance and of the other nine chief categories. Aristotle enumerates, for example, several examples of the second category,
quantity: time, space, speech, lines, solids, and numbers. All
nameable things can be classed under one category or another,
though it is improbable that every attribute would be found in
a given object.

In *Of Interpretation*, Aristotle deals with propositions and
judgments and the distinction between true and false. Consideration is given to the relationship between language and thought.
The combination of notions or ideas in propositions or judgments
is essential, the author states, before truth or error can be discovered. Nouns, verbs, and sentences of various types are defined. Aristotle analyzes the nature of propositions, the necessity
of their containing a verb; the matter of a simple versus a composite proposition; and the fact that for every affirmative proposition there is an opposite denial. He also points out the difference
between contradictory and contrary propositions: in the case of
two contradictory propositions, one must be true, the other false;

*In the philosophic sense of the state or capacity of being affected from
outside oneself.

contraries imply that neither proposition is proven true and both may be false. Here, too, Aristotle introduces the question of "universals." To him, a universal is any common noun, any name that can be universally applied to the members of a class— e.g., man, animal, book, tree. But unlike Plato, he considers such universals as subjective ideas, rather than objective realities— simply as useful mental abstractions. Thus, particular men exist, but not a universal man.

The *Prior Analytics*, a treatise on deductive and inductive reasoning, presents the famous concept of the syllogism, called by Will Durant "the most characteristic and original of Aristotle's contributions to philosophy." In logic, the syllogism is an analysis of a formal argument, consisting of three parts: a major premise, a minor premise, and a conclusion. The conclusion necessarily follows from the premises, for if these are true, the conclusion must be true. For example, every virtue is praiseworthy; generosity is a virtue; therefore, generosity is praiseworthy. The difficulty from a logician's standpoint is that the major premise of the syllogism takes for granted the point to be proved; if not every virtue is necessarily praiseworthy, generosity may not be laudable. Nevertheless, the syllogism is an aid to the clarification of thought and exposition.

Aristotle next turns, in the *Posterior Analytics*, to the problem of knowledge. What is knowledge, how is it acquired, how guaranteed to be true, how is it expanded and systematized? At the outset, it is shown that in the acquisition of knowledge the mind advances from something that is already known, that is, a fact or a meaning. Some of our previous knowledge, however, may be only potential until it is made actual by reasoning. The *Posterior Analytics* treats in detail the characteristics which reasoning must necessarily possess in order to be truly scientific. The features that distinguish scientific from popular reasoning are examined. Particular attention is paid to the function of demonstration, that is, scientific syllogism, syllogism based on full knowledge and not opinion. Demonstration presupposes the knowledge of first premises not themselves known by demonstration. How do the premises come to be known? The first step, Aristotle finds, is perception, inborn in all animals; this is followed by memory of the perception; repeated memories produce experience; and from experience universals are abstracted and generalizations made. Through perception, memory, and experience, intuitive reasoning arrives at the first premises of science.

These first premises are the axioms of science—the propositions which one must know if one is to know anything (e.g., equals subtracted from equals leave equal remainders); the definitions arrived at on the basis of the study of causes; and hypotheses, or assumptions of the existence of the primary objects of science.

The subject matter of the *Topics*, to which the *Sophistic Elenchi* is an appendix, is the modes of reasoning at lower levels, falling short of the conditions of scientific accuracy. Here dealt with are the commonplaces of argument. The purpose of the work, says Aristotle, "is to discover a method by which we shall be able to reason from generally accepted opinions about any problem set before us and shall ourselves, when sustaining an argument, avoid saying anything self-contradictory." Dialectic, or the art of debate and disputation, he states, has three uses: as mental training; for general conversation (to be able to argue with people we meet); and for application to the sciences. Concerning the last value, two points are noted: first, we shall be better prepared to recognize truth and falsehood if we can argue a question pro and con; second, since the first principles of science cannot be scientifically demonstrated, the approach to them must be through the opinions generally held about them. As William D. Ross observes, "Aristotle's motive is to aid his hearers and readers not to win either gain or glory by a false appearance of wisdom, but to discuss questions as sensibly as they can be discussed without special knowledge." The treatise *Sophistic Elenchi* continues the general theme, with Aristotle's study of fallacies or sophisms as they may appear in dialectical discussions.

Out of the *Organon* as a whole emerges Aristotle's theory of knowledge: in essence, that experience is the true source and cause of all our knowledge. This work, George Sarton concludes, "gave the Western world its fundamental instrument, the universal key to philosophic and scientific discussion . . . there is no doubt that Aristotle's immense prestige and excessive authority in medieval times and later was largely due to his creation of the Organon. . . . The creator of the Organon became naturally in the popular opinion the master of all knowledge."

History of Animals

Aristotle was one of the true founders of modern biology. He recorded the main facts of biological life—as he saw them—in his

History of Animals and continued with a series of specialized treatises: *On the Parts of Animals, Generation of Animals, Movement of Animals,* and *Progression of Animals.* "For all his faults," says William Wightman in *The Growth of Scientific Ideas,* "Aristotle is the fountain-head of more ideas in the science of biology than anyone before or since." The greatest of modern biologists, Charles Darwin, offers further tribute: "Linnaeus and Cuvier have been my two gods, though in very different ways, but they were mere schoolboys to old Aristotle."

Biologists of our own time are amazed by the breadth of Aristotle's approach to the field and by the wealth of detail in his writings. He pioneered in the main branches of biologic inquiry, i.e., comparative anatomy and physiology, embryology, ethology (habits of animals), geographic distribution, and ecology (relation between organisms and their environment). Approximately 540 different animals are mentioned by Aristotle, in some instances on the basis of travelers' tales or of legendary lore, but for the most part from personal observation, and, in the case of fifty species, from a knowledge gained by dissection. If no direct knowledge were available, he obtained information from herdsmen, fishermen, hunters, bird-catchers, and apothecaries.

Aristotle defined life as "the power of self-nourishment and of independent growth and decay." He divided zoology into three parts: the general phenomena of animal life, or natural history; the organs and their functions, that is, anatomy and general physiology; and animal reproduction and embryology. Because of religious taboos, he probably never dissected the human body, and was therefore seriously handicapped in this branch of biologic observation and experimentation. The restriction accounts for a number of errors doubtless founded on mere hypotheses. However, that he made a careful and thorough investigation wherever practicable, is apparent throughout Aristotle's zoological treatises. Among the direct results of his inductive-deductive methods were such notable original discoveries as the mammalian character of the cetaceans (whales, dolphins, porpoises, etc.), differences between cartilaginous and bony fishes, the morphology of the four-chambered stomachs of ruminants, the development of the embryo chick (including the presence of the beating heart after the fourth day), the viviparous (producing living young instead of eggs) character of the dogfish shark, the close similarities in structure between birds and reptiles, the place of the monkey's form midway between quadrupeds and man, and the fact that as species become more highly developed and specialized they produce fewer offspring.

Further, Aristotle propounded various biological problems whose solutions were not found until recent times—e.g., the breeding of eels, the anatomy of the hyena, questions of heredity (resolved by the epochal experiments of Gregor Mendel in the nineteenth century), the reproduction of bees (a phenomenon not yet fully understood), and the influence of diet on animal habits.

On the other hand, because he was exploring unknown worlds and blazing new trails, Aristotle was frequently misled into erroneous observations and theories. The lapses may be attributed to a total lack of scientific instruments and of reliable reference books, to the want of opportunity for vivisection and dissection, and on occasion, to preconceived notions. Thus, Aristotle states such propositions—absurd to us—as these: the heart is the seat of intelligence and the brain's function is to cool the heart; man has only eight ribs on each side; woman has fewer teeth than man; the male element in reproduction merely stimulates and quickens; plants do not reproduce sexually; the egg or cell is not at first a living thing; the lowest forms of life are "spontaneously generated"; the lungs serve to temper the body heat by means of the inhaled air; there is no essential difference between arteries and veins; some viviparous quadrupeds lack gall bladders; and female offspring are the result of the failure of form to dominate matter, i.e., they are imperfect or incomplete men.

Of particular interest in the development of the biological sciences is Aristotle's efforts to classify animal species—a field in which his contributions were the most significant up to the time of Linnaeus, more than two thousand years later. Aristotle's classification begins with a fundamental division of the animal kingdom into two parts: those with blood and those without blood—corresponding approximately to the modern groupings of vertebrates and invertebrates. He believed that all life forms one continuous link, each variety shading into the next. Proceeding from the lowest to the highest organisms, there are infinitesimal gradations in structure, manner of life, methods of reproduction and rearing, sensation, and feeling. "Nature makes so gradual a transition from the inanimate to the animate kingdom," states Aristotle, "that the boundary lines which separate them are indistinct and doubtful." The correlation is direct, he holds, between intelligence and complexity of structure and mobility of form.

In his system of classification, Aristotle rejected an earlier theory that animals could be placed in contrasting groups, e.g., land and water animals, and those with or without wings; he noted, for example, the existence of winged and wingless ants. Three kinds of likeness, according to Aristotle, are to be found in the animal kingdom: complete identity of type within a given species, though with minor variations between individuals; likeness between species of the same "greatest genus" possessing the same bodily parts, but those parts differing in such characteristics as number, size, softness or hardness, smoothness or roughness; and, finally, likeness by analogy between the "greatest genera." Concerning the last, Aristotle warns against mistaking apparent similarities due to homology (e.g., bone and fish spine, scales and feathers, nail and hoof, and arm, foreleg, wing, and fin) for real relationships.

Applying all criteria available to him, Aristotle's classification scheme, or "Ladder of Nature," as it came to be called by later naturalists, comprises six major groups of vertebrates, in descending order: man, hairy quadrupeds (land mammals), sea mammals, birds, reptiles and amphibia, and fishes. The invertebrates were reduced to five principal classes—cephalopods (squids, cuttlefishes, octopuses, etc.); crustacea (lobsters, shrimps, crabs, etc.); insects; mollusks other than cephalopods; and zoophytes (corals, sea anemones, hydroids, sponges, etc.)—the last presumed to be produced by spontaneous generation.

The culminating section of Aristotle's zoological works is the *Generation of Animals,* treating the organs of reproduction and the reproductive functions. This work made important contributions to the science of embryology, notably in such steps as the introduction of the comparative method, the classification of animals according to their manner of embryonic development; the conclusion that sex is determined at the very beginning of embryonic growth; and establishment of the correct functions of the placenta and the umbilical cord.

The catholicity of Aristotle's biologic interests is also displayed in his writings on the geographic distribution of plants and animals. He dwells at length on the migration of animals, biological geography, the relation between living beings and their physical environment, the ways in which each animal is affected by other animals and plants, the incredible prolificness of certain animals (such as mice), observations of the fact that some animals prey on others or are preyed upon, and the disappearance of some species because of unfavorable environmental factors.

A peculiar feature of Aristotelian biology is a profound belief in teleology, the doctrine that "Nature never makes anything that is superfluous." As opposed to mechanical explanations of life, teleology holds that every species or individual is being directed toward an end or shaped for a purpose; all parts work for the greatest good of the whole; every organ or part of the body has its distinctive function. This concept is closely allied to Aristotle's idea of the soul. "As every instrument and every bodily member serves some partial end, some special action," he declares, "so the whole body must be destined to minister to some fuller, some completer, some greater sphere of action. The body must somehow be made for the soul and each part thereof for some separate function to which it is adapted." For Aristotle, living things are intelligible only in relation to the idea of the soul. Aristotle is thus a "vitalist," and as Charles Singer observes, "The division between *vitalist* and *mechanist* extends throughout the history of science and still separates students of living things."

Summing up the magnitude of Aristotle's biologic genius, George Sarton remarks, "He was not only the first great one in his field, somewhat like Hippocrates in medicine, but he remained the greatest for two thousand years."

Physics, On the Heavens, Meteorologics, and *Mechanics*

When Aristotle had completed his *History of Animals* and related biological studies, he turned to an examination of the material universe, seeking to fit it into his scheme of classification of the sciences and systematization of knowledge. Several important works grew out of these investigations, notably the *Physics, On the Heavens,* the *Meteorologics,* and *Mechanics.*

From a scientific point of view, unfortunately, Aristotle's physical and astronomical conceptions and conclusions are far inferior to his biological researches. Sir James Jeans calls him "a feeble physicist," adding that "his acute powers of observation led him nowhere in physics, since the physical world is too complex for its secrets to be unravelled by a mere inspection." Aristotle lacked personal knowledge and experience in these matters and apparently undertook no experimentation to prove or disprove his theories. The long-range effects were disastrous, for Aristotle's physical and astronomical conceptions profoundly influenced would-be scientists in the centuries that followed, while his biological works were comparatively neglected.

In the language of Greek philosophy, the word "physics" is broad in meaning. It may be more properly translated as nature or natural philosophy, organic and inorganic. Aristotle's *Physics* treats first the elements of matter. All terrestrial bodies, it is stated, are composed of four elements: earth, water, air, and fire. For celestial bodies, however, a fifth element, ether—"the quintessence"—forms the basic substance of the universe. The four mundane elements, in turn, contain the four "qualities": heat, cold, dryness, and moisture. The doctrine of the four elements (derived by Aristotle from the Pythagoreans, an earlier school of philosophy) was a firm tenet of orthodox medieval theology and was accepted almost unquestioned until the eighteenth century.

According to Aristotle's view of the universe, the earth is surrounded by an atmospheric sphere, and around that are spheres of pure elemental nature. Farther out are seven spheres, each carrying a planet, an eighth sphere bearing the fixed stars, and finally a sphere which, by divine harmony, is responsible for the circular revolution of the whole celestial system.

Aristotle taught further that the universe itself is spherical and finite. It has to be spherical because the sphere is the most perfect shape, and it is finite since the earth is its center. The earth itself is spherical, for reasons of symmetry and equilibrium. The Pythagorean hypothesis that a central fire is the center of our planetary system is rejected in favor of a geocentric or earth-centered scheme. Man is seen as the center of all creation and as its greatest achievement.

There are two kinds of motion in space, says Aristotle: rectilinear and circular. Air and fire, relatively light, move up while earth and water, relatively heavy, move down. Celestial bodies, being made out of the fifth substance, ether, are governed by different laws; their natural motion, therefore, is circular, changeless, and eternal. Circular movement is perfect since the circle is the perfect figure. Celestial motion is "natural" and terrestrial motion is "unnatural," i.e., an earthly body moves only when some external force is exerted upon it, such as a stone being thrown. The acceleration of a falling body, claims Aristotle, depends upon its mass—a fallacious notion, but accepted for two thousand years. Aristotle was led into error by his own famous dictum that nature abhors a vacuum. There can, he maintains, be no void or vacuum in nature. Centuries later, Galileo disregarded the Aristotelian dogma, and considered the possibility of a vacuum and what would happen if resistances were removed; given these conditions, he found that speed is independent of the weight or mass of a falling body.

Four causes, states Aristotle, are at work in nature, and it is the purpose of physics to learn the causes of physical changes. As defined, the first cause is material, i.e., the constituent of an object, such as the bronze in a statue; the second is the form or pattern; the third is the "efficient" cause, i.e., "that from which comes the immediate origin of the movement or rest"; and the fourth is the "final" cause, that is, the end or aim (e.g., health is the cause of our walking). In Aristotle's view, none of the four causes in itself is sufficient to produce an event; instead, all four are necessary for the production of any effect. The causes, then, are the conditions required, but they are not separately capable of explaining the existence of a thing.

Aristotle refers continually to the distinction between potentiality and actuality. Where one thing acts upon another, he points out, the potentialities of the "agent," i.e., the cause, and of the patient that experiences the effect, are separate and distinct potentialities, but when actualized they coincide. A striking example is a magnet and a piece of iron. The magnet has the power of drawing the metal to itself, and the metal has the property of experiencing and answering to the pull of the magnet. The properties are simply potentialities until the two objects are brought into suitable relationship to each other, whereupon they actualize their potentialities simultaneously.

In further discussion of the phenomenon of motion, Aristotle maintains throughout the *Physics* that mechanical movement cannot be self-initiated by inert matter, though matter has a capacity for being moved by forces outside itself (e.g., a falling stone does not move itself, but it can be caused to move by the action of some other body already in motion). Animals, including men, seem to "move themselves"; the impulse toward movement, however, is prompted by a physical desire or mental process. Thus the ultimate origin of movement remains mysterious, leading the author of the *Physics* toward cosmic and theological conclusions.

The *Meteorologics* of Aristotle treats of the region between heaven and earth, the planets, comets, and meteors. Also included are primitive theories of sight, color vision, and the rainbow. As a whole, the work contains not only meteorology in the modern sense, but much of physics, astronomy, geology, and chemistry. Among phenomena described and discussed are meteors, rain, dew, hail, snow, winds, rivers and springs, the saltiness of the sea, thunder and lightning, and earthquakes. The range of interests is impressive, though frequently the conclusions are not valid.

Aristotle's physics dominated European thought until the sixteenth century, when a general revolt against his ideas and prejudices began. Even as late as the eighteenth century, Sarton notes, "Aristotle was still very much alive, though on the defensive."

Nicomachean Ethics

Along with numerous other firsts, Aristotle was the founder of ethics; the earliest formal treatises on the subject are ascribed to him. Of four ethical works in the sum total of Aristotelian writings, the *Nicomachean Ethics* is the most comprehensive and complete. The title is believed to have been taken from the name of the philosopher's son, Nicomachus.

The *Nicomachean Ethics* is divided into ten books: 1, The good for man; 2–5, Moral virtues; 6, Intellectual virtue; 7, Continence and incontinence, pleasure; 8–9, Friendship; 10, Pleasure and happiness.

Aristotle's aim in the study of ethics is to discover what manner of life is the most desirable and best, in order to determine man's highest good. Happiness, he states, is the chief good and everything man does is directed toward its attainment. "Every art and every investigation, and likewise every practical pursuit or undertaking," he writes, "seems to aim at some good . . . the end of the science of medicine is health, that of the art of shipbuilding a vessel, that of strategy victory, that of domestic economy wealth." Aristotle concludes that the purpose of life is not goodness for its own sake, but happiness. "For we choose happiness for itself, and never with a view to anything further; whereas we choose honor, pleasure, intellect . . . because we believe that through them we shall be made happy."

What is happiness? In different individuals, it may be defined in any one of four ways: first, as pleasure, which Aristotle regards as an end for slaves or beasts; second, as honor, an object of political life, assuring us of our own virtue; third, as wealth, which he considers a means not an end; and, fourth, as the life of contemplation or reason, the most exalted end. Man is unique in possessing the power of thought. It follows then that "Happiness is the activity of the highest part of our nature, i.e., reason." Aristotle goes on to observe: "Happiness implies also the absence of great sufferings, and the possession of goods in addition to the virtuous activity of the soul."

Intellectual perfection, says Aristotle, can be acquired through teaching, but moral excellence (courage, temperance, magnanimity, justice, etc.) or goodness of character is developed by habit. We become good by doing good acts, and the truly virtuous person consciously and consistently elects the proper action because he has the motive and disposition to make the right choice. Thus he reenforces his virtue and develops his character.

How may we recognize the distinction between virtue and vice? Here Aristotle introduces his famous principle of the golden mean, the middle way, as a guide to excellence. Qualities or traits of character, he decides, can be classified in groups of three, consisting of two extremes and a center course, which is generally to be preferred. By recognizing what is too little or too much, we come to an understanding of what is right. Thus, between cowardice and rashness is courage; between stinginess and extravagance, liberality; between laziness and greed, ambition; between humility and vanity, self-respect; between obsequiousness and sulkiness, friendliness; between shyness and shamelessness, modesty; between boastfulness and self-depreciation, truthfulness; between buffoonery and boorishness, good humor; between indecisiveness and impulsiveness, self-control. The ideal is the ancient Greek motto, "Nothing in excess."

The concept of the golden mean is not invariably applicable, Aristotle concedes. Certain attitudes and acts—e.g., envy, theft, adultery, and murder—are intrinsically bad—wrongful excesses without redeeming features. Further, it is concluded that men are to be praised or blamed only for voluntary actions, not for those performed under compulsion or through ignorance. By and large, however, the choice between virtue and vice is in our own power—the doctrine of free will.

Aristotle is no puritan. He is opposed to asceticism and views natural impulses as neither good nor bad in themselves. To avoid excesses, each natural inclination or emotion requires control, in terms of time, place, manner, and object. This conclusion reflects, as Will Durant notes, "the Greek feeling that passions are not of themselves vices, but the raw material of both vice and virtue, according as they function in excess and disproportion, or in measure and harmony." Only by being moderate, temperate, and upright in behavior can man be truly happy.

A hard-headed realist, Aristotle discerned that, aside from the golden mean, there are certain external requisites for happiness. Everyone needs a reasonable amount of worldly goods. Poverty is degrading, forcing one to be niggardly and avaricious, while a fair degree of wealth relieves the possessor of care and greed. But most essential of outer circumstances for happiness is friendship—a subject to which Aristotle devotes two of his ten books. Loving is said to be more necessary to friendship than being loved; a man wishes his friend well for the friend's sake, not for his own happiness. Friendship is more needed by the happy than the unhappy, for happiness is multiplied by being shared. Aristotle even places friendship ahead of justice: "When men are friends, justice is unnecessary; but when men are just, friendship is still a boon." Further, "A friend is one soul in two bodies." The higher the state of human development, the wider and more permanent does friendship become. Ultimately, it appears in man as the feeling of union with his kind upon which the family, the state, and all other human associations rest. But close friendships, says Aristotle, are possible only with a limited number of persons: "He who has many friends has no friend," and "to be a friend to many people in the way of perfect friendship is impossible." True friendship implies long duration, stability of character, and equality.

In the tenth and final book of the *Ethics*, Aristotle returns to the thesis that happiness in its most nearly ideal form is achieved through the pleasures of the mind, the intellectual pursuit of truth. "The operation of the intellect," he states, "aims at no end beyond itself, and finds in itself the pleasure which stimulates it to further operation; and since the attributes of self-sufficiency, leisuredness, and freedom from fatigue are found in this activity, it follows that the life of the intellect is the best and pleasantest life for man." In commending the intellectual way of life, Aristotle means the contemplation and study of truth in metaphysics, mathematics, and probably the natural sciences.

Aristotle's concept of the ideal or "great-souled" man sums up his basic ethical principles. In part, he concludes: "To be truly great-minded a man must be good, and whatever is great in each virtue would seem to belong to the great-minded . . . in wealth and power and good or bad fortune of every kind, he will bear himself with moderation . . . he will not be overjoyed in prosperity nor unduly pained in adversity . . . he is not a man to incur little risks, nor does he court danger, but on occasion he will incur great perils, knowing that there are conditions under which his life is not worth living. . . . He is the sort of man to do kindnesses, but he is ashamed to receive them; the former places him in a position of superiority, the latter of inferiority. . . . Further, it is characteristic of the great-minded man not to ask favors, or very reluctantly, but to do a service very readily. . . . He is open in his likes and dislikes, cares more for reality than for appearance, and speaks the truth . . . he is not servile in the presence of the great or wealthy, nor condescending towards people of middle station . . . he does not bear malice nor is he apt to speak ill of his enemies . . . he is slow of motion, speaks in deep tones, and his style of speech is deliberate, avoiding nervousness and a shrill voice . . . his happiness is not dependent on the company of others, he takes pleasure in privacy, unlike the man of no virtue who fears solitude."

Politics

Aristotle's *Politics* is concerned with the philosophy of the state, rather than with government or politics in any narrow sense. A modern authority, Chester C. Maxey, in his *Political Philosophies*, characterizes the treatise as Aristotle's "masterpiece" and asserts that "it clearly entitles him to be recognized as the father of political science." The *Politics* is the general application of the theories presented in the *Ethics*.

As a basis for the *Politics*, Aristotle collected and digested virtually all known constitutions and undertook intensive analyses of past and present political systems. Of 158 such studies made by him, only one survives, the *Constitution of Athens*.

For Aristotle, political science is the large-scale application of ethics. It is the science of human affairs, of man's happiness and good. Seeing man through the eyes of a biologist, Aristotle describes him as "by nature a political animal." Inescapably, a man's life is shaped by his social environment, by the laws, customs, and institutions of his community; if he is to develop his highest capacities, society must be organized to promote the general welfare. Therefore, the purpose of the *Politics* is to discover what factors contribute to man's happiness, and what forms of government and what social institutions are most conducive to attaining these goals.

Aristotle proceeds on the premise that "the State is a creation of nature," an organic evolution from the family, which was formed to satisfy certain needs, and from the villages, which were aggregations of families. Every combination was "for the sake of the good life." He who has no need for society "must be either a beast or a god." The bond which holds men together in states, says Aristotle, is justice, "and the administration of justice, which is the determination of what is just, is the principle of order in political society. . . . Man when perfected is the best of animals, but when separated from law and justice, he is the worst of all."

In an extended discussion of slavery which follows, Aristotle reveals himself as a true product of his own time and class. "Natural slavery," he suggests, is recognized by common sense: "some men are by nature free, and others slaves and for these slavery is both expedient and right." Undoubtedly, Aristotle was influenced in reaching this conclusion by the ancient concept that manual labor is unworthy of a free man, and by his belief that mankind is naturally divided into inferior and superior beings—a reflection of the prejudices of Greek society, of the cultured Greek freemen looking down on the barbarian. Maxey notes that "the learned apologists for Negro slavery in the old South drew their best arguments from Aristotle."

From slaves, one form of property, Aristotle goes on to a consideration of property and money in general. He rejects emphatically the principle of communization of property, holding that private ownership is justified on four counts: it provides incentives to progress; it gives man pleasure in his property; it encourages generosity and liberality; and "we should not disregard the experience of ages," i.e., the idea of private property must be good because it has existed so long. Aristotle regards the acquisition of wealth other than by barter as unnatural; he condemns as morally wrong the unlimited pursuit of wealth beyond what is needed for the purposes of life. Excessive inequalities of wealth, he points out, are perilous to the state's balance and harmony; consequently, a society without extremes of wealth or poverty, in which middle classes are strongest, is best.

Aristotle classifies governments or forms of state into three principal categories: monarchy, aristocracy, and constitutional government, each of which has a perverted form: tyranny, oligarchy, and democracy. Of these, he holds monarchy to be the most nearly ideal type of government. Its success, however, depends upon finding a man "pre-eminent in virtue" (intellectual and moral excellence) and in political capacity. Such men are few. The practical solution that appealed to Aristotle's mind was a compromise, including features of aristocracy, some feudalistic elements, and a certain degree of democracy. The working classes would not rule, and the ruling classes would be properly educated for the tasks of government. The end result would be a moderate constitutional republic, adapted to the kinds of people to be governed and to prevailing conditions.

Education and virtue, according to Aristotle, are the best claims to, and qualifications for, power. Also meriting consideration are wealth, birth, and numbers; in principle, those who contribute most to the common good in the state have most right to power. Citizenship, narrowly interpreted by Aristotle to include the limited number of individuals who had "the power to take part in the deliberative or judicial administration of the state," is best exercised, he thought, by economically independent gentlemen with adequate experience, education, and leisure to devote their undivided attention to government.

Above all, Aristotle demands complete unselfishness in rulers; they must place first the welfare of their subjects. Whether the government is in the hands of one man or many, it should be administered "with a view to the common interest," rather than to serve private purposes. Thus a middle class of "moderate and sufficient property" is preferred to "those who have too much of the goods of fortune, strength, wealth, friends, and the like," who will establish a despotic oligarchy, or to "the very poor, who are in the opposite extreme," from whom will come a degenerate form of government, with power in the hands of the poor and uneducated, called by Aristotle "democracy."

Much space in the *Politics* is devoted to the subject of revolutions, their causes, prevention, and cures. The principal motives for revolution, as analyzed by Aristotle, are: a universal passion for privilege and prerogative; excessive insolence or avarice on the part of rulers; too great concentration of power in one or more individuals; attempts to conceal the misdeeds of men guilty of wrongdoing; disproportionate increases—territorial, social, economic, or otherwise—of any part of the state at the expense of the rest; dissensions and rivalries among people of different races; dynastic and family feuds and quarrels; and struggles for office and political power between rival classes and political parties.

Revolutions may be prevented, Aristotle observes, by avoiding illegality and frauds upon the underprivileged, by maintaining good feelings between the rulers and the people, by keeping a close watch on subversive agencies, by altering property qualifications from time to time, by letting no individual or class become too powerful, by preventing the corruption of magistrates, and by practicing moderation in everything.

The basic issue in government, Aristotle holds, is between the rule of law and the rule of men. While recognizing the inevitable imperfections of laws made by men, he insists that "the rule of the law is preferable to that of any individual," for a government based on the rule of men is always characterized by arbitrariness and passion.

The two final books of the eight contained in the *Politics* describe and discuss the ideal republic, a striking contrast to Plato's *Republic*—the views of Aristotle are far less dogmatic and closer to reality. A model state, Aristotle concludes, must be adapted to the characters and needs of its citizens to enable them to realize the good life. Three prime components are necessary: first, a population not too small or too large for the best common life, properly distributed among husbandmen to provide food, mechanics and artists, soldiers to bear arms, tradesmen, priests to supervise religion, and public men to carry on the political and judicial functions; second, territory sufficient to permit the inhabitants to live comfortably and liberally, well situated for defense and communication, having access to the sea and a maritime force, and located in a temperate climate conducive to mental and physical activity; third, citizens of high character, such as the Greeks, who, Aristotle says, combine intelligence with spirit.

Continuing with his consideration of the ideal state, Aristotle maintains that state regulation of marriage and education is essential to production of the finest human material. The age of marriage should be fixed to prevent the marriage of persons who are too young or too old; persons physically or temperamentally unfit should not be permitted to marry; deformed and feeble-minded children should not be allowed to live; and parents should be forbidden to have children in excess of the state's population requirements.

In Aristotle's model republic, education would be systematic, universal, and public. Citizens should be trained first to be good subjects, from which it will follow that they will become good rulers. Education must be the business of the state, not left to the parents, and ought to be the same for all citizens. The total concentration on military education practiced by the Spartans is insufficient, since it fails to develop all man's powers, and neglects the peaceful virtues of temperance, justice, and intellectual pursuits. To produce the well-rounded citizen, the body, the appetites, and the mind must be trained. Education should train the body for the sake of the soul, and the appetites for the sake of the reason.

Despite dissimilarities between the political philosophies of Aristotle and Plato, as Maxey notes, "both thinkers display the same ethical fervor, the same passion for order, the same love of moderation, the same devotion to justice and reason, the same confidence in education, the same faith in humanity, and the same concern for the realization of the good life. . . . All who believe in new worlds for old are disciples of Plato; all who believe in old worlds made new by the tedious and toilsome use of science are disciples of Aristotle."

Rhetoric

Rhetoric, the art of expressive and persuasive speech, was highly esteemed and practiced among the Greeks from the earliest time. Sterling examples may be found in the *Iliad* and the *Odyssey*, from which arose the tradition that Homer was the father of oratory. After the establishment of democratic institutions in Athens, statesmen and politicians felt compelled to become skilled public speakers, in order to be able to impress and lead their associates and the general populace.

Aristotle's *Rhetoric* is essentially a speaker's manual, composed for sheerly practical purposes, and is in no sense a theoretical work. The treatise became the leading authority on its subject throughout the ancient and medieval eras, and its influence has persisted to modern times.

The *Rhetoric* is divided into three books. In the first, concerned with means of persuasion, three types of speech are differentiated: deliberative, forensic, and academic. Deliberative or political orators must learn to debate political questions in popular assemblies. They are dealing mainly with future contingencies—ways and means, war and peace, defense of the country, imports and exports, and legislation. This type of oratory is designed to show that a proposed course of action is expedient or harmful. Aristotle indicates the kinds of arguments appropriate in such political discussions.

An example of forensic oratory is the pleading of a lawyer before a court. In contrast to the deliberative, the forensic deals with past actions, legal or illegal, involving accusation and defense. The forensic speaker must consider motives for wrongdoing, the mental attitude of the wrongdoer, and the people against whom the wrongs are committed. Here, Aristotle reviews the principles and methods of pleading in the law courts.

The third of the branches of rhetoric, the academic or declamatory, is "show" oratory, pointing with pride or viewing with alarm matters of current concern. It will censure vice and the disgraceful, praise such virtues as justice, courage, self-control, magnanimity, liberality, and wisdom—and incidentally reflect credit on the orator's own moral character. This kind of rhetoric also has its rules, and to be effective requires different techniques from the other types.

In the second book, Aristotle considers the psychological aspects of rhetoric, based upon a knowledge of the human emotions and their causes and of different types of character. Oratory, he says, is fundamentally a conflict of passions, both on the part of the speaker and of his audience. As a preliminary, the speaker must convince the hearers of his own wisdom, virtue, and good will. Many emotions or passions are analyzed by Aristotle, together with their use in shaping thought in the direction desired by the orator, e.g., calmness and anger, friendship and hatred, fear and confidence, shame and shamelessness, kindness and unkindness, pity and indignation, envy and contempt. Also to be kept in mind are the characters of men, their minds, moral habits, weaknesses, and ages. Character will be affected by such factors as noble birth, wealth, power, and good fortune. Passions will vary with age levels: youth, prime of life, and old age. This section of the *Rhetoric* is a little dissertation on practical psychology, highly realistic, even cynical at times, in its keen understanding of human foibles, motivations, and impulses.

The second book deals, in addition, with the "commonplaces" of oratory: the topics or "regions" within which the most general arguments are to be found; a list of fallacies; the proofs common to the several kinds of rhetoric; and methods of refuting arguments. Also discussed is the use of maxims or proverbs— popular sayings epitomizing the people's experience and ancestral wisdom—as valuable vehicles for the orator's own arguments.

The third and last book is concerned with style and language. It is necessary, Aristotle asserts, to know how to say as well as what to say. Elocution, the management of the voice as to loudness, pitch, and rhythm, is considered briefly. In style, the chief goals should be clearness and propriety, i.e., neither pomposity nor triteness. One should avoid stilted, artificial language and frigidity (compound words, uncommon words, too many epithets, unsuitable metaphors). Compositions prepared for speeches should be easy to read and easy to utter. Propriety of style consists of three aspects: emotional, ethical, and proportionate to the subject. The first is to create a feeling of sympathy, the second is to express character, and the third is to avoid treating important subjects in a light manner or employing the grand style on trivial matters.

The conclusion or peroration of a well-planned speech, according to the *Rhetoric*, is composed of four elements: making the audience favorable to oneself and unfavorable to the adversary; amplification or depreciation; putting the hearers into an emotional frame of mind; and recapitulation of the principal arguments or points.

It is strange that Aristotle, who makes frequent reference to the leading orators of his age, never once mentions the greatest of them all, Demosthenes, especially when it is recalled that the two men were exact contemporaries (384–322 B.C.).

Poetics

Like the *Rhetoric*, Aristotle's *Poetics* is believed to have been composed near the end of his life—a possible explanation for the work's incompleteness. In any case, the surviving portion treats primarily of epic and tragic poetry, omitting any detailed analysis of comedy. Though a short treatise of only about fifty pages in ordinary type, the *Poetics* has exerted greater influence and received more intensive consideration than any other single work of literary criticism. A recent commentator, Francis Fergusson, calls it "the most fundamental study we have of the art of drama."

In undertaking to interpret the nature of drama, poetry, and tragedy, Aristotle had before his eyes the dramatic productions of the three supreme masters of the Greek theater: Aeschylus, Sophocles, and Euripides, to all of whom he makes frequent reference to illustrate critical viewpoints.

Poetics, as understood by Aristotle, is something considerably broader than the modern conception of the word. Essentially, the term is meant to cover the literature of imagination, as distinguished from historical and scientific writing. Thus in one of his opening paragraphs, Aristotle specifically mentions epic poetry, tragedy, comedy, dithyrambic poetry, and music as components of poetics. As further analyzed by William D. Ross in his *Aristotle*, poetry in its Aristotelian sense consists of rhythm, language, and tune, in various proportions or combinations, and includes dancing, prose-imitation (mimes and Socratic dialogue), elegies, epics, instrumental music, lyrics, tragedy, and comedy.

At the outset, Aristotle traces the origin of poetry, especially drama. It arises he says, from two instincts in human nature: the instinct to imitate, and the instinct of harmony and rhythm. Imitation is concerned with the intellectual and moral content of art; harmony and rhythm relate to the pleasures of form—the sensuous or esthetic delight we take in color, song, and rhythm.

Poets, Aristotle continues, all "imitate action," as do all artists. The various arts are distinguished from each other by the medium, object, and manner of imitation. "The graver among the poets," remarks Aristotle, "would represent noble actions . . . and the meaner sort the actions of the ignoble." Tragedy and comedy evolved from the introduction of improvised spoken parts in connection with dithyrambs and phallic songs, respectively; the writer of tragedy imitates a "serious and complete action," the comic playwright a "worse" or silly, absurd, ridiculous action.

Aristotle's definition of the art of tragedy is famous:

> Tragedy, then, is an imitation of an action that is serious, complete, and of a certain magnitude; in language embellished with each kind of artistic ornament, the several kinds being found in separate parts of the play; in the form of action, not of narrative; through pity and fear effecting the proper purgation of these emotions.

Poetic license is defended by Aristotle because, unlike the historian, who is dealing with actual events and particular facts, or the philosopher who begins with concrete particulars and proceeds to abstractions, the poet is concerned with general or idealized truth, that is, the universal.

Plato had attacked poetry and poets, charging them with misleading the young and uneducated, misrepresenting the morality of the gods, and undermining faith in heroes by depicting their human weaknesses. Aristotle replies by pointing out that the object of artistic imitation is men in action; some actions are good, some bad; and it is a historical fact that there are good, bad, and indifferent characters among men. Therefore, since poetry is an imitation of human action, the poet is justified in presenting evil as well as virtuous action. Aristotle holds, however, that immoral actions should be represented by the poet as unlawful in deed and tragic in outcome.

The prime object of tragedy, states Aristotle, is to arouse pity and fear—pity for the past and present sufferings of the hero, fear for those predestined to occur. But strangely, imitation in art renders pleasurable that which is painful in life. This paradox is explained by Aristotle's theory of catharsis. Through mysterious psychological processes, the emotions of pity and fear are purged away by tragedy. In keeping with his biological and medical background, Aristotle uses "purgation of the emotions" in the sense of removing or releasing these feelings—accomplished vicariously by poetic tragedy.

From a discussion of the origin and purpose of poetics, Aristotle proceeds to a detailed consideration of the elements of tragedy. The important ingredients are of three types: plot, character, and thought; diction and melody; and spectacle. Of them all, the plot, "the soul of tragedy," is regarded as most significant, giving meaning and unity to otherwise unrelated incidents. The plot is the vision or inspiration which moves the poet to write or sing. Every episode and all dialogue in a well-constructed drama must contribute directly to the organic wholeness of the plot.

Character, as used by Aristotle, generally means revelation of character. Psychological interest is uppermost in the creation of character. It may be achieved through conflict between individuals, conflict between groups, conflict between an individual and society, rebellion of man against the gods, or the effect of environment, accident, or divine action upon an individual. Aristotle maintains that the true tragic hero is fundamentally a good man with a damaging, perhaps fatal, flaw in his character—neither a paragon of perfection nor a villain; otherwise, we would be unsympathetic to his plight and suffering.

Of the remaining elements, thought is conceived as primarily a matter of rhetoric; melody as a pleasant accessory of tragedy, a kind of "sweetening"; and diction or language as "the art of delivery." The writer should avoid too splendid diction, Aristotle admonishes, because it tends to conceal character and thought. The last, spectacle, designed to appeal to the eye, includes the arts of the dancer, the actor, the scene painter, and others concerned with the techniques of production.

The form of tragedy, in another principle enunciated by Aristotle, ought to be perfectly balanced, with a beginning, a middle, and an end, i.e., the action should be complete—unlike life's actual experiences which are seldom, if ever, so neatly rounded out. Also, tragic drama should observe three basic unities: unity of plot, unity of time ("endeavoring to keep as far as possible within a single circuit of the sun"), and unity of action. Another well-known concept, unity of place (that tragedy should not represent actions which happen in different places), developed much later.

Episodes introduced by the dramatist to arouse pity and fear have the greatest effect, Aristotle says, "when they occur unexpectedly and at the same time in consequence of one another." Such incidents are described as "reversals of fortune" and "discovery" or "recognition." Every true tragedy involves a change from happiness to unhappiness, by a "reversal of fortune." Six forms of "discovery," called "a change from ignorance to knowledge," are noted, the most dramatic occurring "when the great surprise comes about through a probable incident," perhaps through accident or chance, as in Sophocles' *Oedipus* when Oedipus learns that he has unwittingly slain his father and married his mother.

George Sarton remarks that "the *Poetics* was not written for poets but for critics and philosophers; it was not written for seers but for men of science." There is justification for the statement in the fact that Aristotle composed the *Poetics* in accordance with principles he had earlier found effective in biology. In epic and drama, as in the study of biology, he was seeking distinct species, and for each species he wished to find the most perfect specimen. Yet, by using the methods of scientific analysis, Aristotle, as Francis X. Connolly notes, "saw poetry as a whole and in its parts, its appeal to eye through spectacle, to the ear through music and diction, to the reason through thought, to all the faculties of sense, intellect and intuition through the synthesis of plot."

6

MASTERS OF DRAMATIC ART

The Greek Playwrights

Insofar as surviving examples can testify, Greek theater reached a high state of perfection from its birth. Five names easily stand out: Aeschylus, Sophocles, Euripides, Aristophanes, and Menander. Their enduring influence is attested by frequent revivals of their work and the use of themes therefrom throughout modern literature and philosophy.

Aeschylus: *Prometheus Bound, Oresteia*

First in time is Aeschylus (526–456 B.C.), master of Greek tragedy. Of ninety-two plays by him, only seven have survived the hazards of twenty-four centuries. But on the basis of his extant works, Aeschylus is universally acclaimed as the supreme dramatist of the ancient world, ranking with Shakespeare in the modern age. Richard W. Livingstone, in his *Pageant of Greece*, writes of Aeschylus: "Nowhere else in literature is such audacious and colossal imagination, nowhere are we so constantly in the presence of the superhuman, nowhere is that superhuman so boldly and nakedly portrayed."

Aeschylus flourished in an epic era—the time of the Persian Wars. Following the defeat of Xerxes' and the Persians' seemingly overwhelming military might, the Greeks were seized with a kind of spiritual ecstasy, manifesting itself in an unparalleled period of creativity—in art, architecture, literature, philosophy, and science. Among the phenomena of that remarkable interlude was the sudden emergence of a highly perfected dramatic art. The four greatest names in drama—Aeschylus, Sophocles, Euripides, and Aristophanes—were near contemporaries.

The vision of a poet in a cloister does not apply to Aeschylus. He is said to have fought with conspicuous bravery at Marathon in 490 B.C. and again at Salamis a decade later. Thus he apparently wrote on armed conflict from firsthand experience and observation.

Aside from his extraordinary productivity as a playwright, Aeschylus revolutionized the techniques of the theater. He found a traditional stage form, a dithyrambic dance and chorus, led by a single actor. Aeschylus is credited with adding a second actor; and later he followed Sophocles in adding a third, thereby changing the nature of the performance, introducing dialogue, and making it possible to enact a complete story. Because the characters frequently represented gods and heroes, Aeschylus designed masks for weird impersonations of natural forces and fantastic mythological figures. To make the figures appear gigantic and awe-inspiring, he added height to his actors by developing the padded shoe, or buskin. He also decorated the stage and began successfully to employ machinery and scenic effects.

The first extant play by Aeschylus is *The Supplicants*, wherein the fifty daughters of the Hellenic patriarch Danaus seek refuge in Argos from the attentions of their cousins, the fifty sons of Aegyptus. They are saved by the Argive King Pelasgus and his people. The play is designed to pay tribute to hospitality and to condemn unholy love. Of greater interest is a second drama, *The Persians*, the only surviving historical Greek tragedy, written to celebrate the Athenian victory over Persia at Salamis in 480 B.C. A third play, *Seven Against Thebes*, deals with the gloomy myth of the house of Laius—an extended saga of parricide, incest, fratricide, and fatal political conflict. In the four other extant plays, *Prometheus Bound* and the trilogy known collectively as the *Oresteia*, Aeschylus reached the peak of his genius.

The story of Prometheus was first told in Hesiod's *Works and Days* and *Theogony*, where it is little more than a simple folk tale. In the hands of Aeschylus, Prometheus becomes the central figure of a cosmic tragedy. He is transformed into a friend and champion of mankind, of incredible fortitude and nobility. Arrayed against him are the harsh and tyrannical forces of Zeus, king of the Olympian gods. Prometheus thwarts the evil designs of Zeus to destroy mankind and to create another race. For defying the ruler of the gods in order to save man, Prometheus suffers dreadful torments, which extend through ages of time.

By way of prologue, it is related that Prometheus, one of the Titans, sided with Zeus in the war between the Titans and the Olympians, and thus aided Zeus to achieve supreme power. But later he turned against Zeus to help men. In the play, Prometheus describes the benefactions he has conferred upon humanity: by giving mankind fire stolen from heaven, he paved the way for numerous arts and handicrafts; he developed in men thought and consciousness; he implanted hope in the human heart; and he taught the race the arts of brick masonry, carpentry, astronomy, arithmetic, writing, the taming of horses, navigation, medicine, methods of divination, and the working of mines. "All human arts are from Prometheus," proclaims the hero; without the gift of fire, civilization could never have been attained. For these acts, Zeus would not forgive him.

To punish Prometheus for his defiance and disobedience, Zeus, at the beginning of the play, has him nailed to a fissure in desolate mountains at the end of the world—a rocky solitude high in the Caucasus. Transported there by Zeus's guards, he has been fastened to the lofty cliff by the reluctant blacksmith god Hephaestus. After their departure, Prometheus appeals to Nature. His suffering and disaster, he confesses, are caused by his own character and actions. "By free will," he says, "I sinned, I will not deny it. By helping mankind, I made my own agony." The twelve daughters of the Titan Oceanus, the play's chorus, hearing the sound of the hammer in their ocean cave, come to him through the air and bewail his wretched plight. Oceanus himself appears upon a winged steed and offers to mediate the dispute—an offer which Prometheus rejects lest Oceanus also be punished. Next comes Io, another victim, a maiden of Argos who has been changed by Zeus's wife, the jealous Hera, into a cow and driven by the sting of a gadfly to wander over the world.

But now the tables are turned to a slight degree. Prometheus has a weapon against Zeus. He knows a secret full of menace to Zeus, prophesies that he will be driven from his throne, unless he, Prometheus himself, aids him, but says that he will reveal the secret only in return for his own release. Zeus is afraid and sends Hermes to force Prometheus to divulge his foreknowledge. Prometheus mocks the messenger. At the climactic end, Zeus hurls his thunderbolts, tempest, and earthquake, blasting and smashing all the crags around Prometheus and hurling him into the depths of the earth, but Prometheus remains silent and unterrified.

Prometheus Bound is the first of a trilogy, of which the last two plays have not survived. There is a tradition that in the lost dramas Zeus releases Prometheus from his bonds, Prometheus reveals the secret, and the two are reconciled. By this time, too, Zeus has become friendly to mankind, apparently converted to the humanitarianism of Prometheus.

Prometheus was for Aeschylus a symbol of humanity—suffering like mankind, and symbolizing the victory of knowledge and art over power inimical to man. The basic theme, often recurring in Greek tragedy, is the conflict between brute force and justice, between man and his champion and a tyrannical god. Aeschylus believed that wisdom is born of suffering, and that good may come of evil. Many commentators have noted the striking parallels between the story of Prometheus and that of Calvary, five hundred years later, wherein Christ intervenes and takes upon himself the sufferings of mankind.

The *Oresteia* is a trilogy—*Agamemnon*, the *Choephoroi*, and the *Eumenides*—connected by a common theme, completed two years prior to the dramatist's death, and preserved intact. The work represents Aeschylus' maturest thought; the classical scholar Werner Jaeger describes it as "the most powerful drama in the entire literature of the world."

The *Oresteia* as a whole is concerned with the tragic repercussions of sin, transmitted from generation to generation, the direful consequences of a hereditary curse upon the members of the royal house of Atreus. As conceived by Aeschylus, crime and violence breed more violence; the sins of the father are visited upon the son; the descendants of a transgressor are driven to follow the same path, until retribution and final destruction overtake them. The original sinner in this instance is the Phrygian king Tantalus, father of Pelops, father of Atreus, father of Agamemnon, father of Orestes.

The scene of *Agamemnon* is the royal palace in Argos. When the play opens, Agamemnon, returning home victorious from the prolonged siege of Troy, receives a lavish but hypocritical welcome from his wife Clytemnestra. The King has brought with him as his prisoner and mistress the Trojan princess Cassandra, daughter of Priam. Cassandra, a prophetess, foretells "horror and the snare of hell," approaching doom, and her own death. The Queen, Clytemnestra, is burning with desire to avenge the death of her daughter, Iphigenia (sacrificed to Artemis by Agamemnon to obtain winds for the Greek fleet), and angered by the presence of Cassandra. With the connivance of her paramour, Aegisthus, she murders the king and then emerges with blood-stained robes, wildly triumphant and proclaiming the justice of her deed. The play closes as Aegisthus mounts the throne, but in the background the chorus utters an ominous warning: a god will guide Orestes back to avenge his father's death.

The *Choephoroi* opens with the return of the exiled Orestes, who has been directed by Apollo to seek revenge. Orestes enters the palace and slays Clytemnestra and Aegisthus. The boy has done his religious duty. His conscience revolts, however, at the terrible act, and he is driven mad by the realization that he is a matricide. As he flees, he is pursued by a band of Furies, the deities of vengeance.

The *Eumenides*, the concluding part of the trilogy, shifts the scene to Delphi, where Orestes has gone to invoke the aid of Apollo. Apollo promises to protect him and tells him to proceed immediately to Athens. Orestes is next seen at the ancient temple of Athena on the Acropolis, clasping the image of the goddess. He is arraigned before a court of Athenian judges, founded on this occasion as a permanent tribunal, presided over by Athena herself. In the end, Orestes is acquitted—Athena casting the deciding vote—and is reconciled with gods and men. The reign of law is thus established to replace blood revenge or the blood feud.

As viewed by Aeschylus, Orestes' guilt is not a natural reflection of his character. His conscience rebels against matricide. He is simply an unfortunate son, bound to avenge his father and bearing the burden of a relentless fate. His final vindication comes from his uprightness, his obedience to divine commands, and his sufferings. The ancient curse loses its power when it is inherited by a man of good will and good faith.

The lesson implicit in the *Oresteia* is that the sufferings of the world are a direct consequence of human sin. Further a fearful aspect of sin is that it casts its shadow over future generations, not of an individual family alone but of all society. In his great trilogy, Aeschylus shows that sin originates in arrogant, willful pride; once committed, it produces other evils; and retribution is inevitable. Aeschylus believed profoundly in the moral structure of the universe and the supremacy of the moral order. In his great dramas he showed that any violation of the natural order sets in motion an inexorable chain of events whose outcome must be punishment but which may end in atonement.

Sophocles: *Oedipus the King, Oedipus at Colonus, Antigone*

A younger contemporary of, and successor to, Aeschylus in classical Greek drama, was Sophocles (495–406 B.C.). Sophocles' first play, produced when he was twenty-seven years of age, won first prize in the annual competition at Athens; the last appeared on the stage four years after his death at the age of nearly ninety. In the interim, he wrote well over one hundred dramas, of which but seven are extant in their entirety: *Ajax, Philoctetes, Electra, The Trachiniae, Oedipus Rex, Oedipus at Colonus,* and *Antigone.* To Aristotle, Sophocles was the model tragedian, and his most famous play, *Oedipus the King,* the "perfect tragedy." A modern commentator, Sir Richard Jebb, says: "Aeschylus was a great creator; Sophocles pre-eminently a great artist."

Significant contributions were made by Sophocles to the techniques of the theater and stage. He added a third speaking actor to Attic drama; abandoned the trilogy form used by Aeschylus, thereby moving close to the dramatic form of the later Western stage; and was highly inventive in scene painting and stage settings.

Among the dramatist's early works is *Ajax,* a study of tragic error. One of the most renowned Greek warriors in the Trojan War, Ajax believes that he should fall heir to the arms of Achilles. Instead, the arms are awarded to Odysseus; and Ajax, in his wrath at being deprived of the honor, plans to murder the responsible leaders of the expedition, Agamemnon and Menelaus. To punish such arrogant pride, Athena comes from Olympus and casts upon Ajax a spell of madness in which he kills a flock of sheep, under the delusion that he is slaying his enemies. Quickly recovering from his insanity, and overcome by shame, Ajax commits suicide by falling upon his sword.

The theme of Sophocles' *Electra* was dealt with also by Aeschylus in the *Choephoroi*, and by Euripides in a play likewise entitled *Electra*—all dealing with the vengeance of Orestes upon his mother Clytemnestra for the treacherous murder of his father Agamemnon. Sophocles concentrates attention on one character in the drama, Electra, sister of Orestes. In a powerful psychological study, he portrays Electra as harsh and uncompromising, devoted to her father's memory, consumed with bitter, impotent hatred of her mother, and, after Orestes' return, goading him on to revenge.

Least highly regarded, perhaps, of Sophocles' surviving plays are the *Trachiniae*, or *The Women of Trachnis*, and *Philoctetes*. The first centers on a tragic and touching study of a jealous woman, Deianira, wife of the national hero and demigod Heracles; the second glorifies the impulsive nobility of youth. Sophocles' richly merited reputation as one of the supreme masters of the dramatic art rests upon three plays, *Oedipus the King*, *Oedipus at Colonus*, and *Antigone*—the so-called Theban Saga.

When the curtain rises on Sophocles' most celebrated play, *Oedipus the King*, a series of events shaping its action has already occurred. Before the birth of Oedipus, his father Laius, the king of Thebes, and his queen Jocasta, had received an oracular warning that their son would be the murderer of his father and commit incest with his mother. In terror of this calamity, they sent a shepherd to take the infant to a neighboring mountain to be exposed, with his ankles pinned together. Too humane to carry out his instructions, the shepherd entrusted the child instead to a stranger, who carried him to Corinth. There he was adopted by the childless King Polybus and his queen. But the oracle of Delphi repeated the prophecy to the grown Oedipus: that he would kill his father and wed his mother. Returning from the shrine, Oedipus met an old man and a retinue of servants. When assailed by them, Oedipus slew all except one servant, who escaped. The elderly man had been Laius. Continuing on to Thebes, Oedipus rid the city of the Sphinx, a monstrous creature which had been preying upon the people. In gratitude, the joyous citizens chose their savior to succeed Laius as king. They also gave him the widowed Queen Jocasta, still young and beautiful, as wife, thus fulfilling the second prophecy. For years the two lived in perfect happiness, producing two sons and two daughters, and the city prospered.

Then, as the play itself opens, in Thebes, before the royal

palace where Oedipus rules, catastrophe strikes. The city is suffering from a plague. Creon, the king's brother-in-law, who has been sent to the shrine of Apollo, returns with a message that the murderer of Laius is in their midst and must be driven from the city before the plague will pass. Oedipus sends for the blind seer Tiresias, who tells the king that he himself is Laius' unwitting slayer. The play's action comes to a rapid climax as incontrovertible proof amasses attesting to the truth of the accusation. Oedipus, a man of courage, nobility, and excellent intentions, beloved by his people, is a victim of fate and human error, guilty of parricide and incest, and, as such, one of the great tragic figures of literature. Unable to face the horrible facts, Jocasta hangs herself and Oedipus strikes out his own eyes. In agony but accepting his fate, he asks Creon to send him into exile which he himself had previously decreed for the unknown murderer whose pollution had brought the plague on the land.

In his *Poetics*, Aristotle derives his definition of the tragic hero chiefly from the character of Oedipus: "A man who is highly renowned and prosperous, but one who is not preeminently virtuous and just, whose misfortune, however, is brought upon him not by vice and depravity but by some error of judgment or frailty."

Near the end of his life, Sophocles returned to the Oedipus theme in his *Oedipus at Colonus*. Exiled from Thebes by Creon and his own sons Polynices and Eteocles, the blind Oedipus, now old and practically a beggar, is forsaken by all except his daughter Antigone. Before going into exile, Oedipus had cursed his sons for failing to protect him. Wandering from place to place, as the play begins, the father and daughter come to the village of Colonus and stop there to rest. Theseus, king of nearby Athens, receives Oedipus as an honored and illustrious guest. Creon comes to try to persuade the exile to return to Thebes, because an oracle has said that the city will suffer unless Oedipus is interred in Theban land. Oedipus' daughter Ismene arrives to inform him that Polynices and Eteocles are engaged in civil war for the throne, and she also begs him to return. Oedipus angrily rejects their pleas. Creon and his attendants seize Antigone and Ismene to carry them back to Thebes, but they are rescued by Theseus.

Oedipus chooses to reward Athens for befriending him and

to punish Creon and his own sons for their disloyalty. Polynices comes to try to win his support, but Oedipus denounces both him and his brother, and prophesies their violent death. Finally, the gods summon Oedipus, and in a splendid scene, heralded by thunder and lightning, he passes into the grove of the Eumenides to his mysterious death. When Antigone begs to know his burial place, Theseus replies that no human being may go near the spot. He tells the daughters to cease their lamentations and proclaims that Oedipus' "destiny has found a perfect end."

In his old age, we see Oedipus as a hero purified by his sufferings, not bitter or broken, but exalted by the ordeals which he has endured. He becomes a superhuman figure, his tomb will be a holy place, and the city in whose soil he is buried will win a great victory. His tragic life has not been without purpose. John Gassner, in his *Masters of the Drama*, observes: "The problem of inexplicable fate posed by *Oedipus the King* is not answered by the later work. But one solution is at least indicated: What man cannot *control* he can at least *accept*; misfortune may be borne with fortitude and be confronted without a sense of guilt."

Though dealing with events subsequent to *Oedipus*, *Antigone* was the first of the unplanned trilogy to be composed by Sophocles. The prevailing motif is conflict between human law and the law of the spirit or individual conscience. The heroine Antigone, loyal daughter of Oedipus, has accompanied her father into exile. She returns to Thebes after her father's death, hoping to reconcile her two brothers, Eteocles and Polynices, who are contending for the Theban throne. In the course of a bitter war, the brothers meet in personal combat and slay each other, fulfilling their father's curse upon them. Thereupon, their uncle Creon becomes king, and issues an edict forbidding anyone upon pain of death to bury the body of Polynices, who has been guilty of leading an invasion against his homeland. Flouting the most sacred duty of a family to bury its dead, Creon decrees that "none shall grace him with sepulture or lament, but leave him unburied, a corpse for birds and dogs to eat, a ghastly sight of shame" and "whoso disobeys in aught, his doom is death by stoning before all the folk."

To the Greeks, no greater disgrace could be inflicted upon the dead than to refuse burial, leaving the deceased without "honor among the dead below." Impelled by family ties and devotion and believing in her sacred duty, Antigone defies Creon's order and buries her brother, after her timid sister Ismene has refused to assist her. In the background, the chorus of the play divides, showing the conflict between the claims of family and of the state. Apprehended by Creon's guard while performing the burial rites, Antigone is condemned to be buried alive, and is shut up in a cave to die, despite an appeal from Creon's son, Haemon, to whom she is betrothed.

As Antigone is taken away, a seer, the old Tiresias, warns Creon that he stands "on the edge of fate" and makes a dark prediction of disaster. Fearful, Creon reverses his decision and orders Antigone to be freed. It is too late. Antigone has hanged herself in the sepulchral chamber, the grief-stricken Haemon commits suicide, and Creon's wife, Eurydice, broken by the death of her son, likewise dies by her own hand. Thus is Creon punished by the gods for his insolence. The closing words of the drama point the moral: "Wisdom is the supreme part of happiness; and reverence toward the gods must be inviolate. Great words of overproud men bring great punishments and in old age teach the chastened to be wise."

Antigone's fearlessness in braving the might of the king in defense of her convictions makes her a truly heroic figure. Even more appealing is her self-denial, through which she overcomes her fear of death and her desire to live. She is a martyr for an act of piety, which in her eyes has caused none to suffer except herself. "Unquestionably," declares Allardyce Nicoll, historian of the drama, "this is the finest and most delicately balanced of all the tragedies the Greek stage has to offer us."

The most memorable impressions made by Sophocles are through his characters. In the depiction of character he created an imperishable place for himself in the world's literature. His men and women are genuine human beings because he is supremely interested in humanity—the individual personality, in particular. His heroes and heroines experience violent passions and tender emotions; they are in a sense playthings of the gods, and yet by the nobility of their own natures, they rise above their conditions to encompass the divine within themselves. Though the idea of destiny is inseparable from the Sophoclean dramas, the spectator's attention is focused on individual character and this becomes the chief interest of a tragedy. Nowhere is Sophocles' power for drawing strong noble characters more in evidence than in his tragic heroines, notably Antigone, Electra, Jocasta in *Oedipus the King*, Deianira in *The Trachiniae*, and Tecmessa in *Ajax*. As poet and playwright, these are Sophocles' greatest achievements.

Euripides: *Medea, Hippolytus, The Trojan Women, The Bacchae*

Euripides (480–406 B.C.), third of the three giants of Greek classical drama, sometimes described as the first modern playwright, was also contemporary with Aeschylus and Sophocles. Euripides was called by Aristotle "the most tragic of poets." The description is apt; Euripides returns again and again to the theme of the pathos of undeserved human suffering at the hands of fickle, capricious gods, over whom man can exert no control. If we seek modern counterparts, close kinships can be traced between Sophocles and Shakespeare and between Euripides and George Bernard Shaw. Like Shaw's, Euripides' approach is characteristically realistic, intellectual, and skeptical. In his preoccupation with social problems, too, Euripides has much in common with both Shaw and Ibsen.

Essentially, Euripides was a nonconformist, a freethinker, and a humanitarian, generally on the side of the radicals and the pacifists of his day. His bitter social dramas, shocking to his fellow Athenians, led to accusations of blasphemy and perjury, ridicule, and harassment, until finally Euripides shook the dust of Athens from his feet and became a voluntary exile to Macedonia, where he spent his last years. In the annual competitions among Greek playwrights, he won highest honors but five times, compared with at least thirteen first prizes for Aeschylus and eighteen for Sophocles.

It is significant, however, that nineteen of Euripides' plays are extant, while only seven each have survived of those of his two great rivals. As a rule, the Greeks and their successors saved those literary productions that they regarded most highly. After Euripides' death, hostile critical opinion swung to the other extreme and eulogized his work.

The plays that we now possess appeared in the last quarter of Euripides' life. Most esteemed by modern commentators and historians of the theater are *Medea, Hippolytus, The Trojan*

Women, and *The Bacchae*. These titles are also illustrative of
the playwright's extraordinary range and versatility.

The motif of the tragedy of *Medea* is of betrayed love turned
to hatred, of a woman's whole soul so dominated by a lust for
vengeance that even maternal feeling is annihilated. The
legendary background of *Medea* is derived from the story of
Jason and the Argonauts who went in search of the Golden
Fleece. In the land of Colchis, the heroes discover that the
treasure they desire is guarded by fire-breathing bulls and dra-
gons. Without supernatural aid, Jason and his men cannot hope
to succeed in their mission. Medea, a princess of the country
who has fallen in love with Jason, betrays her father and uses
her magic arts to allow the Greeks to gain the treasure. She slips
away with them, and when the Colchians pursue the expedition,
she sacrifices her two brothers, held as hostages, to provide
escape. The Greeks proceed to Corinth, where Jason finds favor in
the court of Creon. Medea meanwhile has borne him two sons.

As the play opens, Creon has promised Jason that he shall
succeed to the throne if he will discard Medea and marry the
princess Glauce. Jason consents, failing to reckon with his
scorned wife, a woman threatened by exile and furious with
jealousy. Jason's character and role are far from admirable. He
is self-seeking, willing to accept the benefits of any crimes committed by his wife on his behalf, ungrateful and callous, a
cowardly opportunist; to gain position, ready in middle age to
betray and reject the woman whom he had formerly loved passionately—a nature meant by Euripides to stand for the perpetual
selfishness of men.

On the other hand, it is apparent that Medea and Jason are
mismatched. Here for the first time in dramatic literature appears the theme of miscegenation. Jason is an ordinary Greek.
Medea is a strange barbaric figure from the mysterious East.
She is of royal blood and divine descent, a member of a race
that Jason cannot understand, but toward whom he has an unjustified feeling of racial superiority. Now, having forsaken her
own people, Medea is a stranger in a strange land, an alien without a country, having no one to whom she can turn for protection.

Medea has given her whole being to the man she loved—with
a love which has turned to fierce hatred. She plots a terrible
vengeance: the murder of her children. When Jason comes upon
the stage, she reproaches him violently for his unfaithfulness and

describes with angry despair her present plight. Jason attempts unsuccessfully to mollify her wrath, merely adding fuel to the flame. Aegeus, king of Athens, suddenly appears on his way home from Delphi and promises Medea refuge in his land.

Before destroying her sons by Jason, Medea exacts other vengeance. Pretending to be offering a token of reconciliation, she sends a splendid bridal robe to Glauce. The robe has been poisoned and will consume the flesh of its wearer. Glauce dies a horrible death when she dons the robe, as does Creon, her father, in attempting to save her. A messenger comes to inform Medea, who greets him with an ugly cry of triumph. Thus the stage is set for the final act of the drama. Medea kills the two children with a sword, immediately before Jason reappears. Standing on the roof of the house, Medea mocks him, is untouched by his insults, gloats over her victory. Her last words are spoken from a winged chariot which the sun-god, her ancestor, has provided to carry her safely to Athens.

For Euripides, Medea expresses the elemental nature of women unrepressed and uninhibited by Greek conventions. The play is a study of the conflict of the sexes, a depiction of differences in relative values between men and women, and a powerful defense of women's rights. It is also a landmark of realistic drama as it analyzes the destructive power of jealousy and hate. Allardyce Nicoll notes: "The intensity of the play, its bold presentation of the two main characters, its theme of sex-strife accentuated by racial disparities, and . . . its inherently sensational qualities have made it the happy hunting ground for modern playwrights of the realistic school."

The theme of *Hippolytus* is similar to that in the Biblical story of Joseph and Potiphar's wife. It is a full-length study, probably the first in dramatic literature, of criminal passion: the love of Phaedra, wife of King Theseus, for her husband's illegitimate son Hippolytus. Many critics regard *Hippolytus* as the greatest of all the extant plays of Euripides. The gods are intimately involved with the human drama throughout, and we witness men and women being destroyed unjustly by divine forces with whose power they are unable to cope. The goddesses Artemis and Aphrodite are incarnations of two warring elements in man: asceticism and sexual love.

By way of background, we learn that Theseus as a youth had loved the queen of the Amazons, Hippolyte, and to them had been born a son, Hippolytus. Later Hippolyte had been put aside and Theseus had made Phaedra, a Cretan princess, his queen.

Now having arrived at young manhood, Hippolytus worships the virgin goddess Artemis, his adoration taking the form of a love of Nature and solitude and devotion to athletic pursuits. In the prologue to the play Aphrodite, goddess of love, announces that she will punish him for scorning marriage and carnal desires: "His defiance of me will I avenge." Phaedra is to be inspired with a fatal passion for the young Hippolytus; she will die; and in her death Hippolytus will be destroyed.

In the opening scene, Phaedra, a chaste woman, is portrayed in the midst of an extended struggle to overcome her emotional involvement. She has fasted for three days, and is resolved to die rather than to disgrace her husband and children. Indirectly she reveals her guilty secret to an old nurse, who tries to convince her that it would not be sinful to give her love to another man. But Phaedra will perish before staining her honor. Without her consent, though not forbidden to do so, the nurse informs Hippolytus of Phaedra's passion for him, after first exacting from him an oath of secrecy. The pure young man is deeply outraged, denounces Phaedra and womankind in general, and threatens to break his promise of secrecy. He expresses no pity for Phaedra and gives a thoroughly unpleasant exhibition of self-righteousness. His tirade denounces the source of all life, Aphrodite, and blasphemes against the facts of human birth.

Phaedra's desire now turns to an overwhelming urge for revenge. She writes a letter to her husband, clearing her own reputation, accusing Hippolytus of violating her, and then hangs herself. Theseus finds the message, believes the dead woman rather than his son, and in furious anger curses Hippolytus and calls upon Poseidon to destroy him. The king remains deaf to all his son's pleas and attempts at self-justification. As Hippolytus, being driven into exile, rides along the seashore, his horses are frightened by a monstrous bull coming out of a tidal wave; they stampede, dragging their master to his death. Before he expires, Artemis appears and tells Theseus of his son's innocence and purity. Phaedra, too, is guiltless, for she has simply been an instrument for Aphrodite's revenge.

In *Hippolytus*, and elsewhere in Euripides' writings, the gods are represented as jealous, lustful, moved by mean motives, inferior morally to human beings to whom they bring disaster.

Nevertheless, the play is a powerful and poignant dramatization of an elemental conflict in human nature. Aphrodite clearly represents the overwhelming might of sexual love, the strong sexual instinct in man and woman and in all Nature. Artemis is the personification of asceticism and the rejection of the fundamental sexual instinct. The point is well stated by G. M. A. Grube in *The Drama of Euripides:* "His [Hippolytus'] refusal to recognize the power of sexual love reveals an incompleteness, an aloofness from the realities of life, a preciosity in his search for goodness which his youth may excuse, but cannot justify." John Gassner, in *Masters of the Drama*, adds: "In our day he would be labeled a 'case of arrested development' and his complex would be a field day for psychoanalysts. . . . In modern parlance, he is the victim of a repressed libido."

The Trojan Women has been called the finest war, or more exactly antiwar, play of all time. It is a scathing indictment of man's inhumanity to man. The play has topical interest; the year before it was produced, the Athenians had attacked neutral Melos, whose only crime was a desire to maintain her independence, and with shameless savagery had put to death all men of military age and sold the women and children into slavery. In all history, there has been no more cruel exhibition of power politics. As a reaction to it *The Trojan Women* makes clear that in war there is no real victor; inevitable doom awaits victors and vanquished alike.

As the tragedy of *The Trojan Women* begins, Troy has fallen; its men are all dead and only its wretched women remain, waiting to be assigned as slaves to their new masters. The shrines of the city have been desecrated by the conquerors, who spared no one seeking refuge there. Now the gods are angry, outraged at the brutality and impiety of the Greeks. For their sacrilegious behavior, the conquerors will be plagued on their homeward voyage by storms and lightning. Many of them will be lost. The god Poseidon's parting words are ominous:

> A fool among men is he who sacks cities,
> Brings desolation on the temples, the graves,
> The hallowed places of the dead, and thus
> Has brought destruction too upon himself.

The horrible day dawns after the fall of the city. The wretched women of Troy are heard bewailing their fate and grieving over their dead. There is little action on stage, but a series of episodes, related by the chorus, are building up to the climax: the remnants of Troy being put to the torch and crashing in flames. Three Trojan women have leading parts: Cassandra, the queen's daughter and Apollo's priestess, awarded to the haughty Agamemnon; the widowed mother Andromache, Hector's wife, who falls to Pyrrhus, son of Achilles; and the queen, Hecuba, won by the crafty Odysseus, whom she loathes: "that hateful cheat, that enemy of justice, that lawless beast." Also present, but escaping the sorrows of the Trojan women, is the hypocritical Helen, the adultress, the original cause of the war, who is so irresistible to her husband Menelaus that she goes unpunished.

The woes of the women of Troy accumulate. The virgin Polyxena, another of Hecuba's daughters, is sacrificed on the tomb of Hercules. Astyanax, son of Hector and Andromache, feared as a possible future menace by the Greeks, is thrown from the battlements to his death.

In the few brief moments before the final destruction of the city and the sailing of the Greek fleet, Hecuba prepares the mangled body of her grandson Astyanax for burial. Thus the sham glory of war is revealed in all its horrors. "The fall of Troy, the theme of the most glorious martial poetry ever written," notes Edith Hamilton, "ends in his [Euripides'] play with one old broken-hearted woman, sitting on the ground, holding a dead child in her arms."

The last of Euripides' plays dealt with here, *The Bacchae*, is fundamentally a study of religious frenzy, often strange, intense, and beautiful. It expresses the wild elemental fury of Dionysiac madness, symbolizing the ancient conflict between cold reason and the irrational forces of religious ecstasy. Dionysus has both benign and cruel aspects. Like some followers of Christianity, on the one hand, he preaches love and compassion; on the other, he inspires crusades and massacres. The fanatical devotion of his followers is a force for both good and evil.

The play is set in Thebes during the time of King Pentheus, who has replaced his aged grandfather Cadmus on the throne. The city has been seized by a frenzy of religious enthusiasm, marked by hysterical orgies in honor of Dionysus, the mystic wine god, son of Zeus by Cadmus' daughter Semele. The devotees of the new faith dress themselves in fawn skins, fondle serpents, abandon their homes, and engage in orgiastic dances over the wooded hills.

Pentheus, skeptical of the divinity of Dionysus, and attempting to appeal to reason, bans the exotic religion from the kingdom, imprisons its votaries, and orders the seizure and confinement of the god—thereby inviting his own destruction. His grandfather Cadmus and the old blind seer Tiresias decide, for political reasons, to accept the new religion, though contemptuous of the follies of the worshipers.

Dionysus, imprisoned by Pentheus, is miraculously delivered by an earthquake, and the Bacchae, his female adherents, are likewise freed. A herdsman appears with news of the freeing and relates how the fanatics, led by Pentheus' mother Agave and her sisters, have torn cattle from limb to limb and beaten armed forces sent by the king. Pentheus insists that the bacchanalian revels are merely a pretext for licentiousness and that the votaries of Dionysus are being driven by intoxication and lust to follow an immoral religion.

Dionysus' revenge is not long delayed. Under a mystic spell cast by the god, Pentheus is made to dress in women's garments and to spy on the bacchanals in the forest. The intoxicated women, detecting the spy, attack and rend him to pieces, under the delusion that he is a young lion. His mother, the ecstatic Agave, in one of the most tragic scenes in Greek drama, carries her son's head home, singing a song of triumph. Cadmus enters, carrying the remains of Pentheus' corpse; Agave gradually recovers her sanity, and realizes the dreadful deed she has perpetrated. The play concludes with a lament for Pentheus, heir and protector of Cadmus and the house of Thebes, victim of a mere mortal's futile resistance to a ruthless deity.

In his *Paideia,* Werner Jaeger ably sums up the significance of *The Bacchae,* suggesting that Euripides "as a psychologist found possibilities of enormous and lasting effect in the tragic problem created by the clash of religious mass-hypnotism, awaking all the primitive instinct and energies of its victims, with ordinary society and the established state, based as it was on reason alone . . . the victory of the miraculous and of conversion over reason."

The plays of Euripides to a greater extent than those of any other ancient writer prefigure modern realistic and psychological drama. Their social outlook also blazed new trails. In the Euripidean dramas we are confronted with such problems as the status of women in society, the relation of the sexes, the institution of slavery, the relative merits of democracy and dictatorship, and the morality of the gods. For the first time, slaves and masters are seen as equals, as are men and women, foreigners and natives. Euripides detested military aggression and imperialism, and he condemned all oppressors of mankind, whether human or divine. At the same time, few of his characters are portrayed as unmitigatedly evil or completely good, but rather as blendings of devil and saint. Sophocles is said to have made men as they ought to be, but Euripides made men as they are. Throughout his extant writings, it is crystal clear that Euripides felt a deep pity for the unfortunate and possessed a profound sense of the worth of human life.

Aristophanes: *The Clouds, The Birds, Lysistrata, The Frogs*

Both Sophocles and Euripides were still flourishing when Aristophanes (448–380 B.C.) was born. Aristophanes, greatest of Greek comic dramatists, was an exponent of the so-called Old Comedy which was highly popular in Athens from about 470 to 390 B.C. The chief characteristics of the genre (unlike any modern comic form) were unrestrained license in attacking public personalities, through burlesque, caricature, and invective; broad political, social, and literary satire; and a licentiousness of expression beyond any since tolerated on the stage of any nation. However, the Old Comedy rises above mere buffoonery; it is often directed toward the correction of social abuses: political corruption, misgovernment, weak leaders, war, or any other issues or trends to which the playwright wished to take exception.

The comedies of Aristophanes frequently have been compared to those of Shakespeare in reflecting the spirit of the times. As Edith Hamilton notes, "There is the same tremendous energy and verve and vitality; the same swinging, swashbuckling spirit; the same exuberant, effervescing flow of language; the same rollicking, uproarious fun." Another kindred spirit is Sir William Gilbert, of the team of Gilbert and Sullivan, despite the severe taboos placed on his satirical wit by Victorian conventions. The aim of Aristophanes was to present a "picture of the follies and foibles of a nation," which, according to Voltaire, is the essence of true comedy. His effects were achieved through the devices of fantasy unrestrained and endless exaggeration of detail.

While predominantly a comic artist, Aristophanes used his comedy as an instrument for reform and propaganda. He made slashing attacks on the decadent democracy of Athens, civic corruption, demagogic leadership, militarism and chauvinism, senseless war-making, and what the poet regarded as mistaken tendencies in education, literature, and philosophy. A distinct bias is apparent in the direction of aristocracy and conservatism, a yearning to return to the golden age of Pericles. For these reasons, Aristophanes' favorite targets were Euripides and Socrates, the first of whom he condemned for destroying the old, stately, heroic dramatic art of Aeschylus and Sophocles; and the latter for erroneous educational theories which, in Aristophanes' eyes, were debasing the youth of Athens.

Aristophanes is known to have produced in excess of forty plays, of which eleven are extant. The best-known of the surviving examples are *The Clouds*, which ridicules Socrates and the intelligentsia; *The Birds,* which satirizes Athens in the tale of a utopian city built in the air by birds; *Lysistrata*, which tells of happenings when women take a hand in war and peace; and *The Frogs*, a literary satire which includes as characters Aeschylus, Sophocles, and Euripides.

Aristophanes was a vehement opponent of the educational ideas and practices of his time. He pleaded for a restoration of the simple discipline that had molded the morals, minds, and manners of the heroic men who fought at Marathon. *The Clouds* is a brilliant personal caricature, though notoriously unjust, of Socrates, and a biting attack on the new intellectualism of the Sophists, with their specious rhetoric and inane scientific speculations.

In the play an old man, overwhelmed by debt incurred by his horse-racing son Pheidippides and pursued by creditors, hears that the great philosopher Socrates can teach his students to talk their way out of any predicament. Desiring to learn the art of false reasoning, the father visits the "Thinking Factory" of Socrates. There the master is found swinging above the ground in a basket in order to observe more closely the secrets of the universe, removed from the earth's distractions. His disciples are seen in strange, undignified positions, bent over scanning the sand in order to understand the underworld, exploring the mysteries of the stars, or engaged in ridiculous argumentations.

Strepsiades, the father, enrolls in the school, but unable to absorb the nonsensical teaching, gives up in despair and sends his son, who proves to be a far more apt pupil. Pheidippides is taught to deny all the gods and studies Right Logic and Wrong Logic, the latter advocating every kind of vicious immorality. So well does the wastrel son learn his lesson that he gets rid of the pestiferous creditors and then proves that he has a right to beat his father for disagreeing with his sophistical argument. Disillusioned, cured of his folly, and enraged by his son's un-filial conduct, Strepsiades proceeds to set fire to the humbug philosopher's "Thinking Factory."

The Birds is escape drama, escape by imagination into a care-free world from an Athens weary of war, yet getting ready to embark on the most disastrous adventure of all: the fatal Sicilian expedition. Pure fantasy, with little or no reference to the anxieties of the present, *The Birds* is a wish-picture from which earthly burdens vanish.

In the play, two gentlemen, Peisthetaerus (Plausible) and Euelpides (Hopeful), disgusted with the state of affairs in Athens, journey to Birdland, "a city free from all care and strife," to consult King Epops, the hoopoe. Suddenly, the two Athenians are struck by an inspiration: to turn over supreme power in the universe to the birds. Intrigued by the idea, Epops summons a conference of all the birds, who, skeptical at first, finally give their enthusiastic support to the plan. The birds erect a new city, Nephelococcygia, or "Cloud-Cuckoo-Land," midway between earth and heaven, where the birds are kings and gods. By the wall around the new city separating the upper and lower worlds, the former gods will be deprived of their incense and die of starvation unless they capitulate. Plausible and Hopeful are transformed into birds, and a utopian common-wealth is under way.

Impressed by the wonders of Cloud-Cuckoo-Land, the citizens of Athens become extremely bird-conscious, and applications for citizenship pour in. Rejected summarily are a civic poet, a seer ready to interpret oracles, a geometrician, and a lawmaker—all kicked out by Plausible because he wants none of the Athenian plagues in his ideal city. Among thousands of others seized by the birdmania and applying for wings are such objectionable characters as a parricide who thinks that in Nephelococcygia he can escape punishment for killing his father and an informer whose work would be expedited if he could fly from place to place.

Prometheus arrives and informs Plausible of the pitiful state of the gods, who are ready to surrender and to restore the birds to their ancient godlike position. The old gods are deposed, and as a symbol of submission, Plausible receives a celestial bride Basileia (Sovereignty), the daughter of Zeus. The play ends in happiness and merriment.

Gilbert Murray, great interpreter and translator of Greek literature, observes that *"The Birds* is not perhaps the funniest of Aristophanes' plays, but it is by general agreement the most delightful." Among his other attainments, the playwright was a gifted ornithologist; in *The Birds* he names an extraordinary number of species, some of which modern scientists are unable to identify.

In the autumn of 413 B.C., the Athenians learned of the overwhelming naval catastrophe in Sicily. It was in the mood of this, the darkest period of the Peloponnesian War, that Aristophanes composed *Lysistrata,* an original scheme for bringing peace to the warring Hellenic states.

But despite the tragic temper of the times, the play is a light-hearted, risqué comedy, another vehicle for escape from reality. The plot is simple. The principal character, Lysistrata, a woman of Athens, conceives the idea of stopping the war by persuading all the women of Athens and Sparta to refrain from intercourse with their husbands until the latter cease their stupidities and arrange a truce. At first reluctant to resort to such a drastic measure, the Athenian wives eventually come around to Lysistrata's point of view, leave their husbands and abandon their homes and families. Since without money, war cannot be waged, their initial strategy is to seize the Acropolis, which contains the state treasury.

Next a mission is sent to treat with the women of Sparta. Meanwhile, Lysistrata and her feminine cohorts battle with the old men who have been left behind to guard the city. Episode after episode, each daringly vulgar and amusing, is presented. Some of the women weaken in their stern resolution, vacillating back and forth. But Lysistrata's austere discipline holds firm, and word eventually comes that the women of Sparta have been equally unyielding toward their men. A Spartan herald arrives, empowered by his desperate fellow countrymen to arrange peace. Terms are soon agreed upon, and the play ends in a scene of general jubilation and feasting, with husbands and wives reunited.

The Frogs was written only a few months after the deaths of Sophocles and Euripides. Aeschylus had been gone for fifty years. As the play opens, Dionysus, the Greek national god, is deeply disturbed by the lack of a major tragic dramatist since the passing of the three great masters. Being inordinately fond of the plays of Euripides, he determines to visit Hades to try to bring back to earth that deceased playwright. To Aristophanes, the character of Dionysus in *The Frogs* is the personification of the Athenian public, and the comedy is a subtle rebuke to the political spirit and literary taste of the thoughtless citizens of Athens, in their misguided partiality for Euripides' dramas.

Dressed up as Hercules and accompanied by his servant Xanthias (who bears a striking resemblance to Don Quixote's Sancho Panza), Dionysus is ferried across Charon's lake of the dead, to the raucous accompaniment of the croaking of a band of ghosts of departed Athenian frogs, for whom the play is named. After many ludicrous adventures en route and in the outer precincts of Hades, the travelers arrive at Pluto's court.

Euripides, Dionysus discovers, has in the underworld two formidable rivals, Aeschylus and Sophocles, and is attempting to unseat the former from the throne he occupies as supreme tragedian. Sophocles gracefully withdraws from the contest, and Dionysus is chosen as arbiter between the two remaining competitors.

Aeschylus and Euripides enter and inaugurate the contest by prayer and sacrifice. Euripides is first to plead, pointing out Aeschylus' faults of lofty, bombastic speech far removed from common language, solemn statuesque dramas containing little action; silent, motionless characters who leave most of a play's development to the chorus; obscurity of meaning and mysterious marvels. On the other hand, he says, his own poetry is clear and fluent; his stage is filled with recognizable characters; the ideal and statuesque are changed to the real, the human, and the commonsensical.

Aeschylus replies by stating that the mission of a poet is to ennoble his audience, and he claims that his heroic themes, treated grandly, have made the Athenians honest, vigorous, and warlike. In contrast, his rival has dealt with meaner subjects;

spoken of crimes that ought not to be mentioned; encouraged idle talk instead of noble action; and in general has lowered the characters of the citizens by familiarizing them with immoralities, indelicacies, and low company. Both Aeschylus and Euripides agree that it is the poet's duty to make men better, but they differ in their views on how to effect improvements.

The contestants proceed next to literary style, sharply criticizing the construction, language, meter, and music of each other's compositions. Then, finally, Aeschylus proposes the test of weight: phrases from the works of the two rivals are thrown upon the scales of a balance to determine whose lines are weightier. The words of Aeschylus tip the scales so decisively that Dionysus names him the winner, to return to the earth, while Euripides remains in the underworld.

Aristophanes' attack on the dead Euripides in *The Frogs* is a direct reflection of a bitter antagonism. In earlier plays, as in this one, he held the Euripidean plays up to ridicule, accusing them of corrupting the Athenians, poisoning the patriotic spirit of the citizens, and causing an increase in immorality. Only a return to the solemn, epic, idealistic, moral standards of Aeschylus, he believed, could save Greek tragic drama from complete ruin. For these reasons, it should be noted, in any contest between Aeschylus and Euripides, with Aristophanes serving as judge, the dice are heavily loaded against Euripides.

Menander: *The Girl from Samos, The Dour Man, The Shearing of Glycera, The Arbitration*

Some thirty-seven years after the death of Aristophanes occurred the birth of another comic genius, Menander (343–292 B.C.). Until the recent discovery of a papyrus manuscript containing a complete play, *The Dour Man*, by Menander, only fragments were known to exist of the works of a playwright considered by the Greeks of his own time to be, next to Homer, their greatest poet. The new find is a valuable addition to the Menander corpus, though it is unlikely to change the critical judgments previously reached on the basis of extant portions of missing dramas.

Menander was one of a group of some sixty-four playwrights who, about a half-century after the death of Aristophanes, created the so-called New Comedy, essentially a comedy of manners or a form of domestic comedy. The leading exponents of the genre in Athens were Menander, Philemon, Diphilus, Philippides, and Apollodorus. Of them all, Menander was most prolific (credited with 105 plays) and eventually achieved the greatest popularity.

The New Comedy contains in its liveliness traces of Aristophanes' influence, but it lacks, as Francis G. Allinson, Menander's translator, notes, "the lyric beauty, the rapier wit, the naked licence and the daring personal or political satire of Aristophanes." It more closely resembles the Euripidean dramas, with emphasis upon individual characters (especially including women), carefully contrived and complicated plots, the introduction of love themes, a trend toward realism, and a swing away from unrelieved tragedy to tragicomedy or even sentimentality.

The plays of Menander and his school are best interpreted in the light of the conditions under which they were written. Athens was in the hands of the Macedonians, and political freedom was at an end, though some freedom of speech remained. Theater audiences, and Athenians generally, were bored and disgusted by politics. They could forget and escape the unpleasant political situation by becoming absorbed in domestic affairs. A natural consequence was that playwrights consciously avoided dangerous and unpopular political themes and gave the public what it wanted: diverting but far from world-shaking comedies of domesticity. This form of play, with minor modifications, has continued to hold the stage in the Western world down to the present day.

Far less dramatic ability, unquestionably, was demanded by the New Comedy than by the Old. It produced no figure comparable in poetic genius, imagination, or political discernment to Aeschylus, Sophocles, Euripides, or Aristophanes. The new style is basically realistic, filled with everyday details; the situations are repetitious and stereotyped, the characters commonplace. Menander's plots, for example, almost invariably utilize backgrounds of prosperous, well-ordered homes temporarily upset by young men in love with young girls, parents disturbed by their children's behavior, intriguing servants, and long-lost relatives. Happy endings, after all complications have been satisfactorily resolved, are mandatory. Thus, there is nothing to place an excessive strain on the theatergoer's mind or emotions.

Pliny the Elder calls Menander the unrivaled literary genius of the plain style. Characters drawn by the New Comedy dramatists, typified by Menander, are life size; the superhuman figures created by earlier playwrights have disappeared from the stage. Another change is that Menander's slaves and other humble persons are sometimes more admirable than and morally superior to the wealthy types he depicts. Most unusual for the time are vivid and charming characterizations of women. L. A. Post, in *From Homer to Menander*, observes, "His emphasis on the love of good women as a refining fire by which men learn to know themselves and their duty better seems incredibly modern. There is nothing quite like it either in Molière or in Shakespeare." Thus, over and over, Menander's plays center on such motifs as the reunion of husband and wife, lover and mistress, father and daughter, tensions between the sexes, and the problems of family life. Post notes further that "his use of babies as symbols of married union gives a peculiar color to his dramas." In general, Menander idealizes women, while his men begin by being sinful and then reform.

A special debt is owed by Menander, and doubtless other New Comedy dramatists, to Theophrastus, under whom he studied at the Lyceum. Theophrastus' thumbnail sketches of people, in his *Characters*, shrewdly and sharply drawn, though unvaryingly disagreeable, stupid, or silly, obviously influenced Menander's character-drawing. Also significant in shaping Menander's thought were the ideas of Epicurus, his contemporary, fellow citizen, and companion, who taught a philosophy of happiness and optimism.

The Girl from Samos is the earliest play by Menander of which substantial fragments have survived. Carefree and farcical, it revolves around romantic love, with the action complicated by numerous misunderstandings. The principal characters are two old men, the wealthy and kindly Demeas, and the poor, irascible, touchy Niceratus; Demeas' concubine Chrysis (a refugee from Samos), his confidential slave Parmeno, his adopted son Moschion; and Niceratus' daughter Plangon. The fathers arrange a marriage between Moschion and Plangon, without consulting them, though both young people are delighted with the plan, for they have been pursuing a clandestine love affair and Plangon has had a baby. Fearing her father's wrath, she persuades Chrysis to take the infant into her house and pretend that it is hers by Demeas. But Demeas, just returned from a journey, suspects that his mistress has been unfaithful to him by consorting with his adopted son and, in a fit of jealously, drives Chrysis out of doors. Other complications and misunderstandings ensue with Niceratus too angry to listen to reason, slaves trying to conceal secrets and merely adding to the confusion, and similar mix-ups. The comedy is finally disentangled by a series of confessions and revelations, following which Chrysis is taken back by Demeas, and Moschion is married to Plangon. The dialogue is brisk and witty and the characterization excellent.

Menander's only complete play extant, *The Dour Man*, written early in his career, concerns a misanthropic farmer, Cnemon; his young second wife; his stepson, his daughter Myrrhine, and the son of a neighboring squire. The slapstick element is prominent. The rich squire's son goes hunting, meets the innocent daughter Myrrhine by chance, falls in love with her, and sends an offer of marriage to Cnemon, who chases away the messenger with a shower of clods. But Cnemon accidentally falls down his own well; Myrrhine urges a group of picnickers to save him from drowning; instead, angered because Cnemon has refused to lend them a stew pot, they suggest that a large stone should be dropped on his head. The noble stepson, however, leaps in and rescues him, handicapped rather than aided by the squire's son, who is so busy embracing Myrrhine that he lets go the rope three times. After the near disaster, Cnemon undergoes a change of heart, recalls his wife, whom he had driven away by his ill disposition, adopts his rescuer, marries Myrrhine to the squire's son, and dances in Pan's honor.

A later play, *The Shearing of Glycera*, is less a comedy of errors than is *The Girl from Samos;* nevertheless, misunderstandings abound, symbolized by an allegorical character called Misapprehension. Before the play opens, an elderly man, Pataceus, has given away his twin children, Glycera and Moschion, because he was too poor to support them. The girl Glycera has been brought up by a poor woman and later finds a protector in the soldier Polemon. Moschion, the son, has been adopted by a wealthy old lady, Myrrhine, and reared in luxury. The twins meet, unaware of their relationship, and Moschion imagines himself in love with Glycera. Polemon considers her his wife, however, and enraged by ill-founded jealousy, shears off her hair, as a mark of her shame and disgrace. But by now, Glycera has learned that Moschion is her brother. Pataceus, the father, who has become a wealthy merchant, is reunited with his long-lost children. Polemon is repentant for his impetuous action and promises reform, after which Glycera is reconciled to him and returns as his wife. The play is full of clowning and sentimentality, though again the characters are well-realized, realistic, and believable.

The Arbitration is accepted as Menander's masterpiece. Here we are presented with contrasting forces: generosity, philanthropy, and concern for social justice opposed to narrow selfishness and antisocial behavior. A tight-fisted businessman, Simicrines, marries his daughter Pamphila to a strait-laced, serious, and frugal youth Charisius. But it appears that Charisius had slipped from the path of virtue four months before the wedding, by becoming intoxicated at an all-night festival and assaulting an unidentified girl. Five months after her marriage, Pamphila bears a son, the consequence of an assault made upon her in the dark by a drunken man at one of the city's festivals; she has no idea of the identity of her seducer. Pamphila tries, with the aid of her nurse, to conceal the birth and to get rid of the child. An officious servant reveals the secret to Charisius, who, deeply shocked, but genuinely in love with his wife, drowns his sorrows in prolonged dissipation. Simicrines has no knowledge of the child and is extremely irate with his son-in-law for deserting Pamphila and for squandering his fortune. The title of the play derives from a scene involving a slave, Davus, and a charcoal burner, Syricus; the infant, abandoned by his mother (in accord with Athenian custom for unwanted children), was found by Davus, who in turn has given the baby to Syricus, whose wife could nurse it. Certain keepsakes that had been left with the child, however, were retained by Davus, and these were now the subject of acrimonious dispute between the two men. Simicrines agrees to arbitrate the disagreement, and awards the child and its property to Syricus. After further plots, counterplots, and ramifications, Charisius discovers that he is actually the father of the infant, since the girl he has married is the one he had assaulted. The play concludes with the reconciliation of Charisius and Pamphila. Character drawing again is superior, especially in the exposure of puritanism and hypocrisy, the representation of the gentle, loyal Pamphila, and the transformation of Charisius from a prig, assuming superior virtue, into a courageous, repentant, and potentially reformed personality.

The work of Menander was re-created in the Latin comedies of Plautus and Terence, who proudly proclaimed that their dramas were founded on his, even to the extent of being actual translations. In other instances, Menander's plots were telescoped and materials freely selected from his writings. Four of Terence's six surviving plays are frankly attributed to Menander. Through Plautus and Terence, Robert Graves remarks, in his *Food for Centaurs*, "Menander ended as the father of the English Morality Play, of the Punch and Judy show, and of Classical French comedy."

7

SENSE OF THE PAST

Greek and Roman Historians

Among historians of the ancient world, four Greeks (Herodotus, Thucydides, Xenophon, and Polybius) and four Romans (Sallust, Livy, Plutarch, and, later, Tacitus) stand preeminent. They range in date from early in the fifth to the middle of the first century B.C.

Herodotus: *History of the Persian Wars*

The title "father of history" was conferred upon Herodotus by Cicero. He has also been described as the father of geography, of archeology, of anthropology, of sociology, and not infrequently as the "father of liars." The variety of appellations is indicative of Herodotus' vital interest in the human race and everything that pertained to it.

Before Herodotus, most chronicles of the past had been recordings of legend and mythology, lightly tinged with history, expressed in metrical form. Herodotus was the first major writer in prose, and the first to shape a series of heterogeneous episodes and anecdotes into a connected account of events. Even so, he may have conceived of his role as that of a fascinating storyteller rather than of a historian. Properly speaking, he was a literary man, a moralist, and a reporter, and secondarily a historian in the modern sense.

The story Herodotus had to tell is constructed with consummate artistry, complete with background, unified plot, and logical sequences—all building up toward a dramatic climax. His epic recital deals with the conflict between the freedom-loving

Greeks and the mighty power of a Persian tyrant and his army of slaves, culminating in the great battles of Thermopylae and Salamis. But Herodotus paints on a vast canvas in tracing the antecedents and ramifications of the age-old struggle between Orientalism and Occidentalism.

Herodotus' preparation for his task was superb. He was born on the southwestern coast of Asia Minor and his life covered the period from the Persian to the Peloponnesian wars, which saw the peak of Greek culture. An omnivorous reader, he was intimately familiar with, and deeply influenced by, the classic writings of Homer. In fact, his foremost English translator George Rawlinson comments: "It may be questioned whether there was a single work of importance in the whole range of Greek literature accessible to him, with the contents of which he was not fairly acquainted." Included in this range of knowledge were the works of Greek and Persian historians whose writings have since disappeared.

Further, his active and inquisitive mind led Herodotus to undertake travels lasting for a period of years and extending over virtually all the known world. Edith Hamilton calls him "the first sight-seer." He went as far east as Persia and as far west as Italy. He knew the coast of the Black Sea; he visited Arabia and Egypt (where he went up the Nile to Assouan); and his wanderings also probably included Cyrene, Libya, and Sicily. Altogether, it has been estimated that his wide-ranging journeys took him 1,700 miles from east to west and 1,700 miles from north to south, an incredible achievement considering the hardships and perils of travel in the fifth century B.C.

Herodotus' principal concern, as he roamed the earth, was to observe the customs of various non-Greek peoples: Lydians, Babylonians, Indians, Persians, Arabians, Massagetae, Egyptians, Libyans, Scythians, Thracians, and others who lived within or near the immense Persian Empire. He investigated the effects of geography and climate upon the physical appearances, mores, and institutions of peoples, their progress in the arts and sciences, their religions and laws. He was no less interested in legendary and historical accounts of their past, especially as these may have affected their contemporary attitudes and political behavior.

About 447 B.C., Herodotus is believed to have come to Athens and settled down to the writing of the *History*, a task which remained his principal occupation until his death some twenty-two years later.

Though the Persian Wars are Herodotus' dominant theme, around which the entire narrative turns, the wars are treated in detail only in the last part of the *History*. The first two-thirds of the book relate to the author's travels and what he had learned from them. Here his grand design unfolds. As fitting prologue to the tremendous contest between East and West, the whole of the known world is presented, the growth of the Persian Empire is traced, and previous conflicts between Greece and Persia are reviewed. In summary, the nine parts treat, in order, of these subjects: the rise of the Persian Empire through the downfall of the Lydian; the history of Egypt; the establishment of the Persian Empire under the reigns of Cambyses, Smerdis, and Darius; the conflict of Persia against Scythia and Libya; the developing struggle between Persia and Athens; the growth of the Hellenic spirit in Ionia and Greece and the Battle of Marathon; Xerxes' march against Greece; the Battle of Salamis; the battles of Plataea and Mycale; and the failure of the Persian invasion.

To lighten what might otherwise have been a dull tale, Herodotus digresses again and again from the central motif to introduce historical and geographical data, natural history, and antiquarian anecdotes and information that he had collected about the world and its races. Such asides fill nearly one-half of the entire book. Herodotus is the most gifted of storytellers, however, and the subsidiary episodes not only make delightful reading but also are relevant to and help to illuminate the main narrative. His interests are universal, as Edith Hamilton points out in *The Greek Way*: "He tells us how the homely girls in Illyria get husbands, how the lake dwellers keep their children from falling in the water, what Egyptian mosquito nets are like, that the King of Persia when travelling drinks only boiled water, what the Andrymachidae do to fleas, how the Arabians cut their hair, that the Danube islanders get drunk on smells, how the Scythians milk their mares, that in Libya the woman with the most lovers is honored, how the streets of Babylon are laid out, that physicians in Egypt specialize in diseases, and so on, and so on."

Principally because of these numerous digressions, Herodotus is often accused of inaccuracy and general unreliability by literalists and purists, with some justification. He reported whatever he heard that interested him, without making a clear differentiation between history and folklore. Entire conversations are quoted between famous personages on occasions when

Herodotus could obviously not have been present or had eye-witness sources, a form of poetic license or historical fiction to heighten the effect of his account. On the other hand, he is careful to state that he himself doubts the credibility of some of his amazing stories. "I am under obligation to tell what is reported," he writes, "but I am not obliged to believe it; and let this hold for every narrative in this history." At the same time, he expressed skepticism about some reports later verified, such as the existence of the British Isles and "the earth circular, as if it turned on a lathe."

By way of extenuation, it should be said that for the most part Herodotus gathered his source materials orally from many areas and many races; he was doing research without a library; he knew only Greek but had to deal with a babel of languages; and he wrote about events remote in time, before archeology was born.

A constant religious refrain runs through the *History*. Herodotus believed that omens, oracles, prayers, and prophets play decisive roles in the affairs of men. In his view the great events of history, as well as circumstances of individual lives, are shaped and determined by divine purpose. Further, the gods are jealous: the mighty are laid low, the humble are exalted, the meek inherit the earth, there is a seesaw of happiness and misery among men and nations. Thus is explained the downfall of the proud Xerxes and his mighty Persian army in conflict with the numerically inferior and seemingly nearly defenseless people of Athens.

Herodotus possessed one of the prime requisites of a great historian: objectivity. He was remarkably free of national prejudice and racial bias. Though naturally a partisan of Athens, he admired and praised the bravery, chivalry, and truthfulness of the Persians. From Herodotus' description of the courier system of the Persian King Darius, for example, comes the United States Postal Service motto: "Not snow, nor rain, nor heat, nor gloom of night stays these couriers from the swift completion of their appointed rounds." Herodotus had a broad philosophic appreciation of all nations and invariably found something to praise even among uncivilized peoples.

The strong hold which Herodotus has continued to have on all succeeding generations of readers and writers is explicable in large part by the fact that he is the first European master of the art of writing entertaining prose. Obvious aspects of this talent are his skill in character drawing, his gift for vivid description, the variety of his subject matter, and, not least, the clearness and simplicity of his language.

Thucydides: *History of the Peloponnesian War*

Following the Athenians' near miraculous defeat of the mighty Persian army and navy at the beginning of the fifth century B.C., the victors were chosen to lead the new confederacy of free Greek states. In the ensuing fifty years, the civilization and culture of Greece attained a peak which has continued to excite world admiration to the present day. It was the age of the philosophers Socrates and Anaxagoras; of the sculptor Phidias; of Ictinus, architect of the Parthenon; and of the great dramatists and poets Aeschylus, Euripides, Sophocles, and Aristophanes.

But power corrupts. Athens was mistress of the sea, and her ambitious, vainglorious leaders determined to embark upon further conquests and imperialistic adventures. Shortly, its members found that the free confederacy had become the Athenian Empire. Not, however, without resistance. The Spartans were alarmed at their loss of autonomy and independence, and terrified by the growth of Athenian might and authority. Sparta, with the strongest army of the time, determined to fight to defend herself from the Athenian encroachments. Thus began the long and bloody struggle between the Athenians and the Spartans, which lasted from 431 to 404 B.C.

The events of this war, the Peloponnesian, were recorded with extraordinary fidelity by the Greek historian Thucydides, an Athenian who for a time held an important military command. Subsequently exiled for losing a battle, he spent the remaining years of his life visiting the scenes of battles, reconstructing events from eyewitness accounts, and writing his great historical treatise. From the outbreak of the war, Thucydides believed that it would exceed in importance any other known in history. He undertook, therefore, to record it in detail and to analyze political and military happenings as they developed, almost literally before his eyes. Thucydides may justly be called the first historian of contemporary events, as well as the first critical historian.

Modern historians have frequently contrasted the methodology of Herodotus and Thucydides. In dealing with the Persian invasion, Herodotus branched off from military and political history to bring in social and cultural history, including anecdotes, legends, gossip, superstitions, and unverified reports from a vast miscellany of sources. Thucydides, on the other hand, was preeminently a military and political historian, as he chronicled by seasons—summers and winters—the events of the Peloponnesian War. He omits discussions of literature, philosophy, and art and touches upon state policy and social conditions only as they relate to the progress of the war. "It will perhaps be found," Thucydides noted, in oblique criticism of Herodotus, "that the absence of storytelling in my work makes it less attractive to listen to, but I shall be satisfied if it is considered useful by all who wish to know the plain truth of the events which happened and will according to human nature happen again in the same way. It is written not for the moment, but for all time."

Furthermore, Thucydides maintained an almost Olympian objectivity in his writings. Any personal emotions he may have felt were vigorously suppressed, and he usually abstained from expressing personal judgments, preferring to let the facts speak for themselves or to suggest their own morals. The *History* is as free from bitterness and bias, as coldly impartial as though it pertained to a far-distant past. Thucydides took particular care to test information obtained from others in order to minimize inaccuracies caused by prejudice and unreliable memories.

Modern historians are more in accord with Herodotus than with Thucydides in their concept of history, agreeing that it should record the social, industrial, economic, artistic, moral, and religious life of a people, as well as wars, battles, and political intrigues. But within the narrow confines which Thucydides set for himself, his production is an artistic masterpiece. The story rises far above a mere recital of military campaigns. The author was a master of vivid description; his accounts of battles, for example, read as though he himself had been present. John Stuart Mill considered the *History* perhaps the most powerful piece of narrative writing in all literature. Dramatic scenes are drawn throughout, two among the most memorable being a description of the terrible plague that struck Athens in the midst of the war, killing a quarter of the population, and a portrayal of the naval engagement between the Athenian and Syracusan fleets. Striking dramatic effects are achieved also by placing contrasting events together, usually moments of celebration and smiling fortune followed by disasters of the first magnitude.

A device used successfully by Thucydides to relieve the monotony of factual narration is his insertion of speeches or dialogue attributed to the various actors in the unfolding tragedy, which make up about one-fourth of the entire work. He does not pretend to give the exact words of the speakers. The purpose, rather, is to interpret the forces at work behind events. As he explains: "With reference to the speeches in this history, some were delivered before the war began, others while it was going on; some I heard myself, others I got from various quarters. It was in all cases difficult to carry them word for word in one's memory so that my habit has been to make the speakers say what was in my opinion demanded of them by the various occasions, of course adhering as closely as possible to the general sense of what was really said." Most famous of all the speeches is Pericles' funeral oration over the Athenians who died in the first campaign. Though the technique is viewed somewhat askance by scientific historians, because of its inexactness and dangers of abuse and misrepresentation, it provided an opportunity for Thucydides not only to express indirectly his own political ideas but also to probe deeply into the characters, motives, and beliefs of the leading participants in the struggle.

The central problem in the *History* is the nature of the state; this theme recurs throughout. Piecing together widely scattered references, one sees clearly that Thucydides was opposed both to the rule of a wealthy oligarchy and to that form of extreme democracy scarcely distinguishable from mob rule. He was a moderate democrat who believed that Athens' ultimate defeat in the long war resulted from the taking over of its government by irresponsible and unscrupulous politicians. He believed in the participation by all citizens in the affairs of government, but only under the guidance of high-minded, intelligent, strong leaders. Pericles was his ideal statesman; such men as Alcibiades and Cleon, architects of Athens' tragic downfall, personified the antithesis to this ideal.

In religion, Thucydides is classified as a skeptic. He rejected as senseless superstition the still popular view of the capricious interference of the gods in human affairs. He derided oracles, portents, and omens. Nevertheless, in several passages, he hints that the prevalence of natural calamities—earthquakes, eclipses, tidal waves, plagues, droughts, and famine—concurrently with the Peloponnesian War may not have been mere coincidences, and that these misfortunes were sent perhaps as divine penalties for an unnecessary, degrading, unnatural, and impious war. Even Herodotus' doctrine of divine jealousy and divine compensation—putting down the mighty and exalting the humble and meek—is implied by Thucydides as he paints a dark picture of Athenian ambition and lust for power, and of arrogance and cynicism toward Torone, Scione, Mende, Melos, and the other cities and states which resisted Athens. Nowhere is this point more graphically illustrated than in the account of the mad dream of empire beyond the seas that was the Sicilian expedition, beginning with the holiday-like departure from Athens of the magnificent Athenian navy and ending in total, unmitigated disaster.

With the conclusion of the Peloponnesian War, presumably several years after the death of Thucydides (the *History* ends abruptly in the midst of exciting events), Athens' triumphant career of empire-building ended in ruin. A treaty between Sparta and Persia made the Persian king the arbiter of the affairs of Greece. Most tragic, as Edith Hamilton states, "The cause of humanity was defeated. Greece's contribution to the world was checked and soon ceased. Hundreds of years had to pass before men reached again the point where Greek thought left off." The war wrecked the finest civilization that had evolved up to that time.

Thucydides wrote his *History of the Peloponnesian War* because he believed that men would profit from a knowledge of what brought about that ruinous struggle. He was convinced that human nature never changed but confident that men could learn by experience, could understand the future by a study of the past. History to him was valuable primarily as a record of political experience, not for any religious, ethical, or philosophical content. Thucydides is far superior to all other ancient historians in his remarkable insight into the nature and laws of political events. Some later historians, among them Leopold von Ranke, repudiate the doctrine that a nation can be taught by any experience except its own, concluding that the only thing we learn from experience is that we learn nothing from experience. The validity of that point of view was demonstrated by the war between Rome and Carthage, about three centuries after Thucydides' time, a struggle which began and ended under circumstances similar to those of the Peloponnesian War.

Regardless of the acceptability of his doctrine of history, however, no other historian has more succinctly summed up the basis for all wars than Thucydides, as he declares: "The cause of all these evils was the desire for power which greed and ambition inspire."

Xenophon: *Anabasis*

The historical methods of two contemporaries, Thucydides and Xenophon, have often been compared, usually to the latter's disadvantage. Both gave accounts of contemporaneous military actions in which Greeks were involved; both participated in the events which they described; and both were exiled from their country for conduct regarded as injurious to the state. Here, however, the likenesses end. The philosophical, scientific, impartial observations of Thucydides are in striking contrast to the romantic picturesqueness of Xenophon's writing. Xenophon has aptly been called the inventor of historical romance. A twentieth-century English historian, John Bagnell Bury, suggests that if he were living in modern times, he would be a high-class journalist and pamphleteer, making his fortune as a war correspondent.

Xenophon's later career appears to have been considerably influenced by his association, as a young friend and disciple, with Socrates in Athens. The practical qualities subsequently displayed by Xenophon as a leader of men can be traced directly to Socratic teaching. In the picture of Socrates drawn by Xenophon in the *Memorabilia*, we see facets of that remarkable personality quite different from those depicted by Plato. In Xenophon's eyes the noted philosopher was a sage counselor to his youthful associates, giving them commonsense advice on how to manage their affairs.

The book for which Xenophon is best remembered is the *Anabasis*, the "Retreat of the Ten Thousand," an absorbing narration of a disastrous military expedition in which the author played a star role. It is the story of the force which Cyrus the Younger led against his brother Artaxerxes II, king of Persia, in the hope of winning the Persian throne for himself. Through firsthand observation, Cyrus had learned that Greek soldiers and methods of warfare were immensely superior to the Persian, and it was for this reason that he enlisted Greeks to aid him in the enterprise upon which he was about to embark. The army thus gathered was made up of soldiers of fortune, mercenaries who were willing to go abroad in return for regular pay and food, since there was no fighting to be done at home. Xenophon, then probably less than thirty years of age, joined the expedition at the urging of his friend Proxenus, who was one of the Greek generals in Cyrus' service. Despite his youth and lack of previous experience, Xenophon was destined to save his compatriots from total destruction.

The Greeks marched from the Mediterranean through sandy deserts far into Asia Minor, living on the country as they proceeded. Over terrain at times exceedingly difficult, they traversed a distance of some fifteen-hundred miles from March to September. At the gates of Babylon, the forces commanded by Cyrus confronted a Persian army many times as large. The brilliant generalship and superb fighting qualities of the Greek soldiers prevailed over heavy odds, however, and the battle of Cunaxa was a decisive defeat for the forces of Artaxerxes. But for Cyrus and the Greeks it was a Pyrrhic victory. Cyrus was killed during the fighting, and later, through treachery, five Greek generals were assassinated, leaving their men leaderless, alone in the heart of Asia, without food or ammunition, and surrounded by hostile troops.

Xenophon awoke from a dream during the terrible first night of the retreat convinced that Zeus had chosen him to save the Greek army and to lead it to safety. He fired the young officers with his own enthusiasm, and was elected unanimously to command them on the long trail back. Turning northward, the Greeks followed rivers up to the headwaters of the Tigris and Euphrates, through the wilds of Kurdistan, Georgia, and Armenia, inhabited by savage mountain tribes. Opposed by fierce Kurds every foot of the way, forced to ford rivers, suffering from snow and extreme cold, at times near starvation, the sorely beset forces under Xenophon struggled slowly homeward. At last, nearly a year after the expedition began, a Hellenic city on the Black Sea (modern Trebizond) was reached amid general rejoicing, as the troops in the vanguard shouted, "Thalassa!" ("The sea!").

The march of the Ten Thousand has historical significance aside from being a narrative of enthralling adventures. It revealed the vital weaknesses of the far-flung, much feared Persian Empire. In spite of all efforts of Artaxerxes to destroy them, the vastly outnumbered Greeks accomplished a safe return. This lesson was not lost on Greek statesmen and military commanders, in particular, on Alexander the Great about fifty years later as he undertook to conquer the Eastern world. "Alexander the Great could not have been great had not Xenophon been," commented one ancient Greek.

The *Anabasis* reveals in vivid fashion, also, the extraordinary qualities of the Greek fighting men: their courage and endurance, their willingness to face hardship and danger, their independence and piety. While not lacking in discipline, they demanded to be governed as free men and to have a hand in the making of decisions on matters affecting them. The Ten Thousand have been called "a marching democracy," "a roving commonwealth," deliberating and acting, fighting and voting, "an epitome of Athens set adrift in the center of Asia." As perceptively noted by Edith Hamilton in *The Greek Way*, "What brought the Greeks safely back from Asia was precisely what made Athens great. The Athenian was a law unto himself, but his dominant instinct to stand alone was counterbalanced by his sense of overwhelming obligation to serve the state."

As a manual of the art of war among the Greeks and as a contribution to military science, the *Anabasis* has exerted wide influence. Under attack, Xenophon became an able strategist and tactician. In the most trying situations, the habit of clear and logical thought learned from the teaching of Socrates enabled him to cope with his turbulent troops. Further, not being a professional militarist, he was little concerned with traditional practices, and always ready to devise new tactics to meet new conditions. A modern student of military science and biographer of Alexander, Colonel Theodore A. Dodge, writes: "The soldier of greatest use to us preceding Alexander was unquestionably Xenophon. . . . It is he who has shown the world what should be the tactics of retreat, how to command a rear guard. More tactical originality has come from the *Anabasis* than from any dozen other books. . . . After the lapse of twenty-three centuries, there is no better military textbook than the *Anabasis*."

On numerous occasions, Xenophon's piety shows him to have been a true disciple of Socrates. During the retreat of the Ten Thousand, whenever Xenophon finds himself in a critical situation he refers the problem to the decision of the gods. Once, in apparently desperate straits, he relates how he was encouraged by a heaven-sent dream. Following the successful conclusion of the expedition, he offers sacrifices to Apollo and Artemis.

Perhaps because he had witnessed the dire consequences of war, Xenophon believed that peace should be the goal of all states and disputes ought to be settled by diplomacy. "He who conquers by force," he asserts, "may fancy that he can continue to do so, but the only conquests that last are when men willingly submit to those who are better than themselves. The only way really to conquer a country is through generosity."

The remainder of Xenophon's career was spent in Sparta, rather than Athens. For having sided with the Spartans against the Athenians, he was exiled from his native land. Living the life of a country gentleman and sportsman in semiretirement, he produced a series of books, among them *Hellenica*, a completion of the account of the Peloponnesian War begun by Thucydides; *Oeconomicus*, an exposition on household management and the respective duties of husband and wife; *Memorabilia*, recollections of Socrates; *Cyropaedia*, a fictional work on the education of Cyrus the Elder; and treatises on riding and hunting.

Polybius: *The Histories*

By common consent, Polybius is recognized as the greatest Greek historian after Herodotus and Thucydides. Further, Polybius had the distinction of being an eminent diplomat, statesman, and soldier. His is the first significant universal history, especially valuable for his study of politics. For the historical epoch of which he treats, his writings are the primary source of information.

A native of Megalopolis born into the aristocracy, Polybius early took an active part in the affairs of the great Achaean League or Hellenic Federations, as his father Lycortas had done before him. When the Greeks submitted to the irresistible advance of the Roman Empire, Polybius was taken to Rome as a political hostage and forced to remain there for seventeen years before being allowed to return to his homeland. During this period, he had the good fortune to gain the friendship of some of the most influential Romans. There, too, he conceived the plan for, and wrote a substantial part of, his magnum opus, the

Histories. To this ambitious task, he brought a Greek intellectual background, exceptional abilities as an observer and political analyst, and firsthand experience as a diplomat and traveler in world affairs.

Polybius' *Histories* consist of forty books, of which the first five are fully preserved; of the remaining thirty-five, generous fragments survive. His chief purpose in writing, Polybius tells us, is to demonstrate why, in the short space of about two generations, the ancient world fell under the power of Rome. The *Histories* therefore center on the relatively short era from the Second Punic War (218 B.C.) to the conquest of Macedon by Rome (167 B.C.). In these critical years Rome rose from a small state to world sovereignty. "Can any one," asks Polybius, "be so indifferent as not to care to know by what means, and under what polity, almost the whole inhabited world was conquered and brought under the dominion of the single city of Rome?"

For background purposes, Polybius sketches in the first two books the earlier relations of Rome with Carthage, including the First Punic War, and the previous history of the Achaean League with which he was intimately familiar. The last ten books, an extension of the original plan, give an account of the manner in which Rome exercised her vast power until the destruction of Carthage and final breaking up of the Achaean League, from 168 to 146 B.C.

Throughout his writings, Polybius leaves no doubt of his admiration for Roman achievements. By instinct, as well as birth, he was an aristocrat, with little sympathy for democratic survivals or demagogic outbreaks. Realistically, he saw that the old Greek ideas of freedom and independence, centering in the city-state, were gone, unlikely to return, and that the Greek states had to accept the supremacy of Rome.

The power and greatness of Rome, Polybius maintains, were the consequence of an extraordinarily stable form of government and of high political standards and practices. The secret of success for the Romans, as he analyzes it, was a mixed constitution, a blending of different principles of governmental authority. Each of the three primary forms of government—monarchy, aristocracy, and democracy—contains inherently unstable elements, and constantly tends toward degeneration. But the tendency can be counteracted by setting up a system of checks and balances, that is, by mixing opposing concepts. Otherwise, monarchy is likely to change into tyranny, aristocracy into oligarchy, and democracy into mob rule.

In the Roman constitution, Polybius notes, there was a happy mixture of principles derived from all three of the basic types of government. The consuls exemplified the monarchical concept, the Senate the aristocratic, and the popular assemblies the democratic. Among the three branches the power of government was about equally divided, and none could act independently of the others. The method of checks and balances, Polybius says, "is adequate to all emergencies, so that it is impossible to find a better political system than this."

Forms, however, are not enough to insure the state's growth, vitality, and stability. Of equal significance are leaders of high integrity. In Carthage, Polybius points out, "nothing which results in profit is regarded as disgraceful," while in Rome "unscrupulous gain from forbidden sources" is condemned. Also, "at Carthage candidates for office practice open bribery, whereas at Rome death is the penalty for it."

Polybius' views on the training of historians and the purposes of history are definite and often reiterated. The true historian will be a man of action, familiar with political and military affairs, recording his own experiences of peace and war, describing from personal knowledge men, events, and localities. He will study and compare literary sources, memoirs, archives, and other documents. He must know lands and places, topography, cities, districts, rivers, harbors, and similar geographical features, which knowledge is to be acquired principally by travel. He will ask questions of eyewitnesses and other people connected with the events or places being described but will carefully evaluate their testimony. In terms of these various criteria, it should be noted, Polybius was eminently qualified to write the history of his own age.

In the spirit of Thucydides, Polybius asserts that it is the historian's fundamental duty to record facts accurately and objectively: "If history is deprived of truth, all that remains is an idle tale." He divides historians into three classes: those who write for pay (to cater to the pleasure or preconceived notions of kings or states); those who write for rhetorical display, i.e., literary exercises; and those who write for the truth and the good of mankind. According to Polybius' doctrine, history should be "pragmatic" and universal. In order to be practical, it must deal with political realities and furnish instruction. For this purpose, a mere narrative of events is inadequate, and the historian has an added responsibility: to investigate and explain causes and interconnections. Furthermore, it is only from a view of universal history—not from a study of isolated incidents and limited geographical areas—that one gains a proper understanding of cause and effect and can estimate the real importance of events. Thus Polybius anticipated the modern theory of the unity of history.

In philosophical and religious convictions, Polybius was essentially a Stoic. "To believe things which are beyond the limits of possibility," he comments, "reveals a childish simplicity, and is the mark of a blunted intelligence." As a historian he is little concerned with miracles, and impatient with writers who ascribed public calamities or private adversity to fortune or fate. "When you can discover the cause of an event it is not, in my opinion, admissible to impute it to God." He also repudiates the idea that fortune had anything to do with Rome's greatness. "It was not by fortune, as some of the Greeks think, nor causelessly, that the Romans succeeded; their success was quite natural; it was due to their training and discipline; they aimed at the hegemony and government of the world, and they attained their purpose." Nothing happens without a natural cause. Nevertheless, Polybius regards religion as the foundation of the Roman state, because of its bearing upon the psychology of the masses, whom he sees as ignorant and cowardly, requiring hope from the gods to face dangers and the problems of life.

A modern historian, J. L. Strachan-Davidson, states that "no ancient writer of equal interest and importance finds fewer readers than Polybius"—a viewpoint representing a general consensus. The reasons are obvious. Polybius' literary style is pedantic and tedious in the extreme, lacking in color, romance, or excitement, and he is given to endless arguing, preaching, and moralizing. While his narrative is, in Theodor Mommsen's words, "a model of completeness, simplicity, and clearness," it suffers from its virtues. Contrasted with his two great predecessors, Polybius is wanting in Herodotus' faculty for storytelling and in Thucydides' literary and dramatic force. The *Histories* are valued instead for their variety of subject matter, breadth of view, and acute insight, and the prime importance and fascination of the age with which they deal.

Polybius' influence on Cicero was pronounced, and Cicero aided him in finding a popular audience in ancient and later times. William Ebenstein observes that "in the Middle Ages, Polybius' main ideas are traceable in thinkers as diverse as Marsilio of Padua and St. Thomas of Aquinas, and in the modern era Locke and Montesquieu added new weight to the doctrine of the balance of powers." In specific application of Polybius' theories of political organization, the United States Constitution may be cited as an example. The American political leaders —Madison, Hamilton, Adams, and others—were entirely familiar with the works of Polybius and utilized his concepts in the preparation of a Constitution based on the doctrine of checks and balances, of liberty through limited government.

Gaius Sallustius Crispus: *The War with Catiline,* *The War with Jugurtha*

Gaius Sallustius Crispus is the first Roman historian whose works have survived, at least in part, to the present day. In originality of style, objectivity of approach, and ability to judge men and movements, Sallust has often been compared to Thucydides. Sallust's fame as a historian rests upon two short and specialized monographs: *The War with Catiline,* about twelve thousand words in length, and *The War with Jugurtha,* approximately twice as long. In addition, there are fragments extant of a larger and more ambitious *History,* written in five books.

A plebeian by birth, Sallust led a controversial and eventful political life before settling down to a writing career. At the age of thirty-four, he was elected tribune of the people, but two years later was expelled from the Senate on charges of immorality. The real reason for his expulsion was more probably his opposition to the old Roman aristocracy and his steadfast loyalty to Caesar. Within a short period, Caesar restored him to the Senate by an appointment as quaestor. Subsequently, he served Caesar in several military and naval campaigns, and as proconsul of Africa. In the latter post, Sallust accumulated a vast fortune, quite likely through oppression and extortion. Caesar's influence saved him from criminal charges. Thereafter he retired to a magnificent estate, later the property of Nero and other Roman emperors, and devoted himself to literary pursuits. In Sallust's words: "I resolved to return to a cherished purpose from which ill-starred ambition had diverted me, and write a history of the Roman people, selecting such portions as seemed to me worthy of record."

"The conspiracy of Catiline," Sallust remarks in a prefatory statement, "I regard as worthy of special notice because of the extraordinary nature of the crime and of the danger arising from it." Another motive in Sallust's mind, it has been suspected, was to clear Caesar and Mark Antony's uncle, Gaius Antonius, from the suspicion of complicity in the plot. The *Catiline* monograph is an account of Catiline's famous conspiracy to overthrow the government of Rome, in 63 B.C.—an attempt crushed by Cicero. Sallust professes complete impartiality in presenting the story, but he obviously leans toward the democratic view and against the aristocracy. He portrays in damning fashion senatorial misrule and the moral and economic degeneration of the young nobility. To Sallust, Catiline was the personification of the corrupt, decadent aristocrat, craving luxury and power, who led dissatisfied, disgruntled elements in the state to further his revolutionary schemes.

Though inaccurate in certain historical details, the *Catiline* is a vivid and engrossing piece of reporting. Sallust excels in his delineation of character. The little book is dominated by three brilliantly drawn figures: Catiline, Caesar, and Cato the Younger. Cato is shown as a grand old Roman, iron-willed, stern, and a man of unimpeachable honor, the description of whom is an example of Sallust's fairness, since Cato was an aristocrat and Caesar's unyielding opponent. Nevertheless, Caesar is the hero, the man of the future, the coming liberator, despite faults and failings which Sallust makes no effort to conceal. Curiously, the narrative downgrades and ignores as far as possible the part played by Cicero, who claimed to have saved the state from danger and whose own account of the conspiracy differs in significant respects from Sallust's.

Sallust emulates his great model Thucydides in weaving into the narrative a number of speeches throwing light on particular episodes and the characters involved. The speeches are carefully composed and do not pretend to give the exact words of the speakers; rather, following the Thucydidean tradition, the sentiments expressed are adapted to the individuals represented as delivering them.

Sallust concludes his narration with an account of the defeat and destruction of the conspirators, a striking and memorable recital of the desperate bravery of Catiline and his men before the revolt was finally suppressed, and a portrayal of the tragic scenes characteristic of civil war. As later events demonstrated, the rebellion was a prelude to the overthrow of the republic by Caesar. The Catilinian plot failed for lack of competent leadership and because the time was not yet ripe for the downfall of the governing aristocracy.

In *The War with Jugurtha*, Sallust again uses a historical essay as a weapon with which to attack the corrupt Roman aristocracy. Here he relates the story of the shrewd and ruthless warrior king of Numidia, Jugurtha, who took advantage of the weaknesses of the Senate and the corruption of the aristocratic generals to wage a temporarily successful war against the Roman forces. Sallust comments frankly that he chose to write about the conflict "first and foremost because it was large and alarming and full of surprising reversals, and further because it was this war that marked the beginning of successful resistance to the dominant power of the nobles."

In writing the *Jugurtha*, Sallust had access to a number of literary sources, particularly the memoirs of politician-soldiers, but the work reads like a good historical novel rather than undiluted history. Its chronology and geography are confused and unreliable. Thus, the *Jugurtha* is valuable primarily as a literary masterpiece and for its acute character studies, in which Sallust is again superlative. Here, too, as in the *Catiline*, the essentials of the political situation are effectively dramatized by the insertion of revealing speeches.

Sallust tells how for some six years, relying upon the incompetence and greed of the Roman nobility, and through corrupting generals, Jugurtha was able to defy the might of Rome's armies. When Marius was chosen as commander by the angry Roman people, however, Jugurtha was quickly defeated, forced to surrender, and finally put to death. Marius, the hero of the story, is quoted as describing one of the proud but unfit generals who had preceded him as "a man of the old aristocracy, with many ancestors, but no campaigns."

Sallust expresses the view, in one of his introductory essays, that history is created by only a few persons. Rome's greatness, he says, came from a small number of men, and her present troubles could be attributed to the mediocre individuals who had succeeded the important figures of the past. His hero, Caesar, was determined to add his name to the short list of world movers and shakers.

As a literary stylist, Sallust has been much admired. Einar Löfstedt in *Roman Literary Portraits* describes his manner of expression as "short, pregnant, astringent, and rather archaic, but in its own way extraordinarily powerful." The influence of Thucydides can be detected in his brevity of expression; in turn, Sallust directly influenced Tacitus and has been praised by such modern stylists as Nietzsche. Many of Sallust's pithy phrases have become familiar quotations. Examples are "Plenty of eloquence but little wisdom," "To few is honor dearer than gold," "No one has become immortal by sloth," "Necessity makes even the timid brave," "Terror closes the ears of the mind," "Fame may be won in peace as well as in war."

In considerable measure, Sallust's lasting importance comes from a lack of competitors. So little has survived from the accounts of early Roman historians that excessive dependence has had to be placed on Sallust and his brief treatises. The works of such able contemporaries as Varro, for example, have vanished completely. Also lending interest to Sallust's writings is their interpretation of Roman history during the late republican period, presenting viewpoints frequently at variance with those of other historical and literary sources. Sarton terms Sallust's contributions "brilliant analyses of political events, the first models of their kind in world literature."

Titus Livius: *History of Rome*

The Roman historian Livy (59 B.C.–A.D. 17), generally rated as the greatest prose writer of the Augustan age, is in many particulars the Roman counterpart of the Greek Herodotus. Like Herodotus, Livy has not been highly esteemed for accuracy or critical judgment, but he was a delightful storyteller, had an instinct for lively details, an abhorrence for dullness, a flair for the dramatic, and a charming literary style. Neither Livy nor Herodotus, of course, had any conception of modern standards of historiography and research.

Livy also had much in common with his contemporary Vergil,

and his history is a prose companion to the *Aeneid*. Though Livy was about a decade younger than Vergil, he had been engaged upon his history for a number of years before Vergil died. Each was motivated by a keen sense of patriotism, a desire to glorify Roman history and the Roman Empire. Livy's belief that "the founding of this great city and the establishment of an empire which is now in power is next to the immortal gods" was exactly in accord with the poet's concept in the *Aeneid*. They both viewed Rome as having been founded, built, and governed by a succession of heroic figures, inspired by the gods, and immune to the corruptions of weaker characters. Being moralists, they naturally drew ethical lessons from the study of history. In Livy's words, "This is the most wholesome and most fruitful outcome of historical knowledge, to have before one's eyes conspicuous and authentic examples of every type of conduct, whence the student may choose models for his own imitation and that of his country, and be warned against things ill begun which have likewise ended ill."

Livy's work originally covered all of Roman history, from the mythical Romulus and Remus to recent events, and comprised 142 books—the equivalent of perhaps two dozen modern volumes of average size. The undertaking was spread over a forty-year period. Of the total, about one-fourth survives: the Preface and Books One–Ten, covering the period from Aeneas to 293 B.C.; Books Twenty-one–Thirty, describing the Second Punic War; and Books Thirty-one–Forty-five, telling the story of Rome's conquests down to the year 167 B.C. An epitome or abridgment of the entire work has come down from the fourth century.

In his preface, Livy states his philosophy of history and his purpose in producing yet another history of Rome. He refers to the marvelous tales associated with the beginnings of the city, adding, "It is not my intention either to affirm or deny the truth of the stories. They are better fitted for the imagination of poets than the sober chronicles of history." But here the true patriot intercedes: "If it be reasonably granted to any people to hallow its beginnings and call the gods its founders, surely it is granted to the people of Rome." The glory which the Roman people had won in war and other evidences of their supremacy, Livy felt, gave the legends at least a certain symbolic truth. What really mattered in Rome's history, however, Livy goes on to observe, was that her power was solidly based on morality and discipline. "There never was a nation whose history is richer in noble deeds," he asserts, "nor a community into which greed and luxury have made so late an entrance, or in which plain and thrifty living have been so long or so highly honored."

Despite his remarkable gifts as a literary artist, Livy lacked certain essential qualifications for a great historian. His English translator, B. O. Foster, notes that he was not well-informed, not particularly interested in politics or military arts, and, having no practical experience in government, knew little of constitutional or political matters. Further, his mind was uncritical, his sources were not judiciously chosen, he was indifferent to the use of original documents, even those readily avaliable to him, and he made no effort to acquaint himself with important geographical and topographical information.

Another commentator, Livy's biographer P. G. Walsh, notes a more serious criticism of Livy and one even more damaging to his reputation as an accurate, objective historian: "his occasional attempts to pervert or to cloak the truth for patriotic or moral reasons." For example, Livy invariably represents as men of complete integrity the great leaders who defended or extended the empire, choosing to ignore abundant evidence to the contrary. He similarly idealizes the conduct of Roman troops, glossing over defeats in battle or blaming them on stupid generals.

What then, in the light of numerous deficiencies and shortcomings, is the secret of Livy's success? Added to qualities already cited, are his genius in characterization and his profound psychological insights into the minds, motives, and behavior of men under stress. Like other ancient historians, Livy was drawn to and fascinated by colorful personalities, especially the leading military and political figures. Seneca called him "by nature the most impartial judge of all great characters," a verdict that modern historians would hardly accept, in view of Livy's tendency to exaggerate the merits and overlook human frailties in his heroes. Nonetheless, the procession of soldiers, statesmen, and patriots who move through his pages leave indelible impressions; the reader is swept along by Livy's contagious enthusiasm for his subjects and what Edith Hamilton calls "the fire and power of a great imagination," as a natural consequence of which she rightly concludes "Rome to us is Livy's Rome." We come to admire the Romans' courage, discipline, and ability to rule, and are almost persuaded to concur in Livy's conviction that they were the children of destiny, lords of creation, and divinely ordained to attain world supremacy.

A fair view of Livy's work is to regard it as a great literary creation rather than as a scholarly history. Strong support for this assessment is found in the frequent insertion of fictional speeches, a practice common among all ancient historians after Thucydides. Livy's speeches were composed with artistic care, and much of his literary reputation in Rome rested upon them. No matter how unhistorical the speeches were in literal fact, Livy used them effectively as psychological portraits, to explore character, develop dramatic suspense, inculcate patriotism, and increase historical understanding.

Further illustrating Livy's literary and romantic approach to history are the mentions of prodigies and supernatural occurrences scattered throughout the work. However, these auguries and marvels were, of course, an intimate part of Roman historical tradition, and though Livy relates the old stories of miraculous events, his attitude toward them is generally skeptical. He either disowns them by making clear that he is merely passing on what has been handed down from the past, or he notes that religious interpretations have been attached to the phenomena in earlier times, not by his own.

The exhaustive analysis by Iiro Kajanto, in his *God and Fate in Livy*, demonstrates conclusively that Livy thought that the course of events was mainly determined by human beings rather than by the gods and fate. Passages in which an event is said to have been caused by the gods are few in number and of relatively minor significance. Livy was inclined, however, to view with approval the exploitation of religion for political purposes, citing, for example, the influence on the Roman armies of their belief in the efficacy of prayers and rituals. Livy was also aware of the social value of religion for public morals and recognized that fear of the gods was an effective weapon in controlling the general populace.

Directly or indirectly, Livy has been one of the primary sources of Roman history. It is regettable, therefore, that he so frequently invents and distorts episodes for artistic, dramatic, literary, or patriotic ends. On the other hand, he was an idealist who judged men with sympathetic charity, a lover of noble deeds possessing a rare insight into the workings of the mind and heart, and a writer whose strength of imagination enabled him to bring alive the shadowy names of Rome's past ages.

The work which occupied Livy for all of his adult life met with instant acclaim. It was warmly praised by the younger Pliny, Tacitus, Quintilian, and other Roman commentators, and it virtually superseded earlier histories. Livy shared with Vergil the honor of being the most widely read of Latin writers.

Plutarch: *Parallel Lives of Greeks and Romans*

The great biographer James Boswell conferred upon Plutarch the title "the Prince of Ancient Biographers." The appellation is richly merited, for the world has drawn from Plutarch, more than from any other source, its conception of the heroic men (and occasionally women) of ancient Greece and Rome.

Though Plutarch wrote prolifically of the lives of others, little is known of his own career. He was born about half a century after the beginning of the Christian Era in the province of Boeotia in Greece; he was educated at Athens; he visited Asia Minor, Egypt, and Italy; and he resided for a time in Rome. His lifetime spanned the reigns of the Roman emperors Claudius and Nero to Trajan, and he was a contemporary of Epictetus, Martial, Juvenal, Tacitus, and the two Plinys. He ended his days in literary leisure as priest at Apollo's shrine at Delphi. These bare facts are reasonably well verified.

The Greece into which Plutarch was born had long since lost her political independence; her creative genius was exhausted; and she was merely a vassal state of the mighty Roman Empire. The once proud intellectual center of the world had become a humiliated, conquered country, its population drastically reduced, commerce and agriculture in a sad state, and its people desperately poor.

Plutarch, a highly patriotic Greek, feared that in the midst of all their misfortunes, his countrymen (and others) would lose sight of Greece's former glory. The examples of the mighty dead, he believed, would remind the world of the great deeds, heroic courage, generosity, and notable characters of ancient Hellas' supreme moment in history. Under this motivation, Plutarch started to compose his *Lives*. "It was for the sake of others," he noted, "that I first began to write biographies, but I find myself continuing to do it for my own. The virtues of these great men serve me as a sort of looking glass in which I may see how to adorn and adjust my own life. I can compare it to nothing but living daily with them . . . turning my thoughts happily and calmly to the noble."

Plutarch's fitness for the large task that he had undertaken was extraordinary. He had gathered his materials "out of divers books and authorities," mostly in Rome. His knowledge of Greek literature appears virtually unlimited, and in his writings he incorporated numerous quotations, frequently from authors whose works have otherwise vanished. On his sources, Plutarch brought to bear a richly philosophical mind, though scarcely an original one, and a wide knowledge of men and life.

The *Parallel Lives* were so entitled by their author because of the ingenious plan adopted of writing the accounts in pairs: the biography of a great Greek matched to that of a great Roman, followed by a critical comparison. In this fashion are linked Theseus and Romulus, Demosthenes and Cicero, Alexander and Julius Caesar, and others. A total of forty-six parallel biographies of great and near great men from Greek and Roman history have survived, but the comparison is lacking in a number of cases, some parallels have been lost, and four separate lives have been added, perhaps spuriously.

"My intent," declares Plutarch at the outset, "is not to write histories but only lives," and he clearly understood the difference. His ambition was to paint a gallery of portraits, delineating character rather than narrating historical events. The historian is concerned with economics, politics, and the rise and fall of empires, the biographer with human beings. In Plutarch's view, "The most glorious exploits do not always furnish the clearest indications of virtue or vice in men; sometimes a mere expression, a jest, even, gives us their characters better than the most famous sieges, the bloodiest battles. . . . I must be allowed to give my particular attention to the marks and indications of men's souls, as I endeavor to portray their lives."

Plutarch has been called "a born hero-worshiper," and it is not strange, therefore, that he chose only rulers, leaders, soldiers, and statesmen for subjects. Mere literary personalities, such as Plato or Aristotle, were unworthy, in his estimation, to be immortalized in the same company with famous emperors and military heroes. Further, of thirteen Roman characters included, a majority belonged to a period of less than a century, the era during which the Empire was created. The Greeks were taken from various eras and cities, but all, Greeks and Romans alike, had similar achievements in common: they founded states, defended their states from foreign invasion, extended their dominions, or led political parties.

A curious feature of the *Lives* is the inclusion of legendary figures, as though they were authentic historical personages. The "founders" of Greece and Rome treated by Plutarch— Theseus and Romulus, Lycurgus and Pompilius—are woven out of folklore, legend, and romance. Publicola and Coriolanus are also legendary. Plutarch acknowledged that his sources for such accounts were "full of suspicion and doubt, being delivered to us by poets and inventors of fables"; but he suggests that we "receive with indulgence the stories of antiquity," because "so very difficult it is to find out the truth of anything." In any case, many things that are beyond belief "peradventure will please the reader better for their strangeness and curiosity, than offend or mislead him for their falsehood."

Closely allied to Plutarch's ready acceptance of legend and myth is his confirmed belief in omens, portents, and ghosts. He thought that the supernatural exerted a constant influence on everyday life; that death and disaster, good fortune and victory never came without forewarning. Hence, signs and oracular utterances play decisive roles in the lives of Plutarch's heroes.

Another striking characteristic of the biographies is Plutarch's passion for anecdotes. Again and again, he departs from the main theme to insert a fabulous tale, a picturesque detail, or a miraculous incident to bring color, excitement, and interest to the narrative. Historians have been highly critical of Plutarch for this tendency, and some have even dismissed him as a mere storyteller. In Plutarch's defense, it should be noted that his anecdotes not only add dramatic effect but are generally pertinent illustrations of points of character the author wished to stress. He was looking, he said, for "the signs of the soul in men," and the anecdotes are interwoven with the lives for this sublime purpose. Plutarch did not, of course, meet the standards of historical accuracy prevailing in our own day. He reflected faithfully, however, the historical tradition of his age; he records, in short, what the Greeks and Romans of that era believed or wanted to believe, about their warriors and statesmen of the past.

Plutarch's political theories and ideas often appear incidentally in the biographies. He favored constitutional republics and opposed hereditary monarchies. An enduring constitution and a strong senate of proved men, popularly elected, in his view, are essentials in a well-ordered state. Required, too, above all, are able, courageous leaders, armed with full authority. Viewing political conditions around him, Plutarch concluded that it was by obedience and self-restraint, by "yielding unto reason and virtue" that the "Romans came to command all other and to make themselves the mightiest people of the world."

Plutarch wrote as a moralist, and his digressions on religious, philosophical, and social matters are numerous. He did not choose model characters as subjects, recognizing that there are no perfect human beings. He saw that there were qualities of courage, virtue, and nobleness even in such characters as Alcibiades, Sulla, and Nero, and contrariwise, elements of badness in good men. "Plutarch's heroes," writes the English essayist Robert Lynd, "are men in whom a god dwells at strife with a devil—the devil of sin and imperfection." Plutarch's quest for virtue was unending, and he never paints a biographical portrait without probing deep for evidences of nobility. As Edith Hamilton so discerningly comments in her *Echo of Greece*, "The one he raised to a pedestal was the man who made it easy for people to believe in goodness and greatness, in heroic courage and warm generosity and lofty magnanimity." Other critics have argued that Plutarch was too lenient, condemning him for countenancing or glossing over such crimes and sins committed by his heroes as human slaughter, marital infidelity, perjury, drunkenness, and suicide.

The *Lives* of Plutarch has been the most widely beloved, and perhaps the most widely read, among all the ancient literary treasures of Greece. Traces of its influence are to be found everywhere in modern literature. In the English language, the greatest impact was made by Sir Thomas North's translation, published in 1579. It was this work which introduced Plutarch to the Elizabethan age, and especially to William Shakespeare. Three of Shakespeare's greatest plays—*Coriolanus, Julius Caesar*, and *Antony and Cleopatra*—are based on Plutarch's *Lives*. In *Julius Caesar*, the incidents and much of the language are derived directly from the North translation. Among other notable literary figures who have expressed their admiration for Plutarch, by word or emulation, Montaigne may represent them all when he said, "We dunces had been lost had not this book raised us out of the dust. By this favor of his we dare now speak and write. 'Tis our breviary."

Cornelius Tacitus: *Annals*

For the reputation of the Roman emperor Nero as one of the most vicious, debauched rulers who ever occupied a throne, the historian Tacitus is primarily responsible. Tacitus was no more lenient in treating the lives of other first-century monarchs of the mighty Roman Empire. It was an age of incredible corruption, loose morals, and overall degeneracy, scarcely equaled by any other historical epoch—made to order for Tacitus' bitter pen. John Jackson, English translator of Tacitus' *Annals*, sums up the work as "an amazing chronicle of an amazing era, brilliant, unfair, and unforgettable."

Of Tacitus himself only a few bare facts are known with any assurance, and these do not include his birthplace, the dates of his birth and death, or even his first name. He appears to have been a member of a prominent family and to have held various important governmental posts. Also, he was a lawyer by profession, and married to the daughter of Agricola, Roman governor of Britain.

Tacitus' youth fell in the reign of Nero and he must therefore have known at first hand much of that emperor's dissolute career, the atrocities he committed, and his tragic end. It was under Nero's successor, Domitian, however, that Tacitus suffered his most traumatic experiences. For fifteen years, Domitian exercised an utterly despotic rule. He was a man of unbounded vanity, who forced senators to greet him by kissing his foot, did not permit dinner guests to speak, called himself "master and god," and otherwise demonstrated symptoms of insanity. The execution of some of the ablest and most respected persons in the state, perhaps Agricola among them, was ordered by Domitian, who eventually fell himself at the hands of an assassin. Tacitus emerged from this terror-stricken period with a fundamental hatred of despotism and a markedly pessimistic disposition, strongly disinclined to see any good trait or worthy motive in either the emperors or their consorts.

Under Domitian, Tacitus had not dared to write. "Ancient times," he declared later, "saw the utmost of freedom, we of servitude. Robbed by an inquisition of the common use of speech and hearing, we should have lost our very memory with our voice, were it as much in our power to forget as to be dumb. Now at last our breath has come back, but genius and learning are more easily extinguished than recalled. Fifteen years have been subtracted from our lives."

The incentive that led Tacitus to write history was his desire to teach a great moral lesson; he wrote as a moralist rather than as a historian. His purpose was to leave a record of the evils of tyranny as exemplified in the emperors from Tiberius to Domitian. Throughout his historical works, the indictment of the tyrants was the driving force. He looked back nostalgically to the lost cause of the Roman Republic and viewed the succeeding years as a tragic struggle between liberty and despotism. "This I regard as history's highest function," he writes, "to let no worthy action be uncommemorated, and to hold out the reprobation of posterity as a terror to evil words and deeds."

Tacitus' first major literary production dealt with his own times: the *Histories*, covering the period from A.D. 69, the Year of the Four Emperors, to the death of Domitian in 96. The *Annals*, his last and greatest work, was retrospective, beginning with the death of Augustus in A.D. 14 and concluding with Nero in 68. Of the sixteen original books, several have been lost. The extant portions cover the reign of Tiberius (A.D. 14–37), the last seven years of Claudius' reign (A.D. 47–54), and the first twelve years of Nero's reign (A.D. 54–66). The missing books include all of Caligula's reign and parts of those of Tiberius, Claudius, and Nero.

While nominally a history of the early Roman Empire, the *Annals* is actually a series of psychological biographies, and masterly character sketches, of the several Roman emperors, their families and courtiers, and their opponents. Despite the brilliance of these imperial portraits, they are prejudiced and distorted, though relatively free of factual error. As a whole, they build up indelible impressions of the emperors' cruelty, tyranny, and licentiousness, the servility of the courtiers, the degradation of the Senate, and the complete demoralization of the aristocracy. Describing Tacitus' magic touch, Macaulay writes:

In the delineation of character Tacitus is unrivalled among historians and has very few superiors among dramatists and novelists. By the delineation of character we do not mean the practice of drawing up epigrammatic catalogues of good and bad qualities, and appending them to the names of eminent men. No writer, indeed, has done this more skillfully than Tacitus; but this is not his peculiar glory. All the persons who occupy a large space in his works have an individuality of character which seems to pervade all their words and actions. We know them as if we had lived with them.

Tacitus was one of the first historians to place personality, or the individual, in the center of the historical stage. To him, broad principles, large movements, and great achievements were of interest only as they helped to interpret the characters of the persons associated with them. He saw history as a drama in which the actors have a determining influence. Almost wholly neglected in the *Annals* are the Roman Empire at large, its outlying provinces and peoples, and general administration. Occassionally a military campaign is described (inexpertly), but the chief focus is on the emperors, the court and its intrigues, and on the governing class. The common man was felt to be beneath notice.

In his early youth, Tacitus is said to have occupied himself with writing tragedies, though none of his efforts has survived. In the *Annals*, his biographer Einar Löfstedt comments, "he has given us a series of tragedies—tragedies about human beings, forming together the great tragedy of Rome." Six books of the *Annals* end with catastrophes, involving the deaths of the emperors and of other notable persons. There is a pervading pessimism, an attitude of contempt for mankind, a tendency to dwell upon horrifying details and brutal realism perhaps more characteristic of the dramatist than of the historian. Typical of Tacitus' theatrical style are the description of the violent death of Nero's mother at the hands of her son's emissaries, the accounts of Nero's persecution of Roman Christians, the great fire at Rome, and the last hours and deaths of various personages.

As Löfstedt remarks, Tacitus "has an almost horrifying reluctance to see good motives in persons in power." Thus, Claudius is depicted as weak, eccentric almost to the point of imbecility, cruel, and debauched; Tiberius as a despot under whom a reign of terror grew progressively worse; and Nero as guilty of unrestrained vice and cruelty, murderer of his stepbrother, mother, and wife—to name only a few of his crimes. "I know of no other historian," said Napoleon Bonaparte (doubtless a somewhat prejudiced witness), "who has so calumniated and belittled mankind as Tacitus. In the simplest transactions he seeks for criminal motives; out of every emperor he fashions a complete villain, and so depicts him that we admire the spirit of evil permeating him, and nothing more."

It is not the facts presented by Tacitus but his interpretations that have created doubts and misgivings among modern historians. Tiberius is known to have attended to his imperial duties conscientiously and to have continued Augustus' civilizing mission in Italy and the Empire; under Claudius, government was centralized, new territory was acquired by Rome, and statesmanlike policies were followed toward the neighbors on her vast frontiers. Even under Nero, wise choices of ministers and agents were made, and attention paid to the welfare of the empire at large. Tacitus completely ignored the contemporary social, industrial, and commercial prosperity, and, looking only at Rome itself, could see nothing except the dark side.

Altogether, Tacitus' claim to fame is as a literary artist rather than as a scientific historian, though his narrative is one of the most valuable records that have survived for any period of ancient Rome. He is a supreme master of words, one of the great stylists in Latin literature, but, as various critics have noted, the satirist time and again runs away with the historian.

The literary influence of Tacitus has been extensive and profound. He was one of Montesquieu's idols. Rousseau studied Tacitus to learn the art of writing and even translated part of his works. Among the dramatists and novelists who have drawn freely upon him are Corneille, Racine, Ben Jonson, Alfieri, and Chénier. Sienkiewicz's *Quo Vadis*, Feuchtwanger's Josephus stories, and Robert Graves' Claudius series have adapted many passages from the writings of Tacitus.

8

FATHERS OF THE CHURCH

Among great figures of the early Christian church, two personalities loom largest, one near the beginning and the other toward
the close of the medieval era. St. Augustine (354–430) and St.
Thomas Aquinas (c. 1225–1274), with a span of close to a
millennium between them, represent the most profound theological thought of the Middle Ages.

St. Augustine: Confessions, City of God

The impress on history left by Augustine, bishop of Hippo,
has been equaled by few other men. Various authorities have
estimated him as "the greatest Christian thinker next to the
Apostle Paul," "the greatest Christian between Paul the Apostle
and Luther the Reformer," "the greatest of all Western thinkers,"
"the father of Catholicism and also of Protestantism," "the
towering figure in the early history of Christianity in the Latin
West," and "the chief architect of the Middle Ages." Many of
Augustine's tenets, such as the doctrine of grace, have been
taken over by the Protestants, and he occupies the same commanding position with them as with the Catholics.

Augustine lived in the midst of crisis; at the height of his
career, mankind stood at one of the great crossroads of history.
As Rome perished, a well-ordered world was collapsing about
him. When he was born in the Roman province of Numidia, in
what is now Algeria, about the middle of the fourth century
A.D., the Roman Empire seemed impregnable. But during

Augustine's lifetime the incredible happened: Rome fell before the northern invaders, the Goths and the Vandals overran Italy, and as he died, they had crossed the Mediterranean and were besieging his own town of Hippo. It was, in fact, an age of social disintegration; the classical civilization of pagan antiquity, epitomized by Greece and Rome, was dying, and the new Christendom had not yet arisen to replace this civilization.

Augustine's father was a pagan and his mother a devout Christian. In his early manhood, he himself was a pagan. In his *Confessions*, Augustine describes the experiences which led ultimately to his conversion to Christianity: the excesses of his youth, his subsequent search for truth, and his final adoption of the Christian faith, in 387, at the age of thirty-three, under the influence of St. Ambrose of Milan. Four years later, he was ordained a priest, and in 395 he became Bishop of Hippo, where his prodigious literary and pastoral activity continued for the next thirty-five years.

Augustine's written work is enormous in volume. He stands unsurpassed among the Latin Fathers both in the number of his literary productions and in the variety of subjects treated. The writings comprise sermons, letters, poems, theological and con-troversial treatises, commentaries on the Scriptures, defenses of Christianity, and philosophical and rhetorical essays. Much of his literary activity was devoted to controversy with the heretics of his time; the primary purpose, the desire to defeat heresy, dominates all the Augustinian polemics. In writing against opponents, Augustine develops the doctrines of original sin, predestination, irresistible grace, and final perseverance— each of which left its mark upon later creeds and theologians. Elsewhere, he deals with the nature of matter, the problem of evil, and the possibility of understanding God's plan for the universe. He also develops authoritatively some of the doctrines, originating in Judaism, which have a central place in Paul's theology, especially the guilt of the children of Adam and the necessity for atonement. The Bible, Augustine contends, is the ultimate and supreme authority, an inexhaustible source of truth. In brief, there is no aspect of Christian theology, philoso-phy, and morality which Augustine did not touch and influence.

Amid all of Augustine's prodigious literary output, two works are universally acknowledged as preeminent, the *Confessions* and the *City of God*.

The *Confessions* is the book by which Augustine is best-known in general literature. Sometimes called one of the world's greatest autobiographies, it is the best source for the life of the author, but strictly speaking it is not an autobiography at all. Biographical information is scant. The work was written in 397, ten years after Augustine's conversion to Christianity, and treats of his profound religious experiences against a background of personal unhappiness and moral conflict. A single thread runs throughout: how a skeptical pagan scholar explored the philosophical and religious beliefs of his own and past eras, eventually chose to become a Christian, and became one of the most deeply religious men of all time. In substance the work is a hymn of praise and thanksgiving to God.

The evolution of Augustine's mind may be easily traced in the *Confessions*. The progress from childhood to mature manhood is revealed in the light of his own life and experiences. He recalls the crucial episodes and events, interpreted later as mysterious actions of God, in bringing him to his present state of grace. The windings of his memory are followed through the upheavals of his youth and the disorderly stages of his quest for wisdom. The *Confessions* exposes Augustine's weaknesses and errors, as he saw them, without attempting to justify them. He emphasizes the importance of the senses in the acquisition of knowledge, analyzes the nature and power of memory, treats of learning and thinking, and maintains that all teaching is based on faith and authority.

In his early years, Augustine discloses, he fell into licentious habits. He relates an incident of the theft of pears by him and a gang of ragamuffin friends, an escapade undertaken not from hunger, but simply for delight in doing what was forbidden. The story of his adolescent years includes an account of various other transgressions which he and his youthful playmates thoughtlessly committed, petty derelictions, on the whole, rather than serious crimes. Later, as a student at the University of Carthage, Augustine led a life which he later considered dissolute, having an illegitimate son by a mistress with whom he lived for the next thirteen years. Nevertheless, at the university he made a brilliant scholastic record, became familiar with the teachings of Plato, Cicero, Plotinus, and other classical writers, outstripped all competitors, and mastered the art of rhetoric.

Only after much soul-searching did Augustine decide to become a Christian. While a university student and subsequently as a teacher of rhetoric, his restless, eager mind explored a variety of pagan and heretical faiths, and for a time he was a Manichee. But he found that all these beliefs were ultimately vain and barren. This period of earnest religious inquiry was accompanied by a deepening conviction of sin. Not until after his acceptance of Christianity, Augustine declares, were his doubts resolved; he was then able for the first time to put aside the temptations of the flesh and his besetting sins of lust and pride. Earlier, his intense love of pleasure had stood in opposition to a guilty conscience, which craved spiritual satisfaction.

The first nine of the thirteen books of the *Confessions* relate to Augustine's experiences. The remaining books, quite unrelated, are a commentary on the creation narrative in Genesis, speculative philosophy, and metaphysical treatises on the possibility of knowing God and the nature of time and space. The theological concepts of the *Confessions* have become an integral part of Western Christendom.

J. W. C. Wand, Lord Bishop of London, comments on the *Confessions:* "It is unique in early literature for the extent of its self-revelation. Augustine set the tone, not merely for all introspective literature, but also for introspection as a scientific aid to psychology and philosophy. . . . His analysis of memory, for instance, is of first-rate value in recognizing that one may not merely have memory of past events, but also of past emotions and states of mind." Thus, Augustine's delving into the depths of personality entitles him to high rank as a psychologist, as well as a great religious leader.

Augustine's greatest and most significant book is the *City of God,* designed to vindicate Christianity and the Christian church —a work which laid the foundations of the Holy Roman Empire and paved the way for the subordination of the state to the church.

The *City of God* was written in response to a great disaster. It was begun three years after the Goths had captured and sacked Rome. This was the dreadful penalty visited upon the once proud city, said the enemies of Christianity, for deserting its ancient gods. When Rome had been a pagan city, it had gone from victory to victory, finally reigning supreme; now, almost immediately after the Christians had gained control, catastrophe had struck. Augustine devoted the first ten of the twenty-two books of the *City of God*, a work which required thirteen years to complete, to refuting the pagans' accusation that the agonies of the Roman world should be blamed on the advent of Christianity.

Augustine himself defines the primary objective of his magnum opus: "In the meantime Rome had been overthrown by the invasion of the Goths under King Alaric and by the vehemence of a great defeat. The worshippers of the many and false gods, whom we commonly call pagans, attempted to attribute that overthrow to the Christian religion, and they began to blaspheme the true God with even more than their customary acrimony and bitterness. It was for that reason that I, kindled by zeal for the house of God, undertook to write the books on the *City of God* against their blasphemies and errors."

The tragedy of Rome's fall, Augustine contends, is but an incident in human history, and was foreordained by a divine Providence. The weaknesses and inconsistencies of the pagan beliefs are exposed. Neither Rome nor any other city had ever been saved by its gods. Actually, misfortune had dogged Rome's history long before the coming of Christianity, and the city had fallen because of her sin and error. The worship of many gods, asserts Augustine, is unnecessary for guaranteeing happiness here or in the hereafter, and, furthermore, earthly glory and prosperity are not required for true happiness.

Unwilling to offer simply a defense or apology, Augustine adds: "In order that no one might raise the charge against me that I have merely refuted the opinions of other men but not stated my own, I devoted to this objective the second part of the work." He then proceeded to develop his long and learned essay, perhaps the earliest contribution to the philosophy of history. A complex work, the *City of God* embraces a vast multiplicity of topics in its last twelve books: the resurrection of the body, the future life, the duties of the Christian in his relations with the civil power, and a theological interpretation of the past history of the world in the light of the Christian revelation. The book is, indeed, encyclopedic in range—in most editions exceeding a thousand pages in length; and it can be read from the point of view of theology, philosophy, history, apologetics, ethics, or political theory.

Underlying Augustine's theme is the striking conception of two "cities" or states, the city of God and the city of the earth. Symbolical in nature, without a counterpart in the world as it exists, the city of God represents the godly, the sons and daughters of heaven, the people who live by the laws of God. "The celestial commonwealth is not to be viewed as a kingdom in the skies," observes C. C. Maxey in his *Political Philosophies*, "but as a heavenly regime on earth, the saved being its citizenry and God its ruler." The city of the world, on the other hand, is inhabited by the ungodly, the sons and daughters of earth, full of worldly wisdom and worldly power, but incapable of attaining perfect justice.

The final twelve books of the *City of God* are thus described by Augustine: "The first four contain an account of the origin of these two cities—the city of God and the city of the world. The second four treat of their history or progress; the third and last four, of their deserved destiny." The two opposing societies, he states, have led their separate existences from the beginning of history. Cain, the murderer, is the ancestor of the city of the earth; the slain Abel, of the heavenly city. Since the sin of Adam the vast majority of mankind have been citizens of the earthly city. The minority who belong to the heavenly city are merely pilgrims during their sojourn on earth. In the city of God, rewards are reserved for the good, in happy contrast to the dreadful torments awaiting the wicked who dwell in the earthly city. "Two loves have given origin to these two cities," declares Augustine, "self-love in contempt of God unto the earthly city, love of God in contempt of self to the heavenly city."

Over the wreckage of Rome, Augustine sees rising another city—the city of God—without frontiers, open to all nations and all humanity, whose citizens will embrace a common faith and live in complete obedience to divine law. Because it deals with spiritual matters, the church serves as a concrete embodiment of the heavenly commonwealth, guiding the Christian in his passage from time to eternity. The state, concerned with material affairs, represents the earthly commonwealth. Ideally, the state should function as the secular arm of the church.

Occasional passages in the *City of God* give the impression that Augustine considered the city of God identical with the Christian church, but elsewhere he makes clear that the heavenly city has a wider membership, including both the good angels and the elect who have departed this life; also, the Church on earth has among its members some who are not destined to be saved.

James Bryce, in *The Holy Roman Empire*, concludes: "Dim as the outline of *De Civitate Dei* [*City of God*] may be, St. Augustine had unquestionably drawn a new ideal of the Kingdom of God on earth, in which the Empire should take its place within the Church, and the Church through it should govern the world." Thereby Augustine shaped the political ideology of medieval Europe, directly influencing, for example, the attitude toward the church of Charlemagne, Otto the Great, and other medieval rulers. In effect, Augustine, in the *City of God*, wrote the political platform of the Roman church, establishing the principle that divine authority is higher than human authority, and therefore bound to prevail. According to this theory, men were required to obey the state when it was acting in its proper sphere; in the sphere of religion and morality, however, the church was supreme. Thus, as time went on, the city of God came to be identified in the minds of the faithful with the organized Christian church; hence it was felt that the state could only attain virtue by submitting to the guidance of the church.

Augustine's vision of a city of God emerging from the ruins of the Roman Empire was realized, to a large degree, in the church, which he was instrumental in rejuvenating and reinvigorating. The church undertook the gigantic task of converting to Christianity the heathen conquerors of the Roman state, and it succeeded to such an extent that over the next several centuries the invaders accepted the guidance of the church and acknowledged the Roman pope as the symbol of its unity and power.

William Ebenstein, in his *Great Political Thinkers*, expresses the view that "St. Augustine, the greatest of the Church fathers, stood at the turning point of two worlds, that of antiquity and Christianity. The impact of Plato in particular, but also that of Aristotle, Cicero, and the Stoics, is clearly evident in his work, and he helped to transmit the ancient heritage to the new world that was being born. While the Roman empire was breaking up before his eyes, he sought to construe, as a Christian, the vision of a timeless empire in which peace and justice would forever reign: the City of God." It is crystal clear that wherever one touches the Middle Ages, he finds the marks of Augustine's influence powerful and pervasive.

St. Thomas Aquinas: Summa Theologica

St. Thomas Aquinas, who ranks with St. Augustine as one of the two great fathers of the medieval church, has been given various titles: "universal doctor," "angelic doctor," "prince of scholas-

tics," "doctor of the church," and "father of moral philosophy."
Dante refers to him as "a flame of heavenly wisdom." His
Summa Theologica is one of the most important writings of the
Middle Ages, exerting an almost unrivaled influence on philoso-
phy and theology.

Aquinas was born near Naples into an aristocratic family related to European kings and emperors. Despite the vehement
opposition of his family, at the age of sixteen he joined the men-
dicant order of the Dominicans. Thereafter his life was devoted
to the study, teaching, and writing of philosophy and theology.
Though he died before he was forty-eight, his literary output was
prodigious—some seventy works of encyclopedic range.

During the approximately twelve centuries that elapsed between the death of Jesus and the birth of Thomas, Christian doctrine had evolved a vast literature, begun by Paul and continued by Augustine, Ambrose, Jerome, Boethius, Pope Gregory
I, Alcuin, Anselm, Abelard, Albertus Magnus, Peter Lombard,
and other eminent theologians. The *Summa Theologica* represents the culmination of the long effort of theologians to
codify Christian doctrines into an orderly whole. The historian
Oscar Jaszi observes that "the Roman Catholic Church urgently
needed a comprehensive and systematic theory which would put
the early traditions of Christianity in harmony with the exigen-
cies of the world diplomacy of the papal power."

The complexities and size of the task so admirably accomplished by St. Thomas are summed up by Anton C. Pegis, editor
of the *Basic Writings of Saint Thomas Aquinas:* "Such a codification required the resolution of such vast problems as the relations between revelation and reason; the distinction between
theology and philosophy; the harmonious assimilation of centuries of reflection and discussion on the nature of Christian
thought; the judicious assimilation of the philosophical literature
of the Greek, Jewish, and Arab worlds; the formulation of a
literary form which would be orderly and simple and which could
yet embody this large synthesis." In achieving those manifold
aims, St. Thomas demonstrated an extraordinary ability to combine and unify different elements into an apparently logical and
convincing system. The *Summa* incorporates Platonic teachings,
Aristotelian philosophy, Roman law, the Bible, and the writings
of the great theologians of the church—in short, the sum total of
a complex Christian tradition.

Aquinas did not originate the medieval movement of thought known as scholasticism, but he is universally acknowledged to have been the greatest of the scholastics. The aim of scholasticism was to demonstrate the harmony or compatibility between reason and faith. Knowledge can be obtained, Aquinas argues, through either faith or natural reason. Faith derives its knowledge mainly from the Holy Scripture; the supreme examples of natural reason, derived from the senses, are found in the works of Plato and Aristotle. Both kinds of knowledge come from God, and therefore they cannot be in conflict. Hence it follows that the writings of Plato and Aristotle are in agreement with the doctrines of the Christian religion. Aquinas considered that he had firmly established such harmony in the *Summa Theologica*.

The influence of Aquinas was predominant in the triumph of Aristotelean thought in the thirteenth century. Aristotle's logic had long been known in the West, but his physical and metaphysical writings were not translated into Latin until the late twelfth and thirteenth centuries. At first they were bitterly attacked by theologians. By combining the teachings of Aristotle with Christian dogma, however, Aquinas enlisted the pagan philosopher as a defender of the Christian faith. In the realm of science, Aquinas accepts Aristotle as the supreme authority on biology, psychology, astronomy, and physics, and even in ethics for the moral virtues. He is defective, says Aquinas, in failing to recognize that the world of nature is not the whole world; above it exists the realm of grace.

The method adopted by Aquinas for compilation of the *Summa Theologica* is characteristic of scholasticism: first the question, the arguments for and against, with authorities cited; then the conclusion; and finally the refutation of the arguments rejected. To the question "Whether the Angels Exist in Any Great Number?" for example, the erroneous doctrinal view is stated, followed by presentation of the correct doctrine through a quotation from an authoritative source—in this instance a Biblical passage attesting to the existence of a large number of angels—and ending with Aquinas' own analysis of the problem with answers to the objections. Each of more than three thousand articles follows the same methodology, and in excess of ten thousand objections to points of Christian dogma are answered.

The chief authorities quoted by Aquinas are the Bible, St. Augustine, and Pope Gregory, among the Christian sources, and

Aristotle among the non-Christian. Quotations from the Old and New Testaments are used indiscriminately, verses are taken out of context and sometimes allegorized, as in the explanation that Job's three daughters symbolize the three theological virtues (faith, hope, and charity), and the seven sons, the seven gifts of the Holy Ghost.

In attempting to present a complete science of theology, Aquinas states: "Whereas, the chief aim of this science is to impart a knowledge of God, not only as existing in Himself, but also as the origin and end of all things, and especially of rational creatures, we therefore shall treat first of God; second, of the rational creature's tendency toward God; third, of Christ, who as man is the way whereby we approach unto God." Thus the three parts of the *Summa* deal successively with God, man, and God in the form of man: Christ. Part One is concerned with the existence, nature, and attributes of God and his angels, and God's creation and government of the world; Part Two with general mortality and the nature of man, reviewing moral problems, especially those of a theological nature; and Part Three with Christ and the plan of Redemption, offering a theory of the sacraments. As William Ebenstein comments, in his *Great Political Thinkers*, "A sense of complete certainty pervades the work. There is no slow and groping search toward the discovery of truth, and there are no questions . . . that must be kept open for further thought and inquiry."

Matters of human ethics, dealt with in the second part of the *Summa*, are perhaps of greatest interest to the modern reader. This section, based substantially upon Aristotle's *Nicomachean Ethics*, examines the nature of human happiness, and the relative importance of riches, honor, fame, glory, power, and pleasure. Aquinas discusses in particular types of human passion: love, hatred, desire, pain and sorrow, fear and anger. He studies systematically human conditions, behavior, and habits, including civil and moral law, war and peace, sedition, homicide, theft and robbery, usury, fraudulent dealing, hope and despair, flattery, hypocrisy, cowardliness, courage, nobility, martyrdom, charity, compassion, and faith. The numerous mortal sins are enumerated and discussed in detail along with the seven deadly sins: pride, envy, anger, sloth, covetousness, lust, and gluttony.

Equally elaborate are Aquinas' analyses of the virtues. A discussion of each of the four cardinal virtues—justice, temperance, fortitude, and prudence—is accompanied by a consideration of certain related or subsidiary virtues. Finally there are reflections on the three theological virtues of faith, hope, and charity, and the three monastic virtues of poverty, chastity, and obedience.

As a guide to moral perfection, Aquinas points out the structure of laws; man practices his morality in a law-abiding universe under the governance of a sovereign God. There are, he says, four kinds of law: eternal, natural, divine, and human. Eternal law is the law by which God governs the universe; it is everlasting because God's rule of the world "is not subject to time but is eternal." Natural law is the rule of reason, implanted in all rational men, evolved by their participation in eternal law, whereby they are inclined toward proper acts and ends. Divine law is communicated to man through revelation in the Old and New Testaments, paralleling and going beyond natural law, though never contradicting it. The fourth and lowest form of law is human law, i.e., natural law made active in earthly affairs by the application of human reason, the ordinary law which governs men in society.

Expanding on the theme of human law, Aquinas concludes that the state arose from social necessity and from the fact that man is by nature a social animal. He holds that the organization of the government should be based upon the superior wisdom and morality of the ruler, exercised for the benefit of the ruled. He regards monarchical government as best, but regardless of form, considers secular government as subject to the church, because the state is concerned solely with earthly ends, while the church is concerned with the ultimate end, the salvation of souls. The pope, as the head of Christ's church, has authority covering all matters of sin, placing him on a plane above kings and civil rulers.

Aquinas has been criticized, in dealing with statecraft, for furnishing slaveowners with a comforting argument. Like Augustine, he holds that slavery is a result of original sin—a divine expedient for the punishment of wrongdoing—and therefore is a righteous institution which Christians may conscientiously defend.

Also symptomatic of medieval attitudes is Aquinas' views on heretics, whom he defines as persons who profess the Christian faith, "but corrupt its dogmas." If the heretic remains unyielding in his stand, the church's proper recourse is to "deliver him to the secular tribunal to be exterminated thereby from the world by death." Such treatment of heretics on earth is mild, asserts Aquinas, compared to the eternal hell fire they are condemned to suffer in the hereafter.

The acceptance of Thomas Aquinas' writings as the ultimate authority in all matters, temporal and spiritual, delayed for generations the liberation of scientific thought from theological domination. Academic secular learning, the initial development of modern science during the Renaissance, and the new experimental science after the Renaissance encountered hostility, frequently bitter, from the church. Aquinas had taken over from Aristotle and prevailing Christian doctrine the premise that man is the center and object of creation, and from Ptolemy the system of astronomy that placed the earth as the center of the universe. Any theories not in accord with these doctrines, or running contrary to current human observations and human psychology, were automatically rejected as heretical.

About fifty years after his death Aquinas was canonized. Subsequently, many popes have declared Thomism to be the authoritative guide to doctrine and faith. In an encyclical issued in 1879, for example, Leo XIII ordered that the doctrines of St. Thomas, "the preeminent guardian and glory of the Catholic Church," be henceforth taught in its academies and schools. Later official pronouncements issued by Leo XIII decreed that if other writers and theologians disagree with St. Thomas, "the former must be sacrificed to the latter." Hence, the Thomist philosophy continues to be the fundamental source of Catholic theological teaching.

The writings of St. Thomas Aquinas unquestionably represent the peak of medieval Catholic thought. Aquinas was the master spokesman for the Christian faith in an era when Catholic theology and the power of the Roman church had reached the acme of their influence in Europe. The monumental structure which he built synthesized and articulated the immense body of accepted Christian wisdom that had grown up through the Middle Ages and earlier.

9

ANATOMY OF POWER POLITICS

Niccolò Machiavelli: The Prince

For over four centuries, "Machiavellian" has been synonomous in the world's mind with something diabolical, treacherous, villainous, cruel, and vicious. The term's progenitor, Niccolò Machiavelli, is a popular symbol for the scheming, crafty, hypocritical, immoral, completely unprincipled, and unscrupulous politician whose whole philosophy is that the end justifies the means. The highest law to Machiavelli, it is universally believed, was political expediency. In seventeenth-century England, "Old Nick" was an interchangeable epithet for Machiavelli and Satan. Is there any defense for the accused, or were there any extenuating circumstances?

Machiavelli's sinister reputation rests almost entirely upon a single book, *The Prince*, written in 1513, but unpublished until 1532, five years after the author's death. No book can be dissociated from the period in which it was created, a fact that has never been more aptly illustrated than by *The Prince*. And yet, like every great book, it contains lessons for all times.

Little is known of Machiavelli's life prior to 1498, when, at the age of twenty-nine, he became secretary of the Florentine republic. For eighteen years he served the city-state. Diplomatic missions took him to Tuscany, then across the Apennines to Rome, and later beyond the Alps. He became acquainted with Countess Caterina Sforza; Pandolfo Petrucci, tyrant of Siena; Ferdinand of Aragon; Louis XII of France, the Emperor Maximilian, Pope Alexander VI, Pope Julius II, and Cesare Borgia. Diplomatic conflict between Florence and the other city-states of Venice, Pisa, Milan, and Naples was unceasing. The politics of the era were unbelievably corrupt. Machiavelli, a shrewd student of human nature, was in his element, and on numerous occasions displayed ability and skill in carrying on difficult negotiations. His later realism or cynicism toward political affairs was doubtless based upon experience, for he learned to discount all motives except greed and selfishness.

A turn in the wheel of fortune came for Machiavelli. With Spain's assistance, the Medicis overthrew the republic and restored their rule in Florence. Machiavelli was discharged, imprisoned, tortured, and finally banished to his small country estate near the San Casciano. There, except for brief periods, he remained in retirement until his death in 1527. His principal pastime during those, to him, long dull years was writing: *The Prince, The Discourses, The Art of War*, and the *History of Florence*—all primarily concerned with politics, ancient and contemporary.

Any sentiment in Machiavelli's nature in relation to public affairs is hard to detect, but on one matter he felt deeply. He was a genuine patriot with an ardent longing for a strong, united Italy. He might be a cold, skeptical observer, a cynical man of pure intellect, until he discussed Italian unity, and then he became inspired with passion, eloquence, warmth, and life. Italy's condition in the early sixteenth century was sad enough to make any patriot weep.

A tremendous political, economic, and theological upheaval was under way in Machiavelli's Italy. Elsewhere, in England, France, and Spain, after lengthy struggles, national unification had been substantially achieved. In Italy, on the other hand, the conception of a national or federal organization was unknown. There were five major political units governing the country: Milan, Florence, Venice, the Church State, and Naples. Largest and strongest was Venice. The numerous political divisions were a constant source of weakness for Italy, and practically invited foreign intrigue and intervention. Invasions had started with Charles VIII of France in 1494. Within a few years after his retreat, Louis XII and Ferdinand of Aragon agreed to divide the Kingdom of Naples between them. The Emperor Maximilian sent his troops in to conquer Venice. Armies from Germany, Switzerland, France, and Spain were marching and fighting on Italian soil.

Meanwhile, among the Italians themselves, private quarrels, public feuds, robbery, and murder were rife. Republic warred with republic, each jealous of the other's power, and completely unable to form a common front against foreign foes. The Roman church, at the most degraded period of its history, and dreading the rise of a rival to its temporal power, preferred disunion to union for Italy.

Machiavelli recognized, perhaps more clearly than any man of his time, the dangers threatening Italy. Meditating, in his forced retirement, upon the evils which had befallen his beloved country, he became convinced that the only hope of salvation lay in the rise of a great leader—a leader strong and ruthless enough to force his authority on the petty Italian states, merging them into a single nation capable of defending itself and of driving the hated foreigners from the land.

And so, with patriotic fervor inspired by his vision of a united nation, aware of the critical needs of the hour, and conscious of the golden opportunity open to the new ruler, Machiavelli turned all his pent-up energy and enthusiasm to the composition of *The Prince*. The work was written in the last six months of 1513, and sometime thereafter delivered to Lorenzo's court, with the author's dedicatory statement, "seeing that it is not possible to make a better gift than to offer the opportunity of understanding in the shortest time all that I have learnt in so many years, and with so many troubles and dangers." *The Prince* was Machiavelli's conception of the kind of leader Italy required, and a detailed blueprint of the path he must follow to gain success.

Though *The Prince* is dedicated to Lorenzo de' Medici, new ruler of Florence, the hero of the book is Cesare Borgia, son of Pope Alexander VI, a cardinal at seventeen, able military leader, conqueror of Romagna, and a cruel, pitiless dictator. In 1502, Machiavelli was sent as an envoy to his court, and, as Allan Nevins commented, "saw with admiration how skillfully Borgia alternated the use of caution and audacity, of kindly words and bloody deeds; how coolly he employed perfidy and hypocrisy; how savagely he used terrorism to hold those whom he conquered in subjection; and how tyrannically effective was his grip on a captured state." By his use of duplicity, cruelty, and bad faith, Cesare Borgia attained brilliant, but temporary, success. Machiavelli was a firm partisan of a republican form of government, but when he examined the desperate and deplorable condition of Italy, he was persuaded that a Cesare Borgia would be an ideal leader to end the state of chaos.

The essential argument of *The Prince* is that the welfare of the state justifies everything and there are different standards of morals in public life and private life. It is proper, according to this doctrine, for a statesman to commit in the public interest acts of violence and deceit that would be thoroughly reprehensible and even criminal in private transactions. In effect, Machiavelli separated ethics from politics.

The Prince is a guidebook for princes (or, as some have said, a manual for tyrants) to instruct them in how to gain and to hold power—power not for the ruler's sake, however, but for the good of the people, in order to provide them with a stable government, secure against revolution or invasion. By what means are stability and security to be won?

Hereditary monarchies are dismissed briefly, for, assuming that the ruler has ordinary acumen and intelligence, he will be able to maintain his control of the government. On the other hand, the problems of a new monarchy are far more complex. If recently conquered territories are of the same nationality and language as the state to which they are annexed, control is relatively easy, especially if two principles are followed: "the one, that the blood of the ancient line of princes be destroyed; second, that no change be made in respect of laws or taxes.

"But when states are acquired in a country differing in language, usages, and laws, difficulties multiply, and great good fortune, as well as address, is needed to overcome them." Possible means for their control, Machiavelli goes on to suggest, are for the ruler to go and reside in the area personally, to send colonies (cheaper than maintaining occupying armies), to make friends of feebler neighbors and to endeavor to weaken stronger ones. By disregarding these basic rules, Louis XII of France had suffered defeat and loss of his conquests.

In a consideration of "How Provinces Are to Be Governed," Machiavelli offers three methods by which a state accustomed "to live under its own laws and in freedom . . . may be held. The first is to destroy it; the second, to go and reside there in person; the third, to suffer it to live on under its own laws, subjecting it to tribute, and entrusting its government to a few of the inhabitants who will keep the rest your friends." Of the several choices, either of the first two is recommended as safest.

If, however, the newly acquired city or province has been accustomed to live under a prince, and his line is extinguished, it will be impossible for the citizens, used on the one hand, to obey, and deprived, on the other, of their old ruler, to agree to choose a leader from among themselves; and as they know not how to live as freemen, and are therefore slow to take up arms, a stranger may readily gain them over and attach them to his cause.

In further discussion of "Of New Princedoms," Machiavelli warned, "it should be kept in mind that the temper of the multitude is fickle, and that while it is easy to persuade them of a thing, it is hard to fix them in that persuasion. Wherefore, matters should be so ordered that when men no longer believe of their own accord, they may be compelled to believe by force."

The author then proceeds to extol and glorify the career of Cesare Borgia, as the strong leader par excellence, apologizing for treason and assassination.

When all the actions of the duke are recalled, I do not know how to blame him, but rather it appears to me . . . that I ought to offer him for imitation to all those who, by fortune or the aims of others, are raised to government. Because he, having a lofty spirit and far-reaching aims, could not have regulated his conduct otherwise. . . . Therefore, he who considers it necessary to secure himself in his new principality, to win friends, to overcome either by force or fraud, to make himself beloved and feared by the people, to be followed and revered by the soldiers, to exterminate those who had power or reason to hurt him, to change the old order of things for new, to be severe and gracious, magnanimous and liberal, to destroy a disloyal soldiery, and to create new, to maintain friendship with kings and princes in such a way that they must help him with zeal and offend with caution, cannot find a more lively example than the actions of this man.

A usurper who has seized a state "should make haste to inflict what injuries he must, at a stroke, that he may not have to renew them daily, but be enabled by their discontinuance to reassure men's minds, and afterwards win them over by benefits. . . . Benefits should be conferred little by little, so that they may be more fully enjoyed."

Fear of punishment is but one of the means to be used by a wise sovereign in controlling his subjects:

It is essential for a prince to be on a friendly footing with his people, since, otherwise, he will have no resource in adversity. . . . Let no one quote against me the old proverb, "He who builds on the people builds on sand," for that may be true of a private citizen who presumes on his favor with the people, and counts on being rescued by them when overpowered by his enemies or by the magistrates. But a prince who is a man of courage and is able to command, who knows how to preserve order in his state, need never regret having founded his security on the affection of the people.

For treating of ecclesiastical princedoms, that is, those under direct church government, Machiavelli reserved some of his most scathing and satirical remarks.

They are acquired by merit or good fortune, but are maintained without either; being upheld by the venerable ordinances of religion, which are all of such a nature and efficacy that they secure the authority of their princes in whatever way they may act or live. These princes alone have territories which they do not defend, and subjects whom they do not govern.

Here and elsewhere in his writings, Machiavelli's bitter charge against the Roman church at the beginning of the sixteenth century was that it had not united Italy against the foreigner. His plea was for strict separation of church and state.

Because a strong government requires a good army, Machiavelli considered military affairs of the highest importance, and devoted considerable space to the subject. Most of the Italian states of his time were accustomed to employ hired mercenaries, largely foreigners, to defend them. Such troops, argued Machiavelli, are "useless and dangerous," and a national army composed of citizens would be far more effective and reliable. Inasmuch as national survival may depend on armed might, a ruling prince should regard military matters as his principal study and occupation.

Several chapters are devoted by Machiavelli to the conduct of princes—their proper behavior under various conditions.

There is the greatest difference between the way in which men live and that in which they ought to live. . . . It is essential for a prince who desires to maintain his position, to have learned how to be other than good, and to use or not to use his goodness as necessity requires. . . . Everyone, I know, will admit that it would be laudable for a prince to be endowed with all of the qualities that are reckoned good; but since it is impossible for him to possess or constantly practice them all . . . he must be discreet enough to know how to avoid the infamy of those vices that would deprive him of his government.

A prince should be unconcerned about gaining a reputation for miserliness, as he "spends either what belongs to himself and his subjects, or what belongs to others. . . . Of what does not belong to you or to your subjects you should be a lavish giver . . . for to be liberal with the property of others [acquired by military conquest] does not take from your reputation but adds to it. What injures you is to give away what is your own. And there is no quality so self-destructive as liberality; for while you practice it you lose the means whereby it can be practiced, and become poor and despised, or else, to avoid poverty, you become rapacious and hated."

Cruelty ought to be regarded by the prince as one of the weapons to keep his subjects united and obedient, "For he who quells disorder by a very few signal examples will in the end be more merciful than he who from too great leniency permits things to take their course and so to result in rapine and bloodshed; for these injure the whole state, whereas the severities of the prince injure individuals."

Machiavelli says in a famous passage:

From this arises the question whether it is better to be loved rather than feared, or feared rather than loved. It might perhaps be answered that we should wish to be both: but since love and fear can hardly exist together, if we must choose between them, it is far safer to be feared than loved. For of men it may generally be affirmed that they are thankless, fickle, false, studious to avoid danger, greedy of gain, devoted to you while you are able to confer benefits upon them, and ready, while danger is distant, to shed their blood, and sacrifice their property, their lives, and their children for you; but in the hour of need they turn against you.

Here is utter cynicism, though Machiavelli concludes his weighing of love versus fear by advising the prince that "he must do his utmost to escape hatred."

No part of *The Prince* has been more generally denounced and condemned than chapter eighteen on "How Princes Should Keep Faith." The evil connotations of the term "Machiavellian" are traceable more to this section than to all the remainder of the book. Here the author agrees that keeping faith is praiseworthy, but that deceit, hypocrisy, and perjury are necessary and excusable for the sake of maintaining political power.

There are two ways of contending, one in accordance with the laws, the other by force; the first of which is proper to men, the second to beasts. But since the first method is often ineffectual, it becomes necessary to resort to the second. A prince should, therefore, understand how to use well both the man and the beast. . . . But since a prince should know how to use the beast's nature wisely, he ought of beasts to choose both the lion and the fox; for the lion cannot protect himself from traps and the fox cannot defend himself from wolves . . . a prudent prince neither can nor ought to keep his word when to keep it is hurtful to him and if the causes which led him to pledge it are removed. If all men were good, this would not be good advice, but since they are dishonest and do not keep faith with you, you, in return, need not keep faith with them; and no prince was ever at a loss for plausible reasons to cloak a breach of faith. . . . But men remain so simple, and governed so absolutely by their present needs, that he who wishes to deceive them will never fail in finding willing dupes. . . . Thus, it is well to seem merciful, faithful, humane, re-ligious, and upright, and also to be so; but the mind should remain so balanced that were it needful not to be so, you should be able and know how to change to the contrary. . . . Everyone sees what you seem, but few know what you are.

It is essential, counseled Machiavelli, for a prince to avoid being hated or despised. The two principal ways in which he is likely to incur hatred are "by being rapacious and by interfering with the property and with the women of his subjects. . . . A prince is despised when he is seen to be fickle, frivolous, effeminate, pusillanimous, or irresolute." Furthermore, rulers should make themselves popular by distributing all favors in person, "and leave to the magistrates responsibility for inflicting punishment, and, indeed, the general disposal of all things which are likely to arouse discontent." Not even fortresses will save the prince, if the people hate him.

Instructing the prince on "How he should bear himself," Machiavelli urged that

. . . a prince should show himself a patron of merit, and should honor those who excel in every art. He ought accordingly to encourage his subjects by enabling them to pursue their callings, whether mercantile, agricultural, or any other, in security, so that this man shall not be deterred from beautifying his possessions from the apprehension that they may be taken from him, or that other refrain from opening a trade through fear of taxes.

Reminiscent of ancient Rome, so greatly admired by Machiavelli, is the advice to the prince, "at suitable seasons of the year to entertain the people with festivals and shows."

Machiavelli was a firm believer in fortune or destiny, perhaps a reflection of the attitude in his time toward astrology. "I think it may be the case," he wrote, "that fortune is the mistress of one half our actions, and yet leaves the control of the other half, or a little less, to ourselves." His point of view was only moderately fatalistic, however, for he was convinced that man could exercise some control over his fate, and "that it is better to be impetuous than cautious. For fortune is a woman who to be kept under must be beaten and roughly handled; and we see that she suffers herself to be more readily mastered by those who so treat her than by those who are more timid in their approaches. And always, like a woman, she favors the young, because they are less scrupulous and fiercer, and command her with greater audacity."

The Prince is concluded with "An Exhortation to Liberate Italy," a ringing appeal to patriotism. The time had arrived for a new prince, "some Italian hero" to come forward, for Italy in "her present abject condition" was "more a slave than the Hebrew, more oppressed than the Persian, more disunited than the Athenian, without a leader, without order, beaten, spoiled, torn in pieces, over-run and abandoned to destruction in every shape. . . . We see how she prays God to send someone to rescue her from these barbarous cruelties and oppressions. We see too how ready and eager she is to follow any standard were there only some one to raise it."

Machiavelli ends his eloquent plea with these words:

This opportunity then, for Italy at last to look on her deliverer, ought not to be allowed to pass away. With what love he [the new prince] would be received in all those provinces which have suffered from the foreign inundation, with what thirst for vengeance, with what fixed fidelity, with what devotion, and what tears, no words of mine can declare. What gates would be closed against him? What people would refuse him obedience? What jealousy would stand in his way? What Italian but would yield him homage? This barbarous tyranny stinks in every nostril.

Over three and a half centuries were to elapse before Machiavelli's dream of a united Italy, free of foreign occupation and domination, was to be realized.

Manuscript copies of *The Prince* were circulated during the author's lifetime and for several years afterwards. Its publication in 1532 was approved by Pope Clement VII, cousin of the prince to whom it was dedicated. In the next twenty years, there were twenty-five editions. Then a storm began to gather. The

Council of Trent ordered the destruction of Machiavelli's works. He was denounced as an atheist in Rome, and his writings were banned there and elsewhere in Europe. The Jesuits burned him in effigy in Germany. Both Catholics and Protestants joined in the clamor against him. In 1559 all of Machiavelli's works were placed on the Index of Prohibited Books.

Not until the nineteenth century did Machiavelli's reputation win some measure of exoneration and vindication. Revolutionary movements in America, France, Germany, and elsewhere caused an irresistible trend toward secularization of government, toward separation of church and state. The Italian crusade for freedom, which reached a successful climax in 1870, drew inspiration from the great patriot Machiavelli. In a most perceptive essay, H. Douglas Gregory demonstrated that by following the Machiavellian precepts, the Italian leader, Count Cavour, was able to unite Italy and drive out her invaders, while to have followed any other course would have brought disaster and failure.

That dictators and tyrants of every era have found much useful advice in *The Prince* is undeniable. The list of avid readers is impressive: Emperor Charles V and Catherine de' Medici admired the work; Oliver Cromwell procured a manuscript copy, and adapted its principles to the Commonwealth government in England; Henry III and Henry IV of France were carrying copies when they were murdered; it helped Frederick the Great to shape Prussian policy; Louis XIV used the book as his "favorite night-cap"; an annotated copy was found in Napoleon Bonaparte's coach at Waterloo; Napoleon III's ideas on government were chiefly derived from it; and Bismarck was a devoted disciple. More recently, Adolf Hitler, according to his own word, kept *The Prince* by his bedside, where it served as a constant source of inspiration; and Benito Mussolini stated, "I believe Machiavelli's *Prince* to be the statesman's supreme guide. His doctrine is alive today because in the course of four hundred years no deep changes have occurred in the minds of men or in the actions of nations." (Later, Mussolini changed his mind, for in 1939, on the list of authors, ancient and modern, placed on the Fascist index of books which Roman librarians must not circulate appeared the name of Machiavelli.)

On the other hand, keen analysts of historical events have made it clear that such tyrants as Hitler and Mussolini generally came to bad ends because they disregarded or misinterpreted certain fundamental principles enunciated by Machiavelli.

Students of Machiavelli are agreed that no full understanding of his ideas is possible without reading both his *Discourses* and *The Prince*. The *Discourses*, written over a five-year period, and first published in the same year as *The Prince*, is a considerably larger work. One distinction between them, it has been suggested, is that the *Discourses* deal with "what should be" and *The Prince* with "what is." *The Prince* is concerned entirely with principalities, that is with states ruled by single monarchs. The *Discourses* deal with principles to be followed by republics.

From a comparative reading of the two books, one must come to the startling conclusion that Machiavelli was a convinced republican. He had no liking for despotism, and considered a combination of popular and monarchical government best. No ruler was safe without the favor of his people. The most stable states are those ruled by princes checked by constitutional limitations. The judgment of the people is sound, in Machiavelli's view, as may be noted in his attack on the ancient proverb, "To build on the people is to build on sand." His ideal government was the old Roman republic, and he constantly harked back to it in the *Discourses*.

Why, then, did Machiavelli, valuing above all things a republican government for a free people, produce *The Prince*? The book was written for a specific time and for a specific set of conditions. Machiavelli doubtless realized that it would be impossible to establish a successful republic in sixteenth-century Italy. *The Prince* was written for the sole purpose of enlisting the aid of a strong man to rescue the Italian people from their desperate plight and state of political corruption. Confronted by an acute crisis, Italy could not be too discriminating over the weapons for her salvation.

Widely disparate opinions concerning Machiavelli are still held, despite efforts made to rehabilitate his name. The situation described some years ago by Giuseppe Prezzolini continues to prevail:

We now have the Jesuits' Machiavelli, an enemy of the Church; the patriots' Machiavelli, the messiah of a unified Italy and the House of Savoy; the militarists' Machiavelli, a precursor of national armies; the philosophers' Machiavelli, who invented a new way of thought—

the practical spirit; and the Machiavelli of the writers, who admire his virile style and audacious syntax. And all these Machiavellis are legitimate.

It is hardly disputable that no man previous to Karl Marx has had as revolutionary an impact on political thought as Machiavelli. He has a legitimate claim to the title of "Founder of the Science of Politics."

10

AMERICAN FIREBRAND

Thomas Paine: Common Sense

No rational person would have predicted a brilliant future for Thomas Paine when he arrived in America at the age of thirty-seven. His entire career up to that point had been a succession of failures and frustrations. Every enterprise to which he had set his hand had come to a dismal conclusion. What reason was there to suppose that within a period of a few years the recently arrived immigrant to the New World would emerge as one of the greatest pamphleteers in the English language, one of the most controversial figures in American history, a political agitator and revolutionist whose name was known, feared and hated, or applauded and extolled, throughout the British American colonies, Great Britain, and Western Europe? It appeared as though the ocean voyage had effected a startling metamorphosis in his personality and character, changing him almost overnight from mediocrity to genius.

And yet an examination of Paine's earlier years would give evidence that they had not been lost and, in fact, were a kind of preparation for his new life. Born at Thetford, county of Norfolk, in eastern England, on January 29, 1737, son of a Quaker father and an Anglican mother, he had from the beginning experienced extreme poverty, privation, and drudgery. Until he reached thirteen, he attended grammar school, where, in his own words, he acquired "an exceedingly good moral education and a tolerable stock of useful learning." His flair for science and invention—for the practical as opposed to the theoretical—came to the surface even then and remained with him throughout a busy life.

After this brief formal education, Paine was apprenticed to learn his father's trade of corset-maker. Three years of this work, and then the glamor of the sea and boredom with a monotonous job caused him to run away from home to enlist on the privateer *Terrible*, under a captain bearing the formidable name of Death. Rescued by his father, he resumed stay-making until age nineteen, when he again had a brief fling at privateering, on the *King of Prussia*. Now cured of his romantic conception of a sailor's life, he settled down once again to his trade, but in London rather than Thetford, laboring in a stay-maker's shop near Drury Lane. His leisure was spent attending lectures on astronomy.

There followed years of troubled and indecisive wandering. At Sandwich, he married an orphan servant girl, who died within a year. Her father had been an exciseman; and drawn to the profession because it promised to give him leisure for other interests, Paine obtained an appointment as an excise officer. No surer way could have been found to lose friends and alienate people, for his job was to catch smugglers, and the hands of rich and poor were against him. Discharged from his post for lack of conscientiousness in enforcing the rules, Paine returned briefly to stay-making, then starved as a teacher on £25 a year at Kensington. Reinstated in the excise service, he remarried in 1771, and joined his wife and her mother at Lewes in operating a tobacco and grocery shop, to supplement his income.

During these latter years, Paine spent much of his time in the White Hart Tavern, in meetings of a social club which he had joined. For the edification of the members, he composed humorous verses and patriotic songs, as well as occasional papers on more serious subjects, and frequently engaged in warm arguments on issues of the day. His proficiency in debate led his fellow-excisemen to select him to act as their spokesman in a plea for higher wages and improved working conditions. Many weeks were subsequently spent by Paine in the preparation of a paper entitled "The Case of the Salary of the Officers of Excise and Thoughts on the Corruption Arising from the Poverty of Excise Officers." In the winter of 1772-73, he went to London to present his appeal to members of Parliament and other officials.

Not only was Paine's petition for the excisemen rejected, but he was discharged for neglect of duties, the tobacco shop went into bankruptcy, Paine's furniture and personal belongings had to be sold to save him from debtor's prison, and he was separated from his wife. Thus, approaching middle age, he was left alone and penniless.

Fortunately, during his London sojourn, Paine had met Benjamin Franklin, sent there as commissioner of the colonies, and Franklin, perhaps perceiving his genius, persuaded Paine to try his luck in America. A letter of introduction from Franklin to his son-in-law, Richard Bache, in Philadelphia, characterized Paine as "an ingenious, worthy young man," and recommended his employment as a clerk, assistant tutor in a school, or assistant surveyor. The Franklin letter was Paine's chief asset when he landed in Philadelphia in early December 1774.

However, Paine brought with him an invaluable asset of another kind—his background of experience. He had observed the primitive brutality with which justice was administered in England, he had known abject poverty, he had heard and read much about man's natural rights, he had seen the vast chasm separating the millions of ordinary folk from the few thousand members of the royalty and nobility in Britain, and he knew of the rotten-borough scheme of choosing the House of Commons, and of the corruption and stupidity of the royal family. Having thought deeply on these matters, Paine was possessed with a profound compassion for humanity, a love of democracy, and an urge for universal social and political reform.

Soon after his arrival in Philadelphia, Paine was employed as editor of the *Pennsylvania Magazine*, a newly established journal, and he continued in that position for most of the eighteen months of its existence. Almost immediately his long career as a crusader began, with publication of an essay condemning Negro slavery and strongly advocating emancipation. Five weeks later, the first American antislavery society was formed in Philadelphia. There followed contributions advocating equal rights for women, proposing international copyright laws, denouncing cruelty to animals, ridiculing the custom of dueling, and asking for the abolition of war for the settlement of disputes between nations.

Even as he wrote, however, an international war, in which Paine himself was to play a major role, was rapidly developing. In the spring of 1775 came the battles of Concord, Lexington, and Bunker Hill. After "the massacre at Lexington" in April,

Paine wrote to Benjamin Franklin, "I thought it very hard to have the country set on fire about my ears almost the moment I got into it."

Sentiment in the colonies was seriously divided on the proper course to be followed, ranging from such extremists as Samuel Adams and John Hancock, who were strong for war, to the Tories, ever loyal to the king. George Washington, Benjamin Franklin, and Thomas Jefferson were among the leaders who protested their loyalty to Britain and viewed askance the thought of separation and independence. Both the first and second Continental Congress adopted resolutions affirming their allegiance to the Crown, petitioning only for a just settlement of their grievances.

In the midst of the confused thinking, the conflicting opinions and impulses, the pulling and hauling, one man saw clearly the trend of events and their probable outcome. From the beginning, Thomas Paine viewed separation from England as inevitable. He spent the entire fall of 1775 setting down his ideas. Before publication, the work was shown to several friends, one of whom, Dr. Benjamin Rush, suggested the title *Common Sense* and helped Paine to find a publisher, Robert Bell, a Scotch bookseller and printer in Philadelphia.

Common Sense made its appearance on January 10, 1776, "Written by an Englishman," a pamphlet of forty-seven pages, priced at two shillings. In three months, 120,000 copies had been bought, and estimates of total sales have ranged up to half a million, the equivalent in proportion to population of a sale of 30,000,000 copies in the United States today. Virtually every literate person in the thirteen colonies is believed to have read it. Despite the enormous sales, Paine elected to receive not a penny of royalties.

Nothing comparable to *Common Sense* in its immediate impact is to be found in the history of literature. It was a clarion call to the American colonists to fight for their independence—without compromise or vacillation. Revolution was pointed out to them as the only solution of their conflict with Great Britain and George III. "Since nothing but blows will do," declared Paine, "for God's sake let us come to a final separation. Dearly, dearly do we pay for the repeal of the acts, if that is all we fight for . . . it is as great a folly to pay a Bunker-hill price for law as for land. . . . 'Tis not the affair of a city, a county, a province or a kingdom, but of a *continent*. . . . 'Tis not the concern of a day, a year or an age; posterity are involved in the contest. . . . Now is the seed-time of continental union, faith and honor. . . . The Continental Belt is too loosely buckled . . . independence is the only *bond* that tie and keep us together."

A relatively mild and disarming paragraph introduces *Common Sense:*

Perhaps the sentiments contained in the following pages, are not *yet* sufficiently fashionable to procure them general favor; a long habit of not thinking a thing *wrong*, gives it a superficial appearance of being *right*, and raises at first a formidable outcry in defense of custom. But the tumult soon subsides. Time makes more converts than reason.

The first portion of the pamphlet deals with the origin and nature of government, with particular application to the English constitution. The author's philosophy of government is contained in such sentences as:

Government, even in its best state, is but a necessary evil; in its worst state an intolerable one. . . . Government, like dress, is the badge of lost innocence; the palaces of kings are built upon the ruins of bowers of paradise. . . . The more perfect civilization is, the less occasion has it for government.

The origin and rise of government, Paine argues, was "rendered necessary by the inability of moral virtue to govern the world; here too is the design and end of government, viz., freedom and security."

A sharp distinction is drawn between society and government. Men are attracted into society because through social cooperation certain wants can be satisfied. In this state, man possesses certain natural rights, such as liberty and equality. Ideally, man should be able to live in peace and happiness without government, if the "impulses of conscience" were "clear, uniform and irresistibly obeyed." Since mankind is naturally weak and imperfect morally, some restraining power is required, and this is provided by government. Upon society rather than government, however, depend the security, progress, and comfort of the people. More influential than any political institutions are social usage and custom, the mutual relations and mutual interests of men.

Paine then proceeds to "offer a few remarks on the so much boasted constitution of England," commenting, "That it was noble for the dark and slavish time in which it was erected, is granted. When the world was overrun with tyranny the least remove therefrom was a glorious rescue. But that it is imperfect, subject to convulsions, and incapable of producing what it seems to promise is easily demonstrated." What should be one of the major attributes of government—responsibility—he considered completely lacking in the British constitution. It was so complex that it was impossible to determine who was accountable for anything. The only commendable part of the constitution was the people's right, theoretically at least, to elect members to the House of Commons. Paine proposed a single democratically elected legislative chamber for the colonies, a president and a cabinet, with the executive branch responsible to the congress.

But it was for the institution of hereditary monarchy that Paine reserved his harshest words and most scathing contempt. He attacked the whole principle of monarchy, and the English form in particular.

Government by kings was first introduced into the world by the heathens, from whom the children of Israel copied the custom. It was the most prosperous invention the devil ever set on foot for the pro-motion of idolatry. The heathens paid divine honors to their de-ceased kings, and the Christian world has improved on the plan by doing the same to their living ones. . . . To the evil of monarchy we have added that of hereditary succession; and as the first is a de-gradation and lessening of ourselves, so the second, claimed as a matter of right, is an insult and imposition on posterity. . . . One of the strongest *natural* proofs of the folly of hereditary rights in kings is that nature disproves it, otherwise she would not so frequently turn it into ridicule by giving mankind an Ass for a Lion.

The legitimacy of the English succession as far back as the Conquest was dubious, in Paine's eyes. As he puts it, "A French bastard landing with an armed banditti, and establishing himself King of England against the consent of the natives, is in plain terms a very paltry rascally original.—It certainly has no divinity in it." If the monarchy insured a race of good and wise men, it would not be objectionable, but "it opens a door to the *foolish*, the *wicked*, and the *improper*. . . . Men who look upon them-selves born to reign, and others to obey, soon grow insolent; selected from the rest of mankind their minds are early poisoned by importance . . . when they succeed to the government are often the most ignorant and unfit of any throughout the dominions." Permitting underage and overage kings to sit on the throne also produces a train of evils: in the one case the actual administration of the country is in the hands of a regent, and in the other it is subject to the whims of a senile, worn-out monarch.

To the argument that hereditary succession prevents civil wars, Paine pointed out that since the Conquest, England had suffered "no less than eight civil wars and nineteen rebellions." His conclusion is:

In England a king has little more to do than to make war and give away places; which, in plain terms, is to impoverish the nation and set it together by the ears. A pretty business indeed for a man to be allowed eight hundred thousand sterling a year for, and worshipped into the bargain! Of more worth is one honest man to society, and in the sight of God, than all the crowned ruffians who ever lived.

In several passages Paine paid his respects to George III. After the massacre at Lexington, he wrote, "I rejected the hardened, sullen-tempered Pharaoh of England for ever; and disdain the wretch, that with the pretended title of *Father of his people*, can unfeelingly hear of their slaughter, and composedly sleep with their blood upon his soul." In a later paragraph he adds: "But where, say some, is the King of America? I'll tell you, friend, he reigns above, and doth not make havoc of mankind like the royal brute of Britain."

Having exploded popular ideas of monarchical government, Paine proceeded to "Some thoughts on the present state of the American affairs." Economic arguments for separation from Britain were stressed. To the Tories' contention that America had flourished because of her connection with England, Paine rejoined:

America would have flourished as much, and probably much more, had no European power had any thing to do with her. The articles of commerce, by which she has enriched herself, are the necessaries of life, and will always have a market while eating is the custom of Europe. . . . Our corn will fetch its price in any market in Europe, and our imported goods must be paid for, buy them where we will.

The fact that Britain had protected the colonies against the Spanish, French, and Indians, Paine dismissed with the comment:

"She would have defended Turkey from the same motives, *viz.* for the sake of trade and dominion," and, in any case, the defense was "at our expense as well as her own."

One of the strongest ties holding the colonies against separation, Paine recognized, was a sentimental conception of Britain as the mother country. If this were true, "Then the more shame upon her conduct. Even brutes do not devour their young, nor savages make war upon their families. . . . The phrase *parent* or *mother* country has been jesuitically adopted by the king and his parasites, with a low papistical design of gaining an unfair bias on the credulous weakness of our minds. Europe, and not England, is the parent country of America." The New World, he pointed out, had been "the asylum for the persecuted lovers of civil and religious liberty from *every* part of Europe. . . . Not one third of the inhabitants, even of this province, are of English descent. Wherefore, I reprobate the phrase of parent or mother country applied to England only, as being false, selfish, narrow and ungenerous."

Foreshadowing George Washington's later warning "to steer clear of permanent alliances with any portion of the foreign world," and Thomas Jefferson's policy of "Peace, commerce, and honest friendship with all nations—entangling alliances with none," Paine suggested there would be numerous disadvantages to continued connection with Britain:

. . . because, any submission to or dependance on Great Britain, tends directly to involve this continent in European wars and quarrels; and sets us at variance with nations, who would otherwise seek our friendship, and against whom, we have neither anger nor complaint. As Europe is our market for trade, we ought to form no partial connexion with any part of it. It is the true interest of America to steer clear of European contentions, which she never can do while, by her dependance on Britain, she is made the make-weight in the scale of British politics. Europe is too thickly planted with kingdoms to be long at peace, and whenever a war breaks out between England and any foreign power, the trade of America goes to ruin, *because of her connexion with Britain.*

While the rest of the world was burdened with oppression, America should open her doors wide to freedom, and prepare an asylum for persecuted mankind.

The manifold inconveniences of British government were reviewed, and Paine concluded:

. . . it is not in the power of Britain to do this continent justice; the business of it will soon be too weighty and intricate to be managed with any tolerable degree of convenience, by a power so distant from us, and so very ignorant of us; for if they cannot conquer us, they cannot govern us. To be always running three or four thousand miles with a tale or a petition, waiting four or five months for an answer, which, when obtained, requires five or six more to explain it in, will in a few years be looked upon as folly and childishness. . . . There is something absurd, in supposing a continent to be perpetually governed by an island. In no instance has nature made the satellite larger than its primary planet.

To the doubters and faint of heart who still believed harmony and reconciliation possible, Paine delivered an impassioned plea:

Can ye restore to us the time that is past? Can ye give to prostitution its former innocence? Neither can you reconcile Britain and America. The last cord now is broken, the people of England are presenting addresses against us. There are injuries which nature cannot forgive; she would cease to be nature if she did. As well can the lover forgive the ravisher of his mistress, as the continent forgive the murders of Britain.

Paine devoted his final chapter to some very practical considerations on "the present ability of America," designed to build up the self-confidence of the Americans and to convince them that they had the manpower, manufacturing experience, and natural resources, not only to wage war successfully with Britain, but, if necessary, to win against a hostile world. The colonies already possessed a large body of armed and disciplined men. A navy comparable to Britain's could be constructed in a brief time, for tar, timber, iron, and cordage were available in quantity, and "Ship building is America's greatest pride, and in which she will, in time, excel the whole world." A fleet was needed, in any case, for defense and protection, because the English navy "three or four thousand miles off can be of little use, and on sudden emergencies, none at all."

In the light of the religious controversies in which he subsequently became involved, it is of interest to note Paine's religious views at this stage in his career:

As to religion, I hold it to be the indispensable duty of all governments, to protect all conscientious professors thereof, and I know of no other business which government has to do therewith [an argument apparently against an established church and for separation of church and state]. . . . For myself, I fully and conscientiously believe, that it is the will of the Almighty, that there should be a diversity of religious opinions among us: it affords a larger field for our Christian kindness. Were we all of one way of thinking, our religious dispositions would want matter for probation; and on this liberal principle, I look on the various denominations among us, to be like children of the same family, differing only in what is called their Christian names.

Summarizing the reasons for his conviction that "nothing can settle our affairs so expeditiously as an open and determined declaration for independence," Paine concluded *Common Sense* with the enumeration of four factors: (1) as long as America was regarded as a subject of Britain, no other nation would attempt to mediate the differences between them; (2) no aid could be expected from France or Spain in repairing the breach and strengthening the connection between Britain and America, because such a step would be to their disadvantage; (3) while the Americans professed to be subjects of Britain, they would, in the eyes of foreign nations, be considered rebels, and therefore would win little sympathy; (4) if the Americans would prepare a manifesto setting forth their grievances against Britain, and their intention of breaking off all connections with her, sending copies of the declaration to other countries, expressing their peaceable disposition toward them and their desire to establish trade relations, the results would be highly favorable.

Closing his case, Paine maintained:

. . . until an independence is declared, the continent will feel itself like a man who continues putting off some unpleasant business from day to day, yet knows it must be done, hates to set about it, wishes it over, and is continually haunted with the thoughts of its necessity.

Wherefore, instead of gazing at each other, with suspicious or doubtful curiosity, let each of us hold out to his neighbor the hearty hand of friendship, and unite in drawing a line, which, like an act of oblivion, shall bury in forgetfulness every former dissention. Let the name of whig and tory be extinct; and let none other be heard among us, than those of *a good citizen; an open and resolute friend; and a virtuous supporter of the* RIGHTS OF MANKIND, *and of the* FREE AND INDEPENDENT STATES OF AMERICA.

This was the revolutionary message communicated to the American people by *Common Sense,* running the gamut from down-to-earth, realistic, practical arguments to emotion-charged, violently partisan, and biased appeals of the born agitator.

The immediate and cataclysmic effects of *Common Sense* may be illustrated by quotations from some contemporary leaders. George Washington's doubts evaporated as he wrote to Joseph Reed at Norfolk: "A few more of such flaming arguments as were exhibited at Falmouth and Norfolk, added to the sound doctrine and unanswerable reasoning contained in the pamphlet *Common Sense*, will not leave numbers at a loss to decide upon the propriety of separation"; and a few weeks later, also to Reed, "By private letters which I have lately received from Virginia, I find Paine's *Common Sense* is working a wonderful change there in the minds of many men." John Adams, writing to his wife, "I sent you a pamphlet entitled *Common Sense*, written in vindication of doctrines, which there is reason to expect, that the further encroachments of tyranny and depredations of oppression will soon make the common faith," to which, after reading, Abigail Adams replied, "*Common Sense*, like a ray of revelation, has come in season to clear our doubts and fix our choice." Benjamin Rush said of Paine's writings, "They burst from the press with an effect that has rarely been produced by type and paper in any age or country"; General Charles Lee added, "I own it has convinced me"; Franklin noted, "It has had a prodigious effect"; and William Henry Drayton reported that "This declaration came like an explosion of thunder upon the members" of the Continental Congress.

In his *History of the American Revolution*, Sir George Trevelyan commented:

It would be difficult to name any human composition which has had an effect at once so instant, so extended, and so lasting. . . . It was pirated, parodied and imitated, and translated into the language of every country where the new republic had well wishers. . . . According to contemporary newspapers *Common Sense* turned thousands to independence who before could not endure the thought. It worked nothing short of miracles and turned Tories into Whigs.

Within a few months after the appearance of *Common Sense*, most of the states had instructed their delegates to vote for independence, only Maryland hesitating and New York opposed. On July 4, 1776, less than six months from the date when Paine's famous pamphlet came off the press, the Continental Congress, meeting in the State House at Philadelphia, proclaimed the independence of the United States of America. Though Paine did not write the Declaration, he was closely associated with Thomas Jefferson while it was being composed, and except for the omission of an antislavery clause which Paine advocated, the principles for which he stood were incorporated in the celebrated manifesto.

An account of Paine's subsequent career is only indirectly relevant to the story of *Common Sense*. The highlights may be sketched briefly. He enlisted in the Continental army soon after the Declaration of Independence. As a prolific spokesman for the American cause he contributed tremendously to national unity and spirit through a series of pamphlets, each entitled *The Crisis*. The first of these begins with the much quoted lines: "These are the times that try men's souls. The summer soldier and the sunshine patriot will, in this crisis, shrink from the service of their country; but he that stands it now deserves the love and thanks of man and woman." After a few months, recognizing his value as a propagandist and morale builder, Congress took Paine out of the army and appointed him secretary to the Committee of Foreign Affairs—in effect our first secretary of state. Controversies forced his resignation from this post, following which he was appointed Clerk of the Pennsylvania Assembly. In 1781 he was sent to France with John Laurens, to get financial assistance for the hard-pressed American government; he returned the same year with money and supplies.

The Revolution over, in 1783, Paine turned to mechanical inventions, designing the first iron suspension bridge, and experimenting with steam power. The decision was made to consult engineers in France and England on some of the technical problems, and in 1787 Paine went to Europe, where he remained for fifteen years.

Soon after his arrival abroad, the French Revolution erupted, an event which Paine enthusiastically supported as further vindication of his democratic ideas. In defense of the Revolution, replying to Edmund Burke's attacks, he produced his famed *The Rights of Man*. Forced hurriedly to leave England to avoid arrest for treason, as a result of the doctrines expressed therein, he fled to France, where he had been elected to the Convention as a member representing Calais. In an attempt to save Louis XVI from execution, Paine broke with such extremists as Robespierre and Marat. When these elements took over the government, Paine was arrested, deprived of his honorary French citizenship, imprisoned for ten months, and narrowly escaped the guillotine. Released from prison through the intercession of the American ambassador James Monroe, he was nursed back to health in Monroe's home.

The great work of this period was *The Age of Reason*, sometimes referred to as the "atheist's bible." Actually, Paine was a pious deist, believing in one God and a hereafter, and *The Age of Reason*, though highly critical of the Old Testament, had been written to stem the strong tide of atheism sweeping France in the Revolutionary era: Nevertheless, theologians and orthodox religious groups bitterly condemned Paine as a dangerous radical and unbeliever.

When Paine returned to America in 1802, he found himself received not as a Revolutionary hero, but virtually ostracized by political leaders and churchgoers, because of his authorship of *The Age of Reason* and his radical political theories. In New Rochelle, New York, where he settled, he was denied the right to vote on the ground that he was not an American citizen. An attempt was even made to murder him. After seven incredible years of abuse, hatred, neglect, poverty, and ill health, he died in 1809, at the age of 72. He was denied burial in a Quaker cemetery.

The bitterness, falsehoods, and violent prejudices toward Paine in his last years have persisted to recent times. Theodore Roosevelt referred to him as "a filthy little atheist," though, like the Holy Roman Empire, which was neither holy, Roman, nor an empire, Paine was neither filthy, little, nor an atheist. As late as 1933, a radio program about Paine was banned from a New York City station. Not until 1945, forty-five years after its establishment, was he elected to the Hall of Fame of Great Americans. In the same year, the city of New Rochelle got around to restoring to the Revolutionary hero the rights of citizenship which he lost in 1806.

This was the man who perhaps more than any other deserves the title "Founder of American Independence," who first used the phrase "The United States of America," who foresaw that "The United States of America will sound as pompously in history as the Kingdom of Great Britain," and who proclaimed, "The cause of America is, in a great measure, the cause of all mankind." No better index to Paine's character can be found than his reply to Franklin's remark, "Where liberty is, there is my country." "Where liberty is not," said Paine, "there is mine."

In his own time, the hymn of hate and misrepresentation was not universal. Andrew Jackson dared to say, "Thomas Paine needs no monument made by hands; he has erected a monument in the hearts of all lovers of liberty."

11

PATRON SAINT OF FREE ENTERPRISE

Adam Smith: Wealth of Nations

Two months after Thomas Paine's *Common Sense* had helped precipitate the Declaration of Independence and other momentous events of the American Revolution, a book destined to have profound repercussions in a different sphere of human activity appeared in London. Unlike Paine's fiery tract, Adam Smith's ponderous, two-volume treatise, *An Inquiry into the Nature and Causes of the Wealth of Nations*, was a delayed-action bomb, attracting slight notice at first. Not until the century following the author's death, in fact, did his work reach its full impact.

The year 1776 may logically be regarded as the close of one epoch and the beginning of another. The American Revolution had started, the French Revolution was brewing, and the Industrial Revolution, sparked by the discovery of steam power, was gathering speed. One commentator has characterized the preceding era as "the dark ages of modern time." In England virtually every aspect of economic life was under strict governmental control. Prices were stabilized, wages and hours of labor fixed, production regulated, and foreign trade, both imports and exports, completely dominated by the state. War was almost always present. National policy dictated a strong army and navy, a large population, grabbing of colonies throughout the world, and weakening, by fair means or foul, of rival countries such as France. Any suggestion of an equitable distribution of wealth was violently opposed by the ruling classes. Education was reserved for the privileged few, criminal laws were extremely severe, and political rights for the masses existed largely in theory rather than in practice.

As it had done for generations, the landed aristocracy still held the reins of government; but a new and powerful class of merchants and industrialists had risen, demanding and receiving special privileges for themselves. In the view of this group, exports were blessings, imports calamities; money should not be permitted to leave the country; a "favorable" balance of trade should always be maintained; wages for labor should be low and hours long; high tariffs must protect home industries; a strong merchant marine was essential; and any measures which aided the mercantilists ipso facto were assumed to benefit the nation as a whole. Under highly vocal pressure, Parliament had enacted most of these concepts into law.

Then came Adam Smith, intent on exploding what he considered erroneous and harmful ideas. Smith's adult life up to this point may be regarded as preparation for the monumental task to which he now set himself. A native of Scotland, he matriculated at age fourteen (in 1737) at the University of Glasgow. There he came under the influence of a great teacher, Francis Hutcheson, whose frequently reiterated belief in "the greatest happiness of the greatest number" became Smith's ruling philosophy. Proceeding next to Oxford University, where he remained for six years, Smith devoted most of his time to extensive reading over a wide range of literature. Upon returning to Scotland, he gave public lectures in Edinburgh until 1751, when he was appointed first to the chair of logic and metaphysics and shortly thereafter to the chair of moral philosophy at the University of Glasgow. For twelve years he served as a gifted and popular lecturer, adding to his reputation by publication of a "best-seller," *Theory of Moral Sentiments*—a work regarded by his contemporaries as superior to the *Wealth of Nations*. Tempted by generous financial rewards, Smith resigned his professorship to accompany a young nobleman, as companion and tutor, on a three-year tour of the Continent. There he became acquainted with the leading economists, philosophers, and political thinkers of the time, particularly in France.

As early as 1759, a draft of what subsequently developed into the *Wealth of Nations* existed in Smith's notes, but the work was slow in coming to fruition. Years of meditation, study and reading, firsthand observations, conversations with people in many walks of life, and endless revision were to pass before Smith was ready to turn his magnum opus over to the printer. The three years before publication were mostly spent in London, where he discussed his book with Benjamin Franklin, American colonial agent. Not until March 9, 1776, did the work come from the press. Since that date, it has gone through innumerable editions, and has been translated into most of the world's living languages.

The encyclopedic scope of the *Wealth of Nations* makes it far more than a mere economic treatise. One critic has called it "a history and criticism of all European civilization." Commencing with a discussion of the division of labor, Smith diverges into considerations of the origin and use of money, prices of commodities, wages of labor, profits of stock, rent of land, value of silver, and distinctions between productive and unproductive labor. There follow an account of the economic development of Europe since the fall of the Roman Empire, extended analyses and criticisms of the commercial and colonial policies of European nations, the revenue of the sovereign, different methods of defense and administration of justice in primitive societies, the origin and growth of standing armies in Europe, a history of education in the Middle Ages and a criticism of the universities of Smith's time, a history of the temporal power of the church, the growth of public debts, and, in conclusion, an examination of principles of taxation and systems of public revenue.

Smith's general thesis, on which the *Wealth of Nations* is based, might have been propounded by Niccolò Machiavelli, to wit: every human being is motivated primarily by self-interest. A desire for wealth is only one of the manifestations. Selfish impulses and incentives are the background of all mankind's activities. Furthermore, rather than finding this aspect of human behavior objectionable and undesirable, Smith believed that the selfishness of the individual is conducive to society's welfare. A nation's prosperity can best be provided, he suggested, by allowing the "uniform, constant, and uninterrupted effort of every man to better his condition. . . . It is not from the benevolence of the butcher, the brewer, or the baker that we expect our dinner, but from their regard to their own interest. We address ourselves, not to their humanity, but to their self-love, and never talk to them of our own necessities, but of their advantages." It was because of such passages as these that Ruskin referred to Smith as "the half-breed and half-witted Scotchman who taught the deliberate blasphemy: 'Thou shalt hate the Lord, thy God, damn his law, and covet thy neighbor's goods.' "

Modern industry, Smith contended, is made possible by the division of labor and the accumulation of capital—both of which are explained by self-interest, or the "natural order," as it was referred to by eighteenth-century philosophers. Unconsciously, a "divine hand" leads man so that, in working for his own gain, he is contributing to the good of the whole. It naturally followed that there should be a minimum of government interference with the economic order—the best government, as Thomas Paine argued in another connection, is the government that governs least.

A graphic illustration, pin making, is used by Smith to demonstrate the advantages of division of labor: "A workman not educated in this business . . . nor acquainted with the use of the machinery employed in it . . . could scarce, perhaps, with his utmost industry, make one pin a day, and certainly could not make twenty." By breaking the manufacturing process down "into eighteen distinct operations, which, in some manufactories, are all performed by distinct hands . . . I have seen a small manufactory of this kind where ten men only were employed . . . make among them upwards of forty-eight thousand pins in a day." This was a "consequence of a proper division and combination of their difficult operations."

The division of labor, Smith continued, had its origin among primitive peoples.

In a tribe of hunters or shepherds a particular person makes bows and arrows, for example, with more readiness and dexterity than any other. He frequently exchanges them for cattle or for venison with his companions; and he finds at last that he can in this manner get more cattle and venison, than if he himself went to the field to catch them. From a regard to his own interest, therefore, the making of bows and arrows grows to be his chief business. . . .

Another excels in making the frames and covers of their little huts or moveable houses. . . .

In the same manner a third becomes a smith or a brazier; a fourth a tanner or dresser of hides or skins . . . and thus the certainty of being able to exchange all that surplus part of the produce of his own labour, which is over and above his own consumption, for such parts of the produce of other men's labour as he may have occasion for, encourages every man to apply himself to a particular occupation, and to cultivate and bring to perfection whatever talent or genius he may possess for that particular species of business.

Proceeding next to a consideration of money and commodity prices, Smith states a principle generally condemned as erroneous by orthodox economists, but widely adopted as a rallying cry of socialist thinkers of later eras. "Labour alone," he says, "never varying in its own value, is alone the ultimate and real standard by which the value of all commodities can at all times and places be estimated and compared. It is their real price; money is their nominal price only."

Nowhere in the *Wealth of Nations* is Smith more outspoken, and occasionally indignant, than in his comments on the disparities in bargaining power between employers and workers, and in his opposition to the mercantilist notion that low wages would force laborers to work more and thereby increase England's prosperity. On the first point, he remarks, "The workmen desire to get as much, the masters to give as little as possible. The former are disposed to combine in order to raise, the latter in order to lower the wages of labour."

He continues:

It is not, however, difficult to foresee which of the two parties must, upon all ordinary occasions, have the advantage in the dispute; and force the other into a compliance with their terms. The masters, being fewer in number, can combine much more easily; and the law, besides, authorizes, or at least does not prohibit their combinations, while it prohibits those of the workmen. We have no acts of parliament against combining to lower the price of work; but many against combining to raise it. In all such disputes the masters can hold out much longer. A landlord, a farmer, a master manufacturer, or merchant, though they did not employ a single workman, could generally live a year or two upon the stocks which they have already acquired. Many workmen could not subsist a week, few could subsist a month, and scarce any a year without employment. In the long-run the workman may be as necessary to his master as his master is to him, but the necessity is not so immediate.

Smith's obvious sympathy with the lowly workmen is shown in such passages as these:

Servants, labourers and workmen of different kinds, make up the far greater part of every great political society. But what improves the circumstances of the greater part can never be regarded as an inconveniency to the whole. No society can surely be flourishing and happy, of which the far greater part of the members are poor and miserable. It is but equity, besides, that they who feed, cloath and lodge the whole body of the people, should have such a share of the produce of their own labour as to be themselves tolerably well fed, cloathed and lodged. . . . The liberal reward of labour . . . increases the industry of the common people. The wages of labour are the encouragement of industry, which like every other human quality, improves in proportion to the encouragement it receives. . . . Where wages are high, accordingly, we shall always find the workmen more active, diligent and expeditious, than where they are low.

And again:

Our merchants and master-manufacturers complain much of the bad effects of high wages in raising the price, and thereby lessening the sale of their goods both at home and abroad. They say nothing about the effects of high profits. They are silent with regard to the pernicious effects of their own gains. They complain only of those of other people.

Twenty-two years before publication of the *Principles of Population*, Malthusian theories were forecast by Smith:

Every species of animals naturally multiplies in proportion to their means of subsistence, and no species can ever multiply beyond it. But in civilized society it is only among the inferior ranks of people that the scantiness of subsistence can set limits to the further multiplication of the human species; and it can do so in no other way than by destroying a great part of the children which their fruitful marriages produce.

In view of the gains of labor in modern times, the feudal restraints and restrictions which prevailed in Adam Smith's century are hardly credible. The ban on any form of labor organization was only one of the severe handicaps imposed on workmen. Even more burdensome were apprenticeship laws and the law of settlements.

The apprenticeship statute dated back to Queen Elizabeth's reign. As described by Smith, it provided "that no person should for the future exercise any trade, craft, or mystery at that time exercised in England, unless he had previously served to it an apprenticeship of seven years at least." During these seven years, the employer furnished only subsistence. Unscrupulous employers naturally used the device to exploit their workers, taking much and giving little, while the apprentices were in a virtual state of bondage. In denouncing the practice, Smith maintained that long apprenticeships were unnecessary, for most trades could be learned in a few weeks. Further, apprenticeship regulations were an unfair interference with the workman's right to contract for his own services, to choose his own occupation, and to transfer from a low-wage to a high-wage job.

Equally onerous was the law of settlements. "There is scarce a poor man in England at forty years of age, I will venture to say," wrote Smith, "who has not in some part of his life felt himself most cruelly oppressed by this ill-contrived law of settlements." Like the apprenticeship act, the law of settlements was promulgated in the Elizabethan era. Its original purpose was to establish order in the distribution of poor relief. Each parish was made responsible for the care of its indigent members. To prevent the number of the community's poor from increasing, newcomers were not permitted to take up residence unless they were persons of substantial means. In its application to laborers, the law's practical effect was to create a class of prisoners for life in the town of their birth, placing nearly insuperable obstacles in the way of a workman who wished to move from one locality to another. Here again was an example, in Adam Smith's estimation, of the iniquities of government interference with the rights of man and with the natural workings of the economic system.

An attempt was made by Smith to distinguish between "productive" and "unproductive" labor.

Great nations are never impoverished by private, though they sometimes are by public prodigality and misconduct. The whole, or almost the whole, public revenue, is, in most countries, employed in maintaining unproductive hands. Such are the people who compose a numerous and splendid court, a great ecclesiastical establishment, great fleets and armies, who in time of peace produce nothing, and in time of war acquire nothing, which can compensate the expense of maintaining them, even while the war lasts. Such people, as they themselves produce nothing, are all maintained by the produce of other men's labour. When multiplied, therefore, to an unnecessary number, they may in a particular year consume so great a share of this produce, as not to leave a sufficiency for maintaining the productive labourers.

Sound advice, unfortunately not heeded by the American colonies, was also offered on slave labor.

The experience of all ages and nations, I believe, demonstrates that the work done by slaves, though it appears to cost only their maintenance, is in the end the dearest of any. A person who can acquire no property, can have no other interest but to eat as much, and to labour as little as possible. Whatever work he does beyond what is sufficient to purchase his own maintenance, can be squeezed out of him by violence only, and not by any interest of his own.

From the problems of labor, Smith turned next to the advocacy of land reforms. There, too, he thought unwise governmental regulations and outmoded laws were standing in the path of progress. Much of the land in eighteenth-century Britain was under entail; an owner could thereby establish rules concerning the division and sale of his land binding upon his heirs for centuries after his demise. Another ancient custom was primogeniture, a feudal practice to prevent the breakup of large estates. Under the law of primogeniture, the eldest son was the sole heir. "Nothing," remarked Adam Smith, "can be more contrary to the real interest of a numerous family, than a right which in order to enrich one, beggars all the rest of the children." He urged free trade in land, through the repeal of laws establishing entails, primogenitures, and other restrictions on the free transfer of land by gift, devise, or sale.

A famous chapter in the *Wealth of Nations* deals with colonies. One authority has asserted that it "remains the best summary of colonial policy ever written." The discussion is divided in three parts: (1) "Of the motives for establishing new colonies," in which are reviewed the colonial enterprises of Greece, Rome, Venice, Portugal, and Spain; (2) "Causes of the prosperity of new colonies," enumerating such factors as plentiful and cheap land, high wages, rapid growth of population, and the colonists' knowledge of agriculture and other arts (the comparatively enlightened colonial policies of England are contrasted with the narrow and restrictive policies of Portugal and Spain); (3) "Of the advantages which Europe has derived from the discovery of America, and from that of a passage to the East Indies by the Cape of Good Hope," discoveries ranked by Smith as "the two greatest and most important events recorded in the history of mankind."

Restrictions placed on colonies in order to achieve monopolies of their trade were condemned by Smith as violations of the colonies' "natural rights." The mercantile system applied to the colonies was as absurd and costly as it was to the mother country. Also, there would be a continual financial drain on the colonizing power, for the colonies would never willingly tax themselves sufficiently to pay the expense of their own defense.

Smith was able to view the rebellious American colonists with far more objectivity than were most of his fellow-countrymen. A proper solution to the controversy, he believed, was to represent the American colonists in the British parliament—union rather than separation, with representation based on tax revenues. If eventually, as was not unlikely, the American exceeded the British taxes, the capital might be moved across the Atlantic, "to that part of the Empire which contributed most to the general defense and support of the whole." This would have constituted an effective answer to Tom Paine's assertion that "there is something absurd in supposing a continent to be perpetually governed by an island," for the roles would then have been reversed.

If the differences between England and her American colonies could not be reconciled peaceably, Smith urged independence for the colonies, though he realistically recognized that "to propose that Great Britain should voluntarily give up all authority over her colonies, and leave them to elect their own magistrates, to enact their own laws, and to make peace and war as they might think proper, would be to propose such a measure as never was, and never will be adopted by any nation in the world . . . how troublesome soever it might be to govern it, and how small the revenue which it afforded might be in proportion to the expense which it occasioned."

Smith's clear mind and prescience are revealed in this prophetic passage on America's future:

From shopkeepers, tradesmen, and attornies, they [the American colonists] are become statesmen and legislators, and are employed in contriving a new form of government for an extensive empire, which, they flatter themselves, will become, and which, indeed, seems very likely to become, one of the greatest and most formidable that ever was in the world.

The most celebrated and, undoubtedly, the key part of the *Wealth of Nations* is Book IV, entitled "Of Systems of Political Economy." Here are considered two different systems: the system of commerce, and the system of agriculture, though the space devoted to commerce is eight times as great as that given to agriculture. Therein Smith developed the principles of laissez faire ever since associated with his name. All conclusions concerning labor, land, commodities, money, prices, agriculture, stock, and taxes come to a focus in the argument for free trade, internal and external. Only through unrestricted domestic and foreign commerce could the nation achieve full development and prosperity. Abolish, pleaded Smith, the duties, bounties, and prohibitions of the mercantilist regime and the trading monopolies of the chartered companies, all of which hamstring the natural growth of industry and trade, and the free flow of goods to consumers. Discard the fallacious doctrine of "balance of trade," so revered by the mercantilists. Money is only a tool, and "there is no certain criterion by which we can determine on which side what is called the balance between any two countries lies, or which of them exports to the greatest value. . . . Wealth does not consist in money, or in gold and silver, but in what money purchases, and is valuable only for purchasing."

A division of labor between nations is as desirable and as logical as between individuals.

The natural advantages which one country has over another in producing particular commodities are sometimes so great, that it is acknowledged by all the world to be in vain to struggle with them. By means of glasses, hotbeds, and hotwalls, very good grapes can be raised in Scotland, and very good wine too can be made of them at about thirty times the expense for which at least equally good can be brought from foreign countries. Would it be a reasonable law to prohibit the importation of all foreign wines, merely to encourage the making of claret and burgundy in Scotland?

The economic advantages of free trade are summarized by Smith in these statements:

It is the maxim of every prudent master of a family, never to attempt to make at home what it will cost him more to make than to buy. . . . What is prudence in the conduct of every private family can scarce be folly in that of a great kingdom. If a foreign country can supply us with a commodity cheaper than we ourselves can make it, better buy it of them with some sort of the produce of our own industry, employed in a way in which we have some advantage.

The mutual benefits of foreign trade were stressed by Smith:

Between whatever places foreign trade is carried on, they all of them derive two distinct benefits from it. It carries out that surplus part of the produce of their land and labor for which there is no demand among them, and brings back in return for it something else for which there is a demand. . . . By means of it, the narrowness of the home market does not hinder the division of labor in any particular branch of art or manufacture from being carried to the highest perfection. By opening a more extensive market for whatever part of the produce of their labor may exceed the home consumption, it encourages them to improve its productive powers, and to augment its annual produce to the utmost, and thereby to increase the real revenue and wealth of the society.

That Smith was not absolutely dogmatic in his insistence upon free trade, however, is shown by certain exceptions or limitations he was willing to concede in application of the principle. In a few cases, he pointed out, "it will generally be advantageous to lay some burden upon foreign, for the encouragement of domestic industry. The first is, when some particular sort of industry is necessary for the defence of the country," even though on purely economic grounds it could not be justified, for "defence is more important than opulence." Living in a warring world, Smith granted that rich nations, with which it was profitable to trade in times of peace, might be more dangerous enemies in wartime than poor nations. Also, he agreed that some tariff protection for "infant industries" would enable them to develop more rapidly, perhaps to a point where they could be economically defensible. Further, Smith recommended that all tariff reductions be made "slowly, gradually, and after a very long warning," in order to protect plant investments in industries not capable of meeting foreign competition, and to provide time for workers to seek new jobs. These were realistic concessions to the arguments of free-trade opponents.

If government kept hands off business, industry, agriculture, and most other day-to-day activities of the nation, as Smith advocated, what did he regard as suitable functions for government? The range of responsibilities would be narrow. Essentially, the state should be limited to warding off foreign attack and administering justice. Smith was also willing to have it engage in "erecting and maintaining certain public works and certain public institutions, which it can never be for the interest of any individual, or small number of individuals, to erect and maintain; because the profit could never repay the expense to any individual or small number of individuals, though it may frequently do much more than repay it to a great society." In Smith's brief list of functions properly assignable to the state were included upkeep of the highways, lighting the streets of cities, and water supplies. Thus, Adam Smith saw little excuse for the existence of what he termed that "insidious and crafty animal vulgarly called the statesman or politician" outside of maintaining external peace and internal order.

In one of his exceptions, however, he was far ahead of his time—participation by the government in the general education of the people. In support of his arguments for public education, Smith comments:

A man without the proper use of the intellectual faculties of a man, is, if possible, more contemptible than even a coward, and seems to be mutilated and deformed in a still more essential part of the character of human nature. Though the state was to derive no advantage from the instruction of the inferior ranks of people, it would still deserve its attention that they should not be altogether uninstructed. The state, however, derives no inconsiderable advantage from their instruction. The more they are instructed, the less liable they are to the delusions of enthusiasm and superstition, which, among ignorant nations, frequently occasion the most dreadful disorders. An instructed and intelligent people besides, are always more decent and orderly than an ignorant and stupid one. They feel themselves, each individually more respectable, and more likely to obtain the respect of their lawful superiors, and they are therefore more disposed to respect those superiors. . . . In free countries, where the safety of government depends very much upon the favourable judgment which the people may form of its conduct, it must surely be of the highest importance that they should not be disposed to judge rashly or capriciously concerning it.

An unbiased, impartial estimation of Adam Smith and his work is complex even after two hundred years. There is, for example, the view of Buckle in his *History of Civilization:* "The *Wealth of Nations* is . . . probably the most important book which has ever been written, whether we consider the amount of original thought which it contains, or its practical influence." A writer less sympathetic to Smith's ideas, Max Lerner, nevertheless acknowledged that the *Wealth of Nations* "has done as much perhaps as any modern book thus far to shape the whole landscape of life as we live it today." Lerner observed discerningly that, "those who read it were chiefly those who stood to profit from its view of the world—the rising class of businessmen, their political executive committees in the parliaments of the world, and their intellectual executive committees in the academies. Through them it has had an enormous influence upon the underlying population of the world, although generally unknown to them, and through them also it has had an enormous influence upon economic opinion and national policy."

The judgment of these two authorities is confirmed by the well-known English political economist, J. A. R. Marriott, who remarked that: "There is probably no single work in the language which has in its day exercised an influence so profound alike upon scientific economic thought and upon administrative action. There is every reason why it should exercise it still." Another economist, W. R. Scott, added: "Intellectually, he [Smith] was pre-eminently a master in seeing economic life steadily and whole."

On the other hand, many liberal and radical thinkers have found it difficult to forgive Smith for the excesses of laissez-faire practiced by businessmen and industrialists, who appropriated Smith's writings as their gospel. Doctrines which he had advocated for the protection of the workman, the farmer, the consumer, and society at large, subsequently were twisted by unprincipled interests to mean unbridled license for themselves, free of all government control or interference.

There is also the old argument about the priority of the chicken or the egg. Would Smith's principles have been followed in the development of commerce and industry if he had never written a word, or did the *Wealth of Nations* precipitate the vast changes which followed its publication, furnishing a philosophy and plan for the new movement? Perhaps the truth lies somewhere midway.

Admittedly, Adam Smith picked the right time to be born. Standing on the threshold between two historical eras, he spoke for the new economic liberalism, and a receptive world listened and used his precepts to effect a great economic transformation. British businessmen, as the Industrial Revolution progressed, recognized the validity of Smith's doctrines, discarded mercantilist restrictions and privileges, and in the nineteenth century developed Britain into the world's wealthiest nation. The impact of Smith's ideas was scarcely less striking on other leading trading countries. Few would deny that Adam Smith richly deserves the title "father of modern economics."

12

FIRST OF A NEW GENUS

Mary Wollstonecraft: Vindication of the Rights of Woman

Striking proof of how far in advance Mary Wollstonecraft was of her own time when in 1792 she advocated woman suffrage, is the fact that the Nineteenth Amendment to the Constitution, giving women the right to vote in the United States, was not approved until 1920, and suffrage was not granted them in Great Britain until 1928. Progress has since been rapid, but the battle still rages in many areas of the world.

It is difficult nowadays to conceive of the degrading position and the popular attitude toward women in eighteenth-century society, the conditions that inspired Mary Wollstonecraft's famous polemic, *Vindication of the Rights of Woman*. Not only did women possess no political power, but, under prevailing laws, a wife was regarded as her husband's chattel; she could not dispose of her own property, her husband was permitted to punish her physically, and she had no rights as a parent. Her legal status was in accord with general social opinion, which held that women were placed in the world for the comfort and pleasure of men. This concept was reflected in Rousseau's argument for keeping women in a state of sex subjection:

The education of women should always be relative to that of men. To please, to be useful to us, to make us love and esteem them, to educate us when young, to take care of us when grown up, to advise, to console us, to render our lives easy and agreeable; these are the duties of women at all times, and what they should be taught in their infancy.

Earlier, Milton had viewed a husband as a kind of priest standing between a woman and God: "He for God only, she for God in him." An even more forthright statement came from a Wollstonecraft contemporary, Lord Chesterfield. "Women," he asserted, "are only children of a larger growth. . . . A man of sense only trifles with them, plays with them, humors and flatters them, as he does with a sprightly, forward child; but he neither consults them about, nor trusts them with serious matters."

The one career open to women was marriage, and all their training was directed toward that end. Young girls learned a few accomplishments, were taught a smattering of ornamental knowledge and such virtues as would appeal to a husband in a subject wife, chiefly submission, chastity, and the art of pleasing.

In this strictly man's world, Mary Wollstonecraft threw her bombshell, upsetting the complacency both of the masculine world and of her own sex. It was a period ripe for revolt, the era of the American and French revolutions (Mary Wollstonecraft, in fact, subsequently wrote a history of the French Revolution), when new thoughts about the rights of man were fermenting. To Mary Wollstonecraft, it appeared to be a propitious time to overthrow another despotism, that of men over women. She was, in her own words, "the first of a new genus."

The author based her crusade to win freedom and self-respect for women on the principle that they would thereby become more capable wives and mothers. She opens the book with a picture of the contemporary state of women.

Women are still reckoned a frivolous sex. . . . It is acknowledged that they spend many of the first years of their lives in acquiring a smattering of accomplishments; meanwhile strength of body and mind are sacrificed to libertine notions of beauty, to the desire of establishing themselves—the only way women can rise in the world —by marriage. And this desire making mere animals of them, when they marry they act as such children may be expected to act—they dress, they paint, and nickname God's creatures. Surely these weak beings are only fit for a seraglio! Can they be expected to govern a family with judgement, or take care of the poor babes whom they bring into the world?

The reforms in this pernicious system proposed by Mary Wollstonecraft were momentous and revolutionary for their own time but would scarcely be viewed as anything except moderate today. She urged that women should be educated, for "ignorance is a frail base for virtue." Women, she believed, should have an equal opportunity with men to develop their mental and moral capacities and become the companions, rather than the play-things, of men. To this end, a drastic shake-up in educational practices was recommended. Boarding schools should be abolished, and national day schools should be established and supported by government. In the new public schools, boys and girls would be taught together, to avoid premature sex-consciousness. Further, there would be no distinction based on rank or wealth.

The author suggested that, beginning at age nine, the students should receive more specialized training. The boys would learn mechanical trades and the girls the domestic arts. New careers would open up for women: medicine, agriculture, shop-keeping, and every kind of business. This was written only a few years after Boswell records Samuel Johnson as saying that even portrait painting and writing were "improper employment for a woman." Mary Wollstonecraft, who had observed frequent instances of hardship and tragedy caused by the complete economic dependence of women on men, expanded her ideas further:

> Though I consider that women in the common walks of life are called to fulfill the duties of wives and mothers by religion and reason, I cannot help lamenting that women of a superior cast have not a road open by which they can pursue more extensive plans of usefulness and independence. . . . I really think that women ought to have representatives instead of being arbitrarily governed, without having any direct share allowed them in the deliberations of government.

Thus did the *Vindication* plead for equal educational and economic opportunities for women and a voice for them in government. In the past, the author declared, men "have been more anxious to make women alluring mistresses than affectionate wives and mothers"; future progress depended upon a changed attitude of men toward women and of women toward themselves.

The *Vindication of the Rights of Woman* created a great sensation immediately upon publication. Translations were issued in French and German. The book both shocked and scandalized the conservative and puritanical, who considered it a gross offense against decency and womanly reserve. Horace Walpole called the author "a hyena in petticoats" and a "philosophizing serpent." Mary Wollstonecraft was made more vulnerable to attack by her own unconventional personal life. Her lack of orthodoxy was encouraged by association with such individuals as William Godwin (whom she married shortly before her death), Thomas Paine, and other radical thinkers of the period, though she did not necessarily accept or follow their views of society.

As the feminist cause has advanced, Mary Wollstonecraft's contentions have become commonplace. Nevertheless, her contributions to the principle of education for citizenship instead of sex subordination, to civil rights, and to similar equal prerogatives for women have been of immeasurable importance.

13

TOO MANY MOUTHS

Thomas Malthus: An Essay on the Principle of Population

A favorite amusement of the late eighteenth century was dreaming up utopias. The idealism associated with revolutionary movements in America and France inspired visionaries to conclude that the perfection of man was just over the horizon, and the creation of an earthly paradise was imminent.

Among the dreamers, two, William Godwin in England, and the Marquis de Condorcet in France, had the most devoted followings, voicing for the multitudes the aspirations and visions of a new day. Typical of the incorrigible optimists are views expressed by Godwin in his *Political Justice*. The time would come, he believed, when we would be so full of life that we need not sleep, so full of living that we need not die, and the need of marriage would be superseded by emphasis on developing the intellect; in short, men would be as angels. "Other improvements," he rhapsodized, "may be expected to keep pace with those of health and longevity. There will be no war, no crimes, no administration of justice, as it is called, and no government. Besides this, there will be neither disease, anguish, melancholy nor resentment. Every man will seek with ineffable ardour the good of all."

To dispel the fear of too many people and too little food, Godwin wrote, "Myriads of centuries of still increasing population may pass away and the earth be still found sufficient for the subsistence of its inhabitants." Eventually, he thought, the sexual passion might abate; and Condorcet suggested that it might be gratified without a high rate of reproduction.

These beautiful bubbles invited pricking, and the needle was furnished by an impertinent young cleric. Thomas Robert Malthus, a thirty-two-year-old Fellow of Jesus College, Cambridge. His answer to the social perfectionists, *An Essay on the Principle of Population*, 1798, became one of the great classics of political economy.

A contemporary of Adam Smith and Thomas Paine, though considerably their junior, Malthus was the second son of Daniel Malthus. The father, a country gentleman in easy circumstances, a friend of Rousseau and executor of his estate, was one of Godwin's warmest admirers. Both father and son were fond of debate, and Thomas attacked while Daniel defended utopian views. Finally, at the father's urging, Thomas decided to state his opinions in writing. The celebrated *Essay* was the result, a book which during the past 180 years has had a profound influence on human thought and human practice, and perhaps at no period more pronounced than in the present era. What Adam Smith had done twenty-two years earlier in his inquiry into the nature and causes of wealth, Malthus complemented with his searching analysis of the nature and causes of poverty.

An Essay on the Principle of Population as It Affects the Future Improvement of Society, with Remarks on the Speculations of Mr. Godwin, M. Condorcet, and Other Writers, published anonymously, was little more than a pamphlet (50,000 words) in the 1798 version, and was evidently issued in a small edition, for copies are now exceedingly rare. "It was written," the author later reported, "on the spur of the occasion, and from the few materials which were then within my reach in a country situation." The theme of the *Essay* was not new, for various eighteenth-century writers, including Benjamin Franklin, had discussed the problem of population growth, but none had presented it so forcefully, with so much fervor, or with such clear discernment as did Malthus.

Two basic assumptions are stated by Malthus at the outset:

First, that food is necessary to the existence of man; Secondly, that the passion between the sexes is necessary, and will remain nearly in its present state.

Not even the utopians had supposed that man would ultimately be able to live without food.

But Mr. Godwin has conjectured that the passion between the sexes may in time be extinguished. . . . The best arguments for the perfectibility of man are drawn from a contemplation of the great progress that he has already made from the savage state. . . . But towards the extinction of the passion between the sexes, no progress whatever has hitherto been made. It appears to exist in as much force at present as it did two thousand, or four thousand years ago.

Assuming then that his "postulata" were irrefutable, Malthus proceeded to lay down his famous principle:

. . . that the power of population is indefinitely greater than the power in the earth to produce subsistence for man. Population, when unchecked, increases in a geometrical ratio. Subsistence increases only in an arithmetical ratio. A slight acquaintance with numbers will show the immensity of the first power in comparison to the second.

Elaborating the proposition further, Malthus buttressed his case in this way:

Through the animal and vegetable kingdoms, nature has scattered the seeds of life abroad with the most profuse and liberal hand. She has been comparatively sparing in the room, and the nourishment necessary to rear them . . . The race of plants, and race of animals shrink under this great restrictive law. And the race of man cannot, by any efforts of reason, escape from it. Among plants and animals its effects are waste of seed, sickness, and premature death. Among mankind, misery and vice.

These hard but realistic facts, in Malthus' estimation, placed insurmountable difficulties in the way of the perfectibility of society. No possible reform could remove the pressure of natural laws, obstacles which prevent the "existence of a society, all the members of which, should live in ease, happiness, and comparative leisure; and feel no anxiety about providing the means of subsistence for themselves and families."

Choosing as an illustration of the workings of his geometrical ratio the growth of population in the United States, "where the means of subsistence have been more ample, the manners of the people more pure, and consequently the checks to early marriage fewer," Malthus found the population, exclusive of immigration, had doubled in twenty-five years. From this evidence he deduced that where checks and balances are lacking and no restrictions placed on nature, the rate of increase in any country would double the population every generation. His critics have frequently called attention to flaws in Malthus' rule, for the situation which prevailed in the United States during the era cited was atypical of conditions in any other period of American history or of the history of any other nation.

Applying his yardstick of natural population growth to England, that is, a potential doubling every twenty-five years, Malthus turned to the question of subsistence. His conclusion is "that by the best possible policy, by breaking up more land, and by great encouragements to agriculture, the produce of this Island may be doubled in the first twenty-five years."

Troubles would start to accumulate, however, in the next generation. While the population would be doubling again, that is quadrupling in the fifty-year span, "It is impossible to suppose that the produce could be quadrupled." The best that could be hoped for would be an increase in the food supply triple the beginning rate. Expressed numerically, the Malthus formula would run, for population: 1, 2, 4, 8, 16, 32, 64, etc., and for subsistence: 1, 2, 3, 4, 5, 6, 7, etc.

A logical sequence of Malthus' line of reasoning is that there must be constant checks upon the growth of population. The most drastic check of all is the scarcity of food. A series of "immediate checks" falls into a "positive" group, including unwholesome occupations, severe labor, extreme poverty, diseases, bad nursing of children, great cities, plagues, and famine; and a "preventive" group, namely, moral restraint and vice.

Certain inevitable practical conclusions followed, in Malthus' view. If human beings were to enjoy the greatest possible happiness, they should not assume family obligations unless they could afford them. Those without adequate means to support a family should remain celibate. Furthermore, public policy, such as the poor laws, should avoid encouraging the laboring class and others to bring into the world children whom they could not support.

A man who is born into a world already possessed, if he cannot get subsistence from his parents, on whom he has a just demand, and if the society do not want his labour, has no *claim* of right to the smallest portion of food, and, in fact, has no business to be where he is.

This was written in reply to Paine's *Rights of Man*.

Charity, private or governmental, was undesirable because it gave money to the poor without increasing the amount of food available, thereby raising prices and creating shortages. Also objectionable were public housing schemes, for they had the effect of stimulating early marriages, and consequently of causing a rapid increase in population. Higher wages had a similar catastrophic effect. The sole means of escape from this grim dilemma was delayed marriage with "moral restraint," i.e., continence.

Actually, in Malthus' eyes, any project to better society and alleviate want was likely to end by merely aggravating the evils it sought to cure. This tough-minded, apparently antisocial attitude of the young clergyman alienated humanitarians of his own and succeeding generations. The Malthus doctrines were received enthusiastically, however, by the wealthy and power-holding classes of his time. Mass poverty and other social maladjustments could now be blamed on early marriages and too many children—rather than on maldistribution of wealth.

The Malthus attitude toward government relief programs may be illustrated by this quotation:

The poor-laws of England tend to depress the general condition of the poor in these two ways. This first obvious tendency is to increase population without increasing the food for its support. A poor man may marry with little or no prospect of being able to support a family in independence. They may be said therefore in some measure to create the poor which they maintain; and as the provisions of the country must, in consequence of the increased population, be distributed to every man in smaller proportions, it is evident that the labour of those who are not supported by parish assistance will purchase a smaller quantity of provisions than before, and consequently, more of them must be driven to ask for support. Secondly, the quantity of provisions consumed in work-houses upon a part of the society, that cannot in general be considered the most valuable part, diminishes the shares that would otherwise belong to more worthy members; and thus in the same manner forces more to become dependent.

There is a summary view of Malthus' theories near the end of his essay:

Other circumstances being the same, it may be affirmed that countries are populous according to the quantity of human food which they produce or can acquire, and happy according to the liberality with which this food is divided, or the quantity which a day's labour will purchase. Corn countries are more populous than pasture countries, and rice countries more populous than corn countries. But their happiness does not depend upon their being thinly or fully inhabited, upon their poverty or their richness, their youth or their age, but on the proportion which the population and the food bear to each other.

The appearance of Malthus' essay loosed a storm of criticism, protest, and vituperation, chiefly from two sources: the theological conservatives and the social radicals. "For thirty years," says his chief biographer, James Bonar, "it rained refutations." Malthus was the most abused man of the age, put down as "a man who defended smallpox, slavery and child murder, who denounced soup kitchens, early marriage and parish allowances; who had the impudence to marry after preaching against the evils of a family; who thought the world so badly governed that the best actions do the most harm; who, in short, took all romance out of life."

A few critics dismissed the whole Malthus thesis lightly. Hazlitt "did not see what there was to discover after reading the tables of Noah's descendants, and knowing that the world is round." Coleridge remarked, "Are we now to have a quarto to teach us that great misery and great vice arise from poverty, and that there must be poverty in its worst shape wherever there are more mouths than loaves and more Heads than Brains?"

Other commentators were bitter: William Thompson, leader of early English socialism, wrote:

Insult not the suffering, the great majority of mankind, with the glaring falsehood, that by means of limited population or not eating potatoes their own happiness is in their own hands, whilst the causes are left which render it morally and physically impossible for them to live without potatoes and improvident breeding.

Another violent expression came from William Cobbett: "How can Malthus and his nasty and silly disciples, how can those who want to abolish the Poor Rates, to prevent the poor from marrying; how can this at once stupid and conceited tribe look the labouring man in the face, while they call on him to take up arms, to risk his life in defense of the land."

It was Cobbett, incidentally, who invented the nickname "Parson" for Malthus. Cobbett is addressing a young farmer:

"Why," said I, "how many children do you reckon to have had at last?"

"I do not care how many," said the man, "God never sends mouths without sending meat."

"Did you never hear," said I, "of one Parson Malthus?"

"No sir."

"If he were to hear of your words, he would be outraged, for he wants an Act of Parliament to prevent poor people from marrying young, and from having such lots of children."

"Oh, the brute," exclaimed the wife, while the husband laughed, thinking I was joking.

An objection frequently brought against the Malthusian doctrine when it first appeared was that it was inconsistent with the benevolence of the Creator. Malthus was accused of having published an irreligious book—a damaging accusation against a clergyman of the established church. Because of this criticism, Malthus in the second edition of his *Essay* stressed "moral restraint," a device which would keep the population within bounds, while eliminating misery and vice, and thereby remove "all apparent imputation on the goodness of the Deity."

In a program commemorating the centenary of Malthus' death in 1935, Bonar came to his defense against those who, he believed, had misrepresented, misread, misquoted, and misunderstood Malthus. In his view, Malthus had been affirmative, not negative, in his approach. Bonar suggested that Malthus' "heart's desire for the human race" included (1) a lower death rate for all; (2) a higher standard of life and livelihood for the poor; and (3) an end of the waste of young human lives.

Malthus saw quite clearly that the prevention of a rapid birth rate was practiced increasingly by nations as they became more civilized and better educated, and as they acquired higher living standards. Consequently, his views on the future of human society were guardedly optimistic. In England, itself, Malthus observed that "the most cursory view of society must convince us, that throughout all ranks the preventive check to population prevails in a considerable degree." Realistically, he treated the various social classes—gentlemen, tradesmen and farmers, laborers and domestic servants—separately, because of their different economic circumstances. An anxiety to maintain a certain social position, he thought, would prevent hasty marriages. For example:

A man of liberal education, but with an income only just sufficient to enable him to associate in the rank of gentlemen, must feel absolutely certain, that if he marries and has a family, he shall be obliged, if he mixes at all in society, to rank himself with moderate farmers, and the lower class of tradesmen. Two or three steps of descent in society, particularly at this round of the ladder, where education ends, and ignorance begins, will not be considered by the generality of people, as a fancied and chimerical, but a real and essential evil.

As can be inferred from the contemporary quotations, Malthus was far from ignored in his lifetime. The impression made by the first edition of the *Essay* caused the English government to take a census of population in 1801, the first of any consequence since the coming of the Armada. Earlier proposals for a census had been opposed as anti-Scriptural and un-English. Another aftermath of the *Essay* was the modification of the government's Poor Laws to avoid some of the mistakes pointed out by Malthus.

The impact of Malthusian ideas on natural science was fully as powerful as on the social sciences. Both Charles Darwin and Alfred Russel Wallace freely acknowledged their indebtedness to Malthus in the development of the theory of evolution by natural selection. Darwin wrote:

In October 1838, that is fifteen months after I had begun my systematic enquiry, I happened to read for amusement Malthus' *Population*, and being well prepared to appreciate the struggle for existence [a phrase used by Malthus] which everywhere goes on from long-continued observation of animals and plants, it at once struck me that under these circumstances favourable variations would tend to be preserved and unfavourable ones to be destroyed. The result of this would be a new species. Here then I had at last got hold of a theory by which to work.

In similar vein, Wallace wrote:

It was the first work I had yet read treating any of the problems of philosophical biology, and its main principles remained with me as a permanent possession, and twenty years later gave me the long-sought clue to the effective agent in the evolution of organic species.

The angry protests of the clergy and social rebels, with which the 1798 edition of the *Essay* was received, left Malthus undisturbed; he had become fascinated with the subject and was determined to pursue it further. To reinforce his arguments, he toured Europe in 1799 in search of materials, "through Sweden,

Norway, Finland, and a part of Russia, these being the only countries at the time open to English travellers"; and he made another tour in France and Switzerland during the short peace of 1802. During this period he published a pamphlet entitled *An Investigation of the Cause of the Present High Price of Provisions*, taking the point of view that prices and profits are primarily determined by what he called "effective demand."

Five years after the appearance of the first edition of the *Essay*, a considerably enlarged second version came off the press —a quarto volume of 610 pages. It lacked the verve, sprightly style, and youthful cocksureness of the earlier work, and now assumed the form of a scholarly economic treatise, heavily documented and footnoted, though, except for the development of the idea of "moral restraint," the basic principles were unchanged. Four more editions were brought out in the author's lifetime. By its fifth edition the *Essay* had reached three volumes, totaling about 1,000 pages. The only other major work produced by Malthus, so occupied was he with the successive revisions of the *Essay*, was *The Principles of Political Economy Considered with a View to Their Practical Applications*, published in 1820.

Malthus' personal career was relatively quiet and peaceful. He had been free to pursue his economic studies and writing with little other responsibility until 1804 when he married at the age of thirty-eight. The following year he was appointed professor of modern history and political economy at the newly established East India Company's college at Haileybury, for the general education of civil servants of the East India Company. This was the earliest chair of political economy to be established in an English college or university. Malthus remained at Haileybury for thirty years, until his death in 1834. He had three children, of whom two, a son and a daughter, grew to maturity.

The fires stirred up by Malthus have never died down. The controversies, pro and con, still continue to rage. Such recent titles supporting the Malthusian thesis as the *Challenge of Man's Future*, the *Road to Survival*, *Limits of the Earth*, and *Our Plundered Planet* draw retorts in articles entitled "The Malthusian Scarecrow," "Eat Hearty," "The Malthusian Mischief," and "Mankind Need Not Starve." What is a balanced point of view on the Malthusian theories today?

A major factor in the population problem since the mid-

nineteenth century has been the increasing acceptance of contraceptive techniques, bringing about planned limitations of families except among those lacking knowledge or who are deterred
by religious scruples. This movement, known variously as neo-
Malthusianism, birth control, or planned parenthood, has been
called "the most significant demographic movement in the modern world." Malthus specifically rejected and condemned contra-
ception, however, and the practice in his time was regarded as
something "foul, strange, and unnatural." Nevertheless, it has
become one of the principal population checks of modern society,
adding a fourth to Malthus' trio of "vice, misery, and moral
restraint."

In 1800, when Malthus was writing, the world's population
was estimated at one billion. In the past 175 years it has grown
to more than four billion. A high proportion of the expansion
resulted from an increase in the length of life rather than from
any phenomenal rise in the birth rate. In the advanced nations of
the world, innumerable lives have been saved by changes in
medical, sanitary, and social practices. The Industrial Revolution
brought England an immense increase in the production of manu-
factured goods, and these were exchanged for food and raw
materials from unindustrialized countries. All forms of transpor-
tation were improved to give added mobility. Surplus population
was siphoned off by emigration to mostly unpopulated continents. The dire predictions of Malthus, therefore, were at least
delayed in coming to pass, and perhaps have been postponed
indefinitely, insofar as the Western world is concerned.

There remain, however, critical areas of the globe which serve
as perfect illustrations of Malthusian theories. The Near East,
most of Asia, and a majority of Central and South American
countries are characterized by high fertility, and a correspond-
ingly high death rate. In those areas, lives saved by medicine and
sanitation are likely to be lost by poverty and famine.

As the antithesis of that situation, some of the most highly
civilized and cultured nations of the earth have entered a period
of stabilization or falling population, notably France, Sweden,
Iceland, Austria, England, Wales, and Ireland. Stabilization has
come about through low birth rate, a consequent reduction
in the number of young people, and the increased length of life.

The production of food has been increased immensely since
Malthus' time, and authorities agree it would be possible to make

further substantial gains, through more efficient methods of production, irrigation and reclamation of marginal land, substitution of vegetable foods for animal foods, and by better control over insect pests. The crop surpluses prevailing in the United States and Canada could be cited as evidence of an error in the Malthusian principle. But notwithstanding our vast production of food, there remain hundreds of millions of people in the Orient and elsewhere who exist on a near-starvation or bare-subsistence level. Thus the spectacle of perhaps two-thirds of the world's population enduring malnutrition, famine, ill health, and disease would appear to make the issues raised by Malthus more than a century and a half ago as real and vital today as they were then.

Even those critics who contend that the Malthusian thesis has been invalidated in certain respects by developments which were not, or could not have been foreseen by Malthus, concede that major consequences have flowed from his ideas. As Leonard T. Hobhouse acutely observed, "The Malthusian theory was one cause of the defeat of its own prophecies. It was the belief that population was growing too fast that operated indirectly to check it."

Of many commentators who have written on Malthus' *Essay on the Principle of Population*, perhaps none has given a fairer or more discerning appraisal than John Maynard Keynes, who believed that:

The book can claim a place amongst those which have had great influence on the progress of thought. It is profoundly in the English tradition of humane science—in that tradition of Scotch and English thought, in which there has been, I think, an extraordinary continuity of *feeling*, if I may so express it, from the eighteenth century to the present time—the tradition which is suggested by the names of Locke, Hume, Adam Smith, Paley, Bentham, Darwin, and Mill, a tradition marked by a love of truth and a most noble lucidity, by a prosaic sanity free from sentiment or metaphysic, and by an immense disinterestedness and public spirit. There is a continuity in those writings, not only of feeling, but of actual matter. It is in this company that Malthus belongs.

14

INDIVIDUAL VERSUS STATE

Henry David Thoreau: Civil Disobedience

The name of Henry David Thoreau conjures up in the imagination a keen observer of nature, a lover of solitude and the outdoors, an exponent of the simple life, a poet and mystic, a master of English prose style.

Much less frequently is Thoreau remembered as the author of some of the most extreme radical manifestoes in American history, a spokesman, as described by one of his biographers, for "the most outspoken doctrines of resistance ever penned on this continent." Going far beyond Thomas Jefferson's "That government is best which governs least," Thoreau concluded that "That government is best which governs not at all."

These words introduce Thoreau's celebrated essay "Civil Disobedience," which first appeared in an obscure, short-lived periodical—Elizabeth Peabody's *Aesthetic Papers*—in May 1849. Originally called "Resistance to Civil Government," the title was later changed to "On the Duty of Civil Disobedience," or merely "Civil Disobedience." When first published, the work attracted slight attention and few readers. During the next hundred years, it was read by thousands and affected the lives of millions.

Was Thoreau a philosophical anarchist in his beliefs? An analysis of "Civil Disobedience," its setting and background may provide an answer to that complex question.

As for Thoreau himself, little in his beginnings was calculated to produce a social rebel. Born of French and Scottish stock at Concord, Massachusetts, in 1817, he grew up in a conservative environment of genteel poverty. Four years at Harvard were undistinguished, though there is a glimpse of the future noncon-

217

formist in the fact that he wore a green coat to chapel, "because the rules required black." Much time was spent in the college library, and young Thoreau's interest in writing was stimulated by two excellent teachers: Edward T. Channing and Jones Very.

Happy to return to the green fields and woods of Concord, Thoreau never left them thereafter except for short visits. He turned his hand to a variety of occupations. After a brief, inauspicious fling at public school teaching, three years were spent in partnership with his brother John operating a private school. There followed intermittent periods of assisting his father in the family business of making lead pencils, serving as general handyman for the community, acting as town surveyor, giving occasional lectures, and attempting to become a professional author.

For two brief periods Thoreau lived in the home of Ralph Waldo Emerson. There he became acquainted with members of the Transcendental Club, and participated actively in the discussions of this noted group of New England writers and thinkers. Emerson's influence on Thoreau's intellectual development was strong, and included furnishing some of the ideas for "Civil Disobedience."

Thoreau had no ambition to accumulate wealth, or to perform any work other than enough to provide him the minimum essentials for living. His consuming passion, always, was to achieve leisure time for the fundamentally important matters, as he saw them, of rambling in the Concord fields, studying nature at first hand, meditating, reading, writing—to do the things he wanted to do. His simple needs could be met without engaging in a life of drudgery, such as he observed his neighbors leading. Instead of the Biblical formula of six days of work and one day of rest, Thoreau preferred to reverse the ratios—devoting only the seventh day to labor. In short, everything he stood for was the antithesis of the teachings of Adam Smith, the maxims of Franklin's Poor Richard, and the traditional American ideals of hard work and quick riches.

To exemplify his conception of the simple life, shed of all superfluities, Thoreau spent two years at Walden Pond near Concord. There he built a hut, planted beans and potatoes, ate the plainest food (mainly rice, corn meal, potatoes, and molasses), and lived alone, withdrawn from society. It was a time of concentrated thinking and writing, out of which grew one of the greatest books in American literature: *Walden, or Life in the Woods* (1854).

Ostensibly, *Walden* is a record of Thoreau's life in his rural retreat, and is full of memorable descriptions of the seasons, the scenery, and the animal life about him. But *Walden* is far more than the observations of a naturalist, as Izaak Walton's *Compleat Angler* is more than a manual on fishing. Its comments on the superficialities and limitations of society and government have universal significance. Over the years, the social criticism has drawn as many readers as the portions dealing with natural history. In its way, *Walden* is as radical a document as the earlier published "Civil Disobedience," to which it bears a close kinship.

While visiting in Concord in 1843, soon after he began his sojourn at Walden Pond, Thoreau was arrested and jailed for nonpayment of poll tax. In his refusal to pay the tax, he was following the example of Bronson Alcott, father of the "Little Women," who had been arrested two years earlier for the same offense. Both were using this means to protest against the state's support of slavery. Thoreau was imprisoned for only one night, for an aunt, contrary to his wishes, stepped in and paid the tax.

Not until several years later did Thoreau tell the story, in "Civil Disobedience," of his brush with the law over the poll tax violation. Originally written as a lecture in 1848, the printed version came off the press the following year. The Mexican War of 1846–47 had but recently been concluded and slavery was a burning issue. The Fugitive Slave Law, which was to arouse Thoreau's special indignation, was soon to be enacted. These matters, plus his poll tax battle, were the inspiration for "Civil Disobedience."

Any war was repugnant to Thoreau's ideals, but the Mexican War particularly so, for its main purpose, he believed, was to extend the hated institution of Negro slavery into new territory. Why, he asked, should he be required to provide financial support for a government guilty of such injustices and stupidity? Here was the birth of his doctrine of civil disobedience. Anything except a politician at heart, Thoreau decided the time had come to examine the nature of the state and its government. What should be the relation of the individual to the state, and of the state to the individual? From a consideration of these questions emerged Thoreau's philosophy of personal integrity and of man's place in society.

"Government," wrote Thoreau, "is at best but an expedient; but most governments are sometimes inexpedient. The objections that have been brought against a standing army, and they are many and weighty, and deserve to prevail, may also at last be brought against a standing government."

Thoreau acknowledged that the American government was a relatively excellent one.

Yet, this government never of itself furthered any enterprise, but by the alacrity with which it got out of its way. *It* does not keep the country free. *It* does not settle the West. *It* does not educate. The character inherent in the American people has done all that has been accomplished; and it would have done somewhat more, if the government had not sometimes got in its way. For government is an expedient by which men would fain succeed in letting one another alone; and, as has been said, when it is most expedient the governed are most let alone by it.

Almost immediately after presenting the case for no government, Thoreau recognized that man had not yet reached a state of perfectibility where a complete lack of government was feasible, and began to modify his stand.

To speak practically and as a citizen, unlike those who call themselves no-government men, I ask for, not at once no government, but *at once* a better government. Let every man make known what kind of government would command his respect, and that will be one step toward obtaining it.

The rights of minorities and the fallacies of majority rule were emphatically stated by Thoreau. A majority rules, he argued, "not because they are most likely to be in the right, nor because this seems fairest to the minority, but because they are physically the strongest. But a government in which the majority rule in all cases cannot be based on justice, even as far as men understand it." Never, he believed, should the citizen "resign his conscience to the legislator. . . . We should be men first and subjects afterward. It is not desirable to cultivate a respect for the law, so much as for the right."

Politicians, as a class, Thoreau held in low esteem. "Most legislators, politicians, lawyers, ministers, and office holders," he remarked, "serve the state chiefly with their heads; and as they rarely make any moral distinctions, they are as likely to serve the Devil, without *intending* it, as God. A very few, as heroes, patriots, martyrs, reformers in the great sense, and *men*, serve the state with their consciences also, and so necessarily resist it for the most part; and they are commonly treated as enemies by it."

Thoreau then proceeded to attack the American government of his day. "I cannot for an instant," he declared, "recognize that political organization as *my* government which is the *slave's* government also." It was the duty of citizens to resist evil in the state even to the point of open and deliberate disobedience to its laws.

When a sixth of the population of a nation which has undertaken to be the refuge of liberty are slaves . . . I think it is not too soon for honest men to rebel and revolutionize. . . . This people must cease to hold slaves and to make war on Mexico, though it cost them their existence as a people.

Likewise deplored by Thoreau was the citizen who felt that he had done his full duty merely by casting a ballot.

All voting is a sort of gaming, like checkers or backgammon, with a slight moral tinge to it, a playing with right and wrong, with moral questions, and betting naturally accompanies it. The character of the voters is not staked. . . . Even voting *for the right* is *doing* nothing for it. It is only expressing to men feebly your desire that it should prevail. . . . There is but little virtue in the actions of masses of men.

The proper attitude of the citizen toward unjust laws was debated by Thoreau. Was it better to wait for majority action to change the laws, or to refuse at once to obey the laws? Thoreau's unequivocal answer was, that if the government "requires you to be the agent of injustice to another, then, I say, break the law. . . . What I have to do is to see, at any rate, that I do not lend myself to the wrong which I condemn."

It is of the very nature of government, Thoreau suggested, to oppose changes and reforms, and to mistreat its critics. "Why," he asked, "does it always crucify Christ, and excommunicate Copernicus and Luther, and pronounce Washington and Franklin rebels?"

Those who opposed slavery, Thoreau urged, "should at once effectually withdraw their support, both in person and property, from the government of Massachusetts, and not wait until they constitute a majority of one, before they suffer the right to prevail through them. I think that it is enough if they have God on their side, without waiting for that other one. Moreover, any man more right than his neighbors constitutes a majority of one already."

As a symbol of civil disobedience, a method open to every citizen, Thoreau advocated refusal to pay taxes. If a thousand or even fewer men would express their disapproval of the government in that fashion, Thoreau thought, reform would inevitably follow. Even if resistance to authority meant punishment, "Under a government which imprisons any unjustly, the true place for a just man is also a prison. . . . If the alternative is to keep all just men in prison, or give up war and slavery, the state will not hesitate which to choose." By paying taxes to an unjust government, the citizen condones wrongs committed by the state.

Thoreau saw, however, that the propertied class had too much at stake to rebel, for "the rich man—not to make any invidious comparisons—is always sold to the institution which makes him rich. Absolutely speaking, the more money, the less virtue, for money comes between a man and his objects, and obtains them for him." Not suffering the handicap of wealth, Thoreau could afford to resist. "It costs me less in every sense to incur the penalty of disobedience to the State than it would to obey. I should feel as if I were worth less in that case."

Thoreau was realistic also in seeing the weight of economic objections which held the state of Massachusetts from taking action against slavery.

Practically speaking, the opponents to a reform in Massachusetts are not a hundred thousand politicians at the South, but a hundred thousand merchants and farmers here who are more interested in commerce and agriculture than they are in humanity, and are not prepared to do justice to slave and to Mexico, *cost what it may*.

For six years, adhering to his principles, Thoreau reported that he paid no poll tax. His short prison term left him unshaken in his convictions, but with less regard for the state.

I saw that the State was half-witted, that it was timid as a lone woman with her silver spoons, and that it did not know its friends from its foes, and I lost all my remaining respect for it, and pitied it. Thus the State never intentionally confronts a man's sense, intellectual or moral, but only his body, his senses. It is not armed with superior wit or honesty, but with superior physical strength. I was not born to be forced. I will breathe after my own fashion.

Thoreau differentiated between taxes. He states that he "never declined paying the highway tax," nor the school tax, "because I am as desirous of being a good neighbor as I am of being a bad subject." Where he drew the line was in paying general taxes to support slavery and war. "I simply wish to refuse allegiance to the State, to withdraw and stand aloof from it effectually," in these matters.

There was no desire, either, on Thoreau's part to pose as a martyr or saint.

I do not wish to quarrel with any man or nation. I do not wish to split hairs, to make fine distinctions, or set myself up as better than my neighbors. I seek rather, I may say, even an excuse for conforming to the laws of the land. I am but too ready to conform to them. Indeed, I have reason to suspect myself on this head; and each year as the tax-gathering comes round, I find myself disposed to review the acts and position of the general and State governments, and the spirit of the people, to discover a pretext for conformity.

Furthermore, Thoreau again admitted that, though they fell far below his ideals, "The Constitution, with all its faults is very good; the law and the courts are very respectable; even this State and this American government are, in many respects, very admirable, and rare things, to be thankful for."

Despite his strictures on majority rule, too, Thoreau had some faith in popular judgment. In his view, legislators lacked ability to deal effectively with the "comparatively humble questions of taxation and finance, commerce and manufactures and agriculture. If we were left solely to the wordy wit of legislators in Congress for our guidance, uncorrected by the seasonable experience and the effectual complaints of the people, America would not long retain her rank among the nations."

Thoreau concludes "Civil Disobedience" with a statement of his concept of perfect government, and a resounding reaffirmation of his belief in the dignity and worth of the individual.

To be strictly just, the authority of government . . . must have the sanction and consent of the governed. It can have no pure right over my person and property but what I concede to it. The progress from an absolute to a limited monarchy, from a limited monarchy to a democracy, is a progress toward a true respect for the individual. . . . Is a democracy, such as we know it, the last improvement possible in government? Is it not possible to take a step further towards recognizing and organizing the rights of man? There will never be a really free and enlightened State until the State comes to recognize the individual as a higher and independent power, from which all its own power and authority are derived, and treats him accordingly. I please myself with imagining a State at last which can afford to be just to all men, and to treat the individual with respect as a neighbor; which even would not think it inconsistent with its own repose if a few were to live aloof from it, not meddling with it, nor embraced by it, who fulfilled all the duties of neighbors and fellow-men. A State which bore this kind of fruit, and suffered it to drop off as fast as it ripened, would prepare the way for a still more perfect and glorious State, which also I have imagined, but not yet anywhere seen.

In essence, Thoreau's basic contention in "Civil Disobedience" was that the state exists for individuals, not individuals for the state. A minority should refuse to yield to a majority if moral principles must be compromised in order to do so. Further, the state has no right to offend moral liberty by forcing the citizen to support injustices. Man's conscience should always be his supreme guiding spirit.

The impact of "Civil Disobedience" on Thoreau's own time was negligible. References to the work in the writings of his contemporaries are almost nonexistent. With the Civil War little more than a decade ahead, it might be assumed that the essay would have struck a popular chord. Apparently it was buried under an avalanche of abolitionist literature, and remained obscure and largely forgotten until the following century.

Now, the scene shifts to South Africa and India. In 1907, a copy of "Civil Disobedience" fell into the hands of a Hindu lawyer in Africa, Mohandas Karamchand Gandhi, who was already meditating upon the merits of passive resistance as a defense for his people. Here is an account of the incident, as recollected by the Mahatma, twenty-two years later, to Henry Salt, one of Thoreau's earliest biographers:

My first introduction to Thoreau's writings was, I think, in 1907, or later, when I was in the thick of the passive resistance struggle. A friend sent me the essay on "Civil Disobedience." It left a deep impression upon me. I translated a portion for the readers of "Indian Opinion in South Africa," which I was then editing, and I made copious extracts for the English part of that paper. The essay seemed to be so convincing and truthful that I felt the need of knowing more of Thoreau, and I came across your Life of him, his *Walden*, and other shorter essays, all of which I read with great pleasure and equal profit.

A slightly different version is recounted by one of Gandhi's closest associates in South Africa, Henry Polak:

I cannot now [in 1931] recall, whether, early in 1907, Gandhi or I first came across the volume of Thoreau's Essays (published I believe in Scott's Library), but we were both of us enormously impressed by the confirmation of the rightness of the principle of passive resistance and civil disobedience . . . contained in the essay "On the Duty of Civil Disobedience." After consultation with Mr. Gandhi, I reproduced the essay in the columns of *Indian Opinion* and it was translated into the Gujarati language, in which, as well as in English, the paper was published, and the essay was subsequently circulated in pamphlet form. Later in the same year, *Indian Opinion* organized an essay competition on "The Ethics of Passive Resistance," with special reference to Thoreau's essay and Socrates's writings that had already come to Mr. Gandhi's attention.

Gandhi, who had been dissatisfied with the term "passive resistance," but had found no suitable substitute, at once adopted "civil disobedience" to describe his movement. Here was a statement of principle, he decided, that meant firmness without violence, and a devotion to truth and justice—a political policy completely in accord with Gandhi's philosophy. "Civil Disobedience" in the hands of Mahatma Gandhi became a bible of nonresistance. For his Hindu followers, Gandhi coined an equivalent, *Satyagraha,* a combination of two Sanskrit words, translated as "soul force" or "the force which is born of truth and love or nonviolence."

Thoreau's fight against slavery in the United States, says Gandhi's biographer, Krishnalal Shridharani, "imbued Gandhi with the faith that it is not the number of the resisters that counts in a *Satyagraha,* but the purity of the sacrificial suffering," Gandhi declared:

Writs are impossible when they are confined to a few recalcitrants. They are troublesome when they have to be executed against many high-souled persons who have done no wrong and who refuse payment to vindicate a principle. They may not attract much notice when isolated individuals resort to this method of protest. But clean examples have a curious method of multiplying themselves. They bear publicity and the sufferers instead of incurring odium receive congratulations. Men like Thoreau brought about the abolition of slavery by their personal examples.

In this statement, Gandhi was echoing Thoreau's words on the power of a small but determined minority. Thereby, as

Shridharani commented, Thoreau "not only propounded the weapon of civil disobedience which constitutes one important stratagem in Gandhi's *Satyagraha*, but he also pointed out the potentiality of noncooperation, which Gandhi enlarged upon afterwards as a means to destroy a corrupt state."

Gandhi remained in South Africa through 1914, carrying on a running battle with government forces led by General Jan Smuts. The campaign was marked by persecution, violence of many descriptions, imprisonments, and all the other tools available to a powerful government attempting to suppress an unpopular minority. Gandhi's techniques of noncooperation, nonresistance, civil disobedience, or *Satyagraha*, paid off, however, in the end. Prime Minister Smuts and his government granted every important demand of the Indians, including abolition of fingerprint legislation, repeal of a three-pound head tax, validation of Hindu and Moslem marriages, removal of restrictions on the immigration of educated Indians, and a promise to protect the legal rights of the Indian citizens.

Andrews, another Gandhi biographer, concluded that the South African campaign must stand "not only as the first but as the classic example of the use of nonresistance by organized masses of men for the redress of grievances."

According to Shridharani, Gandhi's interpretation of civil disobedience was that:

Only those who are otherwise willing to obey the law . . . could have a right to practice civil disobedience against unjust laws. It was quite different from the behavior of outlaws, for it was to be practiced openly and after ample notice. It was not likely, therefore, to foster a habit of lawbreaking or to create an atmosphere of anarchy. And it was to be resorted to only when all other peaceful means, such as petitions and negotiations and arbitration, had failed to redress the wrong.

Early in 1915, Gandhi returned to India. There, until his death at the hands of a Hindu assassin in 1948, he led the movement that eventually won freedom from Britain for India and Pakistan. Again there were rioting, massacres, long prison terms, suppression of civil liberties, and unjust laws with which to contend. Civil disobedience was frequently used during these years and was sharpened by Gandhi into a weapon of remarkable effectiveness. The first steps were agitation, demonstrations, negotiations, and, if possible, arbitration. If these did not produce results, such economic sanctions were resorted to as strikes, picketing, general strikes, commercial boycott, and sit-down strikes. Another tactic was nonpayment of taxes.

In August, 1947, dominion status was granted by Britain to Hindu India and Moslem Pakistan.

Undoubtedly, the future will witness further use of the principles of civil disobedience, as conceived by Thoreau and perfected by Gandhi. The power of oppressed peoples everywhere, even in the ruthless dictatorships of modern times, can make itself felt through these means. A current example is the fight of the colored races of South Africa against the Verwoerd government—a renewal of Gandhi's crusade.

"Even the most despotic government," said Gandhi, "cannot stand except for the consent of the governed which consent is often forcibly procured by the despot. Immediately the subject ceases to fear the despotic force, his power is gone."

Thoreau rejected authoritarianism and totalitarianism in any form. His doctrines run absolutely counter to socialism and communism, or to any other ideology that would place the state above individual rights. It must be conceded that trends of government in the twentieth century show Thoreau's ideas fighting a losing battle. Nevertheless, in the world at large the problem of the citizen's relation to his government—the nature and extent of his obedience to the state—has never been more urgent.

"In Thoreau," wrote Vernon L. Parrington, "the eighteenth-century philosophy of individualism, the potent liberalisms let loose on the world by Jean Jacques Rousseau, came to the fullest expression in New England. He was the completest embodiment of the *laissez-faire* reaction against a regimented social order, the severest critic of the lower economics that frustrate the dreams of human freedom. He was fortunate in dying before the age of exploitation had choked his river with its weeds; fortunate in not foreseeing how remote is that future of free men on which his hopes were fixed."

15

CRUSADER FOR THE LOWLY

Harriet Beecher Stowe: Uncle Tom's Cabin

On a single point only do the pro-and-con critics of *Uncle Tom's Cabin* agree. Without exception, all recognize the book's tremendous impact on its time, and its immense influence in instigating the American Civil War. At one extreme, a contemporary commentator described the work as "a monstrous distortion inspired by Abolitionist fanaticism and designed to excite sectional discord." And a well-known lecturer and writer, early in the present century, remarked that *"Uncle Tom's Cabin* has done more harm to the world than any other book ever written."

In contrast, the sentiment of a host of devoted admirers was expressed in a letter from Longfellow, characterizing *Uncle Tom's Cabin* as "one of the greatest triumphs recorded in literary history, to say nothing of its moral effect." Others hailed the book as "a triumph of reality," "immortal," and the author "unquestionably a woman of genius."

Never was a book more topical or better timed psychologically. The struggle over slavery in the United States had grown tense—aggravated by the passage of the Fugitive Slave Law—the abolitionists had for twenty years kept up a crescendo of antislavery agitation, Congress was split down the center by the increasing controversy, the clergy—North and South—boomed from their pulpits Biblical arguments for and against the "peculiar institution" of slavery. The surcharged moral climate awaited only a spark to set off a world-shaking explosion. *Uncle Tom's Cabin* furnished the spark.

Not only was the time ripe, but for generations heredity and environment had been shaping exactly the right person to inaugurate the great crusade against human slavery.

228

Daughter of one of the most noted divines of the nineteenth century, Lyman Beecher, sister of an even more controversial minister, Henry Ward Beecher, married to a minister, sister and mother of other ministers, Harriet Beecher Stowe spent virtually her entire life in an intensely religious atmosphere. Furthermore, her religious training was rigorously Calvinistic, in the spirit of Jonathan Edwards, Samuel Hopkins, and other New England Puritans. Constantly surrounded by fire-and-brimstone theology from her earliest childhood, Harriet Beecher Stowe could hardly avoid becoming a preacher—if not from a pulpit, at least with a pen. Throughout her prolific writings, including *Uncle Tom's Cabin*, the religious background was ever in evidence, inspiring her to evangelistic fervor and scriptural eloquence of expression.

Harriet Beecher Stowe was born in Litchfield, Connecticut, in 1811; and she received a better education, at the Hartford Female Academy, than was customary for women of the period. About two-thirds of it was religious in nature. She was an avid reader. Aside from theology, her favorite authors were Byron and Scott, both of whom influenced her later writing style.

The dynamic and restless Lyman Beecher moved his family from Litchfield to a pastorate in Boston when Harriet was fourteen, and a few years later moved again, to Cincinnati, where he had been called to be president of the Lane Theological Seminary. There Harriet Beecher remained until 1850, teaching school, getting married to a member of the seminary faculty, Calvin Stowe, giving birth to six of her seven children, and occasionally contributing short sketches and stories for magazine publication.

The Cincinnati years were formative in many respects. Located across the Ohio River from large slave plantations in Kentucky, the city was the center of a raging slavery controversy. Antiabolition mobs roamed the streets, destroying the presses of opposition newspapers, and mistreating free Negroes. Violent speeches, for and against slavery, were heard. Cincinnati was a refuge for escaping slaves, on their way north by underground railroad to freedom in Canada. The seminary itself was a hotbed of antislavery sentiment, and only the fact that it was on a rough and muddy road, two miles from the city, saved it from mob attack. Lyman Beecher's home sheltered refugees on several occasions. Harriet heard direct from the runaway slaves stories of broken families, the cruelties of overseers, the horrors of the auction block, and the terrors of being hunted in flight.

On but one occasion did Mrs. Stowe see the slaveholding system in operation. On a brief visit with friends to Maysville, Kentucky, in 1833, she observed a number of plantations, with their great patriarchal manor houses and slave quarters. Here she found the model for the fictional Shelby plantation in *Uncle Tom's Cabin,* and obtained other impressions of the slave system. From her brother Charles, a businessman who traveled to New Orleans and the Red River country, came more ammunition, for he brought back ugly tales of slavery in the Deep South. Mrs. Stowe was indebted to Charles for the prototype of Simon Legree in *Uncle Tom's Cabin,* based on a ruffianly overseer whom Charles had met on a Mississippi riverboat.

Harriet Stowe did not become an out-and-out abolitionist during the Cincinnati years. Perhaps she shared her father's opinion that the abolitionists were "made up of vinegar, aqua fortis and oil of vitriol with brimstone, saltpeter and charcoal to explode and scatter corrosive matter." In fact, Mrs. Stowe was an onlooker rather than an active protagonist in the slavery battle until she returned to New England. Calvin Stowe was appointed to a professorship at Bowdoin College in Maine, and there his family was transplanted in 1850.

All New England was then seething with indignation over passage of the Fugitive Slave Law, and especially over incidents connected with the law's enforcement in Boston. Under the law's provisions, southern slave-owners could pursue escaped slaves into free states, and officials in those states were required to aid them in recovering their property. Negroes who had long been legally free were rounded up and returned to their former masters, and their families were frequently broken up in the process.

A letter reached Harriet Stowe from her sister-in-law, Mrs. Edward Beecher, who implored her to "write something that would make a whole nation feel what an accursed thing slavery is." According to Stowe family tradition, Mrs. Stowe at that moment resolved that "God helping me, I will write something. I will if I live." Meanwhile, one brother, Edward, was thundering against slavery from a Boston church, and another brother, Henry Ward, was holding spectacular auctions of slaves in his Brooklyn church, to redeem them from servitude.

The first portion of *Uncle Tom's Cabin* to be composed was the climax describing Tom's death. While attending church in

Brunswick during a communion service, Mrs. Stowe related, the entire scene unrolled in her mind's eye. The same afternoon, she went to her room, locked the door and wrote out her vision. She ran out of writing paper, but used scraps of brown wrapping paper to complete her story. Subsequently, this account formed the chapter entitled "The Martyr" in *Uncle Tom's Cabin*. It was read to her children and husband, all of whom were deeply affected. Calvin Stowe is said to have exclaimed, "Hattie, this is the climax of that story of slavery which you promised sister Isabel you would write. Begin at the beginning and work up to this and you'll have your book."

After a few weeks, Harriet Stowe wrote Gamaliel Bailey, editor of the *National Era*, an abolition paper published in Washington, D.C. Bailey had known the Beecher family in Cincinnati, where he had edited another antislavery journal, the *Philanthropist,* until driven out by mob violence. In her letter Mrs. Stowe reported that she was planning to write a story called *Uncle Tom's Cabin*, or *The Man That Was a Thing* (a subtitle later changed to *Life Among the Lowly*), in serial form to run to three or four numbers. Bailey offered her three hundred dollars for publication rights and the *National Era* began serialization in June, 1851.

A work which Mrs. Stowe had expected to finish in a month stretched on interminably. Scenes, incidents, characters, and conversations stored up in her memory from past experiences or reading came crowding in, while her powers of imagination and invention were at white heat. The weekly installments ran on for nearly a year before the weary author was able to bring the book to an end. Afterwards, she insisted that "the Lord Himself wrote it. I was but an instrument in his hand."

The essential plot of *Uncle Tom's Cabin* is not complex, though it involves many characters. In the opening scene, a benevolent Kentucky slave-owner, Mr. Shelby, in order to pay his debts, is compelled to sell some of his best slaves, including Uncle Tom, to a New Orleans slave-dealer named Haley. Overhearing a conversation between Shelby and Haley, a mulatto girl named Eliza learns that her child Harry is also to be sold. During the night she flees with the boy across the frozen Ohio River, and seeks freedom in Canada. Her husband, George Harris, a slave on a nearby plantation, also escapes and follows her.

Eventually, after many adventures with pursuing slave-catchers, but aided by Quakers and other sympathetic whites along the way, they reach Canada and later Africa.

Uncle Tom is less fortunate. To avoid embarrassing his master, he refuses to run away, and is separated from his wife and children. On the trip down the Mississippi to New Orleans, Tom saves the life of little Eva, and in gratitude her father, St. Clare, buys him from the dealer. The next two years are pleasant ones for Tom as a servant in St. Clare's elegant New Orleans home, with the saintly child Eva, and her impish little Negro companion, Topsy. Then Eva dies, and, in her memory, St. Clare makes plans to free Tom and his other slaves. But St. Clare is accidentally killed trying to separate two quarreling men, and Mrs. St. Clare orders Tom sent to the slave market. Tom is bought at public auction by a brutal, drunken Red River planter named Simon Legree. Despite impeccable behavior and all efforts to please his cruel master, Tom soon incurs Legree's hatred, and is frequently beaten. Two female slaves, Cassy and Emmeline, decide to make their escape from the plantation and go into hiding. Legree accuses Tom of aiding them, and he suspects Tom of knowing where they are hidden. When Tom refuses to reveal any information, Legree has him flogged into insensibility. A couple of days later, young George Shelby, son of Tom's former owner, arrives to redeem Tom. It is too late. The effects of his vicious beating are mortal and Tom dies. After knocking Legree down, George Shelby returns to Kentucky and frees all of his slaves in the name of Uncle Tom, resolved to devote his future to the cause of abolition.

Though the *National Era*'s circulation was not large, *Uncle Tom's Cabin* won an enthusiastic and zealous following within a few months after publication in 1852. Before the last chapter of the serial appeared, the whole work was published in book form. The small publishing firm of John P. Jewett, in Boston, undertook the work with considerable trepidation, because of its length, its woman author, and its unpopular subject. To hedge against possible financial loss, Jewett offered the Stowes fifty per cent of the profits, in exchange for paying one-half the production costs. Instead, the Stowes elected to receive straight ten per cent royalties on copies sold—a decision that cost them a fortune.

Neither the author nor the publisher was optimistic about *Uncle Tom's* success. Mrs. Stowe expressed the hope that the book would bring in enough to buy her a new silk dress. The original edition was 5,000 copies in two volumes, with a woodcut of a Negro cabin as a frontispiece.

On the day of publication 3,000 copies were sold, the balance went the second day, while orders poured in. Within a week, 10,000 copies had been bought, and over 300,000 by the end of the first year in the United States alone. Eight power presses were running night and day to meet the demand, three paper mills were trying to supply the necessary paper, and still the publisher was "thousands of copies behind orders." Apparently the book was read by every reasonably literate person in the country.

The popularity of *Uncle Tom's Cabin* abroad was immense. A young employee of Putnam's sent a copy to an English publisher, receiving five pounds for his trouble. Pirated editions proliferated, since international copyright protection was lacking. Soon there were eighteen English publishing houses supplying the demand with forty different editions. Within a year it is estimated that a million and a half copies were sold in Great Britain and the colonies, from none of which did Mrs. Stowe receive any royalty. Simultaneously, continental European publishers were busy reaping the golden harvest. Eventually, the book was translated into at least twenty-two languages, and was as phenomenally successful in France, Germany, Sweden, Holland, and other countries as it had been in English-speaking nations.

Furthermore, the novel was promptly dramatized and became one of the most popular plays ever produced on the American stage. Innumerable versions put on by countless theatrical troupes have toured the world during the past century. Again, Mrs. Stowe gained nothing financially, for the copyright law prevailing in 1852 gave her no control over dramatizations. As a matter of fact, she disapproved of the theater, and refused requested permission for her book to be made into a play.

Altogether, the astounding record of publication of *Uncle Tom's Cabin* surpasses anything in the annals of modern publishing. Only the Bible is believed to have beaten the novel's record. In fictional, dramatic, poetical, and musical form it became the property of millions, and circulated round the globe.

The impact of *Uncle Tom's Cabin* on contemporary opinion and passions was as striking as its huge sales. Mrs. Stowe's son and grandson later described its reception as "like the kindling of mighty conflagration, the sky was all aglow with the resistless tide of emotion that swept all before it and even crossed the broad ocean, till it seemed as if the whole world scarcely thought or talked of anything else."

From the South a storm of wrath, denials, and vituperation descended upon Uncle Tom's author. Soon her name was bracketed with the Prince of Evil. Newspapers carried columns of detailed criticism, designed to expose errors and fallacies in Mrs. Stowe's depiction of slavery. Typical of the comments was the *Southern Literary Messenger's* declaration that the book was a "criminal prostitution of the high functions of the imagination," and by her guilt as its author, Mrs. Stowe "placed herself without the pale of kindly treatment at the hands of Southern criticism." Thousands of angry and abusive letters came to Mrs. Stowe personally. At the beginning, *Uncle Tom's Cabin* circulated freely in the South, but after the bitter reaction, possession of a copy in that area became dangerous.

Ironically, Mrs. Stowe had hoped and believed that her novel might be a means of peacefully resolving the prolonged slavery dispute. After reading it, a southern friend had written her, "Your book is going to be the great pacificator; it will unite North and South." In *Uncle Tom's Cabin* Mrs. Stowe attempted to present fairly both sides of the slavery controversy—the picturesque and patriarchal on the one hand, the cruel and sinister on the other. Two slaveholders depicted in the book, Mr. Shelby and Augustine St. Clare, are southern gentlemen of peerless virtue. Little Eva, St. Clare's daughter, is probably the most angelic child in all literature. The arch-villain Simon Legree is a renegade Vermonter, and much of the book's comedy is provided by two other New Englanders, Miss Ophelia and Marks. Mrs. Stowe made it crystal clear that the Northerners had little understanding of the Negro in the concrete, however much they might sympathize with him in the abstract.

But these concessions were insufficient to appease southern resentment. From every side violent attacks continued and Mrs. Stowe was accused of falsifying facts. It was pointed out, for example, that the southern laws were as stringent against the murder of slaves as of whites, and statutes usually forbade the separation of children below the age of ten from their mothers. Also, slaves as property were too valuable to be seriously mistreated.

In the North, *Uncle Tom's Cabin* received a mixed reception.

Even some who disliked slavery condemned the book because they feared it would stir up civil strife. Northern investors in the southern cotton business censured it for fear it would endanger their investments. Their point of view was expressed by the New York *Journal of Commerce* in a scathing editorial questioning Mrs. Stowe's veracity. Generally, however, *Uncle Tom's Cabin* was accepted by northern readers as a just indictment of the slavery system. As nothing else had done, the novel aroused the national conscience and humanitarian instincts. Its strong religious overtones drove home the argument that slavery dealt in human souls.

One of the immediate effects of *Uncle Tom's Cabin* was to make impossible the enforcement of the Fugitive Slave Law. Outside the South, noncooperation with the law was virtually unanimous. More important, the book whipped up an enormous volume of antislavery sentiment and perhaps made inevitable the outbreak of the Civil War. Certainly it was a major catalyst in that catastrophic conflict, as Abraham Lincoln recognized when he greeted Mrs. Stowe, on her visit to the White House in 1862, as "the little lady who wrote the book that made this big war." Charles Sumner remarked, incidentally, that "if *Uncle Tom's Cabin* had not been written, Abraham Lincoln could not have been elected President of the United States."

The literary merits of *Uncle Tom's Cabin* received only cursory attention at first, though they have been much debated among later critics. The historian James Ford Rhodes noted that "the style is commonplace, the language is often trite and inelegant, sometimes degenerating into slang; and the humor is strained." A southern critic, Stark Young, discussing Mrs. Stowe's use of Negro dialect, says, "She has seen plenty of blacks but cannot make them talk. Her ear is impossible; she has no sense of their rhythm or vividness." Van Wyck Brooks refers to the book's "obvious blemishes of structure and sentimentalism," despite which he characterizes it as "a great human document." Another modern commentator, Katharine Anthony, believes that *Uncle Tom's Cabin*, "As a romance and a picture of American manners . . . undoubtedly deserves high rank. Mrs. Stowe apparently had a fondness for the South. While she hated it for being on the side of slavery, she portrayed its atmosphere with fire and sympathy. She was the first American writer to take the Negro seriously and to conceive a novel with a black man as the hero. Although it was written with a moral purpose, the author forgot the purpose sometimes in the joy of telling her tale." But from a historical point of view, of course, the great significance of the novel is as a sociological document rather than as a literary classic or work of art. Certainly it is more than merely a story, as one caustic pen described it, "spattered with murder, lust, illicit love, suicide, sadistic torture, profanity, drunkenness, and barroom brawls."

Uncle Tom's Cabin at once made Mrs. Stowe an international celebrity. The year after the novel's publication, she made the first of three trips abroad, visiting England and Scotland. There she met and was entertained by hundreds of the nobility, royalty, and other eminent persons, among them Queen Victoria, Prince Albert, Dickens, George Eliot, Kingsley, Ruskin, Macaulay, and Gladstone. On her triumphal tour, she was received with like acclaim by the common people, who saw in her the champion of the underdog. In Edinburgh, she was presented with a national penny offering, amounting to 1,000 gold sovereigns, to help carry on her fight against slavery. Never before or since has an American author created so much excitement or been so applauded in the British Isles.

In an attempt to prove that the picture of slavery drawn in her book was not exaggerated or "a tissue of lies," as some charged, Mrs. Stowe compiled *A Key to Uncle Tom's Cabin*, which she said "will contain all the original facts, anecdotes, and documents upon which the story is founded, with some very interesting and affecting stories parallel to those of *Uncle Tom*." The work is divided into four parts. It begins with an explanation of the characters, to prove that they were true to life. The second part relates to slave laws, showing that existing statutes did not protect the slave. Then follows a narration of the experiences of individual slaves, the failure of public opinion to protect the slave, and a discussion of the demoralizing effect of slavery upon free labor in the South. Finally, there is a strong indictment of the churches for their divided and ineffectual stand on slavery.

The *Key* had the weakness and serious shortcoming that its materials had been collected after *Uncle Tom's Cabin* was written, and much of it was based on hearsay; it was not a popular success, and added little strength to the novel's condemnation of slavery. As an instance of poetic justice, the English publisher who had originally pirated *Uncle Tom's Cabin* printed 50,000 copies of the *Key*, anticipating another bonanza, and proceeded into bankruptcy.

Only one other work on slavery came from Mrs. Stowe's prolific pen. This was the novel, *Dred, a Tale of the Great Dismal Swamp*, published in 1856. In four weeks 100,000 copies were sold, though *Dred* never approached the popularity of *Uncle Tom's Cabin*. In *Dred*, the author's theme was the evil effects of the slave system upon the white man—both the owner and the poor white squatter. Miscegenation between the two races and its dire results for all the characters involved were dramatized. *Dred* is rich in sketches of poor whites, revivalist preachers, and plantation life, but there is no one central character, such as Uncle Tom, to win one's sympathy.

Henceforth, for the remainder of her long life of eighty-five years, Mrs. Stowe produced an endless flow of novels, stories, biographies, articles, and religious essays. For nearly thirty years she averaged a book annually, but the subject of slavery was largely abandoned. During the Civil War, her principal contribution was an open letter to the women of England, reminding them of their overwhelmingly favorable response to *Uncle Tom's Cabin* eight or nine years earlier, and reproaching them for pro-southern sentiment and actions after the outbreak of the war. As a result, mass meetings were held throughout the British Isles, helping to change English ruling opinion toward the Union cause. Hence, Mrs. Stowe's letter may have played an important part in preventing English interference at a time when it could have endangered the northern side.

In estimating Harriet Beecher Stowe's place in history, Kirk Monroe declared, "Not only does she stand in the foremost rank of famous women of the world, but, in shaping the destiny of the American people at a most critical period of their history, her influence was probably greater than that of any other individual. . . . Of course, the abolition of slavery was not, and could not be, accomplished by any one person," Monroe pointed out, as he reviewed the elements that had brought final victory, but "the greatest and most far-reaching of all these influences was that of *Uncle Tom's Cabin*."

Perhaps as nearly a definitive evaluation of *Uncle Tom's Cabin* as is possible after the lapse of a century was made by another woman author, Constance Rourke, in her *Trumpets of Jubilee:*

Battered though it has become through an overplus of excitement which has attended its career, defective though it is in certain essentials, it still has qualities which lift it above its contemporary position as a tract, qualities which should dismiss the easy, usual charge of exaggeration. Obviously the book lacks a genuine realism; but perhaps it should not be judged as realism at all. Obviously it lacks the hardiness and purity of view which belong to great writing; its emotion is never free, but intensive, indrawn, morbid, sentimental if one chooses, running an unchecked course which seemed created by hysteria. But the unbroken force of that emotion produced breadth; in its expansions and uncalculated balances, its flowing absorption in large sequences of action and its loose combinations of interwoven fates, the story at least brings to mind what is meant by the epical scale; it has above all that affecting movement toward unknown goals over long distances which becomes the irrestible theme of the greater narrative, rendered here with pathos because the adventure is never free, but always curtailed or fatefully driven.

"Removed from the atmosphere in which it was written," as Van Wyck Brooks asserted, "*Uncle Tom's Cabin* remained a great folk-picture of an age and a nation."

16

PROPHET OF THE PROLETARIAT

Karl Marx: Das Kapital

In his funeral eulogy for Karl Marx, Friedrich Engels concluded that "Marx was above all a revolutionary, and his great aim in life was to cooperate in this or that fashion in the overthrow of capitalist society and the State institutions which it has created." In these words, Marx's collaborator, disciple, and closest friend succinctly summed up the moving force in the famous social rebel's career.

It was a tumultuous age into which Marx was born. Revolt and unrest were in the air. The memory of one French Revolution was fresh, and another was imminent. The following decades were to be marked by widespread popular bitterness and discontent, and criticisms of existing institutions. By 1848, this mood had built up to explosive force, and revolutions erupted throughout Europe. Even in England, the Chartist Movement threatened established government. Pressure for the alleviation of abuses resulting from the new industrialism, and for abolition of the last vestiges of feudalism was everywhere felt. The times were perfectly adapted to Karl Marx's nonconformist temperament and subversive ideas.

Marx was born in 1818 at Trier in the German Rhineland, the son of a prosperous lawyer. On both sides of the family, Karl was descended from rabbinic ancestors, but while he was still a child, the entire family was converted to Christianity. For the remainder of his life, perhaps in reaction against the handicaps imposed by his racial background, Marx was anti-Semitic in his outlook.

Young Marx studied law and philosophy at Bonn and Berlin,

with the ultimate ambition of achieving a professorship. His increasingly unorthodox opinions, however, closed the door to him, and he turned to journalism. A new periodical, the *Rheinische Zeitung*, was being started in 1842, and Marx became first a contributor, and within a short time the editor. Attacks on the Prussian government and the paper's generally radical tone caused its suppression after only a little more than a year.

Marx moved on to Paris to study socialism and to write for another short-lived journal, the *Franco-German Year Books*. There he became acquainted with leading representatives of socialist and communist thought. The most important event of the period, from the standpoint of Marx's future career, was the beginning of his lifelong friendship with Friedrich Engels. A fellow German, Engels was relatively wealthy, the son of a cotton manufacturer, and as devoted to socialist ideals as Marx himself. The foundation for Marx's later *Das Kapital* was laid by Engels in 1845 with the publication of his *Condition of the Working Classes in England*.

Marx's continued agitation against the Prussian government caused the French authorities to expel him as an undesirable alien. He took refuge in Brussels for three years, and then went back to Germany briefly. Exiled again, he returned to Paris during the revolution of 1848. In that year, in collaboration with Engels, he wrote and published the celebrated *Communist Manifesto*. One of the most violent and influential pieces of radical literature ever printed, the pamphlet concludes with the stirring slogan:

The communists consider it superfluous to conceal their opinions and their intentions. They openly declare that their aims can only be achieved by the violent overthrow of the whole contemporary social order. Let the governing classes tremble before the communistic revolution. The workers have nothing to lose but their chains. They have the whole world to gain. Workers of the world, unite!

Wherever Marx went, he was an active and aggressive agitator, organizing workers' movements, editing Communist papers, and instigating rebellion.

The collapse of the European revolutions of 1848-49 made the continent too small to hold Marx. He emigrated to England in the summer of 1849, at the age of thirty-one, and spent the remainder of his life in London. Earlier, he had married Jenny von Westfalen, daughter of a Prussian official, and she remained for nearly forty years his faithful partner, sharing with him a period of incredible poverty, privation, and misfortune. Of their six children, only three survived to grow up, and of the three, two in later life committed suicide. Unquestionably, these years of extreme hardship colored Marx's views and account for much of the rancor and bitterness in his writings. Only frequent financial aid from Friedrich Engels saved the Marx family from actual starvation. Marx's only earned income was a guinea a week, received from the New York *Tribune* for a letter on European affairs, and intermittent pay for jobs of hack writing.

Despite the misery, importunate debtors, sickness, and want with which he was constantly surrounded in the drab Soho district of London where he settled, Marx was as indefatigable as ever in his promotion of socialistic causes. Year after year, often for as much as sixteen hours a day, he went to the British Museum to accumulate the enormous mass of material for the work eventually to be titled *Das Kapital*. Discounting interruptions caused by other activities and illness, the book was over eighteen years in preparation. Engels, who was supporting the Marx family in the meanwhile, was hopeless that it would ever be completed. "The day the manuscript goes to press I shall get gloriously drunk," he said. Both he and Marx referred to it as "the damned book," and Marx admitted that it was "a perfect nightmare."

A major event in Marx's life during these years was the foundation, in 1864, of the International Working Men's Association, now known as the First International. This was an effort to bring the working classes of the world together into international association. Though retiring in public, Marx was the power behind the throne, and wrote most of the association's documents, addresses, rules, and program. Internal quarrels and rivalry for the leadership, together with the disrepute into which the organization fell after the collapse of the Paris Commune in 1871, led to its dissolution. Subsequently, it was succeeded by the Second International, representing western socialist groups, and the Third International, or Comintern, of the communist world.

The prolonged period of gestation for *Das Kapital* finally drew to a close. Late in 1866, the completed manuscript of volume one was sent to Hamburg, and in the fall of the following year, the printed work came off the press. It was written in German, and no English translation was available until about twenty years later. The first rendering into another language—appropriately, in the light of future events—was a Russian edition in 1872.

In Marx's day, England was the prime exhibit of the workings of the capitalist system. Examples to illustrate his economic theories were accordingly drawn almost entirely from that country. Horrible instances were plentiful, for the institution of capitalism in the mid-Victorian period was at its worst. Social conditions in factory communities were indescribably bad. Basing his findings upon official reports of government inspectors, Marx presented the facts accurately in *Capital*—to use the English title. Women pulled canal boats along the towpath with ropes over their shoulders. Women were harnessed, like beasts of burden, to cars pulling coal out of British mines. Children began to work in the textile mills when they were nine or ten years old, and labored twelve to fifteen hours a day. As the practice of night shifts came into vogue the beds in which the children slept were said never to get cold, for they were used in shifts. Tuberculosis and other occupational diseases killed them off at a high rate.

Protests over the terrible conditions were by no means limited to Marx. Such warm-hearted humanitarians as Charles Dickens, John Ruskin, and Thomas Carlyle wrote voluminously and at white heat, demanding reforms. Parliament was being aroused to corrective legislation.

Marx took much pride in his "scientific" approach to economic and social problems. As Engels said, "Just as Darwin discovered the law of evolution in organic nature, so Marx discovered the law of evolution in human history." Economic phenomena, stated Marx, "can be watched and recorded with the precision proper to natural science." Frequently he refers to the work of biologists, chemists, and physicists, and it was clear that he aspired to become the Darwin of sociology or perhaps the Newton of economics. By the scientific analysis of society, Marx believed he had discovered how to transform a capitalistic into a socialistic world.

Marx's "scientific" method contributed immensely to his wide acceptance, for the concept of evolution in all fields had caught the nineteenth-century imagination. By tying his class-struggle theory of history to Darwin's theory of evolution, Marx gave his ideas respectability and, at the same time, he believed, made them irrefutable.

In the view of Marx and his followers, his profoundest contribution to the study of economics, history, and other social sciences was the development of a principle called "dialectical materialism," an abstruse, ambiguous term. Though more fully explained in his earlier writings, the theory is applied in detail in *Capital*.

The dialectic method was taken over by Marx from the German philosopher Hegel. In essence, it maintains that everything in the world is in a constant state of change. Progress is achieved by the reaction of opposing forces on each other. Thus, for example, the English colonial system opposed by the American Revolution produced the United States. As Harold Laski phrased it, "The law of life is the warring of contradictions, with growth as its consequence."

This premise led Marx to the formulation of his theory of historical materialism, or the economic interpretation of history. "The history of all existing society," argued Marx and Engels, "is the history of class struggles. Freeman and slave, patrician and plebeian, lord and serf, guildmaster and journeyman, in a word, oppressor and oppressed, stood in sharp opposition each to the other. They carried on perpetual warfare." In his eulogy of Marx, Engels elaborated further:

He discovered the simple fact, heretofore hidden beneath ideological overgrowths, that human beings must have food and drink, clothing and shelter, first of all, before they can interest themselves in politics, science, art, religion and the like. This implies that the production of the immediately requisite material means of subsistence, and therewith the extant economic developmental phase of a nation or an epoch, constitutes the foundation upon which the State institutions, the legal outlooks, the artistic and even the religious ideas, of those concerned, have been built up.

In brief, the struggle for food and shelter are omnipotent, determining everything else in human affairs.

The history of mankind, according to Marx, is primarily the story of the exploitation of one class by another. In prehistoric ages, there was a tribal or classless type of society. But in historic times, Marx argued, classes had grown up, and the masses of the human population had become, first, slaves, then serfs (the feudal state), and next propertyless wage slaves (the capitalistic era). Applying the theory of dialectical materialism, Marx was convinced that the inevitable further step was a revolt of the workers and "the dictatorship of the proletariat," followed by communal ownership and a return to a classless social organization.

In *Capital*, Marx developed his case against the capitalist system, to demonstrate why, in his estimation, its eventual destruction and disappearance were inescapable. Here he propounded what communists generally regard as his second most important contribution to social science, the theory of labor value. Nor was this an original theory with Marx. Following such older economists as Adam Smith and David Ricardo, he asserted that labor is the source of all value. Marx quoted Benjamin Franklin, who, a century earlier, had remarked that "trade in general being nothing else but the exchange of labor for labor, the value of all things is most justly measured by labor." From Smith he took the definition of capital as "a certain amount of labour amassed and kept in reserve." Ricardo had likewise suggested that the value and price of any commodity should be determined by the amount of labor that goes into it.

Using this as a criterion, Marx developed his theory of "surplus value," first stated in his *Critique of Political Economy* (1859), and in revised form in *Capital*. The worker, lacking property, had only one commodity to sell—his own labor, and to avoid starvation, he must sell it. Given the existing economic system, the employer would purchase the commodity at the lowest possible price. Hence the actual value of the labor was invariably in excess of wages paid. A workingman paid a wage of four shillings a day actually earned that sum in some six hours, but was required to work ten hours. The extra four hours, therefore, were stolen from the worker by the capitalist. So interpreted, profit, interest, and rent were derived entirely from the surplus value of labor's toil, of which the workers have been robbed. It might logically be concluded then, that the capitalist system is nothing more than an evil scheme set up to exploit and to rob the working class.

Though Marx's theories of value and surplus value have been invaluable for purposes of propaganda and agitation, economists generally now consider them invalid and discredited. One of the factors that caused their rejection was the increased use of machinery, which brought about great variations in the amount of labor needed for various commodities. Freehof pointed out that "the chemist will make one discovery with regard to soil fertility and will multiply a hundred fold the productivity of ten million farm laborers. It was the chemist who created the productivity." Also in refutation of the theory, another critic suggested that "Men dive for pearls because they are valuable; pearls are not valuable because men dive for them." Marx does not acknowledge that science, technology, art, or organization add anything to values and prices.

As a matter of fact, economists have never agreed on a method of measuring value, despite two centuries of meditating and writing upon the subject. Demand and utility seem to be the most widely accepted criteria. As Barzun commented, modern economics "has destroyed Marx's theory, but has not replaced it by a tested, 'scientific' one."

His surplus value theory led Marx to the next steps in his thesis. In order to meet fierce competition, each capitalist tries to extract more and more surplus value from the workers by such devices as lengthening hours, or reducing wages, or using the "stretch-out." He introduces more and more machinery to eliminate labor and speed up production. By utilizing machinery which requires less physical strength to operate, men can be replaced by the cheaper labor of women and children. The consequences are thus described by Marx:

> They mutilate the laborer into a fragment of a man, degrade him to the level of an appendage of a machine, destroy every remnant of charm in his work and turn it into a hated toil; they estrange from him the intellectual potentialities of the labor process in the same proportion as science is incorporated in it as an independent power; they distort the conditions under which he works, subject him during the labor process to a despotism the more hateful for its meanness; they transform his lifetime into working time, and drag his wife and child beneath the wheels of the Juggernaut of capital.

So, Marx insists, the installation of machinery to speed up and to increase production not only fails to ease the worker's lot, but has such deleterious effects as causing unemployment (machines displacing men), the exploitation of women and children, overproduction of commodities, and killing the worker's interest in his job. Marx goes on to state:

> Machinery is the most powerful weapon for repressing strikes, those periodical revolts of the working class against the autocracy of capital. The steam engine was from the very first an antagonist that

enabled the capitalist to tread under foot the growing claims of the workmen, who threatened the newly born factory system with a crisis. It would be possible to write quite a history of the inventions made since 1830, for the sole purpose of supplying capital with weapons against the revolts of the working class.

Giving the Malthusian theory a special twist, Marx says that overpopulation always follows in the path of capitalism. The system needs an "industrial reserve army" for periods of great production expansion, when new industries are being created or old ones revived. In the nature of things, the surplus labor force must endure prolonged periods of unemployment. Then appears capitalism's greatest curse: depressions and panics. Since the workers are paid bare subsistence wages, they are unable to buy all the goods the factories pour forth, markets become glutted, the labor force is reduced, and severe depressions ensue.

Seeking outlets for his overstocked warehouses, the capitalist next turns to foreign fields, and tries to find markets in backward countries abroad to unload the commodities his own workers cannot afford to purchase. This endeavor and the search for raw materials to keep the factories operating inexorably lead to international conflicts and imperialistic wars.

The ultimate outcome of capitalist strife and turmoil, Marx believed, is increased concentration and monopoly, for "one capitalist always kills many." The middle class would disappear, as small capitalists were swallowed up by the larger ones. Finally, there would remain only a handful of great capitalists confronting the proletarian multitude. When that time came, the proletariat would have its opportunity. One of the most vivid and memorable passages in *Capital* describes the steps leading up to the denouement:

While there is a progressive diminution in the number of capitalist magnates, there occurs a corresponding increase in the mass of poverty, oppression, enslavement, degeneration, and exploitation. But at the same time there is a steady intensification of the wrath of the working class—a class which grows ever more numerous, and is disciplined, unified, and organized by the very mechanism of the capitalist method of production. Capitalist monopoly becomes a fetter on the method of production which has flourished with it and under it. The centralization of the means of production and the socialization of labor reach a point where they prove incompatible with their capitalist husk. This bursts asunder. The knell of capitalist private property sounds. The expropriators are expropriated.

The class struggle would end with the triumph of the proletariat. Having captured the state, the proletariat would establish its dictatorship. This stage, however, Marx prophesied, "is but the transition to the abolition of all classes and to the creation of a society of the free and equal." How long it would be necessary for the period of dictatorship to continue is not specified—a point of considerable interest in view of Soviet Russia's more than sixty years under an iron-handed authoritarian regime which shows no sign of relaxing its grip. In fact, Marx is extremely vague in describing the nature of his classless society. After the state had carried out its role of education and organization, government would "wither away." There would be no force or struggle, peace and plenty would prevail for everyone. The chief aim of society would be "the full and free development of every individual," and the guiding principle would be "From each according to his abilities, to each according to his needs!"

The inconsistency and glaring contrast of this beautiful dream of utopia with the preceding period of bloody, ruthless class warfare has been commented upon by numerous critics. In any case, as John Hallett wrote:

The "class-less society" of Marx is as dull as the heaven of the orthodox Victorian; and it inspires as little credence and as little enthusiasm. Once the world revolution has been relegated to the background, it is difficult to find in the dry bones of Marxism anything to stir men's passions or steel them to fresh endurance or fresh endeavour.

Nevertheless, Marxism has all the force of a religion to millions of devout Communists. Dialectical materialism serves as a creed to supersede all other faiths. The older religions, such as Christianity, declared Marx, teach a passive acceptance of one's lot in life, glorifying resignation, meekness, and humility. They act, therefore, as "the opium of the people," blinding the proletariat to its destiny and placing major obstacles on the road to revolution.

How much truth is there in Marx? This is a question that has occupied innumerable social scientists, theologians, and other writers and thinkers for the past century. In many essentials, time has shown fundamental errors in his theories and predictions. No non-Marxian economist any longer takes seriously his labor theories of value and surplus value, a foundation piece in

Marx's thought. In no country has there developed the conflict of classes, leading to proletarian revolution, prophesied by Marx. A well-known Marxist, Sidney Hook, emphasized that this doctrine, too, is basic to the Communist creed, for he wrote, "If the facts of the class struggle can be successfully called into question, the whole theoretical structure of Marx crashes to the ground."

The capitalistic system has followed an entirely different course, at least in the most enlightened nations, from that forecast by Marx. Instead of increased misery, poverty, and suffering among the working class, the reverse has occurred. Strong labor unions and government regulation have arisen to hold the excesses of capitalist competition and enterprise in check. Despite Marx's contempt for the "economists, philanthropists, humanitarians, improvers of the condition of the working class, organizers of charity, members of societies for the prevention of cruelty to animals, temperance fanatics, hole-and-corner reformers of every imaginable kind," such people have succeeded in eliminating the worst evils of capitalism, and made the system work with as much smoothness as could reasonably be expected in any exceedingly complex man-made institution. As a recent report of the Twentieth Century Fund commented: "Of all the great industrial nations, the one that has clung the most tenaciously to private capitalism has come closest to the socialist goal of providing an abundance to all in a classless society, a level of material well-being which is beyond even the comprehension of the vast majority of the world's people."

Marx pinned strong hopes on weakening national ties among the "proletariat," aiming to substitute for them a sense of international solidarity among the workers everywhere. Failure to achieve this perhaps desirable goal has been demonstrated in two world wars and by the nationalistic fervor characteristic of the current world scene—nowhere more evident than in Russia, China, and other Communist areas. In Marx's judgment, the proletarian revolution would occur first in the most highly industrialized nations, e.g., England, Germany, and the United States, while Russia was least ripe for revolt—another prediction not borne out by subsequent events.

The dialectic method used by Marx has had considerable weight with later historians, though, as William Henry Chamberlin commented:

Marx's method of historical materialism fails to account for the obvious differences between peoples which are in the same stage of economic development. It leaves out of account such vital factors as race, religion, and nationality. It does not reckon with the immense importance of human personality. It is doubtful whether a single historical event could be correctly interpreted in terms of this theory.

Nevertheless, while recognizing the fallacies in Marx's thought, it would still be difficult to overestimate his impact on our times. In certain important respects, his influence on the capitalistic world has been beneficial. By emphasizing the abuses of the industrial system and playing up the danger of a workers' revolution, fundamental reforms have been effected. In short, the constant reiteration by Communists and Socialists of capitalist shortcomings has forced the correction of many of those evils, and thereby vastly diminished, if not eliminated, the likelihood of the proletarian revolt prophesied by Marx.

But it is the consequences of Marxism's conquest of Russia, China, and other vast areas, bringing a combined population of more than a billion under its sway, that have posed the most urgent problems for the modern world. Ironically, Marx had great scorn for Russians in general and for Russian revolutionaries in particular. His conclusions regarding the Tsarist rule of his day are singularly apt for Communist Russia: "The policy of Russia is changeless. Its methods, its tactics, its maneuvers may change, but the pole star of its policy—world domination—is a fixed star."

Actually, present-day Russia fulfills few of Marx's ideas and ideals for communism. As President Truman remarked, in 1950, Russia is not a Communist state nor was Stalin a real Communist. There is, for example, a dictatorship by the Communist party, or rather a hierarchy thereof, rather than a true dictatorship of the proletariat. The political state which, according to Marx, would soon "wither away" becomes more all-powerful with the passage of time. Beginning with Lenin, the Communist leaders have found it easier to preach Marx than to practice him. While continuing to pay lip service to Marxian philosophy, they have modified the dogma inherited from Marx, as political circumstances and expediency seemed to require. Viewing the activities of his disciples, Marx once said, "I am not a Marxist," and it appears probable that he would have had strong doubts about the application of his theories in the twentieth century. A favorite Socialist saying is that "if Marx had lived under Stalin, he would not have lived long."

Only the first volume of "the Bible of the working classes" was published in Marx's lifetime. After his death in 1883, his copious, but incomplete and badly organized notes for volumes two and three were taken over by Engels. The second volume appeared in 1885 and the third in 1894, the year before Engels died. These contain elaborations and applications of the main thesis, dealing with the "circulation of capital" and the "process of capitalist production as a whole." It is upon the first volume, however, that Marx's reputation rests, and the last two volumes are relatively little read. Still another work, *The Theory of Surplus Value*, which was to have formed the fourth volume of *Capital*, was edited from Marx's manuscripts by Karl Kautsky, and published in Germany from 1905 to 1910.

Capital is admittedly hard reading. One critic (Barzun) describes it as "badly written, ill put together, lacking in order, logic, or homogeneity of material." Another (Croce) mentions "the strange composition of the book, the mixture of general theory, of bitter controversy and satire, and of historical illustrations or digressions," and considers the work "unsymmetrical, badly arranged and out of proportion." A third (Standen), while declaring that "the scheme of the three volumes is magnificent on a grand scale," concedes that "the manner of presentation of *Capital* can be irritating, with its long digressions and ponderous slowness."

It is doubtful that any figure in history has inspired more violently contradictory opinions than Karl Marx. There is practically no middle ground between the view which holds him to have been "a diabolically inspired Jew who plotted the downfall of civilization," and the diametrically opposite picture of him as "the lovable saint who selflessly devoted himself to the world's disinherited class of the nineteenth century." One bitter critic has stated that "In the name of human progress, Marx has probably caused more death, misery, degradation and despair than any man who ever lived."

What is the secret, then, of Marx's appeal for and influence and power over millions of the earth's inhabitants? Thomas Patrick Neill has suggested that Marx is "the symbolical leader of the have-nots in their struggle against the haves." Barzun believes that "The strength of Marx is precisely that he shared the feelings of the downtrodden, that the prejudice of equality was in his very liver, and joined to it the ambition and jealousy of power, both ready to destroy the present moral order in the name of a higher which he saw." Another interpretation comes from Harold Laski: "At bottom, the main passion by which he was moved was the passion for justice. He may have hated too strongly, he was jealous and he was proud. But the mainspring of his life was the desire to take from the shoulders of the people the burden by which it was oppressed." Yet another perceptive evaluation comes from Solomon Bennett Freehof, who wrote, "The great constructive gift of Karl Marx to modern society, socialistic and capitalistic alike, is his picture of the inevitability of a society in which poverty and suffering will cease. This ideal has become a challenge to every social system. Even a social system like ours, which rejects his economics, nevertheless accepts that ideal in its own way. Thus, the man who himself lived in misery gave the world the hope for the complete abolition of poverty. This is the accomplishment of Karl Marx. That is the way in which he has changed the mind of the modern world."

17

LEVIATHAN AGAINST ELEPHANT

Alfred T. Mahan: The Influence of Sea Power upon History, 1660-1783

When a contemporary critic described Admiral Alfred T. Mahan's *The Influence of Sea Power upon History* as "an admirable book, but the most incendiary of modern times," he displayed remarkable perception. More than any other individual, Mahan shaped the modern navies of the world. His pen has been termed "mightier than a flotilla," while "the super-dreadnoughts are his children, the roar of the 16-inch guns are but the echoes of his voice." Certainly, the writings of no other historian have exerted such direct and widespread influence as did those of Mahan.

Throughout recorded time, Mahan demonstrated, sea power has been the deciding factor in world dominion. Command of the sea is essential for any nation aspiring to play a major role in world affairs, and to achieve maximum prosperity and security at home. Land powers, without access to the sea, no matter how great, are doomed to eventual collapse and decay, for the land, Mahan pointed out, "is almost all obstacle, the sea almost all open plain." A nation capable of controlling this plain by its naval power and of maintaining a strong merchant marine can exploit the world's wealth.

What manner of man was "the incendiary Mahan"?—perhaps the last person one would select as a revolutionist, unsettler of the status quo, or disturber of the peace. Born in 1840, the son of a professor of military and civil engineering at West Point, and a graduate of Annapolis, Mahan had spent long, monotonous years as a career naval officer, alternating between shore and sea duty. Except for limited action during the American Civil War, he never experienced armed conflict. His perspective was broadened, however, by service in Brazil and the Orient, and by travels in Europe.

Following these travels, another fifteen years went by without distinction, save for a small volume, *The Gulf and Inland Waters,* relating to Civil War naval history, which Mahan was assigned to write in 1883. Then came the break that would establish his fame and bring about a radical change in his future career. Mahan was invited by Admiral Stephen B. Luce to lecture on tactics and naval history at the newly formed War College in Newport, Rhode Island.

Here was exactly the kind of opportunity for which Mahan had been waiting. Never notably successful as a naval officer, bored with naval routine, still only a captain in rank (he was promoted to rear admiral after retirement), the new assignment seemed heaven-sent. He was given a year's freedom for reading and thinking before reporting at Newport; and then in September, 1886, before a small group of officers, he began the series of lectures which was destined to be published in matured form four years later as *The Influence of Sea Power upon History, 1660-1783.*

In a letter to his English publisher, Mahan noted that the term "sea power" was chosen by design for his title "to compel attention and to receive currency. . . . I deliberately discarded the adjective 'maritime' as being too smooth to arrest men's attention or stick in their minds." It is also apparent that the word "power" hit a responsive chord in an age of steam and electricity and power politics. Thus the title, *The Influence of Sea Power,* was selected with care to make a specific impression upon its readers.

This celebrated book, upon which Mahan's reputation primarily rests, is, in essence, a narration and explanation of the rise and progress of British sea power from the middle of the seventeenth century to the close of the Napoleonic wars.

Mahan begins by tracing in broad outline the rise and decline of the great maritime powers, reviewing in some detail the elements necessary for a nation aiming to achieve power at sea. These conditions he reduces in number to six: geographical position, physical conformation (including natural production and climate), extent of territory, number of population, character of the people, and character of the government.

Elaborating upon these "elements of sea power," Mahan showed in each instance how Britain had gained strength over her opponents. According to his interpretation, sea power is far more than naval power, comprising not only a military fleet but commercial shipping and a strong home base. "The history of sea power," wrote Mahan, "while embracing in its broad sweep all that tends to make a people great upon the sea or by the sea, is largely a military history." Nevertheless, he continually emphasized that navies, campaigns, and battles are only a means to an end. Neither a flourishing merchant marine nor a successful navy is possible without the other. National prosperity depends upon the combination.

In considering geographical position, a matter of prime importance, Mahan stressed the vast advantages accruing to a nation so located "that it is neither forced to defend itself by land nor induced to seek extension of its territory by way of the land . . . as compared with a people one of whose boundaries is continental." Examples are England on one side, and France and Holland on the other. Early in her modern history, Holland's strength was exhausted by having to maintain a large army and to carry on wars to preserve her independence. France was weakened by dividing her wealth and man power between building up naval power and projects of continental expansion. Her position was made more vulnerable, also, by fronting on both the ocean and the Mediterranean Sea, preventing her from making use of a united fleet. Its location on two oceans, Mahan pointed out, placed the United States in a similar position of weakness. A central position, with ports near major trade routes and strong bases for operations against potential enemies, is a great strategic asset. Again, England, with her control of the English Channel and North Sea trade routes, was enabled to gain supremacy.

In analyzing his second element, physical conformation, Mahan stated, "The seaboard of a country is one of its frontiers; and the easier the access offered by the frontier to the region beyond, in this case the sea, the greater will be the tendency of a people toward intercourse with the rest of the world by it." Numerous and deep harbors, however, are vital. Because England and Holland had not been generously treated by nature in soil or climate, they perforce took to the sea, while France, endowed with "delightfulness and richness of the land," and the United States, likewise blessed, had fewer inducements to look seaward.

The third and last "natural condition" affecting the development of a nation as a sea power was extent of territory. By this phrase Mahan meant "not the total number of square miles which a country contains, but the length of its coastline and the characters of its harbors." The proportion of the country's population to the extent of its seacoast was also of paramount significance. An illustration is taken from the American Civil War:

Had the South had a people as numerous as it was warlike, and a navy commensurate to its other resources as a sea power, the great extent of its sea coast and its numerous inlets would have been elements of great strength . . . the South not only had no navy, not only was not a seafaring people, but . . . its population was not proportioned to the extent of the seacoast which it had to defend.

After reviewing the three natural conditions affecting sea power, i.e., geographical position, physical conformation, and extent of territory, Mahan turned next to a consideration of the people and their government. Here stress was still placed on the number of population, but a further distinction was made, for "it is not only the grand total, but the number following the sea, or at least readily available for employment on ship-board and for the creation of naval material that must be counted." Historical instances were provided by England and France. The population of France was considerably greater than that of England, but the latter's maritime and commercial orientation and proclivities gave her a decided edge over the predominantly agricultural population of France. Mahan concluded that "a great population following callings related to the sea is, now as formerly, a great element of sea power," and he found the United States deplorably "deficient in that element."

The effect of national character and aptitudes upon the development of sea power was Mahan's fifth point. "Almost without exception," he wrote, history shows that "aptitude for commercial pursuits must be a distinguishing feature of the nations that have at one time or another been great upon the sea." Though the English and Dutch were often contemptuously referred to as "nations of shopkeepers," they gained far more permanent and substantial rewards from their maritime trade than did the gold-seeking Spanish and Portuguese, or the thrifty, hoarding French, unwilling to risk investments in foreign commerce. "The tendency to trade," remarked Mahan, "involving of necessity the production of something to trade with, is the national characteristic most important in the development of sea power."

National genius was marked too, Mahan believed, by the ability to establish healthy colonies. In this respect the British were superior to the French, because "The English colonist naturally and readily settles down in his new country, identifies his interest with it, and though keeping an affectionate remembrance of the home from which he came, has no restless eagerness to return." Neither were the Spanish effective colonizers, because they were primarily concerned with the rapid exploitation of the new country's wealth, rather than with full development of its resources.

Finally, Mahan considers the character of the government and its institutions in relation to the growth of sea power. The form of government and the character of rulers, he believed, "have exercised a very marked influence upon the development of sea power." While preferring the processes of democratic governments, Mahan noted that "despotic power, wielded with judgment and consistency, has created at times a great sea commerce and a brilliant navy with greater directness than can be reached by the slower processes of a free people. The difficulty . . . is to insure perseverance after the death of a particular despot." Because England had reached the greatest height of sea power of any modern nation, a study of government policies there was considered by Mahan to be especially pertinent. For the most part, English government action over several centuries had consistently been directed toward control of the sea. Regardless of the reigning monarch or of political parties, the English recognized the basic importance to the nation of the maintenance of naval supremacy.

After an extended historical review of the actions of various governments as they pertained to the sea careers of their peoples, Mahan decided that government influence works in two ways: first, in times of peace:

The government by its policy can favor the natural growth of a people's industries and its tendencies to seek adventure and gain by way of the sea; or it can try to develop such industries and such sea-going bent, when they do not naturally exist; or, on the other hand, the government may by mistaken action check and fetter the progress which the people left to themselves would make.

Second, in times of war, sea power is determined by the attitude of the government toward creating, equipping, and adequately maintaining "an armed navy, of a size commensurate with the growth of its shipping and the importance of the interest connected with it." Likewise essential was "the maintenance of suitable naval stations, in those distant parts of the world to which armed shipping must follow the peaceful vessels of commerce." The United States, Mahan found, was weak in that it lacked foreign bases of either a colonial or military nature.

Thus having examined and reflected upon the six basic features affecting sea power, Mahan was ready to proceed to a detailed analysis of European naval wars of the period 1660–1783—approximately a century and a quarter. The remainder of his book is devoted to this historical review. For background, Mahan described the general conditions prevailing in Europe in the late seventeenth century, with particular reference to Spain, France, Holland, and England—the nations that were to be principally involved in future struggles for sea power. In Mahan's eyes, the history of Europe during the tumultuous years that followed was largely a contest among the western powers for the control of the sea. Beginning his survey with the Dutch War of Charles II, he emphasized the extent to which England's commercial interests were involved in the War of the Spanish Succession, from which England emerged as a Mediterranean power, holding Gibraltar and Port Mahon. In the Seven Years' War, Wolfe's success was made possible by the fleet, which opened the St. Lawrence River and prevented the arrival of reinforcements from France. The fundamental meaning of sea power was demonstrated again during the American Revolution, when England, with divided naval forces, was unable to cope with the combined might of France and Spain, and the American colonies were thus able to win their freedom.

Mahan's main thesis, recurring throughout his work, is that

as between sea power and land power, a relentless sea blockade has always proved more decisive than an invincible land army.

"In developing the tactical details of the various battles," his leading biographer, Captain W. D. Puleston, commented, "Mahan made every endeavor to be exact. As his examples were taken from the sailing-ship era, he was at pains to familiarize himself with the technique of sailing and the precise meaning of the old sea terms, which even in his midshipman days had been falling into disuse." In his autobiography Mahan describes the mechanical means he employed, such as paper ship models, to reproduce and re-enact sea battles under sail.

In *The Influence of Sea Power upon History*, Mahan's principal aim was, as he stated to his former commanding officer, Admiral Luce, "to write a critical *military* history of the naval past, not a chronicle of naval events." He might have added also that one of his objects was to indicate the interrelation of naval and political history, for he was fully convinced that the economic power which went with control of the sea gave its possessor a dominant position in world affairs. "Thus England," as Pratt remarked, "because she cultivated sea power while her opponents neglected it, was enabled to thwart the overweening schemes of Louis XIV and Napoleon and, as Mahan firmly believed, to rescue civilization from those who would have destroyed it."

The Influence of Sea Power upon History won world recognition immediately after publication—though far greater abroad than in the United States. Within a short time, translations were available in German, Japanese, French, Italian, Russian, and Spanish. Everywhere the book provided effective ammunition for the period of great naval expansion just getting under way, especially in Great Britain, Germany, and America.

As various critics have suggested, a question will always remain as to whether Mahan's work would have had such a tremendous impact if it had appeared in another period or in a different setting. Without doubt, the times were most propitious, and Mahan's dictums on the significance of maritime might fell upon fertile soil, fitting perfectly the belligerent tendencies of the age. The great powers were flexing their biceps for a disastrous naval race and for the acquisition of new colonial possessions. How natural it was then that Mahan should have been so readily accepted as a prophet. His heavily documented proof that command of the sea was a prerequisite for any nation's welfare furnished justification for policies already adopted or under consideration. As one British writer phrased it, his teaching "was as oil to the flame of colonial expansion everywhere leaping into life."

In Britain, critics hailed Mahan's book as "the gospel of England's greatness." Puleston pointed out that "It might have been written to order for the British Cabinet, so clearly did it support all their contentions." One admiral asserted that for the improved position of the British navy after 1900, "We have not to thank either Conservatives or Liberals, but Mahan and no one else." In a tribute to Mahan at the time of his death in 1914, the London *Post* declared that Britain "owes to the great American a debt which can never be repaid, for he was the first elaborately and comprehensively to formulate the philosophy of British sea-power."

These comments will be more readily appreciated when it is realized that at the time Mahan was writing his *Influence of Sea Power upon History* the English navy had gone through a long period of financial neglect, its personnel had been reduced to a skeleton force, and its might was being rapidly outstripped by more modern French and Italian ships. Britain's navy was described by one seaman as "a menagerie of unruly and curiously assorted ships," over two-thirds of them unarmored. Mahan's support for a modernized, powerful English fleet was therefore extremely timely, and greatly accelerated the movement for naval reorganization and strengthening.

English admiration and esteem for Mahan were demonstrated during two visits which he paid to Britain, in 1893 and 1904. He was a guest of honor at state dinners given by Queen Victoria and the prime minister, was the first foreign guest of honor ever entertained by the Army and Navy Club, and both Oxford and Cambridge universities awarded him honorary degrees within a week's time.

But since *The Influence of Sea Power upon History* was not, as one critic suggested it should have been, published in a language intelligible only to Americans and Englishmen, its impact on Germans and Japanese was as forceful as on the British. Kaiser Wilhelm II reported, "I am just now not reading but devouring Captain Mahan's book. It is on board all my ships. . . . Our future lies upon the water; the trident must be in our fist."

Mahan's work became the inspiration for the new German navy. One of his biographers, Taylor, stated, "There is ample evidence that in the last few months of his life Mahan suffered mental distress about the war [World War I] and the part he had played—although entirely unpremeditated—in stimulating the growth of the German Navy."

Likewise in Japan, every captain of a Japanese ship of war was served out a copy of Mahan's book as part of his equipment. The Japanese were eager to learn Western ways, and began an extensive correspondence with Mahan on the building of navies, the size of guns, and other naval matters. An invitation from the Japanese to become their official naval adviser was declined by Mahan. Nevertheless, taking their cue from him, the Japanese set out to become the supreme naval power of the Far East.

Among the leading countries, only the United States, which Mahan was most anxious to influence, was slow to accept his teachings. Mahan was convinced that the United States must enter into vigorous competition with other powers over foreign markets, build a huge navy, acquire naval bases overseas, and expand by acquiring colonies outside the western hemisphere. Hawaii, he contended, should be annexed and used as an American base. The Caribbean, he pointed out further, bore the same relation to America as did the Mediterranean to Europe, and its importance to the United States would be accentuated by completion of the Panama Canal. Throughout *The Influence of Sea Power upon History* the author gave special attention to the United States and noted its potentialities as a sea power. "Mahan had written his book," said Captain Puleston, "to rekindle among his own countrymen their former interest in sea power. He believed Americans had been so engrossed in developing the interior of the continent that they had unnecessarily thrown away a great heritage. He did not want his country to follow the example of France under Louis XIV and become primarily a land power."

Mahan's arguments made two converts in key positions: Theodore Roosevelt and Henry Cabot Lodge. Roosevelt in the White House and Lodge in the Senate became enthusiasts for a great American navy. Roosevelt found a perfect expression of his philosophy of the "big stick" in Mahan's writings, and he used the sea power theories to help him win American public opinion to a policy of expansion across the seas. The influence of Mahan on the huge program of naval construction in the United States, beginning in the eighteen-nineties, is clear and marked.

Following his first great popular success, Mahan's prolific pen poured forth a cascade of books and magazine articles. Volumes of books and collected essays number some twenty, supplemented by scores of periodical contributions. Most significant were additions to his "sea-power series," notably *The Influence of Sea Power upon the French Revolution and Empire, 1793-1812,* regarded by critics as a more thorough and carefully documented work than *The Influence of Sea Power upon History;* biographies of Farragut and Nelson; and *Sea Power in Its Relations to the War of 1812.*

Mahan readily conceded that his ideas of sea power were not original, and he referred, for example, to what Bacon and Raleigh had written three centuries before on the same theme. Much earlier, such ancients as Thucydides, Xerxes, and Themistocles had recognized the importance of the concept. To a greater extent than any previous writer, however, Mahan succeeded in his special approach, which was, in his own words, "an analysis of history, attempting to show from current events, through a long series of years, precisely what influence the command of the sea had had upon definite issues. . . . This field had been left vacant, yielding me my opportunity." Though, as various commentators have suggested, Mahan's view of history was too narrow, ignoring many vital factors, he provided a new outlook on politics and economics.

Granting that Mahan's doctrines were reasonably valid for his own time and for the preceding centuries, have they been made obsolete by the technological advances of the twentieth century? In particular, has the coming of air power, A-bombs, and H-bombs superseded sea power in today's world? Experts are divided in their opinions. In World War II, sea power played an outstanding part, but it had to be closely coordinated with air power for ships unprotected from the air were highly vulnerable. The postwar development of the "hell-bomb" has cast some shadow on the future of navies. One such bomb could conceivably wholly incapacitate a concentrated fleet. However, Soviet Russia's development of a great fleet of submarines and America's emphasis on aircraft carriers and atomic-powered submarines furnish evidence that sea power may still have a place, even in an atomic age.

In the judgment of scholars, Mahan's permanent rank as a historian will not be on a par with his contemporary fame. His preeminent success was as a propagandist. By the time of his death, the United States had reached the goals he had set for it, i.e., the building of a great navy, the construction of the Panama Canal, and the acquisition of bases in the Caribbean and Pacific. He had witnessed the triumph of his philosophy that "Whoever rules the waves rules the world," with the major nations engaged in a mad competition for sea power. As one acute critic observed, "No other single person has so directly and profoundly influenced the naval doctrines and the national policies of so many nations"; while a French naval expert declared that Mahan "profoundly modified in his own lifetime the history of the age in which he lived."

18

HEARTLAND AND WORLD-ISLAND

Sir Halford J. Mackinder: The Geographical Pivot of History

Within little more than a decade after Admiral Mahan had demonstrated, so convincingly and conclusively, the historical invincibility of sea power, the applicability of his doctrine to the future was seriously undermined, if not invalidated, by two new factors. One, in the material realm, was the Wright brothers' first successful experiments in 1903 with a powered airplane. The second, in the realm of ideas, was a scientific paper written in 1904 by an English geographer, Halford Mackinder, later celebrated as "the father of geopolitics."

In neither case did the world recognize immediately the monumental significance of these two events; nevertheless, the face of the globe was to be irretrievably changed by them.

No more improbable setting could be conceived for the dissemination of revolutionary theories than the meeting of the Royal Geographical Society in London, January 25, 1904, at which Mackinder read his famous paper, "The Geographical Pivot of History." Filling only twenty-four printed pages, the work was no more than an ordinary pamphlet in length, but its remarkable analysis of the interrelations of geography and politics, past and present, throughout the world, introduced concepts that subsequently swayed the thinking of political and military leaders, economists, geographers, and historians everywhere.

At the end of World War I, Mackinder developed his argument in considerably expanded detail in *Democratic Ideals and Reality*, though without essential modification of his original thesis. This book and his earlier essay are the foundation stones for the modern "science" of geopolitics—the combination of geography and political science.

Mackinder was forty-three years old when his renowned lecture was delivered. The son of a country doctor, he had been sent to Epsom College in 1874, and from there to Oxford. After a brilliant scholastic record, he became a traveling lecturer on geography for two years for the Oxford University Extension movement. There followed an appointment as Reader in Geography at Oxford, where he attracted hundreds of students by his dynamic teaching methods. Mainly because of his urgings, the Royal Geographical Society financed the establishment of the first British School of Geography at Oxford, in 1899, with Mackinder as its director. In those years he also found time to win fame as a mountain climber, making the first daring ascent of Mt. Kenya in East Africa. Concurrently with his post at Oxford, Mackinder served as a reader in economic geography at the University of London, a position which led to his becoming director of the London School of Economics from 1903 to 1908. Always keenly interested in politics, he was elected to several terms in Parliament, from 1910 to 1922. His entire career, however, was primarily in academic circles, and devoted to promoting the scientific study of geography, especially geography as seen "from the human standpoint."

In "The Geographical Pivot of History," destined to have such wide repercussions, Mackinder first presented his theory of closed space, an idea popularized forty years later by Wendell Willkie in his "One World" slogan. Mackinder believed that "the Columbian epoch," a period of four centuries of geographic exploration and expansion, had ended at the beginning of the twentieth century. "In 400 years," he wrote, "the outline of the map of the world has been completed with approximate accuracy."

Pursuing the same thought in *Democratic Ideals and Democracy*, Mackinder stated:

We have lately attained to the North Pole and found that it is in the midst of a deep sea, and to the South Pole, and have found it upon a high plateau. With these final discoveries the book of the pioneers has been closed. No considerable fertile new land, no important mountain-range, and no first-class river can any more be the reward of adventure. Moreover, the map of the world had hardly been sketched before claims to the political ownership of all the dry land had been pegged out. . . . The missionary, the conqueror, the farmer, the miner, and, of late, the engineer, have followed so closely in the traveller's footsteps that the world, in its remoter borders, has hardly been revealed before we must chronicle its virtually complete political appropriation. In Europe, North America, South America, Africa, and Australasia there is scarcely a region left for the pegging out of a claim of ownership, unless as the result of a war between civilized or half-civilized powers.

In the 1890s, the brilliant American historian, Frederick Jackson Turner, had expressed a similar, though more limited, closed-space concept in his writings on the passing of the frontier and its significance in American history. Now, Mackinder maintained, the frontier had vanished throughout the world. He described the probable effects of his premise.

From the present time forth, in the post-Columbian age, we shall again have to deal with a closed political system, and none the less that it will be one of world-wide scope. Every explosion of social forces, instead of being dissipated in a surrounding circuit of unknown space and barbaric chaos, will be sharply reechoed from the far side of the globe, and weak elements in the political and economic organism of the world will be shattered in consequence. . . . Every shock, every disaster or super-fluity, is now felt even to the antipodes, and may indeed return from the antipodes. . . . Every deed of humanity will henceforth be echoed and reechoed . . . round the world.

In the closed system characteristic of our era, and the almost limitless mobility which has accompanied it, both on land and in the air, the age of dominant sea power, in Mackinder's view, had gone. If this were true, then an age of land power had arrived. Where was the natural center for the new epoch? In the world's greatest land mass, of course; that is, the immense area of Eurasia, termed by Mackinder the "pivot region of the world's politics." Among five maps used to illustrate his essay, the last is entitled "The Natural Seats of Power," and delineates the "pivot area." Mackinder envisaged the geographical pivot as the north and interior of Euro-Asia, extending from the Arctic to the central deserts and westward to the broad isthmus between the Baltic and Black Seas.

According to the historical analysis, with which much of his paper is concerned, Europe and the rest of the world have, for centuries, been under constant pressure from the pivot area.

It was under the pressure of external barbarism that Europe achieved her civilization. I ask you, therefore, for a moment to look upon Europe and European history as subordinate to Asia and Asiatic history, for European civilization is, in a very real sense, the outcome of the secular struggle against Asiatic invasion. The most remarkable contrast in the political map of modern Europe is that presented by the vast area of Russia occupying half of the Continent and a group of smaller territories tenanted by the Western Powers.

Tracing the ebb and flow of early European history, Mackinder continued:

For a thousand years a series of horse-riding peoples emerged from Asia through the broad interval between the Ural mountains and the Caspian sea, rode through the open spaces of southern Russia, and struck home into Hungary in the very heart of the European peninsula, shaping by the necessity of opposing them the history of each of the great peoples around—the Russians, the Germans, the French, the Italians, and the Byzantine Greeks.

From the point of view of permanent influence, the Mongol invasions of the fourteenth and fifteenth centuries left the deepest impress, overrunning much of central Europe, Russia, Persia, India, and China. These invasions came from what Mackinder called the "pivot area," and "all the settled margins of the Old World sooner or later felt the expansive force of mobile power originating in the steppe."

Projecting his story to our own times, Mackinder saw the pivot area as increasing its weight in world affairs, coincidentally with its growth in economic and military power. Viewed historically, he saw as evidence "a certain persistence of geographical relationship," for—

Is not the pivot region of the world's politics that vast area of Euro-Asia which is inaccessible to ships, but in antiquity lay open to the horse-riding nomads, and is today about to be covered with a network of railways? There have been and are here the conditions of a mobility of military and economic power of a far-reaching and yet limiting character. Russia replaces the Mongol Empire. Her pressure on Finland, on Scandinavia, on Poland, on Turkey, on Persia, on India, and on China replaces the centrifugal raids of the Steppe-men. In the world at large she occupies the central strategical position held by Germany in Europe. She can strike on all sides and be struck on all sides, save the North.

Outside the pivot area, Mackinder defines two "crescents." In a great inner crescent, are placed Germany, Austria, India, and China, while in an "outer crescent" are found Britain, South Africa, Australia, the United States, Canada, and Japan. In reality, the power of the pivot area was not equivalent to the peripheral states, but, and here Mackinder voiced his greatest fear, "This might happen if Germany were to ally herself with Russia." In that event, the pivot state could expand over the marginal lands of Euro-Asia, use "vast continental resources for fleet-building, and the empire of the world would then be in sight."

Mackinder concluded his notable address by emphasizing that he spoke as a geographer. "The actual balance of political power at any given time is," he pointed out, "of course, the product, on the one hand, of geographical conditions, both economic and strategic, and, on the other hand, of the relative number, virility, equipment, and organization of the competing peoples." In his estimation, "the geographical quantities in the calculation are more measurable and more nearly constant than the human." The geographical significance of the pivot position would not be altered if it were occupied by some people other than the Russian.

Were the Chinese, for instance, organized by the Japanese, to overthrow the Russian Empire and conquer its territory, they might constitute the yellow peril to the world's freedom just because they would add an oceanic frontage to the resources of the great continent, an advantage as yet denied to the Russian tenant of the pivot region.

Writing at the close of the first World War, Mackinder felt "that the War has established, and not shaken, my former points of view." In *Democratic Ideals and Reality* he pursued further the concept of the "pivot area," now referred to as the "Heartland," set in the center of the "World-Island."

As Mackinder viewed them, Europe, Asia, and Africa are not three continents but one: the "World-Island." Since man's thinking in the past has been dominated by the sea, this massive area has not been regarded as an island because it was impossible to circumnavigate it. "An ice-cap, two thousand miles across, floats on the Polar Sea," Mackinder pointed out, "with one edge aground on the shoals off the north of Asia. For the common purposes of navigation, therefore, the continent is not an island."

Except for this fact and its vast size, however, it does not differ from other islands. Both in area and population, the World-Island overshadows the remainder of the earth. Of the land, the World-Island has two-thirds, while North and South America, Australia, and lesser regions have the rest. Furthermore, seven-eighths of the earth's population are contained on the World-Island, while the other land areas have only one-eighth. The Old World then, Mackinder observed, is "incomparably the largest geographical unit on our globe."

Citing "the proportions and relations" of the World-Island, Mackinder continued:

It is set as it were on the shoulder of the earth with reference to the North Pole. Measuring from Pole to Pole along the central meridian of Asia, we have first a thousand miles of ice-clad sea as far as the northern shore of Siberia, then five thousand miles of land to the southern part of India, and then seven thousand miles of sea to the Antarctic cap of ice-clad land. But measured along the meridian of the Bay of Bengal or the Arabian Sea, Asia is only some three thousand five hundred miles across. From Paris to Vladivostok is six thousand miles, and from Paris to the Cape of Good Hope is a similar distance.

Not only are the two Americas and Australia relatively small from the standpoint of area, Mackinder argued, but the man-power and natural resources available to them are far inferior to the "Great Continent" or World-Island. "What if the Great Continent, the whole World-Island or a large part of it," asked Mackinder, "were at some future time to become a single and united base of sea power? Would not the other insular bases be outbuilt as regards ships and outmanned as regards seamen?" Though Germany had been defeated in World War I, the possibility still existed "that a large part of the Great Continent might some day be united under a single sway, and that an invincible sea power might be based upon it." Had Germany won, Mackinder warned, "she would have established her sea power on a wider basis than any in history, and in fact on the widest possible base."

Mackinder's Heartland had substantially the same boundaries as his earlier "pivot area." The Heartland is the central region of Europe and Asia, remote from and beyond the control of sea power. It "includes the Baltic Sea, the navigable Middle and Lower Danube, the Black Sea, Asia Minor, Armenia, Persia, Tibet and Mongolia. Within it, therefore, were Brandenburg-

Prussia and Austria-Hungary, as well as Russia—a vast triple base of manpower, which was lacking to the horse-riders of history." The Baltic and Black seas were included by Mackinder because it had been shown during World War I that they could not be reached or controlled by outside sea power.

The Heartland, Mackinder went on to say, by way of further definition, has "one striking physical circumstance which knits it graphically together; the whole of it, even to the brink of the Persian Mountains overlooking torrid Mesopotamia, lies under snow in the winter time. . . . At mid-winter, as seen from the moon, a vast white shield would reveal the Heartland in its largest meaning." This area, Mackinder was convinced, was the key to the World-Island. Extending roughly from the Himalayas to the Arctic Ocean, and from the Volga to the Yangtze, it stretched 2,500 miles north and south and another 2,500 miles east and west. Invulnerable to sea power because of its inland position, the Heartland could, if properly developed and organized militarily, become the seat and pivot of effective world power.

His arguments were reduced by Mackinder to an oft-quoted formula:

> *Who rules East Europe commands the Heartland:*
> *Who rules the Heartland commands the World-Island:*
> *Who rules the World-Island commands the World.*

To prevent any one nation, especially Russia or Germany, from becoming supreme in the Heartland following World War I, Mackinder advocated setting up a barrier of buffer states from the Baltic to the Black Sea. The independent states, as visualized by Mackinder, were to be Esthonia, Lithuania, Poland, Great Bohemia, Hungary, Great Serbia, Great Roumania, Bulgaria and Greece—a list only slightly at variance with the decisions of the Paris Peace Conference. In the light of recent history, of course, Mackinder made a bad guess. The buffer zone did not accomplish its purpose. First Germany and then Russia broke through the barrier. Germany broke through the barrier as a prelude to World War II; Russia took over all of Eastern Europe after the war's conclusion.

During World War II, in 1943, four years before his death, Mackinder for the third time examined the Heartland theory. In an article, "The Round World and the Winning of the Peace," he found his concept "more valid and useful today than it was either twenty or forty years ago." He went on to prophesy that "if the Soviet Union emerges from the war as conqueror of Germany, she must rank as the greatest land power on the globe. Moreover, she will be the Power in the strategically strongest defensive position. The Heartland is the greatest natural fortress on earth. For the first time in history it is manned by a garrison sufficient both in number and quality."

Nowhere were Mackinder's theories more avidly seized upon than in Nazi Germany. As interpreted by Karl Haushofer, prolific writer on geopolitical subjects, Mackinder's root idea of the Heartland set in a World-Island dominated German political thought for two decades, 1925-45.

Haushofer came into prominence as early as 1908, when he was sent to Japan as a military observer for the German General Staff. Concentrating upon mastery of Far Eastern affairs, he became recognized as an expert. Through exceptional linguistic ability he learned to speak six foreign languages, including Chinese, Japanese, Korean, and Russian. Also, he traveled widely to gain firsthand acquaintance with the Middle and Far East. During World War I, Haushofer rose rapidly in military rank, retiring as a major general. After the German surrender, and for the remainder of his career, he engaged in writing and in teaching political geography and military history at the University of Munich. From his pen came innumerable books, pamphlets, and articles expounding upon two key words in Nazi ideology: *Geopolitik*, dealing with the dynamics of world political change, and *Lebensraum*, the German people's need for living space, for room to expand and grow.

It is not certain when Haushofer first encountered Mackinder's work—probably in the early nineteen-twenties. Immediately Haushofer recognized that he had found his master, and freely acknowledged his debt. Writing in 1937, for example, he described Mackinder's 1904 paper as "the greatest of all geographical world views" and added that he had never "seen anything greater than these few pages of a geopolitical masterpiece." Two years later he argued for a German-Russian alliance, pointing out that Mackinder, taking the British view, had expressed fear of the power these two countries united might exert. Haushofer frequently repeated Ovid's maxim, "It is a duty to learn from the enemy." At least four times, he reproduced Mackinder's map of the Heartland in the periodical *Zeitschrift für Geopolitik,* and admitted without hesitation that his own ideas were based upon the foundation supplied by Mackinder.

A mutual friend, Rudolf Hess, was the link between Haushofer and Hitler. While Hitler was in jail, following the abortive Beer Hall Putsch of 1923, he was visited on several occasions by Haushofer. That Hitler absorbed some of Haushofer's geopolitical indoctrination is revealed by various passages in *Mein Kampf.* With the Nazi triumph a decade later, Haushofer was in a key position to influence German policy. Appointed head of the Nazi Geopolitical Institute, he recruited a huge staff to comb the earth for data on the nature, living conditions, and cultural influences of peoples, and other geographic information of potential military importance.

Fascinated by Mackinder's ideas, Haushofer was obsessed with the conviction that Germany must win control of the Heartland. His blueprints called for a "transcontinental bloc," reaching from the Rhine to the Yangtze. Central to his scheme was to be a monster alliance of Germany, Japan, China, Russia, and India against the British Empire. His teachings were strongly endorsed and supported by the German General Staff. The signing of the Nazi-Soviet Pact in 1939 seemed to make Haushofer's dream come true, but his whole policy was tossed overboard when Hitler committed the most decisive blunder of World War II by ordering his generals to attack the Soviet Union. Shortly after the war ended, Haushofer and his wife committed suicide at their Bavarian home.

As was natural, the implication by critics that he had helped to lay the foundation of Nazi militarism was resented by Mackinder. In a 1944 speech, he remarked:

It has, I am told, been rumored that I inspired Haushofer, who inspired Hess, who in turn suggested to Hitler while he was dictating *Mein Kampf* certain geo-political ideas which are said to have originated with me. Those are three links in a chain, but of the second and third I know nothing. This however I do know from the evidence of his own pen that whatever Haushofer adopted from me he took from an address ["The Geographical Pivot of History"] I gave before the Royal Geographical Society just forty years ago, long before there was any question of a Nazi Party.

The spread of geopolitical doctrines was not confined, of course, to Germany. Hardly less active have been the Russians.

A flourishing geopolitical bureau, Moscow's Institute for World Economy and Politics, has long concerned itself with the conflict between the United States and the World-Island, which the Soviet Union hopes to dominate. It is of interest in this connection to recall Mackinder's view of Russia in 1919 when the Communist government was young. The leopard, he was convinced, never changes his spots. The British and American brand of government and the ideals of the League of Nations "are all of them opposed to the policies cast in the tyrannical molds of East Europe and the Heartland, whether Dynastic or Bolshevik. It may be the case that Bolshevik tyranny is an extreme reaction from Dynastic tyranny, but it is none the less true that the Russian, Prussian, and Hungarian plains, with their widespread uniformity of social conditions, are favorable alike to the march of militarism and to the propaganda of syndicalism."

The validity of Mackinder's geographical theories has been frequently debated, and the flaws in his argument pointed out. An obvious defect is Mackinder's failure to take into account the immense potentialities of air power. In his later writing he recognized that the conquest of the air had forced a new kind of unity on the world, but insisted this development supported rather than weakened the Heartland—World-Island thesis. Critics maintain, however, that air power has become such a formidable weapon that the conception of the Heartland has lost its strategic significance. Air lines now crisscross the oceans and the continent. As Herrick commented:

The air is universal. Within range of the necessary bases, it is one vast highway to be traversed at will over land and sea alike. Air power can be blocked only by air power; it knows no Heartland from which it is inevitably excluded. . . . Today's strategical formula might well read: *Who rules the planes commands the bases: who rules the bases commands the air: who rules the air commands the world.*

This view is reinforced by examination of a globe, where one sees the proximity of the Heartland and North America. "Seen from North America and in terms of new communications," Hans Werner Weigert points out, "inaccessibility and vastness no longer conceal the Heartland from us. It lies no longer behind an impenetrable wall of isolation." Modern long-range aircraft have conquered the arctic regions in the seventy years since Mackinder first delivered his ominous warnings. Further, the very size of the Heartland is a serious handicap to a defending power. The great length of Soviet Russia's land and sea frontiers, for example, increases vulnerability to hostile aircraft and presents a defense problem of enormous complexity. While being able, in Mackinder's words, to "strike on all sides," she can also be struck on all sides.

Another blind side shown by Mackinder was his failure to realize the powerful place occupied by the Americas. At the time he was writing *Democratic Ideals and Reality*, he had just recently witnessed, in World War I, a demonstration of American vigor and strength. Apparently preoccupied with the Heartland—World-Island way of looking at the earth, however, he could see the New World only as peripheral, as "merely satellites of the old continent."

Nevertheless, despite Mackinder's shortcomings as a seer, there are weighty arguments sustaining his judgments. The Soviet Union has established an iron rule over the Heartland, and through agricultural and industrial development, mineral exploitation, railway and airfield construction has made the area one of the strongest in the world, economically and militarily. On the other hand, though proceeding under the forced draft of several five-year plans for the past several decades, the region has not yet attained the productive efficiency of the United States. Also, though ruling the Heartland, the Soviet Union is still remote from its goal of commanding the World-Island, much less the world.

Criticism has exposed the weakness of some details of Mackinder's views, but it has not invalidated his basic premises. As "the first to provide us with a global concept of the world and its affairs," in John C. Winant's phrase, he will be long remembered. "There is," declared Mackinder, "no complete geographical region either less than or greater than the whole of the earth's surface." He was instrumental in obtaining wide acceptance of the belief he expressed as early as 1889, that the "political geographer's is the crowning chapter of geography." His primary concern was to persuade his own countrymen and the peoples of other democracies that geographical facts are of basic importance in the growth of peoples and states. He believed and taught that the world cannot be made safe for democracy unless the geographical realities are fully understood. Upon Mackinder's ideas of the world and its regions the foundations of modern geography are laid.

19

STUDY IN MEGALOMANIA

Adolf Hitler: Mein Kampf

The funeral pyre which consumed the mortal remains of Adolf Hitler and Eva Braun on April 30, 1945, deep underground in the Berlin chancellery, was a climax that might have been imagined by the operatic composer Hitler most ardently admired, Richard Wagner, for a new Götterdämmerung, or *Twilight of the Gods*. The scene rang down the curtain on a vast melodrama that had opened a generation earlier, when the future Führer began his march to power.

At the time the Nazi Party under Hitler's leadership took over the reins of government in Germany in 1933 after more than a decade of agitation and violence, the world was appalled by its actions. The regime was coldly ruthless in establishing its control; all vestiges of democratic government were abolished; dissenting views mercilessly suppressed; churches, fraternal orders, and labor unions persecuted or "coordinated"; Jews murdered in large numbers; and territorial threats against ostensibly friendly neighboring nations thundered in waves of propaganda.

Yet, if non-Germans had taken the trouble to peruse a fat tome entitled *Mein Kampf* ("My Struggle"), they would have found the entire program spelled out in all its shocking detail. Thanks to the protection of international copyright, its author had succeeded in restricting the full story to the original German. It is improbable, though, that even if the unexpurgated text had been freely available in English, French, and other languages, many persons would have taken seriously "the fantastic dream of a frenzied visionary"—so vast in scope and incredibly ambitious did it appear. *Mein Kampf* has rightly been called the "propagandistic masterpiece of the age" and, viewed from the standpoint of a trial judge, the "most incriminating book of the twentieth century." A great nation and its allies committed themselves to carrying out the fanatical ideas in the book. By the outbreak of World War II, 5,000,000 copies had been distributed in Germany alone.

Growing up in Vienna (as another Viennese, Sigmund Freud, might have predicted), Hitler formed at a tender age the impressions, prejudices, and hatreds that were to govern him for the remainder of his life. All are poured out in *Mein Kampf*. The opening chapters provide a brief but significant sketch of those early years. Born in 1889, at Braunau, Austria, just across the river from the German border, Hitler always felt himself a German rather than an Austrian, and especially despised the easygoing Viennese. According to his own account, the first years were full of privation, suffering, failure, frustration, and maladjustment. His formal schooling ceased at thirteen, and both parents were lost about the same time. In Vienna, his struggles to become an artist and, failing that, an architect, were handicapped by lack of education and lack of talent.

During the Vienna period, Hitler claims to have read widely, with emphasis on history. His ideas were influenced particularly by a book on the Franco-Prussian War, which inspired in him a fervent pride in the German race and convinced him of the God-given destiny of that people. At the same time he began to form an intense dislike for the Jews, and complete contempt for the Slavs and all other "non-Aryans." The Jew is primarily an international-minded money-maker and exploiter, usually a Socialist or Communist, Hitler declared, while the Slavs are an inferior race, with no culture of their own.

Association with the Social Democrats in Vienna caused Hitler to loathe Socialist and Communist propaganda, and, though he was an apt student of the party's tactics, his hatred of Marxism was lifelong. Despite his omnivorous reading habits, there is no evidence that he ever opened *Das Kapital*. Scarcely less profound was his detestation of democracy and democratic institutions, an aversion which began when he attended sessions of the Austrian Reichsrath in Vienna and observed what he regarded as its inefficient methods.

Finally, no longer willing to breathe the abominable cosmopolitan air of Vienna, Hitler settled in 1912 in Munich, which he called "a thoroughly German city." Two years later, to his delight, the World War came. He enlisted in a Bavarian regiment, and before the war ended had been wounded, gassed, twice decorated, and promoted to the rank of corporal. Germany's defeat both grieved and enraged him—a defeat, he believed, that had been caused by Jews, Marxists, and pacifists. The creation of a democratic German government following the war likewise angered and embittered him. It was then that Hitler resolved to become a politician.

Hitler's entry into politics came after his return to Munich. For a time he served as a paid political informer for the army or *Wehrmacht*. He was invited to, and accepted, membership in a small group called the German Workers' party, soon renamed the National Socialist German Workers' party, the nucleus of the Nazi party. Within a short time, by internal maneuvering, Hitler gained tight control of the organization, and abolished the "senseless" practice of making party decisions by vote of the members. The Party's program, as it developed under Hitler's command, was designed to win the sympathies of the working classes, to exterminate "the international poisoners," to abolish legislative bodies, and to establish the principle of blind, unquestioning obedience to a leader or *Führer*.

By 1923, with 27,000 party members, and supported by a military clique under General Ludendorff, while the Stresemann government appeared to be tottering, Hitler concluded that the time had come to seize power. He had his followers stage the famous Beer Hall Putsch in Munich. The attempt ended in complete fiasco, and sixteen of Hitler's adherents were shot down in the streets. Hitler himself was arrested and sentenced to five years in prison, a term later reduced to one year.

As a prisoner in the Bavarian fortress at Landsberg, Hitler had leisure for the first time to write his autobiography. Actually, *Mein Kampf* is a spoken rather than a written book. Sharing the prison with Hitler was his loyal disciple, Rudolf Hess. To Hess, who typed it directly, Hitler dictated the first volume of the work. Dedicated to the sixteen Nazis who had fallen in the Munich uprising, the book was originally titled "Four and a Half Years of Struggle Against Lies, Stupidity, and Cowardice." The second volume was completed in 1926 at Berchtesgaden.

Otto Tolischus has described the contents of *Mein Kampf* as

"10 per cent autobiography, 90 per cent dogma, and 100 per cent propaganda"—a fair analysis. It seems incredible today that such a crude, long-winded, badly written, contradictory, and repetitious book could have captured the emotions of a highly cultured nation. But the situation was made to order. Ludwig Lore's comments are enlightening:

The German people in 1933 were in a mood that made them dangerously susceptible to the Fascist bacillus. They had tried to find a way back to normal living and national self-respect and had found the way blocked by prejudice and blind misunderstanding. The great nations were interested only in reparations. The German labor parties which might have helped were split into half a dozen warring camps. All this was played against a background colored by a century of high-pressure nationalism. The German people had reached a point where order and security seemed to matter more than a political freedom that had become synonymous with brawls and bloodshed. Hitler understood these things and used them for his purposes, aided by a phenomenal capacity for organization and propaganda and by the readiness of Germany's great industrialists to finance his campaigns. Once established, the Germans' innate respect for authority made it simple to establish Fascist leadership.

Mein Kampf's theme song, recurring again and again, is race, race purity, race supremacy—though nowhere did Hitler attempt to define race. Mankind, he said, is divided into three groups: the culture-creators, of whom there is only one example, the Aryan or Nordic (more specifically the German); the culture-bearers, such as the Japanese; and the culture-destroyers, e.g., Jews and Negroes. It was never intended by nature, Hitler claimed, that all races should be equal, any more than individuals are equal. Some are created superior to others. The Germans, as the world's strongest race, should rule over the inferior races of the earth. A few characteristic passages from *Mein Kampf* will illustrate Hitler's views on "inferior" races.

Writing of the Austrian Empire:

I was repelled by the conglomeration of races which the capital showed me, repelled by this whole mixture of Czechs, Poles, Hungarians, Ruthenians, Serbs, Croats, and everywhere, the eternal mushroom of humanity—Jews and more Jews.

About Africans:

. . . it is criminal lunacy to keep on drilling a born half-ape until people think they have made a lawyer out of him, while millions of members

of the highest culture-race must remain in entirely unworthy positions;
. . . it is a sin against the will of the Eternal Creator if His most gifted
beings by the hundreds and hundreds of thousands are allowed to
degenerate in the present proletarian morass, while Hottentots and
Zulu Kaffirs are trained for intellectual professions.

Hindu nationalists "individually always impressed me as gab-
bling pomposities without any realistic background." Poles,
Czechs, Jews, Negroes, and Asiatics are lumped together as unworthy of German citizenship, even though they may be born
in Germany and speak the German language. France was regarded with special contempt:

. . . racially; . . . she is making such great progress in negrification
that we can actually speak of an African state arising on European
soil. The colonial policy of present-day France cannot be compared
with that of Germany in the past. If the development of France in the
present style were to be continued for three hundred years, the last
remnants of Frankish blood would be submerged in the developing
European-African mulatto state.

It is in the attacks on the Jews, however, that Hitler's race
prejudice reaches its frenzied height, as, for example, in this
passage:

The Jewish train of thought in all this is clear. The Bolshevization of
Germany—that is, the extermination of the national folkish Jewish
intelligentsia to make possible the sweating of the German working
class under the yoke of Jewish world finance—is conceived only as a
preliminary to the further extension of this Jewish tendency of world
conquest. As often in history, Germany is the great pivot in the mighty
struggle. If our people and our state become the victim of these blood-
thirsty and avaricious Jewish tyrants of nations, the whole earth will
sink into the snares of this octopus; if Germany frees herself from
this embrace, this greatest of dangers to nations may be regarded as
broken for the whole world. . . .
In general, the Jews will always fight within the various national
bodies with those weapons which on the basis of the recognized men-
tality of these nations seem most effective and promise the greatest
success. In our national body, so torn with regard to blood, it is therefore the more or less "cosmopolitan," pacifistic-ideological ideas, arising from this fact; in short, the international tendencies which they
utilize in their struggle for power . . . until they have turned one state
after another into a heap of rubble on which they can then establish
the sovereignty of the eternal Jewish empire.

To maintain the pristine purity of the Aryan, i.e., the German
master race, there must be no "bastardization" by admixture

with inferior stocks. The decline of great nations in the past, asserted Hitler, had invariably resulted from the mixture of blood and the loss of race purity. To prevent such a calamity, it is the state's duty to intervene. Even though "cowards and weaklings" may protest the invasion of their rights, the state must "see that the nation's blood be kept pure so that humanity may reach its highest development. The state must lift marriage from the abyss of racial shame and sanctify it as an institution for the procreation of likenesses of God instead of monstrosities which are a cross between men and apes."

Fanatically believing in the innate superiority of the Aryan "race" over all others, Hitler preached that it is the duty, and privilege, of the master race to conquer, exploit, dispossess, or exterminate other races for its own advantage. Since Germany was crowded and needed *Lebensraum*, more living space, it was her right, as the great Nordic power, to grab Slavic land, remove the Slavs, and settle Germans on it. All humanity in the long run would benefit through having the habitat of the highest race extended and the scattered Germanic peoples united under one rule. "Only an adequately large space on this earth assures a nation of freedom of existence. . . . Germany will either be a world power or there will be no Germany."

The vast expansion visualized by Hitler would take place principally at the expense of Russia. Looking hungrily to the east, he speculated on what could be accomplished "if the Ural, with its immeasurable raw material and the Ukraine with its immeasurable grain fields lay within Germany." It was Germany's duty to rescue the Russian people from the Bolshevist leaders. "If we speak of soil in Europe today," continued Hitler, "we can primarily have in mind only Russia and her vassal border states. Here Fate itself seems desirous of giving us a sign. By handing Russia to Bolshevism, it robbed the Russian nation of that intelligentsia which previously brought about and guaranteed its existence as a state. . . . The giant empire in the east is ripe for collapse."

Power, Hitler said, is the justification for invasion.

. . . no people on this earth possesses so much as a square yard of territory on the strength of a higher will or superior right. . . . State boundaries are made by man and changed by man. The fact that a nation has succeeded in acquiring an undue amount of soil constitutes no higher obligation that it should be recognized eternally. At most it proves the strength of the conquerors and the weakness of the nations. And in this case, right lies in this strength alone.

Hitler recognized that there were other possible solutions than territorial expansion to Germany's rapid population growth. One alternative would be contraceptive limitation of births—rejected because it was not in accord with the master race theory. Another, followed by Germany's prewar rulers, was to expand factory production for foreign markets, that is, increased industrialization, a solution not acceptable to Hitler, for he wanted Germany to feed herself and be self-sufficient. Furthermore, he was violently opposed to the creation of a large urban proletariat, the result of a great factory system. A third way out was to increase the productivity of the already available land, but this, argued Hitler, was but a partial and temporary answer. The only real remedy, he concluded, was for Germany to acquire new territory beyond existing frontiers, enabling more Germans to live on the land.

Hitler's long-range goals in population and territory were summarized in this paragraph:

. . . Today we count eighty million Germans in Europe! This foreign policy will be acknowledged as correct only if, after scarcely a hundred years, there are two hundred and fifty million Germans on this continent, and not living penned in as factory coolies for the rest of the world, but: as peasants and workers, who guarantee each other's livelihood by their labor.

In short, Hitler foresaw the German population as more than tripled in the next hundred years, and, per capita, possessing twice as much room as was then available. The idea of a widely spaced population also appealed to Hitler for "military-geographical" reasons, because it would be less vulnerable to an enemy. (Shades of Mackinder-Haushofer!)

To attain the objectives set by his soaring ambition, Hitler proposed to use three methods: propaganda, diplomacy, and force. Nowhere in *Mein Kampf* is the author more revealing of himself and his tactics than in his discussion of propaganda techniques, correctly believed by him to be one of the Nazis' most effective and formidable weapons. Max Lerner called Hitler "probably the greatest master of propaganda and organization in modern history," adding that, "to find his equal one must go

back to Loyola and the Jesuits." To perfect his own understanding of the propaganda art, Hitler studied the propaganda techniques of the Marxists, the organization and methods of the
Catholic Church, British propaganda of World War I, American
advertising, and Freudian psychology. He wrote:

The function of propaganda . . . is not to weigh and ponder the rights
of different people, but exclusively to emphasize the one right which
it has set out to argue for. Its task is not to make an objective study
of the truth, in so far as it favors the enemy, and then set it before the
masses with academic fairness; its task is to serve our own right,
always and unflinchingly. It was absolutely wrong to discuss war-guilt
from the standpoint that Germany alone could not be held responsible
for the outbreak of the catastrophe; it would have been correct to
load every bit of the blame on the shoulders of the enemy, even if this
had not really corresponded to the true facts, as it actually did. . . .
The purpose of propaganda is not to provide interesting distraction
for blasé young gentlemen, but to convince, and what I mean is to
convince the masses.

The importance of concentration and repetition was stressed.

The receptivity of the great masses is very limited, their intelligence
is small, but their power of forgetting is enormous. In consequence of
these facts, all effective propaganda must be limited to a very few
points and must harp on these in slogans until the last member of
the public understands what you want him to understand by your
slogan. As soon as you sacrifice this slogan and try to be manysided,
the effect will piddle away, for the crowd can neither digest nor retain
the material offered. In this way the result is weakened and in the end
entirely cancelled out.

Hitler's faith in propaganda is illustrated by his statement that
"It is possible by means of shrewd and unremitting propaganda,
to make people believe that heaven is hell—and hell heaven."
For its greatest potential, propaganda must be adapted to the
most limited intelligence, "aimed always and primarily at the
emotions, and very little at men's alleged reason." Propaganda
has "no more to do with scientific accuracy than a poster has to
do with art. . . . The greater the mass of men to be reached, the
lower its intellectual level must be."
Also useful to the propagandist are certain psychological
tricks. One should not, for example, attempt to convert a crowd
to a different point of view in the morning. Dim lights are useful,
and in the evening when people are tired and their powers of

resistance low, their "complete emotional capitulation" is relatively easy to achieve. Another mighty tool is mass suggestion, when the mob has a chance to join in parades and spectacular demonstrations, so typical of the Nazi regime. As Hitler put it:

> . . . the gigantic mass demonstrations, these parades of hundreds of thousands of men, which burned into the small, wretched individual the proud conviction that, paltry worm as he was, he was nevertheless a part of a great dragon, beneath whose burning breath the hated bourgeois world would some day go up in fire and flame and the proletarian dictatorship would celebrate its ultimate final victory.

Hitler's supreme contempt for the masses appears again and again, in such phrases as "an empty-headed herd of sheep," "the incarnation of stupidity," and his frequently expressed belief that mankind in the mass is lazy, cowardly, feminine, emotional, and incapable of rational thought.

The ultimate in Hitlerian propaganda technique is the principle of the big lie. The doctrine is "wholly correct," Hitler declared, "that the very greatness of the lie is a factor in getting it believed. . . . With the primitive simplicity of the masses a great lie is more effective than a small one, because they often lie in small matters, but would be too ashamed to tell a great big lie. Hence it will never occur to the broad mass to suspect so large a lie, and the mass will be quite unable to believe that anyone could possibly have the infernal impudence to pervert the truth to such an extent." In brief, the bigger the lie, the more likely it will be believed by the masses.

Another major propaganda principle is that of the single devil. Do not confuse the populace by offering too many enemies for it to hate at the same time. Concentrate upon one adversary, and focus the people's hatred upon this enemy. For Hitler, of course, the Jew served as the universal scapegoat. Regardless of whether he was ranting against democracy, Marxism, the Versailles Treaty, France, or some other favorite target, the Jew was always present, scheming and plotting, trying with devilish ingenuity to undermine Germany and Aryan culture. A sample is this hysterical outburst:

> . . . France is and remains by far the most terrible enemy. This people, which is basically becoming more and more negrified, constitutes in its tie with the aims of Jewish world domination an endur-

ing danger for the existence of the white race in Europe. For the contamination by Negro blood on the Rhine in the heart of Europe is just as much in keeping with the perverted sadistic thirst for vengeance of this hereditary enemy of our people as is the ice-cold calculation of the Jew thus to begin bastardizing the European continent at its core and to deprive the white race of the foundations for a sovereign existence through infection with lower humanity.

The task of the propagandist is facilitated, Hitler said, by state control of education. Too much book-learning is an error. Physical education and physical health should take first place. Second is the development of character, especially such military virtues as obedience, loyalty, strength of will, self-control, capacity for sacrifice, and pride in responsibility. Relegated to third place is intellectual activity. For girls, training must be for motherhood. The concept of educaton for all was repugnant to Hitler, who described it as a disintegrating poison invented by liberalism for its own destruction. Each class and each subdivision of a class had only one possible education. He thought that the great mass of people should enjoy the blessings of illiteracy.

For the last group, education is to be limited to an indoctrination with "general ideas, carved by eternal repetition into the heart and memory of the people." Always the guiding principle is that the child belongs to the state, and the sole object of education is to train tools for the state.

Hitler's views on popular education are of a piece with his opinion of democracy in general. At every opportunity he ridiculed the ineffectiveness of the democratic state:

The Western democracy of today is the forerunner of Marxism which without it would not be thinkable. It provides this world plague with the culture in which its germs can spread. In its most extreme form, parliamentarianism created a "monstrosity of excrement and fire," in which, however, sad to say, the "fire" seems to me at the moment to be burned out. . . . For there is one thing which we must never forget: in this, too, the majority can never replace the man. It is not only a representative of stupidity, but of cowardice as well. And no more that a hundred empty heads makes one wise man will an heroic decision arise from a hundred cowards.

Hitler saw democracy as "the deceitful theory that the Jew would insinuate—namely, the theory that all men are created equal"; while any doctrine of universal suffrage and equal rights is "pernicious and destructive."

Hitler substituted the leader principle for democracy. He put heads over the mass who were supposed to obey orders without question. Over all was the Führer, taking full responsibility for all he did or failed to do.

Having drawn his blueprint for Germany and the world in *Mein Kampf*, Hitler faithfully adhered to it, except for one important, though, as it turned out, temporary deviation—the Nazi-Soviet Pact of 1939. How difficult it must have been for him to swallow the Russian agreement is indicated by this diatribe in *Mein Kampf*.

Never forget that the rulers of present-day Russia are common blood-stained criminals; that they are the scum of humanity which, favored by circumstances, overran a great state in a tragic hour, slaughtered and wiped out thousands of her leading intelligentsia in a wild blood lust. . . .

Since Hitler, in *Mein Kampf*, had so plainly revealed his intentions years before he came to power in Germany, and more than a decade prior to the beginning of World War II, why did the statesmen of the world pay so little heed to his warnings? In part, he was ignored because of the general atmosphere of appeasement, wishful thinking, and peace-at-any-price that prevailed. Another factor was an amazing story of international censorship. Because Hitler refused to authorize a complete translation of *Mein Kampf*, only a much expurgated, bowdlerized version was available in English until 1939. In that year, on the eve of war, two American publishers, one with Hitler's approval and one without, brought out uncensored editions. In France, in 1936, Hitler, through his publisher, sued and restrained the issue of a full translation, pleading infringement of copyright. A condensed edition published in London omitted most of the passages attacking France, eliminated a section justifying war, and so softened the tone of the book as to be false and misleading.

Meanwhile, millions of copies of the complete *Mein Kampf* were being sold and circulated in Germany. Every newly married couple was presented with a copy, while every member of the Nazi party and every civil servant was expected to possess the book. Later editions in Germany did, however, leave out the attacks on Russia and France, to conceal Hitler's purposes and to lull potential enemies to sleep.

Viewing *Mein Kampf* retrospectively, historians would maintain that Hitler had no understanding of history, anthropologists that his racial views were nonsense, educators that his theories of education were altogether medieval and reactionary, political scientists would protest his authoritarian doctrines of government and his misrepresentation of democracy, while literary experts would hold that he did not know how to write a paragraph or organize a chapter. Weigert summed it up in this way:

The half-educated Hitler was a mosaic of influences: the amoral statecraft of Machiavelli, the mystic nationalism and romanticism of Wagner, the organic evolution of Darwin, the grossly exaggerated racialism of Gobineau and Houston Stewart Chamberlain, the messianic complex of Fichte and Hegel, the military braggadocio of Treitschke and Bernhardi, and the financial conspiracy of the Prussian Junker caste. . . . Haushofer served as a channel of unification between theory and action.

And yet, despite such glaring defects, *Mein Kampf* is, as one of its bitterest critics, Hendrik Willem Van Loon, described it, "one of the most extraordinary historical documents of all time," combining "the naiveté of Jean-Jacques Rousseau with the frenzied wrath of an Old Testament prophet." Norman Cousins called it "by far the most effective book of the twentieth century. . . . For every word in 'Mein Kampf,' 125 lives were to be lost; for every page, 4,700 lives; for every chapter, more than 1,200,-000 lives." Its power was derived, of course, from the fact that it was the political bible of the German people, and guided the policies of the Third Reich from 1933 until the end of World War II.

It is the world's misfortune that Hitler's ideas did not expire with him. Their adherents are still numerous in Germany, while Communist governments have borrowed and are making extensive use of many of them. Dictators everywhere will continue to find primary source material for their evil purposes in *Mein Kampf*, in the same manner that, for the past four centuries, they have been drawing upon Machiavelli.

THE WORLD OF SCIENCE

20

GREEK AND ROMAN SCIENTISTS

Along with their enormous contributions to history and literature, Greece and Rome advanced the field of science on many
fronts. Certain names stand out: Hippocrates in medicine, Theophrastus in botany, Euclid and Archimedes in mathematics,
Aristotle in all-encompassing fashion, Pliny in natural history,
and Lucretius on the philosophy of science.

Hippocrates: Aphorisms

A period of not less than one hundred centuries in the history of
mankind elapsed before the man of medicine prevailed over the
medicine man. Among both primitive tribes and advanced civilizations, disease was fought by exorcising or propitiating spirits,
ghosts, and demons. Illness was attributed to attacks by supernatural beings, or to their actual entry into the body of the
sufferer—afflictions sent as a punishment for sin. Hag-ridden and
god-ridden, men fought with shadows. The priests were the
doctors. Imhetep with his magic became the god of healing in
Egypt; Aesculapius with like divine powers became the god of
healing in ancient Greece. Temples were erected to these gods by
grateful worshipers.

The laying of a scientific basis for medicine did not come until
approximately the fifth century B.C. in Greece. For the first time,
practical medicine then began to be separated from religion and
philosophy, and the belief became established that all diseases
are due not to the interference of the gods but to natural causes.
Greek medicine culminated, about 420 B.C., in the school of
Hippocrates, who had an approach to the art far in advance of

anything preceding it and similar in spirit to modern medical theory and practice. There are few traces of superstition and hardly any reference to religion in the Hippocratic writings. His method was to ignore all the gods and to hold instead that disease is a natural phenomenon governed by natural laws.

Hippocrates as a historical figure, aside from his writings, is little known. Tradition dates his birth at 460 B.C., and he is reputed to have lived to an advanced age, variously recorded as between ninety and a hundred and ten. He is mentioned in Plato's dialogues and in the writings of Aristotle, by whom he was venerated as the Great Physician.

Although Hippocrates has been called "a symbol rather than a doctor, a name more than a man," the knowledge that the medical profession has accumulated since his time has been gained through the basic principle established by him: precise observation. He urged a clear differentiation between speculation and guesses on the one hand and exact knowledge obtained from observation on the other. "To know is one thing," he stated, "merely to believe one knows is another. To know is science, but merely to believe one knows is ignorance."

In attempting to discover the true causes of disease, Hippocrates believed that the four elements, earth, air, fire, and water—or, as sometimes described, heat, cold, dryness, and moisture—are represented in the body by four body fluids or "humors": blood, phlegm, black bile, and yellow bile. When a person is in sound health, the fluids exist in his body in harmonious proportions. The fundamental condition of life is the innate heat, greatest in youth and gradually declining with age. These fanciful notions remained the accepted doctrine among physicians as to the causes of diseases as late as the mid-nineteenth century.

According to the Hippocratic view, diseases were to be cured by restoring the disturbed harmony in the relation of the elements and humors. In actual treatment, however, Hippocrates departed from beautiful theories and depended upon common sense. Primarily, he believed in the healing power of Nature. He considered health as a normal state, disease as an abnormal condition. Hence if the disease is not too serious, he held, Nature will assert itself and health will be promptly regained. The main duty of the physician is to stand by and to help Nature, to relieve pain whenever possible, and to strengthen the patient's body and spirit.

The therapeutic means at Hippocrates' disposal were few and weak. As listed by George Sarton, historian of science, "He used purgatives, emetics, cordials, emmenagogues, enemata and clysters, bloodletting, starvation diets in order to evacuate the body, fomentations and baths, frictions and massage, barley water and barley gruel, wine, hydromel (honey with water), oxymel (honey with vinegar)."

But more valuable than drugs, Hippocrates taught, are diet and exercise. His diets were prescribed according to certain sensible rules. The age of the patient was to be considered: "Old persons use less nutriment than young." The seasons: "In winter abundant nourishment is wholesome; in summer a more frugal diet." The physical state of the person: "Lean persons should take little food, but this little should be fat; fat persons, on the other hand, should take much food, but it should be lean." Digestibility of the food: "White meat is more digestible than dark." The best guarantee of health is a moderate amount of nourishment with a moderate amount of exercise. Sedentary persons are advised to walk. To prevent disease Hippocrates also recommended moderation in working, eating, drinking, exercising, and sleeping.

From a clinical standpoint, the most famous of all Hippocratic writings are his records of actual cases. Some forty-two have survived, all short and clear. Here are to be found classical descriptions of gout, arthritis, puerperal septicemia, tuberculosis, mumps, hysteria, epilepsy, and different types of malaria. Often cited is the appearance of the face at the point of death in many acute diseases: "Nose sharp, eyes hollow, temples sunken, ears cold and contracted with their lobes turned outwards, the skin about the face hard and tense and parched, the color of the face as a whole being yellow or black"—observations used by Shakespeare in describing the death of Falstaff.

Hippocrates was less concerned with diagnosis than with prognosis, i.e., predicting the course of a disease and the possibility of cure or of death. Through prognosis the doctor could recognize, and eventually foretell, different stages that occur in every disease. For this purpose, the clinical records of previous cases were essential. Hippocrates paid close attention to variations in the appearance of the eyes, the color of the skin, the prominence of the veins, pulsations in the arteries, the existence of fevers, chills, tremors, and sweating, frequency of respiration, the position of the patient in bed, the condition of the tongue, and the influence of environment on health and disease.

Hippocrates knew little of anatomy except of the bones. In the field of surgery, his principal contributions relate to fractures and dislocations. His knowledge of the internal organs, arteries, veins, and nerves was practically nonexistent, because among the Greeks dissection of the human body was forbidden by the prejudice of religion and custom.

Hippocrates was meticulous in his directions to physicians, including such details as preparation of the operating room, the employment of artificial and natural light, scrupulous cleanliness of the hands, the care and use of instruments, method of bandaging, placing of the patient, use of splints, and the necessity for general tidiness, order, and cleanliness. He held that the physician himself should be a man of honor, in good health, sympathetic and friendly, personally clean and properly dressed, careful to avoid notoriety and self-seeking, temperate in eating and drinking, and a philosopher in outlook.

Out of these high standards for the physician came the celebrated Hippocratic Oath—in a modern form administered to candidates for the Doctor of Medicine degree. As revised, the vow reads:

I do solemnly swear by that which I hold most sacred: That I will be loyal to the profession of medicine and just and generous to its members; that I will lead my life and practice my art in uprightness and honor; that into whatsoever house I shall enter, it shall be for the good of the sick to the utmost of my power, I holding myself aloof from wrong, from corruption, from the tempting of others to vice; that I will exercise my art solely for the cure of my patients, and I will give no drug, perform no operation for a criminal purpose, even if solicited, far less suggest it; that whatsoever I shall see or hear of the lives of men which is not fitted to be spoken, I will keep inviolably secret; these things I do promise and in proportion as I am faithful to this my oath may happiness and good repute be ever mine—the opposite if I shall be foresworn.

Most widely circulated and best known of the works of Hippocrates are his *Aphorisms,* consisting of precepts, observations, and summations drawn from his medical treatises, mainly *The Prognostics, On the Articulations,* and *On Airs, Waters, and Places.* The so-called Hippocratic writings total eighty-seven treatises. The number ascribed directly to Hippocrates himself varies from four to thirteen. Critics have concluded that the remainder were written by no less than nineteen different authors, some of whom lived after Hippocrates' time.

With Hippocrates, we come, as Sir William Osler phrases it, "out of the murky night of the East, heavy with phantoms, into the bright daylight of the West." To which Sarton adds, "The main achievement of Hippocrates was the introduction of a scientific point of view and scientific method in the cure of diseases, and the beginning of scientific medical literature and clinical archives. The importance of this can hardly be exaggerated." Rebelling against the ancient myths and superstitions prevalent among the physicians of his day and against the intrusions of philosophy into medical doctrine, Hippocrates laid a solid foundation for the study and for the practice of the healing arts.

Theophrastus: On the History of Plants, On the Causes of Plants

The foundation stone of the scientific study of plant life was laid by the Greek philosopher Theophrastus, at the end of the fourth and the beginning of the third century B.C. Born Tyrtamus of Eresus in Lesbos, he received the nickname Theophrastus ("divine of speech") from Aristotle. At an early age, Theophrastus traveled to Athens and there became a member of the Platonic circle, a fellow student of Aristotle, though about fifteen years the latter's junior. After Plato's death, he attached himself to Aristotle and later succeeded his great teacher as head of the famous Lyceum. As evidence of Aristotle's high esteem, he bequeathed to Theophrastus his library and garden and designated him guardian of his children.

In his writings, Theophrastus was as prolific and versatile as Aristotle. The biographer Diogenes Laërtius credits him with some 227 treatises on subjects as diverse as religion, politics, ethics, education, rhetoric, mathematics, astronomy, logic, meteorology, music, poetry, love, epilepsy, water, fire, odors, dreams, inventions, and natural history. Of his writings of a literary nature, the most popular is the *Characters:* thirty sketches of moral weaknesses, e.g., arrogance, backbiting, superstition, boorishness, and buffoonery—which subsequently had considerable influence on drama and other branches of literature.

The most important of Theophrastus' multiple works are two large botanical treatises: *On the History of Plants*, originally composed in ten books, of which nine have survived; and *On the Causes of Plants,* of which six of the original eight books are extant. Together they form the most significant contributions to botanical science during ancient and medieval times, becoming the ultimate authority on all botanical matters for the next two thousand years. Therein is recorded all the botanical knowledge available in the ancient world. Theophrastus may be said to have done for the vegetable kingdom what Hippocrates had previously accomplished for surgery and clinical medicine: the organization of a mass of scattered lore into a systematic treatise.

Theophrastus appears to have journeyed abroad little, if at all, and to have relied chiefly on information and observations brought to him by his students and other travelers. For example, his sponsor Alexander the Great took scientifically trained observers with him to the East, and these men provided Theophrastus with descriptions of such plants and plant derivatives as cotton, banyan (fig), pepper, cinnamon, coconut, myrrh, and frankincense. Facts and fancies were also drawn from diverse sources nearer home: philosophers, drug collectors, root diggers, farmers, woodmen, and charcoal burners. In addition, Theophrastus, a keen observer of natural phenomena, frequently based his accounts on what he had seen over a period of many years in his own garden.

In the course of his collecting activities, Theophrastus learned of much curious folklore and superstitions associated with plants, about most of which he was skeptical but recorded because he thought it too interesting to omit. The root diggers' calling, he found, was governed by various strange beliefs, such as the following: if taboos were broken, the herbs collected lost their efficacy; it was necessary to eat garlic before going to gather certain plants; some had to be gathered by day and others only by night; in given instances, the best quality of drugs could be obtained by approaching on the windward side; with others, top-quality material required the digger to face east while lifting the roots; one had to beware, too, of the woodpecker, buzzard hawk, and eagle, while plucking, respectively, peony, feverwort, and black hellebore, taking the precaution of drawing circles around the plant with a sword or placing fruit and cakes in the hole in the ground from which the plant had been uprooted.

It is likely that both Plato and Aristotle taught Theophrastus the essential role of classification in science. In any case, he was the first to apply principles of classification to the vegetable world. For each of about five hundred plants identified and described in his botanical treatises he attempted to note the characteristic features which distinguish it from other plants, and to indicate its individual "nature" or peculiar character. Theophrastus evidently felt an acute need of botanical terms, then largely nonexistent, and on occasion he was impelled to give special technical meanings to words in more or less current use, a method common to modern scientific nomenclature.

On the History of Plants is chiefly concerned with descriptions, discussions of structural parts of plants, and differences between plants. The nine books cover the following topics: (1) parts of plants and their nature and classification; (2) propagation, especially of trees; (3) wild trees; (4) trees and other plants found in particular areas or under special conditions (i.e., geographic botany); (5) timbers of various trees and their uses; (6) undershrubs; (7–8) herbaceous plants; (9) juices of plants and the medicinal properties of herbs.

In treating of trees, Theophrastus enumerates such external parts as roots, stems, branches, buds, leaves, flowers, and fruits, and refers to the sap, fibers, vessels, flesh, wood, bark, and pith. The *History* distinguishes woody from herbaceous plants, land from aquatic plants, and permanent organs from the deciduous ones. It also considers the lack of seed in elms and willows; the dissemination of seeds by rain and floods; the bleeding of turpentine from the stems of needle-leaved trees; and the use of roses for the manufacture of attar. Theophrastus recognizes fungi, algae, and lichens as plants, and he divides the plant world into the two kingdoms of flowering and flowerless plants. Another plant classification that he found useful was based on duration: annual, biennial, and perennial.

His second work, *On the Causes of Plants*, delves more deeply into the physiological features and philosophical implications of plants. Granting the striking differences between plants and their organs, how are the variations to be explained? Following the Aristotelian doctrine that Nature does nothing in vain, what could one learn of her intentions? Theophrastus sought for answers by finding out how plants live, grow, and multiply. Though less descriptive than the *History*, the *Causes* is also full of facts. Its six books relate to the following topics: (1) generation and propagation of plants, fructification and maturity of fruits; (2) means to increase plants (including the effects of weather and soil), horticulture, and silviculture; (3) planting shrubs, preparing the soil, and grape cultivation; (4) quality of seeds and their degeneration, culture of legumes; (5) plant diseases and other causes for crop failure; (6) tastes and odors of plants.

Theophrastus distinguishes what he considered the various modes of plant reproduction. "A plant," he says, "has power of germination in all its parts, for it has life in them all. . . . The manner of generation of trees and plants are these: spontaneous, from a seed, from a root, from a piece torn off, from a branch or twig, from the trunk itself, or from pieces of the wood cut up small." Theophrastus, like Aristotle, was fascinated by the miracle of germination, and comments in detail on closely observed behavior of germinating seeds: wheat, barley, beans, chick peas, lupines, and so on. A clear distinction is drawn between plants having single or multiple seed leaves: monocotyledon and dicotyledon, in modern botanical terminology.

One of the most remarkable passages in Theophrastus' *History* deals with plant sexuality. Explaining the fecundation of palm trees, he states: "With dates it is helpful to bring the male to the female; for it is the male which causes the fruit to persist and ripen." The process of pollination is then described, with specific directions for pollinating by hand. Sarton reminds us that Theophrastus' discovery "was almost completely forgotten until its reintroduction more than two millennia later." Ignorance on the subject is demonstrated as late as the seventeenth century, when the English herbalist Parkinson, in his *Theatre of Plants*, scoffed at Theophrastus' theory: "The ancient writers have set down many things of dates," he wrote, "but I pray you account this among the rest of their fables."

Both the *History* and *Causes* contain a considerable discussion of phytopathology—damage to plants, especially farm crops, by insects, worms, and other parasites. Theophrastus describes flea beetles, caterpillars, "horned worms" (a beetle), pea weevils, red spiders, codling moths, and other destructive insects that made life difficult for the Greek farmer. The particular plants attacked by each pest are noted, and control measures recommended.

Though Theophrastus does not treat of ecology (relations between organisms and their environment) in modern terms, he deals with wild plants in what are in effect ecological groups, e.g., marine herbs (algae), submerged marine trees (chiefly corals), marine shore plants, and plants found in deep fresh water, shallow lake shores, river banks, and marshes. Charles Singer, historian of medicine, notes that "Theophrastus has a perfectly clear idea of plant distribution as dependent on soil and climate, and at times seems to be on the point of passing from a statement of climatic distribution into one of real geographical regions."

The amount of botanic information Theophrastus was able to compile is truly astounding, especially in view of his lack of scientific instruments; the practical difficulties that he faced in gathering, sorting, and classifying data; and the almost complete absence in his time of useful guidelines in a new field. Little, if anything, worthwhile was added to his findings in ancient times or during the Middle Ages. In Sarton's judgment, "Theophrastus is not only the first botanic writer but also the greatest until the Renaissance of the sixteenth century in Germany. . . . The botany of Theophrastus and the zoology of Aristotle represent the climax of natural history in antiquity."

Archimedes: On the Sphere and Cylinder

The consensus among historians of science is that Archimedes (287?–212 B.C.) was the greatest mathematician of antiquity and conceivably the greatest mathematical genius of all time. Both in theories and in practical applications, his achievements were phenomenal.

Archimedes, a native of Syracuse, Sicily, was too young to have studied under Euclid. His instructors in mathematics at Alexandria, where he went to study, however, were students and followers of Euclid. Despite the fact that his versatile mind touched many fields, Archimedes always considered himself, like Euclid, a geometer. His mechanical inventions, as he saw them, were simply "the diversions of geometry at play."

The discoveries with which the name of Archimedes is most intimately associated are in hydrostatics and statics, of which sciences he is generally acknowledged to be the founder. According to an often-told story, the fundamental concept of hydrostatics came to Archimedes while bathing. Hiero, king of Syracuse, had ordered a pure gold crown. When it was delivered, he suspected the artisan had used silver as well as gold in its making. Archimedes was assigned the problem of finding the facts without destroying the crown. Noticing the buoyancy and loss of weight of his own body in the bath water, he suddenly realized that here was the solution: Any body immersed in a liquid must lose weight equal to the weight of the liquid displaced. He knew that a pound of silver occupies nearly twice as much space as a pound of gold. Using a piece of silver and a piece of gold, each of equal weight to that of the crown, and a full vessel, he measured how much water ran over, and thereby ascertained by mathematics exactly how much silver had been mixed with the gold.

Thus was established the "Archimedes principle" that every substance has a characteristic density or specific gravity. Briefly described, the principle is that a solid body, when surrounded by a fluid, will be buoyed up by a force equal to the weight of the fluid it displaces. When bodies lighter than water are pushed down into it, they displace an amount of water of greater weight than their own, so that, when let free, they rise to the surface of the water and float. Only as much of their bulk remains submerged as will displace a quantity of water of exactly equal weight. Bodies having the same density as water have no tendency to rise or sink, since their weights are identical. The principle applies also to bodies surrounded by other liquids, gases, and the air. An example of Archimedes' theory is the buoyancy of balloons.

Subsequently, Archimedes worked out methods for calculating the stability of floating bodies, a practical application of which was to design ships that would not turn over, introducing the basic idea of equilibrium.

Density is known as an intensive property, and modern physics and engineering are based on intensive properties which can be measured, such as temperature, electrical conductivity, heat conductivity, hardness, elasticity, melting point, boiling point, solubility in water, and viscosity.

Scarcely less celebrated than Archimedes' discovery of the first law of hydrostatics is his theoretical and practical approach to laws of the lever. He concludes: "Weights which balance at equal distances are equal, unequal weights at equal distance will not balance, and unequal weights at unequal distances will balance, the greater weight being at the lesser distance." These laws are the basis of operation, for example, of elevators and steam cranes. In brief, make the lever long enough, push the long end down far enough, and any weight can be lifted at the short end.

Out of his experiments with levers came another traditional tale about Archimedes. "Give me a place to stand on and I will move the earth," he stated to King Hiero. Impressed but skeptical, Hiero asked for a demonstration. As Plutarch relates the episode, the king possessed a large ship, a vessel which could be drawn out of the dock only with the labor of many men. "Loading her with many passengers and a full freight, sitting himself the while off, with no great endeavor, but only holding the head of the pulley in his hand and drawing the cord by degrees, Archimedes drew the ship in a straight line, as smoothly and evenly as if she had been in the sea." Archimedes had devised for the occasion a combination of pulleys now known as a pulley block or a block and tackle.

Most spectacular of Archimedes' inventions were those designed to defend Syracuse against invading Roman forces. Again as told by Plutarch, a colossal catapult hurled "immense masses of stone" that "came down with incredible noise and violence, against which no man could stand." Cranes caught ships that ventured in too close and up-ended them or hoisted them high in the air and then flung them back into the sea. Iron beaks seized other ships and smashed them into jutting cliffs, or held them fast while giant boulders were dropped on them. The Roman legions fled in panic from the devastation wrought by Archimedes' war machines. Syracuse was saved until three years later, when the Roman general Marcellus took it from the rear while the inhabitants were sleeping.

Though Archimedes' great mechanical ingenuity had to serve mainly military ends, he devised several ingenious contrivances for peaceful purposes. One of the best-known was a form of pump, called the Screw of Archimedes, a device for raising water, seeming to make water run uphill, and long used in irrigation and water pumping. This simple device was in effect a pipe twisted in the form of a corkscrew, confined within a cylinder; as it revolved about its axis, the "screw" drew the water up until it came out at the top. Also invented by Archimedes was a device for demonstrating the motions of the planets. This orrery, the first planetarium, was actually seen by Cicero, according to whom it represented the motions of sun and moon so well that eclipses could be demonstrated.

Nevertheless, Archimedes held his inventions in low esteem. He had been taught at Syracuse that a scientist was above practical affairs and everyday problems. Plutarch wrote, "although they [the inventions] had obtained for him the reputation of more than human sagacity, he did not deign to leave behind him any written work on such subject, but, regarding as ignoble and sordid the business of mechanics and every sort of art which is directed to use and profit, he placed his whole ambition in those speculations the beauty and subtlety of which are untainted by any admixture of the common needs of life."

Like that of other great Greek mathematicians before him— Thales, Pythagoras, Eudoxus, Euclid—such an attitude reflected intellectual snobbery, a contempt for practical applications, considered fit only for merchants and slaves. Yet, the practical problems fascinated Archimedes throughout his career.

Archimedes was correct, in a sense, in viewing his "speculations" as of first importance. Nearly two thousand years before Isaac Newton and Leibniz devised the modern calculus, Archimedes invented the integral calculus and in one of his problems anticipated the invention of the differential calculus. His chief interest was in pure geometry, and he regarded his discovery of the ratio of the volume of a cylinder to that of a sphere inscribed in it as his greatest achievement. He deduced the centers of gravity of many figures, including parabolic areas. He showed *pi*, the ratio of the circumference of a circle to its diameter, to be almost exactly the figure used in modern mathematics. Many of the common formulas of geometry are attributed to him. He has also been credited by recent writers on the history of mathematics with fundamental developments in trigonometry. In short, his work in mathematics was of immense range and variety.

Of Archimedes, George Sarton comments, "When one bears in mind that he had formulated and solved a good many abstruse problems without having any of the analytic instruments that we have, his genius fills us with awe." To which Bell, in his *Men of Mathematics*, adds: "Archimedes, the greatest intellect of antiquity, is modern to the core. He and Newton would have understood each other perfectly, and it is just possible that Archimedes, could he come to life long enough to take a postgraduate course in mathematics and physics, would understand Einstein,

Bohr, Heisenberg, and Dirac better than they understand themselves."

Archimedes met his end as a true scientist. Again according to our chief authority, Plutarch, when the Romans finally conquered Syracuse in 212 B.C., the Roman general Marcellus gave orders that Archimedes' life was to be spared. Archimedes refused to surrender, however, until he had completed a mathematical design on which he was engaged, and was slain by an irate soldier. In accordance with his expressed wish, the Roman conquerors built a tomb for him on which was engraved a diagram of a cylinder circumscribing a sphere, to commemorate the way in which he had calculated the area of a spherical surface.

Titus Lucretius Carus: De Rerum Natura

Of all the great figures of literature, Lucretius is a rare, perhaps a unique, example of a writer who is known by a single composition, a work upon which he spent his life, and, even so, left unfinished. *De Rerum Natura* ("On the Nature of Things") has the epic qualities of the *Iliad* and the *Aeneid*, but differs radically from them in being an epic, in poetical form, of scientific philosophy.

Lucretius (99–55 B.C.) lived in an age of famous personalities. Cicero, Caesar, Catullus, and Vergil were his Roman contemporaries. Of himself as an individual, virtually nothing is known. It is probable that his short life was spent in study and retirement. According to an ancient tradition, unverified, he was subject to fits of insanity and died by suicide.

Early in life, Lucretius apparently became an ardent convert to Epicurean philosophy, a system which he regarded as the final and complete solution of "the riddle of this painful earth." In *De Rerum Natura*, he represents himself as a disciple of the great master, Epicurus (c. 342–270 B.C.). Since only fragments of Epicurus' own writings have survived, Lucretius' magnificent poem, extending to 7,415 lines, is the most complete and systematic statement in existence of Epicurean thought.

The popular conception of Epicureanism is of a philosophy preaching pleasure and self-indulgence as the highest good, emphasizing sensual enjoyment and even debauchery. According to the moral teachings of Epicurus and his followers, such as Lucretius, however, man's true happiness is derived through freedom from superstitious fear, the renunciation of excessive ambition and of the pursuit of wealth, and delight in the simpler forms of pleasure, especially those of the mind.

The main purpose of *De Rerum Natura* is to show the way to the ideal life, to the tranquility of spirit and soul which was Epicurus' aim. As viewed by Lucretius, mankind is confronted by two major obstacles in its search for happiness and peace of mind: fear of the gods and fear of death. These impediments can be overcome, he maintains, by an understanding of the true nature of things. A rational approach will show that everything can be explained in natural, nothing in supernatural, terms. Further, the soul is mortal, and therefore death should hold no terrors. Hence, Lucretius' exposition of natural science was designed first of all to remove fear. We will cease to fear the gods, he believed, when we learn the laws of natural science, and we will no longer dread death when we learn the nature of the soul.

Lucretius was a bitter enemy of superstition and religion in all its forms, repudiating the concept of a divine providence watching over the ways and fates of men. He also condemned the idea of unseen powers hostile to man and capable of doing him evil as gross superstition, disproved by all nature. Because of their ignorance of natural phenomena and of the great forces of nature, men had come to believe that the gods were responsible for them and that these gods lived in the sky. Lucretius does not deny the existence of the gods; instead, he concludes that they dwell outside the world, in a state of untroubled bliss; that they have no control over nature; and that they are totally unconcerned with the affairs of the world. However, despite his opposition to the religion of his time, Lucretius showed a devout reverence for the powers of nature, which he in effect deified.

To drive out and to dispel miracles and superstitions, and to explain the universe in rational terms, Lucretius adopted the atomic theory. "All nature," he stated, "is composed of two things; for there are atoms and vacuum in which the atoms are situated and in which they move hither and thither. . . . The atoms are now in motion with the same motion as they had in ages past and to all eternity will continue to move in the same way."

An atomic theory had been invented by Leucippus (fl. 475

B.C.), and formulated more specifically by Democritus (460–370 B.C.), who used the word "atom" to signify a fundamental particle of matter so firm and small that it could not be further divided or smashed. The theory reached Lucretius several centuries later through the writings of Epicurus. As developed by Lucretius, it holds that all nature can be made intelligible by the concept of atoms in void space. The atoms are exceedingly small (though varying in size and shape); they are indestructible; they are in creaseless motion; and they are infinite in number. Collisions force atoms to combine into groups, thus bringing into existence things as we see them. Nothing can be destroyed; all change occurs by way of combination and separation of atoms, a hypothesis leading directly to the modern doctrines of the indestructibility of matter and the conservation of energy. In the Lucretian view, the sum of matter and the sum of energy in the universe are constant factors.

From his atomic conceptions, Lucretius draws certain startling conclusions: space and time are infinite; the laws of nature are universal and immutable; the variety of things is infinite; there are many worlds, all in process of change; and evolution is everywhere in evidence.

Foreshadowing Mendelian principles of heredity, Lucretius notes that germ seeds descend from parent to offspring, reproducing characteristics even of remote ancestors. The idea of evolution of species is lacking in his work, but, prefiguring the doctrine of the survival of the fittest is his observation that many plants and animals have disappeared from the earth because they failed to adapt to changing conditions.

In the evolution of man himself, Lucretius shows himself in harmony with modern anthropology. The fifth book of *De Rerum Natura* undertakes to trace the origin of life and the gradual advance of man from the most primitive cave dweller (the speechless subhuman prowler) to the most civilized Roman citizen. It tells how, step by step, man began social life, originated language, discovered fire, learned the use of metals, developed the art of war (next to religion, the most detestable of practices in Lucretius' eyes), and as civilization progressed developed clothing, horticulture, music, and writing. According to this account, nothing has a divine origin; everything evolves and grows from the operation of natural causes. Lucretius was thus the first to advance the idea of human progress.

Even grander in concept are Lucretius' theories of the cosmos. He considers possible processes by which the earth, the sky, sun, moon, and stars were formed. There are, Lucretius holds, an infinite number of universes, each having infinite potentialities for differences in natural phenomena.

The last of the six books is occupied with meteorology, seeking to explain, in accordance with natural causes, abnormal phenomena which are frequent sources of supernatural fear, such as thunder, lightning, hurricanes, clouds, rain and rainbow, earthquakes, volcanoes, and eclipses. For the most part, the theories offered are not in accord with present-day science, but Lucretius' principal aim was not so much to discover final scientific answers as to suggest a number of possible natural causes, thereby eliminating superstitious dread.

Lengthy passages in *De Rerum Natura* explain the nature of the soul and endeavor to destroy the fear of death. Lucretius argues that when the body dies, the soul also dies, because body and soul are made of atoms which are freed and separate when life ends. If men understood the finality of death, he felt, they would cease to worry about the hereafter and be happy. Man's fear of death and his efforts to shut out thoughts of it from his mind are responsible for avarice, uncontrolled ambition, war, murder, and even suicide. To Lucretius, the extinction of life is not a sad thing; it is a blessing, a relief, an emancipation. The endless chain of life-death-life must continue. From a universal view, the individual is insignificant.

To a great majority of mankind, doubtless, the Epicurean philosophy as thus propounded by Lucretius is unconvincing and unsatisfying. Except for Vergil, on whose writings the Lucretian influence is clear and profound, *De Rerum Natura* received slight attention from ancient authors. In fact, there is little to show that the work received any considerable notice prior to the Renaissance. Curiously, despite its antireligious bias, the poem was carefully preserved in the Christian monastic libraries, possibly because it attacks heathen gods. However, beginning with the rationalist thought of the sixteenth century, Lucretius became a great seminal influence. Giordano Bruno (1548–1600) was one of the first to be deeply attracted to him and to discuss the atomic theory. Sir Isaac Newton (1642–1727) was a convinced atomist, and his ideas of the atom closely resemble those of Lucretius. Under the influence of Newton, John Dalton (1766–

1844) revived the atomic theory and used it to explain his observations on the action of gases, thus laying the foundation for modern chemistry. In the nineteenth century, Clerk Maxwell and Lord Kelvin, and in the twentieth, Albert Einstein, are among the great scientists who have paid tribute to Lucretius. Though our knowledge of atomic science and of other fields for scientific inquiry explored by Lucretius has vastly expanded and changed since his era, his teachings have had a direct and beneficial influence upon the development of modern science.

Summing up a critical review of Lucretius and his work, Thomas Macaulay writes: "In energy, perspicuity, variety of illustration, knowledge of life and manners, talent for description, sense of the beauty of the external world, and elevation and dignity of moral feeling, Lucretius had hardly ever an equal."

Pliny the Elder: Natural History

To Gais Plinius Secundus, usually called Pliny the Elder (23–79)—to distinguish him from his famous nephew and protégé of the same name—we are indebted for the preservation of excerpts from hundreds of ancient writers whose works have otherwise vanished completely. According to a list appended by Pliny to the first book of his *Natural History*, he consulted some two thousand works by 147 Latin and 327 foreign authors in the preparation of this encyclopedic treatise.

Writing was more of an avocation than a vocation for Pliny. Following his birth in northern Italy and a period of study in Rome, he began, in his early twenties, an active military and governmental career that occupied him for the remainder of his life. Before completing his formal education, he had become interested in the study of plants. Shortly thereafter, under Seneca's influence, he had turned to philosophy and rhetoric and had begun the practice of law. On official missions, he traveled in Germany, Spain, Gaul, Africa, and possibly in Judea and Syria.

Despite multiple demands made on his time as soldier, lawyer, governor of provinces, and adviser to the Roman court, Pliny was a prolific author. A record left by the younger Pliny notes that his uncle wrote on the use of the javelin by cavalry, a history of the German wars, the training of the orator, a treatise on grammar, a history of Rome, and finally the *Natural History*, largest and most important of his works, and the only one that has survived. To account for such extraordinary literary productivity, Pliny the Younger describes his uncle's working habits. The elder Pliny was accustomed to reading or having books read to him at meals, in the bath, while traveling, or taking exercise, in brief, during every available minute. As he read or listened, he made notes or extracts from the material at hand, and when traveling he was accompanied by a corps of secretaries to take down his words. By these methodical practices, he gradually amassed a vast store of data for subsequent use.

In his preface to the *Natural History*, Pliny claims to have dealt with no less than twenty thousand subjects, to elucidate which he draws principally upon one hundred selected authors. In the main, therefore, the *Natural History* is a secondhand compilation from the works of others, though Pliny intersperses many observations of his own. Critics agree that he showed little judgment or discrimination in his selections, mixed the true and the false in hodgepodge fashion, neglected to arrange the mass of material by any intelligible method, and often failed to understand his authorities.

Natural history as interpreted by Pliny encompassed considerably more than does the modern definition of the term. In his work, he attempted to give a comprehensive survey of all contemporary knowledge of the physical universe, and of this world in particular as well as all of its constituents—animal, vegetable, and mineral. The compilation is thus an encyclopedia of astronomy, meteorology, geography, mineralogy, zoology, and botany. But, in addition, it treats of the fine arts, painting and sculpture, human inventions and institutions, and the author's views on religion, ethics, and literature.

The thirty-seven books of the *Natural History* are logically arranged, even though the contents are unsystematic. They are distributed as follows: mathematical and physical description of the world; geography and ethnography of Europe, Africa, and Asia; anthropology and human physiology; zoology of land animals, sea creatures, birds, and insects; botany, including agriculture and materia medica; medical zoology; mineralogy; history of ancient art, silver chasing, bronze statuary, painting, marble statuary, and precious stones. The portions relating to the fine arts, painting, and sculpture, while irrelevant from the point of view of natural history proper, are now regarded as among the most important parts of the work.

The main theme running through Pliny's *Natural History* is that nature is designed to serve the human race. Natural objects are usually described, therefore, only in their relation to man, for Pliny believed that all things were intended for some useful purpose. "Nature and Earth fill us with admiration," writes Pliny, "as we contemplate the great variety of plants and find that they are created for the wants or enjoyments of mankind." In his view, every plant has some special medicinal value, if it can be discovered, and for every disease there is a curative plant. It was this belief in an omniscient and omnipotent Nature that won great favor for the non-Christian Pliny and his works among the early Christians.

Through his writings on medical botany and materia medica, Pliny influenced the progress of medicine for the next fifteen hundred years. He offered a vast collection of remedies based on what he had heard or what he himself believed, though naturally without foundation in scientific experiment. His credulity is attested, for example, by the statement: "The herb dittany has power to extract arrows. This was proved by stags who had been struck by these missiles, which were loosened when they fed on this plant." Obviously, this is folklore, as were many of the current superstitions and notions Pliny subscribes to about the medicinal properties of various waters and of fishes and other aquatic creatures.

It is characteristic of Pliny that he accepted uncritically almost everything that he heard or read, without attempting to verify his facts by trial or observation. The marvelous and the monstrous held a special fascination for him. Thus, in writing about faraway places, he told of men whose feet were turned the wrong way, of mouthless men who fed upon the fragrance of flowers and fruit, of men whose feet were so large that they could hold them over their heads as parasols to protect them from the sun, of winged horses, unicorns, mermaids, near-human dolphins, and many other prodigies. Some of these yarns may be found later scattered through the *Arabian Nights* and the folk tales of Europe. On the other hand, Pliny rejected the prevailing belief in the astrological influences of the stars upon the human race, including the superstition that each falling star marked the death of the particular human to whom fate had attached it.

In religion, Pliny tended to be a Stoic. The *Natural History* contains numerous digressions on human morals and puritanical tirades. The author is critical of luxury and artificiality and urges simplicity in living. In general, he has a low estimate of human ability, deplores human wickedness, and mistrusts the wisdom of Providence.

Literature also receives Pliny's attention. His evaluation of great literary figures placed Homer and Cicero at the summit, with Vergil ranking only slightly below them.

Scientific curiosity cost Pliny his life. In A.D. 79, fifty-six years of age, he was in command of a Roman fleet in the Bay of Naples. The volcano Vesuvius began to erupt, and Pliny landed to get a closer view. While he was on shore, a terrific eruption, which buried the city of Pompeii, occurred, and Pliny was suffocated by sulphur fumes. A vivid account of this disaster is furnished by Pliny the Younger.

After Pliny's time, the *Natural History* was copied and recopied. For fifty generations, it was the paramount authority in its field among medieval and Renaissance scholars. At least two hundred manuscript copies prior to the invention of printing are in existence, and it is significant that Pliny's *Natural History* was the first scientific work to be printed (Venice, 1469).

The progress of modern science has made virtually all of Pliny's knowledge obsolete, and his work is read at present for its antiquarian and historical interest. In the *Natural History*, however, we have an encyclopedic mine of classical data, even though often inaccurate, on the natural sciences; and the compilation marks an important stage in the development of scientific knowledge. Further, the sections on sculpture, painting, and ancient culture in general contain valuable information available in no other extant writings of the period.

21

CELESTIAL REVOLUTION

Nicolaus Copernicus: De Revolutionibus Orbium Coelestium

Since primitive ages, man has been fascinated by the pageant of the skies—the sun, the moon, the planets, the stars, and their ceaseless movements. The rising and setting of the sun, the waxing and waning of the moon, the succession of the seasons, the advance and retreat of the planets were not only observable facts, but in numerous respects affected mankind's daily existence. It is not strange, therefore, that a vast body of legends, and even religions, grew up around celestial phenomena.

As civilizations advanced, philosophers attempted to explain the moving heavens in rational terms. Most advanced of the ancient scientists and thinkers on matters of astronomy were the Greeks, starting with Pythagoras in the fifth century B.C. and Aristotle in the next century. An Egyptian, Claudius Ptolemy, living in Alexandria about A.D. 150, organized and systematized the classical learning of his own and preceding eras into a comprehensive set of theories. For nearly 1,500 years, the Ptolemaic system, as set forth in "The Almagest," dominated the minds of men and was universally accepted as the true conception of the universe.

Ptolemy's theory was built around the notion that the earth was a fixed, inert, immovable mass, located at the center of the universe, and all celestial bodies, including the sun and the fixed stars, revolved around it. The earth, it was believed, was the hub of a system of spheres. To these the planets were rigidly attached. The stars were attached to another sphere outside this system, and all rotated each twenty-four hours. The complicated motions of the planets were explained by epicycles, with the

307

planetary spheres rotating in the opposite direction from the sphere of stars, but pulled along by a stronger force. Saturn was considered the most distant planet, nearest to stellar space, and consequently took longest to complete a revolution. The moon, being nearest the center, completed a revolution in the briefest time. Edward Rosen describes the Ptolemaic conception in these terms:

The traditional doctrine held that the planets, moving eastward most of the time, periodically slowed down until they actually came to a halt, then reversed themselves a second time, resuming their eastward journey, and repeating this cycle of changes endlessly.

The universe was thus a closed space bounded by a spherical envelope. Beyond this universe there was nothing.

General assent to the Ptolemaic theories was made easier by two factors, both a reflection of human nature: first, the system rested upon natural appearances, upon things as they were seen by any casual observer; and, second, they fed man's ego. How pleasing it was to believe that the earth was the center of the heavens, with the planets and stars revolving about it. The whole universe seemed to be made for man.

This beautiful structure remained substantially intact until the coming of the great era of intellectual awakening in Europe— the Renaissance. The theory's destruction was the work of Nicolaus Copernicus, "a churchman, a painter and a poet, a physician, an economist, a statesman, a soldier, and a scientist"—one of the "universal men" for whom the Renaissance was celebrated.

Copernicus' seventy-year life span, 1473-1543, was one of the most exciting and adventurous periods in Europe's history. Columbus discovered new continents. Magellan circumnavigated the globe, Vasco da Gama made the first sea voyage to India, Martin Luther waged the Protestant Reformation, Michelangelo created a new world of art, Paracelsus and Vesalius laid the groundwork for modern medicine, and Leonardo da Vinci, "that tremendous universal genius," flourished as painter, sculptor, engineer, architect, physicist, biologist, and philosopher. What a fitting age for another brilliant mind, Copernicus, to give the world a new system for the universe.

Nicolaus Copernicus was born on the banks of the Vistula in Torun, Poland, an old Hanseatic League city. His early career was largely directed by an influential uncle, Lucas Watzelrode, later the prince-bishop of Ermeland. A long and varied education for Nicolaus began with the preparatory school at Torun, and continued, in 1491, at the University of Krakow. He had been attracted to this institution by its reputation as one of the leading European centers for mathematics and astronomy. Five years later he traveled to Italy to continue his education at Bologna, one of the oldest and most famous of European universities. The study of canon law and astronomy occupied his time. Subsequently, he spent a year in Rome, lecturing on mathematics and astronomy. About five years in Padua and Ferrara, studying medicine and church law, completed Copernicus' academic career. His degree of Doctor of Canon Law was received from Ferrara in 1503.

Meanwhile, through his uncle's influence, Copernicus had been nominated canon in the cathedral of Frauenburg, and it was there that he spent the remaining thirty-seven years of his life, after returning from Italy in 1506.

Copernicus' canonical duties were multifarious: he carried on an active medical practice among churchmen and laity; aided in the military defense of his district in the recurring wars between Poles, Prussians and Teutonic knights; participated in the peace conferences which followed; advised on the reform of the coinage and currency; administered the remoter parts of the diocese; and for relaxation, painted and translated Greek poetry into Latin.

Astronomy, then, was only one of the varied activities carried on by the versatile Copernicus. But increasingly it became his primary interest, as he developed his ideas on astronomical phenomena—ideas which apparently had come to him early in life and had been intensified by his studies at Krakow and in Italy. His investigations were carried on quietly and alone, without help or consultation. For an observatory, he used a turret on a protective wall built around the cathedral.

Astronomical instruments available to Copernicus were crude and primitive. His work was done nearly a century before the telescope was invented. For measuring purposes, he possessed a sundial; a triquetrum (an awkward three-sided wooden affair) which he made himself, to obtain the altitudes of the stars and planets; and an astrolabe, a sphere within vertical and horizontal rings. Further, the climate was unfavorable to astronomical observations; proximity to the Baltic Sea and rivers brought fogs and clouds. Completely clear days and nights were rare. Nevertheless, on every possible occasion, year after year, Copernicus labored over his calculations.

The revolutionary theory which Copernicus was attempting to prove or disprove through his prolonged studies went directly contrary to the time-honored and revered Ptolemaic system. The theory was, in short, that the earth was not stationary but rotated on an axis once daily and traveled around the sun once yearly. So fantastic was such a concept in the sixteenth century that Copernicus did not dare to advance it until he was convinced his data were irrefutable. Hence the delay of more than thirty years before the Copernican system was revealed to the world.

Actually, certain of the ancient Greek astronomers had suggested that ours might be a sun-centered rather than an earth-centered universe. Aristarchus, "the ancient Copernicus," in the third century, B.C., for example, accounted for the daily rising and setting of the sun by supposing that the earth turned around once a day on its axis. But his hypothesis, along with those of other astronomers with similar ideas, was rejected by Aristotle and Ptolemy in favor of a geocentric or earth-centered scheme. These early theories were known to Copernicus from his reading of classical literature, and may well have inspired him to a reexamination of the problem. To Copernicus, it seemed that Aristarchus, 1,800 years before, had given a much simpler explanation of the motions of the sky than were contained in the complicated Ptolemaic system.

Perhaps as early as 1510, Copernicus wrote a short general account of his new theory. Entitled the *Commentariolus*, or "Little Commentary," the tract was not published during the author's lifetime, but a number of handwritten copies were circulated among students of astronomy. At least two of the manuscripts are still extant. In the *Commentariolus* Copernicus indicated that he had begun his researches because it appeared to him that the Ptolemaic theories of the cosmos were too complex, too irrational, and did not provide satisfactory explanations for celestial phenomena. The main conclusions to which Copernicus had come were reported: the earth was not the center of the solar system, but only of the moon orbit, and all the planets revolved around the sun. The "Little Commentary" represented a distinct stage in the development of the great astronomer's ideas.

It is conceivable that Copernicus' master work, on which he had toiled for thirty years, might never have reached the printing press, and consequently would have been lost to the world, except for the efforts of a young German scholar. In the summer of 1539 there came to Frauenburg to visit Copernicus a twenty-five-year-old professor of mathematics from the University of Wittenberg. This was George Joachim Rheticus. Attracted by Copernicus' growing fame, Rheticus had come to verify at first hand the true merits of his reputation. He expected to remain only a few weeks, but he was warmly welcomed by Copernicus and actually stayed for over two years. He speedily became convinced that his host was a genius of the first rank. For three months he studied Copernicus' writings and discussed them with the author. Rheticus then wrote an account of the Copernican ideas and sent it, in the form of a letter, to his former teacher Johann Schöner, at Nuremberg. The letter was printed at Danzig in 1540. The *Narratio Prima*, or "First Account," by Rheticus, was the first published statement of the Polish astronomer's world-shaking theories. Actually, the little book dealt in detail only with a portion of the Copernican system, that is, with a consideration of the earth's movements. Rheticus had anticipated following his "First Account" with other "accounts," but these were never required. His admiration, amounting almost to adulation, was shown by the warm praise he gave his "Dominus Doctor" throughout his treatise.

Up to this point, Copernicus had been extremely reluctant to permit publication of his complete work. He was a perfectionist, and felt every observation had to be checked and rechecked; the original manuscript, rediscovered in Prague in the middle of the nineteenth century, after being lost for three hundred years, shows evidence of a half-dozen extensive revisions. In addition to these hesitations, Copernicus may also have been deterred by the potential disapproval of the Church. The Protestant Reformation and the intellectual ferment of the Renaissance were making religious circles suspicious of revolutionary theories as well as of any ideas that might cause other departures from orthodox teachings. Copernicus, a faithful churchman, had no desire to play the heretic or the martyr.

So favorably received, however, was the *Narratio Prima*, and so urgent were the pleadings of Rheticus and others to permit full publication, that Copernicus finally yielded. The manuscript was entrusted to Rheticus, who was to take it to Nuremberg and see it through the press. Before this task could be accomplished, however, Rheticus was appointed to a professorship at the University of Leipzig, and a local Lutheran clergyman, Andreas Osiander, was assigned the responsibility.

Apparently Osiander was worried about the radical ideas expressed by Copernicus. Without authorization and anonymously, he proceeded to remove Copernicus' introduction to Book I. For it he substituted his own preface, stating that the book merely contained hypotheses for the convenience of astronomers; it was not necessarily true or even probable that the earth moves; in other words, the book was not to be taken seriously. Osiander was doubtless well intentioned in his attempt to avoid hostile criticism; and, as Stephen Paul Mizwa pointed out, "Perhaps, unwittingly, Osiander rendered a much greater service than he realized for the preservation of this great work. Because of this spurious and disarming foreword, cleverly addressed as though in the name of the author, 'to the reader of the hypotheses of this work,' the church overlooked the revolutionary importance of *De Revolutionibus* and did not put it on the Index until 1616."

Before the printing was finished, Copernicus suffered a severe stroke. A well-authenticated story relates that, in one of the most dramatic moments in history, a messenger arrived in Frauenberg bringing from Nuremberg the first copy of Copernicus' masterpiece and placed it in his hands only a few hours before the author's death. The date was May 24, 1543. The book was entitled *De Revolutionibus Orbium Coelestium*, "Concerning the Revolutions of the Heavenly Spheres." Like other scholarly productions of the time, it was written in Latin.

Wisely and diplomatically, Copernicus dedicated his work to Pope Paul III. It is obvious from the dedicatory statement that Copernicus anticipated some difficulties.

I can well believe, most holy father, that certain people, when they hear of my attributing motion to the earth in these books of mine, will at once declare that such an opinion ought to be rejected. Now, my own theories do not please me so much as not to consider what others may judge of them. Accordingly, when I began to reflect upon what those persons who accept the stability of the earth, as confirmed by the opinion of many centuries, would say when I claimed that the earth moves, I hesitated for a long time as to whether I should publish that which I have written to demonstrate its motion, or whether it would not be better to follow the example of the Pythagoreans, who used to hand down the secrets of philosophy to their relatives and friends in oral form. As I well considered this, I was almost impelled to put the finished work wholly aside, through the scorn I had reason to anticipate on account of the newness and apparent contrariness to reason of my theory.

My friends, however, dissuaded me from such a course and admonished me that I ought to publish my book which has lain concealed in my possession not only nine years, but already into four times the ninth year. Not a few other distinguished and very learned men asked me to do the same thing, and told me that I ought not on account of my anxiety, to delay any longer in consecrating my work to the general service of mathematicians. . . .

I do not doubt that clever and learned men will agree with me if they are willing fully to comprehend and to consider the proofs which I advance in the book before us. In order, however, that both the learned and the unlearned may see that I fear no man's judgment, I wanted to dedicate these, my night labors, to your Holiness, rather than to anyone else, because you, even in this remote corner of the Earth where I live, are held to be the greatest in dignity of station and in love for all sciences and for mathematics, so that you, through your position and judgment, can easily suppress the bites of slanderers, although the proverb says that there is no remedy against the bite of calumny. It may fall out, too, that idle babblers, ignorant of mathematics, may claim a right to pronounce a judgment on my work, by reason of a certain passage of Scripture basely twisted to suit their purpose. Should any such venture to criticize and carp at my project I heed them not and look upon their judgments as rash and contemptible.

His conception of the universe is summarized by Copernicus in these words:

Most distant of all is the Sphere of the Fixed Stars, containing all things and for that very reason immovable; in truth the frame of the Universe, to which the motion and position of all other stars are referred. Though some men think it to move in some way, we assign another reason why it appears to do so in our theory of the movement of the Earth. Of the moving bodies first comes Saturn, who completes his circuit in 30 years. After him, Jupiter, moving in a twelve year revolution. Then, Mars, who revolves biennially. Fourth in order an annual cycle takes place in which we have said is contained the Earth with the lunar orbit as an epicycle. In the fifth place Venus is carried around in nine months. Then Mercury holds the sixth place, circulating in the space of eighty days. In the middle of all dwells the Sun. Who, indeed, in this most beautiful temple would place the torch in any other or better place than one whence it can illuminate the whole at the same time? . . . We find, therefore, under this orderly arrangement a wonderful symmetry in the Universe, and a definite relation of harmony in the motion and magnitude of the orbs, of a kind it is not possible to obtain in any other way.

An outline of the contents of *De Revolutionibus* will show the plan of its development. Following the dedicatory preface to Pope Paul III, and the fake introduction by Osiander, the work is divided into six "Books," or main divisions, each subdivided by chapters. In Book I are Copernicus' views of the universe, arguments in favor of his heliocentric or sun-centered theory, including the idea that the earth, like other planets, revolves around the sun, and a discussion of the seasons. Several chapters at the end of this book constitute a textbook on trigonometry, and the principles of this branch of mathematics were utilized by Copernicus in later sections.

Book II deals with the motions of the celestial bodies, measured mathematically, and closes with a catalog of stars, showing the position of each in the sky—a list taken over from Ptolemy for the most part, though with some corrections.

The other four books contain detailed descriptions of the motions of the earth, the moon, and the planets. In each case, explanation of the motions is accompanied by a geometrical diagram showing the course followed by the sphere on the basis of Copernicus' calculations.

One of the principal reasons advanced against the theory of a moving earth had been stated by Ptolemy. The earth must remain stationary, he contended, for otherwise anything floating in the air, such as a cloud or a bird, would be left behind, and an object tossed in the air would descend a considerable distance westward. Most cataclysmic of all, if the earth turned at such a tremendous speed, it would soon break into pieces, disintegrate, and fly off into space. Before Galileo's discovery of the mechanics involved and Newton's law of gravitation, these ancient Ptolemaic arguments were difficult to refute. Copernicus answered them by suggesting that the air around the earth is carried along by the earth's motion and that it is more logical to assume that the earth turns instead of the entire universe, for if the earth did not rotate, the sky would have to revolve to produce day and night. The defense was further reinforced by a philosophical speculation: nature is not self-destructive, and God would not have created a universe merely to have it destroy itself.

For Copernicus, the sun was inert and passive, stationary amid revolving planets, much like Ptolemy's conception of the earth. The sun's only functions were to supply light and heat. The universe was strictly limited. Outside the sphere of the stars, as Ptolemy had taught, space ceased to exist. The concept of infinite space was probably as unknown to Copernicus as it had been 1,400 years earlier to Ptolemy. Neither did he depart from Ptolemy's system of epicycles. There was a different center for each of the orbits, and the sun was not placed in the true center of any of the planetary orbits. These were features of the Copernican system to be corrected by later astronomers.

Acceptance of the Copernican system was slow, both among scientists and the general populace. With a few exceptions, expressions of contemporary opinion were in violent opposition. According to one tale, the printer's shop where *De Revolutionibus* was being printed was attacked by university students who tried to destroy the press and the manuscript; the printers barricaded themselves to finish the job. A burlesque play ridiculing Copernicus was produced by a group of strolling players at Elbing; it depicted the astronomer as having given his soul to Satan.

More serious, however, was the reaction of the powerful Church organizations. The new theories upset the standard philosophical and religious beliefs of the medieval era. If the Copernican doctrines were true, man no longer occupied a central place in the universe; he had been removed from his pedestal, and his home was reduced to but one of many planets.

But because it was occupied with other matters and in part perhaps because of Osiander's misleading preface, the Catholic Church took no immediate action against the Copernican treatise. Less restrained were the Reformation leaders. Martin Luther severely criticized Copernicus on a number of occasions. He referred to him as "the new astronomer who wants to prove that the Earth goes round, and not the Heavens, the Sun, and the Moon; just as if someone sitting in a moving wagon or ship were to suppose that he was at rest, and that the Earth and the trees were moving past him. But that is the way nowadays; whoever wants to be clever must needs produce something of his own, which is bound to be the best since *he* has produced it! The fool will turn the whole science of Astronomy upside down. But, as Holy Writ declares, it was the Sun and not the Earth which

Joshua commanded to stand still." Luther's loyal disciple Melanchthon remarked disparagingly of Copernicus, "He stopped the sun and set the earth in motion."

John Calvin was equally emphatic in his condemnation, quoting Psalm 93: "The world also is established, that it cannot be moved," and demanded indignantly, "Who will venture to place the authority of a Copernicus above that of the Holy Spirit?"

Not until 1615 did the Catholic Church take stern measures against the *De Revolutionibus,* and its action then was in the nature of reprisal against such advocates of the Copernican theories as Galileo and Bruno. The Copernican principles were disposed of in this fashion:

The first proposition, that the sun is the center and does not revolve about the earth, is foolish, absurd, false in theology, and heretical, because expressly contrary to Holy Scripture. The second proposition, that the earth revolves about the sun and is not the center, is absurd, false in philosophy and from a theological point of view at least, opposed to the true faith.

The following year, 1616, the writings of Copernicus were placed on the Index of prohibited books "until they should be corrected," and, at the same time, "all writings which affirm the motion of the Earth" were condemned. For more than two centuries, Copernicus remained on the Index. The ban was finally removed in 1835.

The fates suffered by Galileo and Bruno may well have deterred others from embracing the Copernican system. Giordano Bruno, an ardent follower of Copernicus, went beyond the latter in advocating the theory that space is boundless and that the sun and its planets are only one of many similar systems. He suggested further that there might be other inhabited worlds, with rational beings equal or superior to ourselves. For such blasphemy, Bruno was tried before the Inquisition, condemned, and burned at the stake in February, 1600. Only slightly less drastic was the treatment of the great Italian astronomer Galileo, who, in 1633, under threat of torture and death by the Inquisition, was forced on his knees to renounce all belief in Copernican theories, and was sentenced to imprisonment for the remainder of his days.

The hesitation of Catholic and Protestant theologians to accept the Copernican theory was matched by the attitude of philosophers and scientists. One of the founders of modern scientific methods, Francis Bacon, for example, argued against the conception of the earth rotating on an axis and circling in an orbit around the sun. The hold of Aristotle and Ptolemy on the European universities was unbroken long after *De Revolutionibus* saw the light. Actually, as Joel Stebbins points out, "The slow adoption of the Copernican system was characteristic of all countries. In America the Ptolemaic and Copernican systems were taught concurrently at Harvard and also at Yale."

Nevertheless, slowly and gradually the Copernican theories won inevitable acceptance. Continued investigations by such dedicated scientists as Giordano Bruno, Tycho Brahe, Johann Kepler, Galileo Galilei, and Isaac Newton during the succeeding decades constructed a pyramid of irrefutable evidence. Defects in the Copernican system were removed by these and other investigators as better instruments for observation were perfected, and as each individual could build upon the researches of his predecessors.

The greatest astronomer immediately following Copernicus was a Dane, Tycho Brahe. Brahe did not subscribe to the theory that the earth revolves around the sun, but, with excellent instruments given to him by the King of Denmark, he was able to make astronomical observations and measurements far superior to those of Copernicus. On the basis of these data, his German assistant, Johann Kepler, after Brahe's death, was able to formulate his three famous laws: (1) that planets travel in ellipses, rather than in circles, with the sun in one focus; (2) that as the earth or other planet revolves around the sun in its elliptical orbit it does not move uniformly, but in such a way that as it is nearest the sun it moves fastest; (3) the distance of a planet from the sun is proportional to the period of its revolutions around the sun.

Galileo was the first observer to apply the telescope to astronomy, and many of his telescopic discoveries substantiated the findings of Copernicus. A scientific foundation was provided by Galileo when he established fundamental principles in dynamics, the science of motion. Conclusive proof of the validity of the Copernican theory was furnished by Sir Isaac Newton, with his discovery of the law of gravitation and his formulation of the

laws under which the planets moved. And some of the remaining
mysteries of the universe were unveiled by Einstein's theory of
relativity in the twentieth century.

In the light of numerous modifications made by scientists in
later centuries, the question is frequently and reasonably asked:
Is the Copernican theory true? Undeniably, Copernicus left his
system incomplete and inaccurate at various points. His conception of the perfectly circular motion of the celestial bodies was
demonstrated to be erroneous; instead, they move in ellipses.
Copernicus thought of the universe with very finite limitations,
contrary to the modern theory of an infinite number of solar
systems. In other details, likewise, the principles stated by Copernicus over four centuries ago do not conform to present-day
knowledge. But in its essential feature—the choice of the sun as
the center of our planetary system—Copernicus discovered fundamental truth and furnished a foundation for the modern science of astronomy.

Copernicus' place in the history of science is lastingly established. His influence on his contemporaries and on all subsequent
thought entitle him to a preeminent position. As Goethe wrote:

Of all discoveries and opinions, none may have exerted a greater effect on the human spirit than the doctrine of Copernicus. The world
had scarcely become known as round and complete in itself when it
was asked to waive the tremendous privilege of being the center of
the universe. Never, perhaps, was a greater demand made on mankind
—for by this admission so many things vanished in mist and smoke!
What became of our Eden, our world of innocence, piety and poetry;
the testimony of the senses; the conviction of a poetic—religious faith?
No wonder his contemporaries did not wish to let all this go and
offered every possible resistance to a doctrine which in its converts
authorized and demanded a freedom of view and greatness of thought
so far unknown, indeed not even dreamed of.

In conclusion, consider the judgments of three notable American scientists. Commented Vannevar Bush, "Publication of the
master work of Copernicus . . . marked a turning point of such
great importance as to influence every phase of human thought.
It affords an outstanding example of the effect of scientific truth
in the freeing of man's mind and in clearing his vision for future
conquests of ignorance and intolerance." Nobel prize winner
Harold C. Urey affirmed, "All superlatives fail when describing
the work of Nicolaus Copernicus. He broke with a conception

of the solar system that had stood for one thousand years, and introduced an entirely new concept of the relation of the planets to the sun. In so doing he initiated the whole modern method of scientific thought, and modified our thinking on all phases of human life." Last, there is the opinion of the distinguished astronomer Harlan True Stetson:

It is always embarrassing to survey the long list of true notables that have contributed to the progress of science in the world's history and to give any small number as preeminently outstanding. Yet, if I were called upon to select three names, I should say without much hesitation, Copernicus, Newton, and Darwin. These three have certain characteristics in common that make them inseparable in the triumph of progress. These characteristics are imagination, the boldness of genius, and an originality exhibiting extraordinary comprehensiveness of the concept. Of the greatest of these, all things considered, I believe the laurels would go to Copernicus, for it was he who laid the foundations of modern astronomy without which Newton could not have built his law of gravity and he opened the gates to a revolutionary type of thinking challenging the orthodox which had to take place before the doctrine of evolution could gain a foothold in our thinking.

22

FATHER OF SCIENTIFIC ANATOMY

Andreas Vesalius: De Humani Corporis Fabrica

It is an amazing coincidence that Nicolaus Copernicus' *De Revolutionibus Orbium Coelestium* (May 25, 1543) preceded by only one week publication of another monumental scientific work, Andreas Vesalius' *De Humani Corporis Fabrica* (June 1, 1543). Scholars agree that, as definitely as such events can be traced, these two books represent the end of the medieval era and the birth of modern science. A striking difference may be noted, however, between the ages of the authors: Copernicus was seventy and Vesalius only twenty-eight when their books appeared.

Vesalius came from a Belgian family that had produced five generations of psysicians, and he was determined from the outset to follow in their footsteps. His specific interest in anatomy began early. As a boy, fascinated by the physical characteristics of small animals, he dissected hundreds of them—moles, toads, rats, pigs, cats, dogs, and monkeys. After a preliminary education at Louvain, he chose to go to Paris to study anatomy. The chief attraction there appears to have been a renowned teacher, Jacobus Sylvius. But Vesalius was destined to be bitterly disappointed in Sylvius' lectures and demonstrations.

The teaching of anatomy and the sciences in general was, at the time, highly formalized, a practice handed down from the Middle Ages. The professor of anatomy sat on a raised platform, high above the class, reading appropriately sanctioned passages from Galen, a second-century Greek physician. At his feet was a body, usually of an animal, and beside it a barber-surgeon, who dissected the specimen in crude fashion and pointed out the parts described by the physician.

In the preface to his celebrated book, Vesalius referred contemptuously to "the detestable procedure now in vogue, that one man should carry out the dissection of the body, and another give the description of the parts." He continued:

These latter are perched up aloft in a pulpit like jackdaws, and with a notable air of disdain they drone out information about facts they have never approached at first hand, but which they merely commit to memory from the books of others, or of which they have descriptions before their eyes; the former are so ignorant of languages that they are unable to explain their dissections to the onlookers and botch what ought to be exhibited in accordance with the instruction of the physician, who never applies his hand to the dissection, and contemptuously steers the ship out of the manual. Thus everything is wrongly taught, days are wasted in absurd questions, and in the confusion less is offered to the onlooker than a butcher in his stall could teach a doctor.

During the medieval era and until well into the sixteenth century Galen's writings were read with almost idolatrous reverence. For fourteen centuries his treatise on the organization of the human body was the accepted text for the entire medical world. Galen was the final authority in everything relating to anatomy, physiology, diagnosis, therapy, and medical theory. To doubt him might well lead to death for heresy. Scant attention was paid to the work of critics, such as Leonardo da Vinci (1452–1519), whose remarkable anatomical dissections and drawings disproved some of Galen's conclusions. In dissections, if the specimen differed in any particular from Galen's descriptions, the explanation was that the human body had changed since the master's time.

Dissatisfied with the type of instruction he had encountered in Paris, Vesalius concluded that anatomy could be learned only through firsthand dissection of human bodies. Cadavers, however, were extremely difficult to come by. His search for material led him, at great personal risk, to undertake body-snatching expeditions. On one occasion, he stole a corpse from the gallows outside the Louvain city walls, the body being that of a criminal who had been left hanging as a warning to other malefactors.

After Paris and a period in Venice, Vesalius was appointed professor of surgery and anatomy at Padua. There he lectured to overflowing classes of students, personally performing all dissections, and unhesitatingly corrected Galen when his own observations showed Galen in error. Meanwhile, work continued on his great anatomical treatise, conceived by Vesalius several years earlier.

By late summer of 1542, Vesalius had ready the text and illustrations for *De Humani Corporis Fabrica* ("On the Structure of the Human Body"). The magnificent drawings are believed to have been done under Vesalius' direction by Jan Stephen van Calcar, a pupil of Titian. The *Fabrica*, as one commentator wrote, "is more than a milestone in the history of medicine; it is a great work of creative art." The woodcuts combine scientific exactness and artistic beauty, while the printing is a superb example of the typography of Oporinus of Basel, the Swiss city where the book was produced.

The subject matter in the *Fabrica* was arranged in the same order of topics as Vesalius' lectures: the bones, the muscles, blood vessels and nerves, the internal organs, and the brain. Though Vesalius' anatomical descriptions have great merit, chief interest centers in the plates, frequently described as the finest anatomical drawings ever made. Even the initial letters are works of art, showing cherubs engaged in dissection and other activities. In the frontispiece, Vesalius himself is shown standing beside the dissecting table, on which a body lies, with a panoramic view of the dissection theatre as a background. Here is depicted the birth of scientific anatomy, man's first clear and accurate knowledge of the foundation stone of medical science and of the whole science of the human body.

The effect of such a radical publication as the *Fabrica* on a superstitious age was explosive. Because it denied concepts of the structure of the human body accepted for centuries and attacked the sacred writings of Galen himself, Vesalius was uncompromisingly condemned by the stubborn forces of tradition. Leading the attack was Sylvius, Vesalius' old teacher at Paris, who spoke of Vesalius as a madman, and added:

I implore his Majesty the Emperor to punish severely as he deserves, this monster, born and reared in his own home, this most pernicious exemplar of ignorance, ingratitude, arrogance, and impiety: and to suppress him completely lest he poison the rest of Europe with his pestilential breath.

Highly sensitive to criticism, Vesalius resigned his post at Padua, burned all his notebooks, and moved to Spain to become personal physician to Charles V and later to Philip II. His career in anatomical research was finished.

Vesalius was more than the founder of a real science of anatomy; along with Harvey, he was instrumental in establishing sound principles of scientific research, science based on fact rather than tradition. Sir William Osler, the noted Canadian authority, called the *Fabrica* "the greatest medical book ever written—from which modern medicine starts." The famous British physiologist, Sir Michael Foster, concurred:

This book is the beginning, not only of modern anatomy, but of modern physiology. . . . Upon the publication of the "Fabrica" the pall of authority was once and for ever removed. It ended, for all time, the long reign of fourteen centuries of precedent; it began in a true sense the renaissance of medicine.

23

DAWN OF SCIENTIFIC MEDICINE

William Harvey: De Motu Cordis

Biological science and research at the beginning of the seventeenth century were little more advanced than had been the study of astronomy prior to Copernicus. Physicians and medical schools still practiced and taught the anatomical and physiological theories concerning the heart, arteries, veins, and blood handed down from the great Asiatic-Greek physician Galen in the second century as Vesalius had found earlier.

For more than a thousand years, no substantial additions had been made to man's knowledge of blood circulation and the functions of the heart. Aristotle had taught that blood originated in the liver, went from there to the heart, and then through the body to the veins. The heart, he believed, was also the source of body heat and the seat of intelligence. Erasistratus of the Alexandrian school maintained that the arteries carried a subtle kind of air or spirits. This conception had been corrected by Galen, who discovered that the arteries carried blood, not air, but for centuries after his time physicians were convinced that a spirit of some sort had a part in the blood system, perhaps animating the heart.

Only the boldest of scientists dared to question the precedents and sayings received from the ancients. Galen's writings were regarded as of almost divine origin—not to be disputed or doubted. According to Galen, too, the liver was the center of the blood system. Digested food was carried to the liver and there transformed into blood, with "natural spirits" added. Blood

324

moved backward and forward in the body, by way of both the veins and the arteries, like the slow ebb and flow of the tides. Arterial blood from one side of the heart mixed with venous blood from the other side through minute pores.

To natural facts there had become attached, over the centuries, much superstitious lore about the blood. More than any other part of the body, blood possessed a sacred quality, as is shown by its use in religious sacrifices and the pouring of blood upon the altars of the gods.

By 1600, however, change was everywhere in the air. The Renaissance in Europe brought not only a revival of literature, but an intellectual awakening immediately affecting the natural sciences. It was the age of Galileo, Kepler, Harvey, Bacon, and Descartes. In Italy, fifty years earlier, "the founder of modern anatomy," Andreas Vesalius, proved that the "pores" described by Galen were nonexistent, and that there was no direct connection between the two chambers of the heart. About the same time, Servetus, later burned at the stake by John Calvin, stated his belief that the blood circulates through the lungs, but he did not recognize the heart as a pumping organ. The pulmonary circulation idea was likewise suggested by Realdo Colombo, anatomy professor at Rome. Another important link was supplied by Fabricius of Padua in 1603, when he discovered that the veins have valves, though he misunderstood their purpose, surmising they were merely meant to slow the flow of blood into the extremities.

Thus, these and a few other brave souls had the temerity to cast doubt on ancient dogma that had held medical progress enchained throughout the medieval era. None, on the other hand, was able to arrive at the whole truth. Each made a significant contribution toward unveiling the mystery of blood circulation and heart functions, but in every instance stopped short, with a partial and incomplete answer. The task of discovering and formulating an orderly, systematic, and scientific set of principles fell to the brilliant and incisive mind of an English physician, William Harvey.

The renascence of learning came to England later than to the Continent, particularly Italy, but at the time of Harvey's birth in 1578, the nation was entering one of its greatest periods. During the reign of Queen Elizabeth, Britain's naval might would be established by the defeat of the Spanish Armada, English explorers would open up new lands, and Shakespeare, Donne, Spenser, Dryden, Milton, Jonson, and Bacon would flourish in the literary world. The repression of thought, characteristic of preceding centuries, was beginning to lift, and men's minds were free, within certain limits, to create new ideas and to open new fields.

For the study of medicine, it was natural for Harvey to go to Italy. The renowned university at Padua has been called the alma mater of the Renaissance, and for generations it was the medical center of Europe. There, after graduating from Cambridge, young Harvey spent four years, principally under the guidance of a famous and inspiring teacher, Fabricius, discoverer of valves in the veins. He learned to dissect and experiment on various kinds of animals, and it is probable that his lifetime interest in blood circulation was first aroused by Fabricius' theories.

Returning to England in 1602, Harvey began a career destined to last for the next fifty years, as physician, lecturer, and writer. He married the daughter of Queen Elizabeth's personal physician, and subsequently served as a fellow of the Royal College of Physicians, physician to St. Bartholomew's Hospital, and physician to James I and Charles I.

Throughout his life, however, Harvey was more fascinated by medical research and experimentation than by the practice of medicine. In 1616 he began lecturing before the College of Physicians on the circulation of the blood. His manuscript lecture notes still survive, written in an almost illegible mixture of Latin and English. The notes describe some of his experiments and reveal that by this date he had already become convinced of the validity of his now celebrated theories on blood circulation. "The movement of the blood," he wrote, "is constantly in a circle, and is brought about by the beat of the heart."

Twelve years passed before Harvey was ready to publish his conclusions. Why the long delay in reporting such a notable discovery to the world? There are various conjectures. Sir William Osler suggested that "Perhaps it was the motive of Copernicus, who so dreaded the prejudices of mankind that for thirty years he is said to have detained in his closet the *Treatise of Revolutions*." In Harvey's own words, his theory of general circulation of the blood "is of so novel and unheard-of character, that I not only fear injury to myself from the envy of a few, but I tremble lest I have mankind at large for my enemies, so much does wont and custom, that has become as another nature, and doctrine once sown and that has struck deep root and rested from antiquity, influence all men."

Neither was Harvey a man to rush into print lightly, for, in his opinion, "The crowd of foolish scribblers is scarcely less than the swarms of flies in the height of summer, and threatens with their crude and flimsy productions to stifle us as with smoke."

But eventually, after years of further experimentation and observation, Harvey decided the time was ripe. In 1628, in Frankfurt, Germany, there appeared a small volume of seventy-two pages, considered by many authorities not given to overstatement to be the most important medical book ever written. Naturally, it was in Latin, the universal scholarly language. The full title was *Exercitatio Anatomica de Motu Cordis et Sanguinis in Animalibus,* "Anatomical Exercise on the Motion of the Heart and Blood in Animals." Exactly why it was issued in Germany is not known—perhaps because the annual book fair held in Frankfurt would insure its more rapid circulation amongst scientists on the continent. Harvey's atrocious handwriting was doubtless to blame for numerous typographical errors.

Two dedications graced *De Motu Cordis.* The first is to Charles I, in which the king in his kingdom is compared to the heart in the body, and this is followed by an address to Doctor Argent, President of the Royal College, "and the rest of the doctors and physicians, his most esteemed colleagues." In the latter statement, Harvey expresses the view that truth should be accepted regardless of its source and that truth is of more value than antiquity. "I profess," he said, "both to learn and to teach anatomy, not from books but from dissections; not from the positions of philosophers but from the fabric of nature." In this sentence, Harvey caught the design and spirit of modern scientific methodology.

An introduction and seventeen brief chapters, which make up the main body of the book, give a clear, connected account of the action of the heart and of the circular movement of the blood around the body. The introduction reviews the theories of Galen, Fabricius, Realdo Colombo, and other earlier writers, effectively demonstrating their errors.

In his first chapter, Harvey related some of the problems that had confronted him in his research:

When I first gave my mind to vivisections, as a means of discovering the motions and uses of the heart, and sought to discover these from actual inspection, and not from the writings of others, I found the task so truly arduous, so full of difficulties, that I was almost tempted to think, with Fracastorius, that the motion of the heart was only to be comprehended by God. For I could neither rightly perceive at first when the systole [contraction] and when the diastole [dilation] took place, nor when and where dilation and contraction occurred, by reason of the rapidity of the movement, which in many animals is accomplished in the twinkling of an eye, coming and going like a flash of lightning.

Harvey at length became convinced that the heart's movements could be studied with less difficulty in the colder animals, such as toads, frogs, serpents, small fishes, crabs, shrimps, snails, and shellfish, than in the warm-blooded animals. In the former, he saw that the movements were "slower and rarer." The same phenomena were easily observable in dying warm-blooded animals, as the heart's action slowed down.

On the basis of his experiments Harvey noted that the heart's contraction forces the blood out; as the heart contracts, the arteries dilate to receive the blood. The heart, a muscle serving as a kind of pump, forces continuous circulation of the blood. The blood impelled into the arteries gives rise to the pulse, "as when one blows into a glove." Contrary to the ancient ebb and flow belief, the movement is all in one direction. Harvey demonstrated that the blood passes from the left side of the heart through the arteries to the extremities, and then back by way of the veins to the right side of the heart. The direction of the circulation he determined by tying ligatures around arteries and veins at various points. The momentous discovery, in short, was that the same blood carried out by the arteries is returned by the veins, performing a complete circulation.

Harvey's description of this process is picturesque:

These two motions, one of the ventricles, another of the auricles, take place consecutively, but in such a manner that there is a kind of harmony and rhythm preserved between them, the two concurring in such wise that but one motion is apparent, especially in the warmer blooded animals, in which the movements in question are rapid. Nor is this for any other reason than it is in a piece of machinery, in which, though one wheel gives motion to another, yet all the wheels seem to move simultaneously; or like the mechanism in firearms, where the trigger being touched, down comes the flint, strikes the steel, elicits a spark, which falling among the powder, it is ignited, upon which the flame extends, enters the barrel, causes the explosion, propels the ball, and the mark is attained—all of which incidents, by reason of the celerity with which they happen, seem to take place in the twinkling of an eye.

In thinking of the blood's movements as circular, Harvey may conceivably have been influenced by the ancient philosophers, such as Aristotle, who taught that the circular motion is perfect and the noblest of all movements. Harvey's contemporary, the astronomer Giordano Bruno, concluded that the circle is "the fundamental symbol and pattern of all life and action in the cosmos." It is significant that Harvey in his treatise uses such phrases as "motion as it were in a circle" and "motion of the blood we may be allowed to call circular."

Harvey's line of reasoning on the circulation was remarkably accurate on the whole, but there was one missing link. How did the blood get from the arteries to the veins? Harvey knew that the blood went to the arteries from the left heart and from the veins back to the right heart. However, he said, "I have never succeeded in tracing any connection between the arteries and veins by a direct anastomosis of their orifices." Lacking a microscope, he could not see the capillaries, the minute vessels through which the blood cells pass from the arteries to the veins, though he was convinced there must be such channels. The riddle was solved a few years after Harvey's death by an anatomy professor at Bologna, Marcello Malpighi. Examining a frog's lung under the newly-invented microscope, Malpighi saw the network of capillaries connecting the arteries and veins, exactly as Harvey had predicted. Thus the final step in demonstrating the circulation of the blood was completed.

To win over the skeptics, further proofs of circulation were produced by Harvey. One was the application of what is known to scientists as the quantitative method. He demonstrated that in an hour's time the heart, in its some 4,000 beats, pumps out far more than the total amount of blood in the body. If the blood sent out by the heart in a single day is measured, the quantity is much in excess of all the food taken in and digested—thereby disproving the ancient Galen's theory. "In short," wrote Harvey, "the blood could be furnished in no other way than by making a circuit and returning."

Additional evidence of circulation comes from the effect of poisons on the body.

We see in contagious diseases, in poisoned wounds, the bites of serpents or mad dogs, in the French pox, and the like the whole body may become diseased while the place of contact is often unharmed or healed. . . . Without doubt the contagion first being deposited in a certain spot is carried by the returning blood to the heart, from which later it is spread to the whole body. . . . This may also explain why some medical agents applied to the skin have almost as much effect as if taken by mouth.

Harvey's use of animals for experimental purposes was an innovation. He believed that "Had anatomists only been as conversant with the dissection of the lower animals as they are with that of the human body, the matters that have hitherto kept them in a perplexity of doubt would, in my opinion, have left them freed from every kind of difficulty." Harvey may be rightly regarded as one of the founders of the science of comparative anatomy. He mentions, for example, experiments on sheep, dogs, deer, pigs, birds, chicks in eggs, snakes, fish, eels, toads, frogs, snails, shrimps, crabfish, oysters, mussels, sponges, worms, bees, wasps, hornets, gnats, flies, and lice.

I have observed that there is a heart in almost all animals, not only in the larger ones with blood, as Aristotle claims, but in the smaller bloodless ones also, as snails, slugs, crabs, shrimps, and many others. Even in wasps, hornets, and flies, have I seen with a lens a beating heart at the upper part of what is called the tail, and I have shown it living to others. In these bloodless animals the heart beats slowly, contracting sluggishly as in moribund higher animals. This is easily seen in the snail, where the heart lies at the bottom of that opening on the right side which seems to open and close as saliva is expelled. . . . There is a small squid . . . caught at sea and in the Thames, whose entire body is transparent. Placing this creature in water, I have often shown some of my friends the movements of its heart with great clearness.

Aside from his remarkable discoveries, Harvey's greatest contribution to science and medical research was his introduction of experimental or laboratory methods. He laid the foundation upon which for more than three centuries physiology and medicine have been built. The essence was as Harvey himself stated, "to search and study out the secrets of Nature by way of experiment." Medicine had a history going back several millenniums before the birth of Harvey. Physicians had learned to recognize and to describe accurately the principal diseases afflicting mankind. Observation, while important, is not in itself enough, and frequently leads to erroneous conclusions. This was the major difference between Harvey and his predecessors. Going beyond superficial observation, little handicapped by superstitions or by reverence for antiquated theories, Harvey drew up hypotheses and tested them by experiments. He was the first to adopt the scientific method of experiment for the solution of a biological problem. All his successors of significance since 1628 have followed the same path.

The reception of Harvey's discoveries at the time is of interest. His book was not a literary sensation; its profound import was probably not recognized even by Harvey himself. Some opposition rising from conservatism and prejudice was expressed. A contemporary society gossip, John Aubrey, wrote that "he had heard him [Harvey] say that after his book on the Circulation of the Blood came out, he fell mightily in his practice; 'twas believed by the vulgar that he was crack-brained, and all the physicians were against him."

The attitude of one of the intellectuals of the time was expressed by Sir William Temple, writing of the work of Copernicus and Harvey:

Whether either of these be modern discoveries or derived from old foundations is disputed; nay, it is so too, whether they are true or no; for though reason may seem to favour them more than the contrary opinions, yet sense can hardly allow them, and to satisfy mankind both these must concur. But if they are true, yet these two great discoveries have made no change in the conclusions of Astronomy nor in the practice of Physic, and so have been but little use to the world, though, perhaps, of much honour to the authors.

For the most part, Harvey ignored his critics. The prolonged hostility of the University of Paris medical school, however, finally induced him to break his silence. John Riolan, professor of anatomy in the Paris school, had persuaded the faculty there to prohibit the teaching of Harvey's doctrine. In an attempt to overcome his objections, Harvey addressed to Riolan two *Anatomical Disquisitions* on the subject of the circulation of the blood. These were published in a small book in 1649, twenty-one years after *De Motu Cordis*. Therein, Harvey replied in detail to those who had condemned his work.

In the second of the *Disquisitions*, Harvey laments:

But scarce a day, scarce an hour has passed since the birthday of the circulation of the blood that I have not heard something for good or for evil, said of this my discovery. Some abuse it as a feeble infant and yet unworthy to have seen the light; others again think the baby deserves to be cherished and cared for. These oppose it with much ado, those patronize it with abundant commendation. One party holds that I have completely demonstrated the circulation of the blood by experiments, observations, and ocular inspection against all force and strength of argument; another thinks it scarcely sufficiently illustrated, not yet cleared of all objections. There are some, too, who say that I have shown a vainglorious love of dissection of living creatures, and who scoff at and deride the introduction of frogs and serpents, flies and other of the lower animals upon the scene. . . . To return evil speaking with evil speaking, however, I hold to be unworthy in a philosopher and searcher after truth. I believe that I shall do better and more advisedly if I meet so many indications of ill breeding with the light of faithful and conclusive observation.

Fortunately, Harvey lived to see general acceptance of his theories among those competent to judge them. His election to the presidency of the College of Physicians in 1654, three years before his death, is evidence of his high standing among his professional colleagues.

Also indicative of contemporary opinion is the Latin inscription on Harvey's tomb:

William Harvey, to whose honorable name all academies rise up out of respect, who was the first after many thousand years to discover the daily movement of the blood, and so brought health to the world and immortality to himself, who was the only one to free from false philosophy the origin and generation of animals, to whom the human race owes its acquirements of knowledge, to whom Medicine owes its very existence, chief Physician and friend of their Serene Highnesses James and Charles, Monarchs of the British Isles, a diligent and highly successful Professor of Anatomy and Surgery at the College of Medicine at London; for them he built a famous Library and endowed it and enriched it with his own patrimony. Finally after triumphal exertions in observation, healing and discovery, after various statues had been erected to him at home and abroad, when he had traversed the full circle of his life, a teacher of Medicine and of medical men, he died childless on June 3 in the year of grace 1657, in the eightieth year of his age, full of years and fame.

There has been little of a *basic* nature added to Harvey's discovery of the circulation, though, of course a vast body of knowledge has accumulated dealing with the physiology of the heart, blood vessels, and lungs. Much is known now concerning the heart's structure, its behavior in health and disease, its complex movements, and the functions of the blood that were not even imagined in Harvey's day.

Nevertheless, as Kilgour commented:

The direct contributions of Harvey's discovery to medicine and surgery are obviously beyond measuring. It is the basis for all work in the repair of damaged or diseased blood vessels, the surgical treatment of high blood pressure and coronary disease, the well-known "blue baby" operation, and so on. It is general physiology, however, that is most in his debt. For the notion of the circulating blood is what underlies our present understanding of the self-stabilizing internal environment of the body. In the dynamics of the human system the most important role is played by the fluid whose circulation Harvey discovered by a feat of great insight.

Perhaps no one has better summed up the meaning of Harvey's career to the progress of medicine than a great medical leader of our own time. In the annual Harveian Oration delivered at the Royal College of Physicians in London, in 1906, Sir William Osler said of *De Motu Cordis:*

. . . . It marks the break of the modern spirit with the old traditions. No longer were men to rest content with careful observation and with accurate description; no longer were men to be content with finely spun theories and dreams, which "serve as a common subterfuge of ignorance"; but here for the first time a great physiological problem was approached from the experimental side by a man with modern scientific mind, who could weigh evidence and not go beyond it, and who had the sense to let the conclusions emerge naturally but firmly from the observations. To the age of the hearer, in which men had heard, and heard only, had succeeded the age of the eye, in which men had seen and had been content only to see. But at last came the age of the hand—the thinking, devising, planning hand; the hand as an instrument of the mind, now reintroduced into the world in a modest little monograph of seventy-two pages, from which we may date the beginning of experimental medicine.

24

SYSTEM OF THE WORLD

Sir Isaac Newton: Principia Mathematica

Of all the books which have profoundly influenced human affairs, few have been more celebrated and none read by fewer people than Sir Isaac Newton's *Philosophiae Naturalis Principia Mathematica* ("Mathematical Principles of Natural Philosophy"). Deliberately written in the most abstruse and technical Latin, profusely illustrated by complex geometrical diagrams, the work's direct audience has been limited to highly erudite astronomers, mathematicians, and physicists.

One of Newton's chief biographers has stated that when the *Principia* was published in the last quarter of the seventeenth century there were not more than three or four men living who could comprehend it; another generously stretched the number to ten or a dozen. The author himself admitted that it was "a hard book," but he had no apologies, for he planned it that way, making no concessions to the mathematically illiterate.

Yet, notable men of science hold Newton to be one of the great intellectual figures of all time. Laplace, a brilliant French astronomer, termed the *Principia* "pre-eminent above any other production of human genius." Lagrange, famous mathematician, asserted that Newton was the greatest genius who ever lived. Boltzmann, a pioneer of modern mathematical physics, called the *Principia* the first and greatest work ever written on theoretical physics. An eminent American astronomer, W. W. Campbell, remarked, "To me it is clear that Sir Isaac Newton, easily the greatest man of physical science in historic time, was uniquely the great pioneer of astro-physics." Comments from other leading scientists over the past two-and-a-half centuries have been phrased in like superlatives. The layman must necessarily accept these judgments on faith, and on the basis of results.

Newton was born almost exactly a century after the death of Copernicus, and in the same year as Galileo's death. These giants in the world of astronomy, together with Johannes Kepler, furnished the foundations upon which Newton continued to build.

Newton was a mathematical wizard in an age of gifted mathematicians. As Marvin pointed out, "the seventeenth century was the flowering age of mathematics, as the eighteenth was of chemistry and the nineteenth of biology, and the last four decades of the seventeenth saw more forward steps taken than any other period in history." Newton combined in himself the major physical sciences—mathematics, chemistry, physics, and astronomy—for in the seventeenth century, before the era of extreme specialization, a scientist could encompass all fields.

Newton, born on Christmas Day, 1642, in his early years saw the rise and fall of Oliver Cromwell's Commonwealth Government, the Great Fire which practically destroyed London, and the Great Plague which wiped out a third of the city's population. After eighteen years spent in the little hamlet of Woolsthorpe, Newton was sent to Cambridge University. There he was fortunate to come under the guidance of an able and inspiring teacher, Isaac Barrow, professor of mathematics, who has been called Newton's "intellectual father." Barrow recognized, encouraged, and stimulated the growing genius of young Newton. While still in college, Newton discovered the binomial theorem.

Because of the plague, Cambridge was closed in 1665, and Newton returned to the country. For the next two years, largely cut off from the world, he devoted himself to scientific experimentation and meditation. The consequences were astounding. Before he had reached the age of twenty-five, Newton had made three discoveries that entitle him to be ranked among the supreme scientific minds of all time. First was the invention of the differential calculus, termed "fluxions" by Newton, because it deals with variable or "flowing" quantities. The calculus is involved in all problems of flow, movement of bodies, and waves, and is essential to the solution of physical problems concerned with any kind of movement. "It seemed to unlock the gates guarding the storehouse of mathematical treasures; to lay the mathe-matical world at the feet of Newton and his followers," according to one commentator.

Newton's second major discovery was the law of composition of light, from which he proceeded to analyze the nature of color and of white light. It was shown that the white light of the sun is compounded of rays of light of all the colors of the rainbow. Color is therefore a characteristic of light, and the appearance of white light—as Newton's experiments with a prism demon-strated—comes from mixing the colors of the spectrum. Through knowledge gained from this discovery, Newton was able to con-struct the first satisfactory reflecting telescope.

Even more noteworthy was Newton's third revelation: the law of universal gravitation, which is said to have stirred the imagi-nations of scientists more than any theoretical discovery of modern times. According to a well-known anecdote, the flash of intuition which came to Newton when he observed the fall of an apple led to formulation of the law. There was nothing particularly new in the idea of the earth's attraction for bodies near its surface. Newton's great contribution was in conceiving the gravitation law to be universal in application—a force no less powerful in relation to celestial bodies than to the earth—and then producing mathematical proof of his theory.

Curiously enough, Newton published nothing at the time on these three highly significant discoveries on the calculus, color, and gravitation. Possessed of an extremely reticent, even secre-tive nature, he had an almost morbid dislike of public attention and controversy. Consequently, he was inclined to suppress the results of his experiments. Whatever he published later was done under pressure from friends, and afterward he nearly always regretted surrendering to their entreaties. Publication led to criti-cism and discussion of his work by fellow-scientists, something which Newton, with his sensitive nature, completely detested and resented.

Following the enforced isolation and leisure of the plague years, Newton returned to Cambridge, received a master's de-gree, and was appointed a fellow of Trinity College. Shortly thereafter his old teacher, Barrow, withdrew, and Newton, at the age of twenty-seven, became professor of mathematics, a position which he held for the next twenty-seven years. For the next decade or two little was heard of Newton. It is known that he continued his investigations of light, and published a paper on his discovery of the composite nature of white light. Immediately he became involved in controversy, first because his conclusions on the subject of light were in opposition to those then prevailing; and, second, because he had included in the paper a statement on his philosophy of science. In the latter, he had expressed the point of view that the chief function of science is to carry out carefully planned experiments, to record observations of the experiments, and lastly to prepare mathematical laws based on the results. As Newton stated it, the "proper method for enquiring after the properties of things is to deduce them from experiments." While these principles are in complete accord with modern scientific research, they were by no means fully accepted in Newton's day. Beliefs founded on imagination, reason, and the appearance of things, usually inherited from ancient philosophers, were preferred to experimental evidence.

Attacks on his paper by such established scientists as Huygens and Hooke so angered Newton that he resolved to escape future irritations by doing no more publishing. "I was so persecuted," he said, "with discussions arising from the publication of my theory of light, that I blamed my own imprudence for parting with so substantial a blessing as my quiet to run after a shadow." He even expressed an acute distaste for science itself, insisting that he had lost his former "affection" for it. Later, he had to be "spurred, cajoled and importuned" into writing his greatest work, the *Principia*. In fact, creation of the *Principia* appears to have come about more or less by chance.

In 1684, through computations by Picard, the earth's exact circumference was determined for the first time. Using the French astronomer's data, Newton applied the principle of gravitation to prove that the power which guides the moon around the earth and the planets around the sun is the force of gravity. The force varies directly with the mass of the attracted bodies and inversely as the square of their distances. Newton went on to show that this accounts for the elliptical orbits of the planets. The pull of gravity kept the moon and the planets in their paths, balancing the centrifugal forces of their motions.

Again, Newton failed to reveal his phenomenal discovery of nature's greatest secret. As it happened, however, other scientists were engaged in a search for a solution of the same problem. Several astronomers had suggested that the planets were bound to the sun by the force of gravity. Among these was Robert Hooke, Newton's severest and most persistent critic. But none of the theorists had been able to offer mathematical proof. By now Newton had won considerable reputation as a mathematician, and he was visited at Cambridge by the astronomer Edmund Halley who requested his help. When Halley stated the problem, he learned that it had been solved two years before by Newton. Further, Newton had worked out the principal laws of motion of bodies moving under the force of gravity. Characteristically, though, Newton had no intention of publishing his findings.

Halley at once recognized the significance of Newton's accomplishment, and used all his powers of persuasion to convince the stubborn Newton that his discovery should be developed and exploited. Moved by Halley's enthusiasm and with his own interest rekindled, Newton began the writing of his masterpiece, the *Principia*, termed by Langer "a veritable reservoir of mechanistic philosophy, one of the most original works ever produced."

Not the least remarkable feature of the *Principia* was that its composition was completed in eighteen months, during which, it is said, Newton was so engrossed that he often went without food and took little time to sleep. Only the most intense and prolonged concentration could have brought forth such a monumental intellectual achievement in so brief a period. It left Newton mentally and physically exhausted.

Furthermore, during the time of writing, Newton's peace of mind was intensely disturbed by the usual controversies, particularly with Hooke, who maintained he should receive credit for originating the theory that the motion of the planets could be explained by an inverse square law of attraction. Newton, who had finished two-thirds of the *Principia*, was so incensed by what he considered an unjustified claim, that he threatened to omit the third and most important section of his treatise. Again Halley used his influence and prevailed on Newton to complete the work as first planned.

The role played by Edmund Halley in the whole history of the *Principia* deserves the highest commendation. Not only was he responsible for inducing Newton to undertake the work in the first place, but he obtained an agreement with the Royal Society to publish it, and unselfishly dropped everything he was doing to supervise the final printing. Finally, when the Royal Society reneged on its promise to finance the publication, Halley stepped in and paid the entire expense out of his own pocket, though he was a man of moderate means, with a family to support.

Surmounting all obstacles, the *Principia* came from the press in 1687, in a small edition, selling for ten or twelve shillings a copy. The title page bore the imprimatur of Samuel Pepys, then President of the Royal Society, "although it is to be doubted," remarked one commentator, "whether the learned diarist could have understood so much as a single sentence of it."

Any brief summary of the *Principia* in nontechnical language is a difficult, if not impossible, undertaking, but some highlights may be indicated. The work as a whole deals with the motions of bodies treated mathematically, in particular, the application of dynamics and universal gravitation to the solar system. It begins with an explanation of the differential calculus or "fluxions," invented by Newton and used as a tool for calculations throughout the *Principia*. There follow definitions of the meaning of space and time, and a statement of the laws of motion, as formulated by Newton, with illustrations of their application. The fundamental principle is stated that every particle of matter is attracted by every other particle of matter with a force inversely proportional to the square of their distances apart. Also given are the laws governing the problem of bodies colliding with each other. Everything is expressed in classical geometrical forms.

The first book of the *Principia* is concerned with the motion of bodies in free space, while the second treats of "motion in a resisting medium," such as water. In the latter section, the complex problems of the motion of fluids are considered and solved, methods discussed for determining the velocity of sound, and wave motions described mathematically. Herein is laid the groundwork for the modern science of mathematical physics, hydrostatics, and hydrodynamics.

In the second book Newton effectively demolished the world system of Descartes, then in popular vogue. According to Descartes' theory, the motions of the heavenly bodies were due to vortexes. All space is filled with a thin fluid, and at certain points the fluid matter forms vortexes. For example, the solar system has fourteen vortexes, the largest of them containing the sun. The planets are carried around like chips in an eddy. These whirlpools were Descartes' explanation for the phenomena of gravitation. Newton proceeded to demonstrate experimentally and mathematically that "the Vortex Theory is in complete conflict with astronomical facts, and so far from explaining celestial motions would tend to upset them."

In the third book, entitled "The System of the World," Newton was at his greatest as he dealt with the astronomical consequences of the law of gravitation.

In the preceding books I have laid down the principles of philosophy [science]; principles not philosophical but mathematical. . . . These principles are the laws and conditions of certain motions, and powers or forces. . . . I have illustrated them here and there . . . with . . . an account of such things as are of more general nature . . . such as the density and the resistance of bodies, spaces void of all bodies, and the motion of light and sound. It remains that, from the same principles, I now demonstrate the frame of the System of the World.

Explaining why he had not popularized his work, Newton revealed that—

Upon this subject I had, indeed, composed the third Book in a popular method, that it might be read by many, but afterwards, considering that such as had not sufficiently entered into the principles could not easily discern the strength of the consequences, nor lay aside the prejudices to which they had been many years accustomed, therefore, to prevent the disputes which might be raised upon such accounts, I chose to reduce the substance of this Book in the form of Propositions (in the mathematical way), which should be read by those only who had first made themselves masters of the principles established in the preceding Books; not that I would advise anyone to the previous study of every Proposition of those Books; for they abound with such as might cost too much time, even to readers of good mathematical learning.

For this reason, the style of the *Principia* has been described as "glacial remoteness, written in the aloof manner of a high priest."

At the outset, Newton makes a fundamental break with the past by insisting that there is no difference between earthly and celestial phenomena. "Like effects in nature are producd by like causes," he asserted, "as breathing in man and in beast, the fall of stones in Europe and in America, the light of the kitchen fire and of the sun, the reflection of light on the earth and on the planets." Thus was discarded the ancient belief that other worlds are perfect and only the earth is imperfect. Now all were governed by the same rational laws, "bringing order and system," as John MacMurray said, "where chaos and mystery had reigned before."

A mere listing of the principal topics covered in the third book is impressive. The motions of the planets and of the satellites around the planets are established; methods for measuring the masses of the sun and planets are shown; and the density of the earth, the precession of the equinoxes, theory of tides, orbits of the comets, the moon's motion, and related matters discussed and resolved.

By his theory of "perturbations" Newton proved that the moon is attracted by both the earth and the sun, and therefore the moon's orbit is disturbed by the sun's pull, though the earth provides the stronger attraction. Likewise, the planets are subject to perturbations. The sun is not the stationary center of the universe, contrary to previous beliefs, but is attracted by the planets, just as they are attracted to it, and moves in the same way. In later centuries, application of the perturbations theory led to the discovery of the planets Neptune and Pluto.

The masses of different planets and the masses of the sun Newton determined by relating them to the earth's mass. He estimated that the earth's density is between five and six times that of water (the figure used by scientists today is 5.5), and on this basis Newton calculated the masses of the sun and of the planets with satellites, an achievement which Adam Smith called "above the reach of human reason and experience."

Next, the fact that the earth is not an exact sphere, but is flattened at the poles because of rotation, was explained, and the amount of flattening was calculated. Because of the flattening at the poles and the slight bulge at the equator, Newton deducted that the force of gravity must be less at the poles than at the equator—a phenomenon that accounts for the precession of the equinoxes, the conical motion of the earth's axis, resembling a gyroscope. By studying the shape of the planet, furthermore, the possibility of estimating the length of day and night on the planet was shown.

Another application of the law of universal gravitation was Newton's exploration of the tides. When the moon is fullest, the earth's waters experience their maximum attraction, and high tide results. The sun also affects the tides, and when the sun and moon are in line, the tide is highest.

Still another subject of popular interest on which Newton shed light was comets. His theory was that comets, moving under the sun's attraction, travel elliptical paths of incredible magnitude, requiring many years to complete. Henceforth, comets, which were once regarded by the superstitious as evil omens, took their proper place as beautiful and harmless celestial phenomena. By using Newton's theories of comets, Edmund Halley was able to identify and to predict accurately the reappearance about every seventy-five years of the famous Halley's Comet. Once a comet has been observed, its future path can be accurately determined.

One of the most amazing discoveries made by Newton was his method for estimating the distance of a fixed star, based on the amount of light received by reflection of the sun's light from a planet.

The *Principia* made no attempt to explain the *why* but only the *how* of the universe. Later, in response to charges that his was a completely mechanistic scheme, making no provision for ultimate causes or for a Supreme Creator, Newton added a confession of faith to the second edition of his work.

This most beautiful system of the sun, planets, and comets could only proceed from the counsel and dominion of an intelligent and powerful Being. . . . As a blind man has no idea of colours, so have we no idea of the manner by which the all-wise God perceives and understands all things.

The function of science, he believed, was to go on building knowledge, and the more complete our knowledge is, the nearer are we brought to an understanding of the Cause, though man might never discover the true and exact scientific laws of nature.

Brilliant achievement that the *Principia* was, it was not written in a vacuum as Newton's most ardent admirers concede. I. Bernard Cohen stated:

The great Newtonian synthesis was based on the work of predecessors. The immediate past had produced the analytical geometry of Descartes and Fermat, the algebra of Oughtred, Harriot and Wallis, Kepler's law of motion, Galileo's law of falling bodies. It had also produced Galileo's law of the composition of velocities—a law stating that a motion may be divided into component parts, each independent of the other (for example the motion of a projectile is composed of a uniform forward velocity and a downward accelerated velocity like that of a freely falling body). The afore-mentioned are but a few of the ingredients present and waiting for the grand Newtonian synthesis. But it remained for the genius of Newton to add the master touch; to show finally, and once and for all, in just what manner the ordered universe is regulated by mathematical law.

It was evident that the world needed, as Sir James Jeans described Newton, "a man who could systematize, synthesize and extend the whole, and it found him in superlative excellence in Newton."

Newton himself recognized that his "System of the World," his mechanics of the universe, was built upon the work begun by Copernicus and so notably carried forward by Tycho Brahe, Kepler, and Galileo. "If I have seen farther than other men," Newton said, "it is by standing on the shoulders of giants."

In fact, the probable cause of the controversies that dogged Newton's life was the intellectual ferment prevailing in his time. The air was full of new theories, and many able scientists were exploring them. It is not surprising that two men would make the same discovery almost simultaneously and quite independently. Precisely this appears to have happened in Newton's two principal controversies, those with Leibniz and Hooke. Leibniz invented the differential calculus, and Hooke advanced a theory of universal gravitation, both somewhat later than Newton's, but announced to the world first, because Newton had neglected to publish his work.

The contemporary reception of the *Principia* was more cordial in England and Scotland than on the Continent, but everywhere slow. As Newton had foreseen, an understanding of it required great mathematical ability. The extraordinary nature of the performance was acknowledged, however, even by those who had only a dim conception of Newton's contribution. Gradually, scientists everywhere accepted the Newtonian system, and by the eighteenth century it was firmly established in the world of science.

After the *Principia*, Newton appears to have lost any active interest in scientific research, though he lived for forty years after its publication. During this period he was the recipient of many honors: he was appointed Master of the Mint, knighted by Queen Anne, elected President of the Royal Society from 1703 until his death in 1727, saw publication of the second and third editions of the *Principia*, and, in general, was held in the highest respect and esteem.

Scientific discoveries in the twentieth century have modified or shown inadequacies in Newton's work, especially in relation to astronomy. Einstein's theory of relativity, for example, maintains that space and time are not absolute, as Newton had taught. Nevertheless, as various authorities in science and technology have pointed out, the structure of a skyscraper, the safety of a railroad bridge, the motion of a motor car, the flight of an airplane, the navigation of a ship across the ocean, the measure of time, and other evidences of our contemporary civilization still depend fundamentally on Newton's laws. As Sir James Jean wrote, the Newtonian principles are "inadequate only with reference to the ultra-refinements of modern science. When the astronomer wishes to prepare his 'Nautical Almanac,' or to discuss the motions of the planets, he uses the Newtonian scheme almost exclusively. The engineer who is building a bridge or a ship or a locomotive does precisely what he would have done had Newton's scheme never been proved inadequate. The same is true of the electrical engineer, whether he is mending a telephone or designing a power station. The science of everyday life is still wholly Newtonian; and it is impossible to estimate how much this science owes to Newton's clear and penetrating mind having set it on the right road, and this so firmly and convincingly that none who understood his methods could doubt their rightness."

The tribute paid Newton by Einstein should remove any question of rival philosophies: "Nature to him was an open book, whose letters he could read without effort. In one person he combined the experimenter, the theorist, the mechanic and, not least, the artist in expression."

Newton's own estimate of his career, made near the end of a long life, was characteristic of his modesty: "I do not know what I may appear to the world, but to myself I seem to have been only like a boy on the seashore, and diverting myself in now and then finding a smoother pebble or a prettier shell than ordinary, while the great ocean of truth lay all undiscovered before me."

25

DISCOVERER OF VACCINATION

**Edward Jenner: An Inquiry into the Causes and Effects
of the Variolae Vaccinae**

Of all the ancient scourges of mankind, the most deadly and
devastating was smallpox, a disease which can be traced back at
least to Egyptian mummies more than three thousand years ago.
Only leprosy, influenza, cholera, typhus fever, and bubonic
plague were as dreaded, and over the centuries none of these
had rivaled smallpox in its dire consequences. In Europe alone,
sixty million people died of smallpox in the eighteenth century.
One out of every fourteen persons born in England during these
years succumbed to the disease, which attacked the high and
the low, the young and the old alike. Many occupants of the
French throne, among them Louis XV, died of the affliction, as
did Mary II (at age thirty-two), Queen of England and consort
of William II. A favorite theme of novelists was the pathetic
disfigurement of beautiful women by smallpox. Victims of the
disease who survived were usually marred for life and frequently
blinded.

Credit for relieving the human race of this awful pestilence
belongs to an English country physician, Edward Jenner. The
idea of preventive inoculation for smallpox was not original with
Jenner. Long before his time, the practice of injecting small doses
of matter, from a smallpox sore on a patient with a mild case,
under the skin of a well person, to cause the latter to build up
an immunity, had been known in the East. An English traveler,
Lady Mary Wortley Montague, had brought the idea from Turkey as early as 1721. The method, however, had serious faults;
the resulting disease was often not mild, and sometimes it proved
fatal. Furthermore, each inoculated person was a source of infection to other persons.

345

A tradition among the dairy folk of the Gloucestershire countryside led to Jenner's epochal discovery. Dairy maids who had contracted cowpox when milking were believed by the farmers to be ever afterward immune from smallpox. Jenner noted also that persons who had had smallpox in a mild form thereby acquired immunity against a second attack. He determined to undertake a series of experiments to test the prevailing folklore. His first operation was performed in 1796 upon an eight-year-old country boy, James Phipps, using matter from the hand of a milkmaid, Sarah Nelmes, who was suffering from a typical case of cowpox. About eight weeks after the operation, the boy was inoculated with smallpox virus. In a letter to a friend Jenner described the results:

A boy named Phipps was inoculated in the arm from a pustule on the hand of a young woman who was infected by her master's cows. Having never seen the disease but in its casual way before, that is, when communicated from the cow to the hand of the milker, I was astonished at the close resemblance of the pustules in some of their stages to the variolous [smallpox] pustules. But now listen to the most delightful part of my story. The boy has since been inoculated for the small-pox which, as I ventured to predict, produced no effect. I shall now pursue my experiments with redoubled ardour.

Thus was marked the first successful vaccination for smallpox in history. Over the next two years Jenner continued his experiments, by the end of which period he had demonstrated in twenty-two cases that vaccination with cowpox matter gave complete protection against smallpox. Sixteen of the cases had occurred accidentally among people working with cows and horses; the others were contrived under Jenner's direction.

The evidence was beyond question. To announce the great medical triumph, Jenner published in 1798 one of the masterpieces of scientific literature, *An Inquiry into the Causes and Effects of the Variolae Vaccinae*, a thin quarto of seventy-five pages with four colored plates. Full descriptions were included of the cases personally directed or observed by Jenner. In somewhat florid opening paragraphs the author began:

The deviation of Man from the state in which he was originally placed by Nature seems to have proved to him a prolific source of diseases. From the love of splendour, from the indulgencies of luxury, and from his fondness for amusement, he has familiarized himself with a great number of animals, which may not originally have been intended for his associates.

The Wolf, disarmed of ferocity, is now pillowed in the lady's lap. The Cat, the little Tyger of our island, whose natural home is forest, is equally domesticated and caressed. The Cow, the Hog, the Sheep, and the Horse, are all, for a variety of purposes, brought under his care and dominion.

The *Inquiry* went through several editions and within a few years had been translated into a number of other languages, spreading knowledge of Jenner's discovery around the world. Soon the results of vaccination began to be felt in the declining death rate from smallpox. Napoleon Bonaparte, for example, had all of his soldiers vaccinated, and his armies were thereafter free of the disease.

Nevertheless, conservative opposition in medical and lay circles was vociferous. Ministers denounced vaccination from their pulpits as man's interference with the ways of God. Antivaccinationist societies, some of which are still in existence, were formed. The fantastic idea was circulated that vaccination would cause the human subject to sprout horns, grow a tail, low like a cow, bellow like a bull, and acquire other bovine characteristics. Overzealous advocates of vaccination harmed its reputation by using contaminated vaccine matter producing serious illnesses.

Such obstacles, however, were gradually surmounted. A grateful Parliament recognized Jenner's work by two grants, totaling £30,000, to cover his expenses, and in his later years he was accorded numerous honors.

In succeeding generations, Jenner's original discovery has been vastly expanded by other research workers in the development of a formidable battery of toxins and antitoxins and various forms of inoculation to protect the individual against many contagious diseases.

Jenner's successful solution to the smallpox problem has probably saved more lives and suffering than any other single accomplishment in the history of medicine. As Thomas Jefferson stated in a letter to Jenner, May 14, 1806: "You have erased from the calendar of human afflictions one of the greatest. Yours is the comfortable reflection that mankind can never forget that you have lived; future nations will know by history only that the loathsome small-pox has existed, and by you has been extirpated."

In December 1977, the World Health Organization announced the end of the last known case of virulent smallpox anywhere in the world.

26

SURVIVAL OF THE FITTEST

Charles Darwin: Origin of Species

By curious coincidence, the year 1809 witnessed the births of more extraordinary leaders than perhaps any other single year in history. Each was destined to gain preeminence in his career. Two of them, Charles Darwin, "the Newton of biology," and Abraham Lincoln, "the great emancipator," were born on the same day and nearly in the same hour. Other remarkable individuals who first saw the light in this year included William Gladstone, Tennyson, Edgar Allan Poe, Oliver Wendell Holmes, Elizabeth Barrett Browning, and Felix Mendelssohn.

Of these celebrated names, and in fact among all the millions born in the nineteenth century, none, with the possible exception of Karl Marx, did as much as Darwin to change the main trends of thought, and to produce a new outlook in human affairs. "Darwinism" is a concept as firmly fixed in the popular mind as Marxism, Malthusianism, and Machiavellianism.

Though the basic principles of Darwin's theories are today almost universally accepted in the scientific world, controversies have raged around them for nearly a century. The fundamentalist-modernist battles of the nineteen-twenties, culminating in the Scopes "monkey trial" in Tennessee, are among the most publicized instances of a war which began in 1859. Only recently have there been signs of an armistice in the hostilities.

As a youth, Darwin showed little promise of becoming a world-famed scientist. He was descended from a family of distinguished scholars and professional men, but even his father expressed strong doubt that he would ever amount to anything. In grammar school, young Charles was bored by the study of dead languages and by the rigid classical curriculum. He was rebuked by the headmaster for wasting his time on chemical experiments and in collecting insects and minerals. Following in his father's footsteps, he was sent to Edinburgh University at sixteen to study medicine. After two years there, he decided that the medical profession was not for him. Whereupon he was transferred to Cambridge to train for the ministry in the Church of England.

From the point of view of formal study, Darwin considered the three Cambridge years wasted. But he did have the good fortune to form firm friendships with two influential teachers. With John Stevens Henslow, professor of botany, and Adam Sedgwick, professor of geology, he spent much time in field excursions, collecting beetles, and in natural history observations.

It was through Sedgwick that Darwin received an offer to sail as naturalist on board the naval ship *Beagle*, starting out on an extensive surveying expedition in the southern hemisphere. Looking back on this voyage in later years, Darwin rated it "by far the most important event in my life." It determined his whole career. The idea of becoming a clergyman "died a natural death" on the *Beagle*.

During the five years from 1831 to 1836, the *Beagle* touched on nearly every continent and major island, as she circled the world. Darwin was called upon to serve as geologist, botanist, zoologist, and general man of science—superb preparation for his subsequent life of research and writing. Everywhere he went, he made extensive collections of plants and animals, fossil and living, earth-dwelling and marine forms. He investigated, with the eye of a naturalist, the flora and fauna of land and sea—the pampas of Argentina, the dry slopes of the Andes, the salt lakes and deserts of Chile and Australia, the dense forest of Brazil, Tierra del Fuego, and Tahiti, the deforested Cape Verde Islands, geological formations of the South American coast and mountains, active and dead volcanoes on islands and mainland, coral reefs, fossil mammals of Patagonia, traces of extinct races of man in Peru, and the aborigines of Tierra del Fuego and Patagonia.

Of all the regions visited, none impressed Darwin as forcibly as the Galápagos Islands, 500 miles off the west coast of South America. On these isolated, uninhabited, and rather barren volcanic islands, he saw giant tortoises, elsewhere found only as fossils, huge lizards long since extinct in other parts of the world, enormous crabs, and sea lions. He was particularly struck by the fact that the birds were similar to those on the neighboring continent, but not identical. Furthermore, there were variations among the different species of birds from island to island.

The strange phenomena of the Galápagos Islands, added to certain facts previously noted in South America, reinforced the ideas on evolution beginning to take shape in Darwin's mind. According to his own account:

I had been deeply impressed by discovering in the Pampean formation great fossil animals covered with armour like that on the existing armadillos; secondly, by the manner in which closely allied animals replace one another in proceeding southwards over the Continent; and thirdly, by the South American character of most of the productions of the Galápagos archipelago, and more especially by the manner in which they differ slightly on each island of the group; none of the islands appearing to be very ancient in a geological sense.

Never again could Darwin accept as credible the teachings of Genesis, that every species had been created whole and had come down through the ages unchanged.

Immediately upon his return to England, Darwin began keeping a notebook on evolution, collecting facts on variation of species, the beginning of the *Origin of Species*. The first rough draft of his theory was written out in thirty-five pages in 1842, and enlarged in 1844 to a fuller sketch of 230 pages. In the beginning, the great riddle was how to explain the appearance and disappearance of species. Why did species originate, become modified with the passage of time, diverge into numerous branches, and often vanish from the scene completely?

The key to the mystery for Darwin came through a chance reading of Malthus' *Essay on Population*. Malthus had shown that mankind's rate of increase was retarded by such "positive checks" as disease, accidents, war, and famine. It occurred to Darwin that similar factors might keep down the populations of animals and plants.

Being well prepared to appreciate the struggle for existence which everywhere goes on from long-continued observation of the habits of animals and plants, it at once struck me that under these circumstances favourable species would tend to be preserved, and unfavourable ones to be destroyed. The result of this would be the formation of new species. Here then I had at last got a theory by which to work.

Thus was born the famous Darwinian doctrine of "natural selection," "struggle for existence," or "survival of the fittest," the foundation stone for the *Origin of Species*.

For twenty years Darwin compiled his notebooks, substantiating his theories. He read a vast range of literature—whole series of periodicals, travel books, books on sport, horticulture, breeding of animals, and general natural history. "When I see the list of books of all kinds which I read and abstracted, including whole series of Journals and Transactions, I am surprised at my industry," wrote Darwin. He talked with expert breeders of animals and plants, and sent lists of questions to everyone who might have useful information. Skeletons of many kinds of domesticated birds were prepared, and the age and weight of their bones compared with those of wild species. Tame pigeons were kept and extensive crossing experiments made. He experimented with floating fruits and seeds in sea water, and investigated other questions relating to seed transport. All the botanical, geological, zoological, and paleontological knowledge he had acquired on the *Beagle* expedition was brought to bear on the problem. To this mass of data were added Darwin's own ideas as he gave constant thought to his revolutionary theories.

Strong support for the principle of natural selection, Darwin thought, came from a study of "artificial selection." In the case of domestic animals and plants—horses, dogs, cats, wheat, barley, garden flowers, etc.—man has selected and bred the varieties that were most advantageous to his own needs. So radically modified have domestic animals, crops, and flowers become in the process, they can scarcely be recognized as related to their wild ancestors. New species are developed by selection. The breeder picks out animals and plants possessing the characters he wants, breeds only these generation after generation, and eventually produces species different from any that had previously existed. Dogs as unlike as the dachshund, the collie, the spaniel, and the greyhound, for example, were descended from the wolf.

If evolution could be brought about by artificial selection, reasoned Darwin, is it not possible that nature functions in the same manner, by natural selection? In nature, however, the breeder's place is taken by the struggle for existence. Among all forms of life, Darwin observed, an enormous number of individuals must perish. Only a fraction of those that were born can survive. Some species furnish food for other species. The battle goes on ceaselessly, and the fierce competition eliminates animals and plants unfitted to survive. Variations in species take place to meet the conditions necessary for survival.

So intent was Darwin in building a tower of irrefutable proof for his theories that he neglected publication until the eighteen-fifties. Then, at the urging of close friends, he began preparation of a monumental work to be issued in several volumes. But when the task was approximately half finished a thunderbolt struck. Darwin received a letter from Alfred Russel Wallace, a fellow scientist, who was carrying on natural history explorations in the Malay archipelago. Wallace revealed that he, too, was meditating on the origin of species, and like Darwin had been inspired by reading Malthus. With the letter was enclosed an "Essay on the Tendency of Varieties to Depart Indefinitely from the Original Type." It was precisely a statement of Darwin's own theory, for, said Darwin, "if Wallace had had my MS. sketch written out in 1842, he could not have made a better short abstract! Even his terms now stand as heads of my chapters."

Darwin was in a dilemma. It was obvious that both men had arrived at identical conclusions quite independently, though Darwin had given years of study and thought to the subject, while Wallace's ideas had come to him in a sudden flash of intuition. At length it was decided that papers by both Darwin and Wallace would be presented at the next meeting of the Linnaean Society. Accordingly, the first public announcement of the theory of evolution by natural selection was made on the evening of July 1, 1858. Shortly thereafter, both papers were issued in the Society's *Journal*.

Spurred on by the Wallace incident, Darwin abandoned the huge work on which he had been engaged, and settled down to writing what he called an "abstract." Near the end of 1859, the book that was to become a milestone in the history of science was published by John Murray in London. The first edition was 1,200 copies, all of which were sold the first day. Other editions followed, until, by the end of Darwin's lifetime (in 1882), 24,000 copies had been sold in England alone, and it had been translated into almost every civilized language. The original was entitled *On the Origin of Species by Means of Natural Selection, or the Preservation of Favoured Races in the Struggle for Life*. Time has shortened this unwieldy title to *Origin of Species*.

The fundamentals of Darwin's theory are discussed in the first four chapters of the *Origin*. The following four consider possible objections to the theory, after which several chapters deal with geology, the geographic distribution of plants and animals, and pertinent facts concerning classification, morphology, and embryology. The final chapter summarizes the entire argument.

At the outset, the *Origin of Species* describes the changes that have taken place in domesticated animals and plants as a result of human control. The variations that have come about by "artificial selection" are compared with changes in nature, or "natural selection." Wherever there is life, it is concluded, change is constant. No two individuals are ever exactly identical.

To variation there is added the struggle for existence. Some striking illustrations are used to demonstrate how far the ability of all living organisms to reproduce outstrips their capacity to survive. Even the slowest breeding animals, like elephants, would soon fill the world. If every elephant grew to maturity and reproduced naturally, "After a period of from 740 to 750 years," said Darwin, "there would be nearly nineteen million elephants alive, descended from the first pair." From this and other examples, it is deduced that "As more individuals are produced than can possibly survive, there must in every case be a struggle for existence, either one individual with another of the same species, or with the individuals of distinct species, or with the physical conditions of life." There is no exception to the rule that every plant, fish, bird, and animal, including the human race, produces infinitely more seed than will ever be born or could be accommodated in a crowded world. The rate of increase is geometrical.

The interdependence of species is also graphically illustrated. Darwin found that pollination by "humble-bees" is necessary for the fertilization of heartsease flowers and some kinds of clover.

The number of humble-bees in any district depends in a great measure upon the number of field-mice, which destroy their combs and nests. . . . Now the number of mice is largely dependent, as every one knows, on the number of cats. . . . Hence it is quite credible that the presence of a feline animal in large numbers in a district might determine, through the intervention first of mice and then of bees, the frequency of certain flowers in that district.

The *Origin of Species* proceeds to show how the principle of "natural selection" operates to check population increases. Some individuals in a species will be stronger, can run faster, are more intelligent, more immune to disease, or better able to endure the rigors of climate than their fellows. These will survive and reproduce as the weaker members perish. A white rabbit will survive in Arctic regions, while more conspicuous brown rabbits will be exterminated by foxes and wolves. Long-necked giraffes have survived, because in drought years they were able to reach a food supply at the tops of trees, while the short-necked giraffes starved. These favorable variations insured the survival of the fittest. In the course of many millenniums they led to the creation of essentially new species.

The law of tooth, fang, and claw, as it operates everywhere, was aptly dramatized by Darwin:

We behold the face of nature bright with gladness, we often see superabundance of food; we do not see, or we forget, that the birds which are idly singing round us mostly live on insects or seeds, and are thus constantly destroying life; or we forget how largely these songsters, or their eggs, or their nestlings, are destroyed by birds and beasts of prey; we do not always bear in mind, that, though now food may be superabundant, it is not so at all seasons of each recurring year.

An important aspect of natural selection, Darwin pointed out, is sexual selection. "Generally, the most vigorous males, those which are best fitted for their places in nature, will leave most progeny. . . . A hornless stag or spurless cock would have a poor chance of leaving numerous offspring." Among birds, "the contest is often of a more peaceful character," as the males of different species seek to attract the females by beautiful singing, gorgeous plumage, or by performing strange antics.

Climate is also a major factor in natural selection, for "seasons of extreme cold or drought seem to be the most effective of all checks. . . . The action of climate seems at first sight to be quite independent of the struggle for existence; but in so far as climate chiefly acts in reducing food, it brings on the most severe struggle between the individuals, whether of the same or of distinct species, which subsist on the same kind of food." Most likely to survive are the vigorous individuals able to withstand heat or cold and most capable of obtaining food. Darwin wrote:

Natural Selection is daily and hourly scrutinizing, throughout the world, the slightest variations; rejecting those that are bad, preserving and adding up all that are good; silently and insensibly working, *whenever and wherever opportunity offers,* at the improvement of each organic being in relation to its organic and inorganic conditions of life. We see nothing of these slow changes in progress until the hand of time has marked the lapse of ages, and then so imperfect is our view into long-past geological ages, that we see only that the forms of life are now different from what they formerly were.

In his final chapter, Darwin implied that the power of natural selection is virtually without limit, and suggested that one could "infer from analogy that probably all the organic beings which have ever lived on this earth have descended from some one primordial form, into which life was first breathed." All the complex forms of life, he believed, owed their existence to natural laws. He found the results of natural selection inspiring.

Thus from the war of Nature, from famine and death, the most exalted object which we are capable of conceiving, namely the production of the higher animals, directly follows. There is a grandeur in this view of life, with its several powers having been originally breathed by the Creator into a few forms or into one; and that, whilst this planet has gone circling on according to the fixed law of gravity, from so simple a beginning endless forms most beautiful and most wonderful have been, and are being, evolved.

In this fashion was the theory of unending evolution presented by the *Origin of Species.* Contrary to popular belief, however, Darwin did not originate the evolutionary theory. The idea is older than Aristotle and Lucretius. Such brilliant minds as Buffon, Goethe, Erasmus Darwin (Charles' grandfather), Lamarck, and Herbert Spencer had supported the doctrine. Charles Darwin's contribution was notable in two directions. First, he accumulated more indisputable evidence to show the *fact* of evolution than had ever been offered before. Second, he advanced his famous theory of natural selection as a reasonable explanation for the *method* of evolution.

The contemporary reception of the *Origin of Species* has been compared to "a conflagration like lightning in a full barn." If the revolutionary new theory were valid, the Biblical story of creation could no longer be accepted. The church immediately viewed the Darwinian thesis as dangerous to religion, and roused a storm of opposition. Though Darwin had carefully omitted any application of his theory to mankind, the charge was spread that the author had represented men as having descended from monkeys.

Attempts were made to discredit Darwin by ridicule. An article in the *Quarterly Review* called him a "flighty person" attempting, in his book, "to prop up his utterly rotten fabric of guess and speculation," and whose "mode of dealing with nature" was "utterly dishonourable to science." The *Spectator* disliked the theory "because it utterly repudiates final causes and thereby indicates a demoralized understanding on the part of its advocates"; furthermore, Darwin was accused of collecting a mass of facts to substantiate a false principle, and "You cannot make a good rope out of a string of air bubbles." One reviewer asked if it were "credible that all favourable varieties of turnips are tending to become men." Since England had no Inquisition, the *Athenaeum*, in another scathing review, consigned Darwin "to the mercies of the Divinity Hall, the College, the Lecture Room, and the Museum." Darwin's comment on this was: "He [the reviewer] would, on no account, burn me, but he would get the wood ready and tell the black beasts how to catch me." At Darwin's alma mater, William Whewell would not permit a copy of the *Origin of Species* to be placed in the Trinity College library at Cambridge.

From fellow scientists, Darwin won strong support and met bitter opposition. The ultraconservative point of view was represented by such figures as Owen in England and Agassiz in America, both of whom held that the Darwinian ideas were scientific heresy and would soon be forgotten. The astronomer Sir John Herschel described Darwinism as "the law of higgledy-piggledy." Darwin's old geological professor at Cambridge, Sedgwick, held the theory to be "false and grievously mischievous," and wrote Darwin that he had "laughed till his sides ached" at his book, considering it was "machinery as wild as Bishop Wilkins's locomotive that was to sail with us to the moon."

But Darwin was not lacking in stalwart champions. Foremost among these were Charles Lyell, the geologist, Thomas Huxley, biologist, Joseph Hooker, botanist, and Asa Gray, the famous American botanist. Of them all, Darwin leaned most heavily on Huxley, whom he called his "agent general" and who referred to himself as "Darwin's bulldog." Darwin was not a controversialist, and never appeared in public to defend his theories. The brunt of the defense was carried by the able and aggressive Huxley.

It was Huxley who played one of the two leading roles in a dramatic conflict over Darwin's *Origin.* The stage was provided by a meeting of the British Association at Oxford in 1860. Darwinism was the conference theme. The big gun on the opposition side was Bishop Wilberforce of Oxford. At the conclusion of a forceful address which he believed had smashed Darwin's theory, the Bishop turned to Huxley, sitting on the platform. "I should like to ask Professor Huxley," he demanded sarcastically, "is it on his grandfather's or his grandmother's side that the ape ancestry comes in?" In an aside to a friend, Huxley exclaimed, "The Lord hath delivered him into my hands." Rising to reply, Huxley is reported to have said:

A man has no reason to be ashamed of having an ape for his grandfather. If there were an ancestor whom I should feel shame in recalling, it would be a man of restless and versatile intellect, who, not content with success in his own sphere of activity, plunges into scientific questions with which he has no real acquaintance, only to obscure them by an aimless rhetoric, and distract the attention of his hearers from the point at issue by eloquent digressions and skilled appeals to religious prejudice.

This was one of the first of innumerable clashes between church and science on the issue of Darwinism and evolution to rage in the succeeding years.

Darwin's own views on religion were modified as he grew older. As a young man, he had accepted the idea of special creation without question. In his *Life and Letters,* he expressed the belief that "man in the distant future will be a far more perfect creature than he is now."

Darwin added further:

Another source of conviction in the existence of God, connected with the reason, and not with the feelings, impresses me as having much more weight. This follows from the extreme difficulty or rather impossibility of conceiving this immense and wonderful universe, including man, with his capacity of looking far backward and far into futurity, as the result of blind chance or necessity. When thus reflecting I feel compelled to look to a First Cause, having an intelligent mind to some degree analogous to that of man; and I deserve to be called a Theist. This conclusion was strong in my mind about the time, as far as I can remember, when I wrote the *Origin of Species;* and it is since that time that it has very gradually, with many fluctuations, become weaker. But then arises the doubt: Can the mind of man, which has, as I fully believe, been developed from a mind as low as that possessed by the lowest animals, be trusted when it draws such grand conclusions?

Darwin threw up his hands at this point, and ended by declaring:

I cannot pretend to throw the least light on such abstruse problems. The mystery of the beginning of all things is insoluble by us; and I for one must be content to remain an agnostic.

Following the *Origin of Species*, a stream of books flowed from Darwin's active pen. They dealt with more specialized topics, but all, in essence, were designed to elaborate, supplement, and substantiate the case for evolution by natural selection—presented comprehensively in the *Origin of Species*. First came two little volumes entitled *On the Various Contrivances by Which Orchids Are Fertilized by Insects* and *The Movements and Habits of Climbing Plants*. Next appeared two major works: *The Variation of Animals and Plants under Domestication* and *The Descent of Man and Selection in Relation to Sex*. Succeeding books were concerned with the expression of emotion in man and animals, insectivorous plants, the effects of cross-fertilization, the power of movement in plants, and the formation of vegetable mold.

In the *Origin of Species*, Darwin had intentionally soft-pedaled any discussion of man's beginnings, because he thought any emphasis on this phase of evolution would cause his entire theory to be rejected. In the *Descent of Man*, however, a massive amount of evidence was advanced to demonstrate that the human race is also a product of evolution from lower forms.

Viewed in retrospect, Darwin's impress on nearly all major fields of learning was, and continues to be, profound. The doctrine of organic evolution has been accepted by biologists, geologists, chemists, and physicists, by anthropologists, psychologists, educators, philosophers, and sociologists, and even by historians, political scientists, and philologists. Charles Ellwood declared:

When one reflects upon the immense influence which Darwin's work has had on practically all lines of human thought, and especially on the biological, psychological, and social sciences, one is forced to conclude that . . . Darwin must be given the seat of highest honor as the most fructifying thinker which the nineteenth century produced, not only in England, but in the whole world. And the social significance of Darwin's teachings is even yet only beginning to be apprehended.

Anthony West concurred, in writing of the *Origin of Species:* "The effect was truly tremendous. Almost by the mere statement of a new principle of approach, dynamic, not static, he revolutionized every department of study, from astronomy to history, from paleontology to psychology, from embryology to religion."

On the other hand, there have been applications of Darwin's theories of which he undoubtedly would have passionately disapproved. An example is fascism's use of the idea of natural selection, or survival of the fittest, to justify the liquidation of certain races. Similarly, wars between nations have been defended as a means of eliminating the weak and perpetuating the strong. Darwinism has been twisted further, by Marxists, to apply to the class struggle. And ruthless business corporations have justified methods of destroying smaller companies on the same grounds.

Because he was an extraordinarily acute observer and experimenter, Darwin's work has stood up well, for the most part, as scientific knowledge has expanded. Even though his theories have been modified by the findings of modern science, Darwin succeeded in foreshadowing in a remarkable fashion the ideas prevailing today in genetics, paleontology, and a variety of other fields.

A masterly summing-up of Darwin's place in the history of science has come from another great biologist, Julian Huxley, grandson of Darwin's coworker, defender, and friend:

Darwin's work . . . put the world of life into the domain of natural law. It was no longer necessary or possible to imagine that every kind of animal or plant had been specially created, nor that the beautiful and ingenious devices by which they get their food or escape their enemies have been thought out by some supernatural power, or that there is any conscious purpose behind the evolutionary process. If the idea of natural selection holds good, then animals and plants and man himself have become what they are by natural causes, as blind and automatic as those which go to mould the shape of a mountain, or make the earth and the other planets move in ellipses round the sun. The blind struggle for existence, the blind process of heredity, automatically result in the selection of the best adapted types, and a steady evolution of the stock in the direction of progress. . . .

Darwin's work has enabled us to see the position of man and of our present civilization in a truer light. Man is not a finished product incapable of further progress. He has a long history behind him, and it is a history not of a fall, but of an ascent. And he has the possibility of further progressive evolution before him. Further, in the light of evolution we learn to be more patient. The few thousand years of recorded history are nothing compared to the million years during which man has been on earth, and the thousand million years of life's progress. And we can afford to be patient when the astronomers assure us of at least another thousand million years ahead of us in which to carry evolution onwards to new heights.

27

PSYCHOLOGIST OF THE UNCONSCIOUS

Sigmund Freud: The Interpretation of Dreams

Of all branches of learning, it is generally conceded that psychology is most mystical and obscure, the least susceptible of scientific proof of any of the sciences. In the nature of things, the elusiveness and unpredictability are inescapable, because the psychologist is dealing with the most mysterious of natural phenomena: the mind of man. A theory in chemistry or physics can be verified or disproved by laboratory techniques, but the validity of a psychological theory may be impossible to demonstrate. Thus the storm of controversy that has raged around Sigmund Freud and psychoanalysis for over seventy-five years.

But whether demonstrable or not, Freudian theories have exerted an unrivaled influence on modern thought. Not even Einstein has touched the imaginations or permeated the lives of his contemporaries as has Freud. In exploring the unknown regions of the mind, Freud formulated ideas and terms that have now become part of our daily living. Virtually every field of knowledge—literature, art, religion, anthropology, education, law, sociology, criminology, history, biography, and other studies of society and the individual—has felt the effects of his teachings.

There is little, however, of sweetness and light in these teachings. A rather facetious critic has remarked:

For laymen, as Freud's theories spread, he emerged as the greatest killjoy in the history of human thought, transforming man's jokes and gentle pleasures into dreary and mysterious repressions, discovering hatreds at the root of love, malice at the heart of tenderness, incest in filial affections, guilt in generosity, and the repressed hatred of one's father as a normal human inheritance.

Nevertheless, because of Freud, people think very differently about themselves today. They accept as commonplace such Freudian concepts as the influence of the subconscious on consciousness, the sexual basis of neuroses, the existence and importance of infantile sexuality, the function of dreams, the Oedipus complex, repression, resistance, and transference. Human foibles, like slips of the tongue, forgetting of names, and failure to remember social engagements take on new significance when viewed from a Freudian standpoint. It is now difficult to realize that the prejudices which Freud had to overcome to spread his doctrines were even more intense than those encountered by Copernicus and Darwin.

When Freud was born at Freiberg in Moravia, the *Origin of Species* had not yet appeared. The year was 1856. Like Karl Marx, Freud had ancestors who included several rabbis; but unlike Marx, Freud said: "I have remained a Jew." He was taken to Vienna at the age of four, and spent practically all his adult life there. To his father, a wool merchant, he owed, according to his principal biographer, Ernest Jones, his "shrewd scepticism about the uncertain vicissitudes of life, his custom of pointing a moral by quoting a Jewish anecdote, his disbelief in matters of religion." Freud's mother lived to the age of ninety-five, a warm, lively personality. Sigmund was her firstborn and favorite son. Later he wrote, "A man who has been the indisputable favorite of his mother keeps for life the feeling of a conqueror, that confidence of success that often induces real success."

In the early years, Freud was strongly attracted by Darwin's theories, for he felt that "they held out hopes of an extraordinary advance in our understanding of the world." Deciding to become a physician, he entered the University of Vienna to study medicine, receiving a degree in 1881. As a junior resident physician in the general hospital, he continued his studies in neurology and cerebral anatomy. A few years later came the turn in his fortunes that was eventually to establish his worldwide renown. A traveling fellowship took him to Paris to work under Jean Charcot, then a celebrated French pathologist and neurologist. Here he had his firsthand contact with Charcot's work on hysteria and his treatment of it by hypnotic suggestion. Charcot proved, to Freud's satisfaction, "the genuineness of hysterical phenomena, their frequent occurrence in men, the production of hysterical paralyses and contractures by hypnotic suggestion," and their close similarity in appearance to real attacks.

But back in Vienna, Freud was unable to convince his medical colleagues of any scientific basis for the treatment of nervous disorders by hypnotic methods. He was even punished for his radical ideas by being excluded from the cerebral anatomy laboratory. Henceforth, he was a lonely figure, withdrawn from academic life and ceasing to attend meetings of learned societies. In his private practice of medicine, he continued to experiment with hypnosis for several years, but gradually abandoned it because few people make good subjects and hypnosis sometimes has unfortunate effects on the personality. Instead, Freud began development of the technique termed "free association," ever since a standard psychoanalytic practice.

Freud is, without question, the founder of modern psychiatry. Prior to his time, psychiatry was concerned with such symptoms of insanity as schizophrenia and manic-depressive psychosis, requiring confinement in an institution. Beginning his clinical work with the treatment of repressions and conflicts of neurotics, Freud soon came to the conclusion that such conflicts were not peculiar to neurotics, but were also characteristic of well-adjusted persons. Further, neuroses were not diseases in the accepted sense, but psychological states of mind. The great problem was how to treat these widely prevalent mental disturbances. Upon his observations, experiments, and experience with many Viennese patients, around the turn of the century, Freud built the foundation of psychoanalysis.

Freud was one of the most prolific scientific writers of our time, and the variety of new concepts and psychological contributions which emanated from his pen cannot be found in any single book or paper. In his own eyes, probably the favorite was his earliest major work, *The Interpretation of Dreams*, issued in 1900, which contains nearly all of his fundamental observations and ideas. In an earlier work, *Studies in Hysteria*, 1895, he had indicated his belief that sexual disturbances were the *"essential* factor in the etiology of both neuroses and psychoneuroses"—one of the cornerstones of psychoanalytic theory. Within the next few years, Freud had also worked out his concepts of resistance, transference, childhood sexuality, relationship between unpleasant memories and fantasies, defense mechanisms, and repression.

A brief summary of its principal doctrines will reveal something of the complexity of psychoanalysis. In the first place, psychiatry and psychoanalysis are not synonymous. Psychoanalysis may be considered a subdivision of psychiatry, and is generally applied only to the most difficult cases of personality disturbances. Psychoanalysis, then, can be defined as a therapy in the treatment of nervous and psychic disorders. According to a 1977 report, a mere 2,389 of over 24,000 accredited psychiatrists in the United States are psychoanalysts.

Freud was interested only incidentally in individual therapy. The cases of maladjusted individuals, he regarded as but symptoms of the economic, social, and cultural derangements of the contemporary world. His aim was to attack the disease at its source.

Most critics would agree that Freud's claim to enduring fame rests on his discovery and exploration of the unconscious mind. Comparing the human mind to an iceberg, eight-ninths of which is submerged, he held that the mind is mainly hidden in the unconscious. Beneath the surface there are motives, feelings, and purposes which the individual conceals not only from others but even from himself. In Freudian psychology, the unconscious is supreme and conscious activity is reduced to a subordinate position. By coming to understand the profound and unknown depths of the unconscious, we learn the inner nature of man. Most of our thinking, declared Freud, is unconscious and only occasionally becomes conscious. The unconscious mind is the source of neuroses, because the individual tries to banish to that region his disagreeable memories and frustrated wishes, but only succeeds in storing them up for future trouble.

Freud classified mental activity in an individual as being carried on at three levels, which he named the Id, the Ego, and the Superego. Of first importance is the Id. "The domain of the Id," said Freud, "is the dark, inaccessible part of our personality; the little that we know of it we have learned through the study of dreams and of the formation of neurotic symptoms." The Id is the center of primitive instincts and impulses, reaching back to man's animal past, and is animal and sexual in nature. It is unconscious. The Id, continued Freud, "contains everything that is inherited, that is present at birth, that is fixed in the constitution." The Id is blind and ruthless, its sole purpose the gratification of desires and pleasures, without reckoning the consequences. In Thomas Mann's words, "It knows no values, no good or evil, no morality."

The new-born infant is the personification of the Id. Gradually, the Ego develops out of the Id as the child grows older. Instead of being guided entirely by the pleasure principle, the Ego is governed by the reality principle. The Ego is aware of the world around it, recognizing that the lawless tendencies of the Id must be curbed to prevent conflict with the rules of society. As Freud put it, the Ego is the mediator "between the reckless claims of the Id and the checks of the outer world." In effect, therefore, the Ego acts as censor of the Id's urges, adapting them to realistic situations, realizing that avoidance of punishment, or even self-preservation, may depend upon such repressions. Out of conflicts between the Ego and the Id, however, may develop neuroses seriously affecting the individual personality.

Finally, there is the third element in the mental process, the Superego, which may be broadly defined as conscience. The leading Freudian disciple in America, A. A. Brill, wrote:

The Super-Ego is the highest mental evolution attainable by man, and consists of a precipitate of all prohibitions, all the rules of conduct which are impressed on the child by his parents and parental substitutes. The feeling of *conscience* depends altogether on the development of the Super-Ego.

Like the Id, the Superego is unconscious, and the two are in perpetual conflict, with the Ego acting as referee. Moral ideals and rules of behavior have the Superego as their home.

When the Id, Ego, and Superego are in reasonable harmony, the individual is well adjusted and happy. If the Ego permits the Id to break the rules, however, the Superego causes worry, feelings of guilt, and other manifestations of conscience.

Closely associated with the Id is another concept originated by Freud: his theory of the *libido*. All the Id's impulses, he taught, are charged with a form of "psychic energy," termed *libido*, primarily sexual in character. The libido theory has been called "the essence of psychoanalytic doctrine." All man's cultural achievements, art, law, religion, etc., are regarded as developments of libido. While referred to as sexual energy, actually the word "sexual" is used in a very broad sense. In infants, it includes such activities as thumb-sucking, bottle-nursing, and excreting. In later years, the libido may be transferred to another person through marriage, take the form of sex perversion, or be expressed through artistic, literary, or musical creation—a process entitled "displacement." The sex instinct, in Freud's opinion, is the greatest source of creative work.

Under the influence of libido, Freud maintained, in perhaps the most controversial of all psychoanalytic theories, the child develops sexual feelings toward its parents. Beginning with its first sensual pleasures derived from feeding at the maternal breast, the infant forms a love attachment for its mother. As he matures, but at an early age, the male child develops strong sexual urges for the mother, while hating and fearing his father as a rival. The female child, on the other hand, may move away from the close relationship with her mother and fall in love with her father, with the mother becoming an object of dislike and rivalry. As applied to the male, this is called the Oedipus complex, named after the ancient Greek mythological figure who killed his father and married his own mother. The Oedipus complex, Freud said, is a heritage from our primitive ancestors who killed their fathers in jealous rages. As he reaches maturity, a normal person outgrows the Oedipus impulses. Weak individuals, on the other hand, may never succeed in breaking the parental attachment, and thus are led into a series of neuroses.

In fact, Freud declared, "The neuroses are without exception disturbances of the sexual function." Furthermore, neuroses cannot be blamed upon unsuccessful marriages or unfortunate adult love affairs, but all can be traced back to sex complexes of early childhood. Applying his theory to the field of anthropology, in his book *Totem and Taboo*, Freud concluded that nature and religious myths of primitive man are the product of father and mother complexes. Religion itself, he believed, is merely an expression of the father complex. After detailed analyses of hundreds of cases who came to him for treatment, Freud elevated sexual instinct and sexual desires to a preeminent role in the shaping of personality, as well as identifying them as the chief cause of neuroses. This is a judgment that has been rejected by some other prominent psychoanalysts, as will be indicated later.

Because he is forced by society to suppress many of his urges, the individual unconsciously accumulates many "repressions," to use Freud's term. Normally, one's consciousness succeeds in preventing the "dark unconscious forces" that have been repressed from again emerging. Neurotic persons, though, may go through periods of deep emotional disturbances because of such censorship. It is the task of psychoanalytic therapy, said Freud, to "uncover repressions and replace them by acts of judgment which might result either in the acceptance or in the rejection of what had formerly been repudiated." Because of the painful nature of the repressed material, the patient usually tries to prevent the uncovering of his repressions. Freud termed these efforts "resistances," which it is the physician's object to overcome.

The technique invented by Freud for dealing with repressions and resistances is the method now known as "free association"— stream-of-consciousness talk by a patient reclining on the psychoanalyst's couch, in a dimly lighted room. The patient is encouraged "to say whatever comes into his head, while ceasing to give any conscious direction to his thoughts." It was claimed by Freud that the method of free association is the only effective way of treating neurosis, and that it "achieved what was expected of it, namely the bringing into consciousness of the repressed material which was held back by resistances." As Brill described Freud's procedure with patients, "He persuaded them to give up all conscious reflection, abandon themselves to calm concentration, follow their spontaneous mental occurrences, and impart everything to him. In this way he finally obtained those *free associations* which lead to the origin of the symptoms." The forgotten material, dredged up by the subject out of his unconscious, after perhaps months of psychoanalytical treatment, usually represents something painful, disagreeable, frightening, or otherwise obnoxious out of his past, matters he dislikes to remember consciously.

Inevitably, in such a process, the rambling reminiscences produce a mass of diffuse, irrelevant, and apparently useless data. Everything, therefore, depends upon the ability of the physician to psychoanalyze his material, which, as various critics have pointed out, can be interpreted in an almost infinite number of ways. The intelligence and skill of the psychoanalyst, therefore, are of basic significance.

In the course of psychoanalytic treatment of patients, Freud discovered what he called "a factor of undreamt-of importance," an intense emotional relationship between the subject and the analyst. This is called "transference."

The patient is not satisfied with regarding the analyst in the light of reality as a helper and adviser . . . on the contrary, the patient sees in his analyst the return—the reincarnation—of some important figure out of his childhood or past, and consequently transfers on to him feelings and reactions that undoubtedly applied to this model.

The transference "can vary between the extremes of a passionate, completely sensual love and the unbridled expression of an embittered defiance and hatred." In this situation, the analyst, "as a rule, is put in the place of one or other of the patient's parents, his father or his mother." The fact of transference, Freud regarded as "the best instrument of the analytic treatment," but "nevertheless its handling remains the most difficult as well as the most important part of the technique of analysis." The problem "is resolved," stated Freud, "by convincing the patient that he is re-experiencing emotional relations which had their origin in early childhood."

Another fruitful device for probing into inner conflicts and emotions developed by Freud was the analysis of dreams. Here again Freud was a pioneer. Before his time, dreams were regarded as without meaning or purpose. His *The Interpretation of Dreams* was the first attempt at a serious scientific study of the phenomenon. Thirty-one years after publication of the book, Freud remarked that "It contains, even according to my present-day judgment, the most valuable of all the discoveries it has been my good fortune to make." According to Freud, "We are justified in asserting that a dream is the disguised fulfillment of a repressed wish." Each dream represents a drama in the inner world. "Dreams are invariably the product of a conflict," stated Freud, and "The dream is the guardian of sleep." Its function is to aid rather than disturb sleep, releasing tensions that come from unattainable wishes.

The dream world, in the Freudian view, is dominated by the unconscious, by the Id, and dreams are important to the psychoanalyst because they lead him into the patient's unconscious. In the unconscious are all the primitive wishes and emotional desires suppressed from conscious life by the Ego and Superego. The animal desires are always present under the surface, and force themselves forward in dreams. Even in sleep, however, the Ego and Superego stand on guard as censors. For that reason, the meanings of dreams are not always clear, they are expressed in symbols, and require expert interpretation. As symbols, they cannot be taken literally, except perhaps in the simple dreams of children. *The Interpretation of Dreams* offers numerous examples of dreams psychoanalyzed by Freud.

Likewise indicative of the workings of the unconscious are misspellings, slips of the tongue, and odd tricks of absentmindedness. "In the same way that psychoanalysis makes use of dream-interpretation," said Freud, "it also profits by the numerous little slips and mistakes which people make—symptomatic actions, as they are called." The subject was investigated by Freud in 1904 in his *The Psychopathology of Everyday Life*. In this work, he maintained that "these phenomena are not accidental . . . they have a meaning and can be interpreted, and one is justified in inferring from them the presence of restrained or repressed impulses and intentions." To forget a name may mean that one dislikes the person with that name. If a man misses his train because of confusion over schedules, it may indicate he did not desire to catch it. A husband who loses or forgets his house key may be unhappy at home and not desire to return. A study of such blunders can lead the psychoanalyst into the mazes of the unconscious mind.

The similar release is obtained with jokes, which Freud termed "the best safety valve modern man has evolved," for through them we are temporarily freed of repressions that polite society otherwise requires us to keep hidden.

Perhaps because of premonitions, increasing disillusionment, or extreme pessimism, toward the end of his life, Freud became preoccupied with the "death instinct." Eventually, he came to regard this conception as almost on a par in importance with the sexual instinct. Freud held that there is a death instinct driving all living matter to return to the inorganic state from which it came. According to this view, man is constantly torn between the urge to life, that is the sexual instinct, and a counter force, the urge to annihilation, or the death instinct. In the end, of course, the death instinct wins out. The instinct is responsible for war, and for such examples of sadism as prejudice against races and classes, the vicarious enjoyment of criminal trials, bullfighting, and lynching.

The foregoing, in brief, are the principal facets of Freudian theory. Present-day psychiatrists are split into two or more opposing camps, pro and con Freud. Even his disciples have modified their full acceptance of the theories over the past fifty years. One of the early followers, Alfred Adler, seceded from the Freudian camp because he believed that Freud had overemphasized the sexual instincts. As an alternative doctrine, Adler taught that every man's desire to prove his superiority is the mainspring in human behavior. He developed the idea of an "inferiority complex" which impels the individual to strive for recognition in some activity. Another famous secessionist was Carl Jung, of Zurich, who also tried to minimize the role of sex. Jung divided mankind into two psychological types: extroverts and introverts, though he recognized that every individual is a mixture of the two. Unlike Freud, Jung emphasized hereditary factors in the development of personality. In general, Freud's critics part company with him on such issues as his insistence on the prime significance of childhood neuroses, his conviction that men are controlled by primeval, rigid instincts, and on his elevating the libido or sexual energy to a central place in the formation of personality. Some disagree with Freud also in his belief that free association is an infallible technique for exploring the unconscious, pointing out most particularly the difficulties in interpreting data produced by that method.

Nevertheless, as one psychiatrist observed:

The changes and developments of sixty years have in no way diminished Freud's stature or influence. He opened up the realm of the unconscious. He showed how it helps to make us what we are and how to reach it. Many of his ideas and concepts have had to be modified by his successors in the light of further experience. You might say that they have been writing a New Testament for psychiatry. But Sigmund Freud wrote the Old Testament. His work will remain basic.

Much of our modern attitude toward insanity we owe to Freud. There is an increasing tendency to suggest that "Neurotics and psychotics are just like ourselves, only more so." Alexander Reid Martin stressed that "Whether acknowledged or not, all psychiatric and psychotherapeutic hospitals today utilize elements and fundamentals of Freudian psychology. What formerly was regarded as an unknown world, forbidding, grotesque, purposeless and meaningless, through Freud became enlightened and charged with meaning, attracting the interest and recognition not only of medicine, but of all the social sciences."

The impact of Freudian thought on literature and art has been equally noticeable. In fiction, poetry, drama, and other literary forms, Freudian motifs have flourished in recent years. Bernard De Voto has expressed the opinion that "no other scientist has ever had so strong and so widespread an influence on literature." The effect on painting, sculpture, and the world of art in general has been no less profound.

To sum up the manifold contribution of Freud's genius is difficult because of the breadth of his interests and the controversial nature of his findings. One attempt was made by an English writer, Robert Hamilton, whose conclusion was this:

Freud put psychology on the map. He was a great pioneer and much of his success was due to his originality and literary style. In spite of its nihilistic character, there has never been a system more interesting and original, nor, outside pure literature, a more attractive style. He made the world think psychologically—an essential need for our time; and he forced men to ask themselves questions vital to human welfare. Out of the thesis of the sterile academic psychology of the nineteenth century he brought the antithesis of psycho-analysis with its dark negations.

A noted American psychiatrist, Frederic Wertham, stated the case from another point of view:

One should make clear that, aside from the host of new clinical facts about patients that he observed, Freud brought about three fundamental changes in the approach to the study of personality and mental pathology. The first was to speak of psychological processes at all, and to think of them with the logic of natural science. This became possible only when Freud introduced the realistic concept of the unconscious and practical methods for its investigation. The second was his introduction of a new dimension into psychopathology: childhood. Before Freud, psychiatry was practiced as if every patient was Adam—who never was a child. The third was his inauguration of the genetic understanding of the sexual instinct. His real discovery here was not so much that children have a sex life, but that the sexual instinct has a childhood.

A similar judgment was expressed by A. G. Tansley, in an obituary prepared for the Royal Society of London:

The revolutionary nature of Freud's conclusions becomes intelligible when we remember that he was investigating an entirely unexplored field, a region of the human mind into which no one had penetrated before, and whose overt manifestations had been regarded as inexplicable or as degenerative aberrations, or had been ignored because they lay under the strongest human taboos. The very existence of this field was unrecognized. Freud was forced to assume the reality of an unconscious region of the mind, and then to attempt to explore it, by the apparent discontinuities in the chains of conscious mental events.

Finally, Winfred Overholser suggests that "There is every reason to think that one hundred years hence Freud will be classed with Copernicus and Newton as one of the men who opened up new vistas of thought. Certain it is that in our time no man has cast so much light upon the workings of the mind of man as Freud."

The last months of Freud's long lifetime were spent in exile. Following the Nazi occupation of Austria, he was forced to leave Vienna in 1938. England granted him asylum, but cancer of the mouth caused his death in September, 1939, a little more than a year later.

28

HARBINGER OF THE ATOMIC AGE

Albert Einstein: Relativity, the Special and General Theories

Albert Einstein is one of the rare figures in history who succeeded in becoming a legend of heroic proportions during his own lifetime. The more incomprehensible to the lay public his ideas appeared, the more intriguing they seemed, and the more Olympian their progenitor. As Bertrand Russell aptly remarked, "Everybody knows that Einstein has done something astonishing, but very few people know exactly what it is that he has done." To be told, though inaccurately, that there are scarcely a dozen men in the entire world who fully grasp Einstein's theories of the universe, challenges and intrigues. The incomprehensibility of Einstein's theories stems from the complex nature of his field of operation. One point of view was expressed by George W. Gray:

Inasmuch as the theory of relativity is presented by its author in mathematical language, and in strictness of speaking cannot be expressed in any other, there is a certain presumption in every attempt to translate it into the vernacular. One might as well try to interpret Beethoven's Fifth Symphony on a saxophone.

Nevertheless, Einstein himself, Bertrand Russell, Lev Davidovitch Landau, and others have shown that it is possible to describe the Einstein cosmos intelligibly without resort to mathematical symbolism. And a fantastic world it is, extremely upsetting to ideas firmly established for centuries, "a strange pudding for the layman to digest." We are asked, for example, to accept such incredible conceptions as these: space is curved, the shortest distance between two points is not a straight line, the universe is finite but unbounded, parallel lines eventually meet, light rays are curved, time is relative and cannot be measured in exactly the same way everywhere, measurements of length vary with speed, a body in motion will contract in size but increase in mass, and a fourth dimension—an interweaving of space and time—is added to the familiar three of height, length, and width.

Though Einstein's contributions to science have been innumerable, his fame rests primarily upon the theory of relativity, an achievement which, Banesh Hoffman concluded, "has a monumental quality that places its author among the truly great scientists of all time, in the select company of Isaac Newton and Archimedes. With its fascinating paradoxes and spectacular successes it fired the imagination of the public."

The revolution in concepts brought about by Einstein began in 1905, with the appearance in a German journal, *Annalen der Physik*, of a thirty-page paper carrying the unexciting title "On the Electrodynamics of Moving Bodies." At the time, Einstein was only twenty-six years of age, and serving as a minor official in the Swiss patent office. He had been born into a middle-class Jewish family at Ulm, Bavaria, in 1879. As a student, he was not precocious even in mathematics. Because of failure of the family fortune, Einstein was forced out on his own at fifteen. Emigrating to Switzerland, he was able to continue his scientific education at the Polytechnic Academy in Zurich, married a fellow student, and became a Swiss citizen. To earn a living he settled in a job making preliminary reports and rewriting inventors' applications for the patent office. His spare time was used for intensive study of the works of philosophers, scientists, and mathematicians. Soon he was ready to launch the first of a flood of original contributions to science, destined to have far-ranging repercussions.

In his 1905 paper, Einstein set forth the Special Theory of Relativity, challenging man's existing concepts of time and space, of matter and energy. The foundations for the theory were laid down in two basic assumptions. The first was the principle of relativity: all motion is relative. A familiar illustration of the principle is a moving train or ship. A person sitting in a train with darkened windows would have, if there was little commotion, no idea of speed or direction, or perhaps even that the train was moving at all. A man on a ship with portholes closed would be in a similar predicament. We conceive motion only in relative terms, that is in respect to other objects. On a vastly greater scale, the forward movement of the earth could not be detected if there were no heavenly bodies for comparisons. It should be noted that this principle was stated explicitly by Newton in his *Principia,* and was not a new contribution; Einstein merely affirmed its relevance to electrodynamics as well as in mechanics.

Einstein's second major hypothesis was that the velocity of light is independent of the motion of its source. The speed of light, 186,000 miles a second, is always the same, anywhere in the universe, regardless of place, time or direction. Light travels in a moving train, for instance, at exactly the same speed as it does outside the train. No force can make it go faster or slower. Furthermore, nothing can exceed the velocity of light, though electrons closely approximate it. The speed of light is, in fact, the only constant, unvarying factor in all of nature.

A famous experiment carried out in 1887 by two American scientists, Michelson and Morley, furnished the basis of Einstein's theory on light. They attempted to determine the velocity of the earth as it passed through the ether (a hypothetical substance which was believed to pervade all space not occupied by matter). No velocity could be determined, and most physicists abandoned the ether theory.

Einstein's paper in 1905 answered the question which had puzzled Michelson, Morley, and their fellow physicists. The essential point deduced by Einstein was that light always travels at the same velocity no matter under what conditions it is measured, and the motion of the earth in regard to the sun has no influence upon the speed of light.

Newton stated, "It may be that there is no body really at rest to which the place and motions of others may be referred." Today's scientists do not say that there is or is not such a thing as absolute motion. The question, only to be determined by experiment, is whether absolute motion can be detected. Einstein asserted that every body's movement is relative to that of another. Motion is the natural state of all things. Nowhere on earth or in the universe is there anything absolutely at rest. Throughout our restless cosmos, movement is constant, from the infinitesimally small atom to the largest celestial galaxies. For example, the earth is moving around the sun at the rate of twenty miles a second. In a universe where all is motion and fixed points of reference are lacking, there are no established standards for comparing velocities, length, size, mass, and time, except as they might be measured by relative motions. Only light is not relative, its velocity remaining changeless regardless of its source or the observer's position.

Doubtless the most difficult of all Einsteinian concepts to comprehend and the most unsettling to traditional beliefs is the relativity of time. Einstein held that events at different places occurring at the same moment for one observer do not occur at the same moment for another observer moving at a speed relative to the first. For example, two events judged as taking place at the same time by an observer on the ground are not simultaneous for an observer in a train or an airplane. Time is relative to the position and speed of the observer, and is not absolute.

As speed increases, time seems to slow down. We are accustomed to the thought that every physical object has three dimensions, but Einstein maintained that time is also a dimension of space, and space is a dimension of time. Neither time nor space can exist without the other and they are interdependent. Movement and change are constant, we live in a four-dimensional universe, with time as the fourth dimension.

Thus the two basic premises of Einstein's theory, as first presented seventy years ago, were the relativity of all motion and the concept of light as the only unvarying quantity in the universe.

In developing the principle of relativity of motion, Einstein upset another firmly established belief. Previously, length and mass had been regarded as absolute and constant under every conceivable circumstance. Now, Einstein came along to state that the mass or weight of an object and its length depend on how fast the body is moving relative to uniform motion of the observer. As an example, he imagined a train one thousand feet long, traveling at four-fifths of the speed of light. To a stationary observer, watching it pass by, the length of the train would be reduced to only six hundred feet, though it would remain a thousand feet to a passenger on the train. Similarly, any material body traveling through space contracts according to velocity. A yardstick, if it could be shot through space at 161,000 miles per second would shrink to a half-yard.

Mass, too is changeable. As velocity increases, the mass of an object becomes greater. Experiments have shown indirectly that particles of matter speeded up to 86 per cent of the speed of light weigh twice as much as they do when at rest. Movement and change and relativity had been recognized long before Einstein. The novel results of his theory come from the combination of the well-known principle of relativity with the new assumption of the constancy of the velocity of light.

Einstein's original statement of 1905, known as the special theory of relativity, is limited to uniform motion of the reference frames that are used in the description. It tells us how things look from a train moving uniformly in a straight line, but they do not tell us how things look from a rotating merry-go-round. In our cosmos, stars, planets, and other celestial bodies seldom move uniformly in a straight line. Any theory, therefore, which fails to include every type of motion offers an incomplete description of the universe. Einstein's next step, accordingly, was the formulation of his general theory of relativity, a process which required ten years of intensive application. In the general theory, Einstein studies the mysterious force that guides the movements of the stars, comets, meteors, galaxies, and other bodies whirling around in the vast universe. The general theory is valid for all kinds of observers, whether their motion is uniform or accelerated.

In his general theory of relativity, published in 1915, Einstein advanced a new concept of gravitation, making fundamental changes in the ideas of gravity and light which had been generally accepted since the time of Sir Isaac Newton. Gravity had been regarded by Newton as a "force." Einstein proved, however, that the space around a planet or other celestial body is a gravitational field similar to the magnetic field around a magnet. Tremendous bodies, such as the sun or stars, are surrounded by enormous gravitational fields. The theory also explained the erratic movements of Mercury, the planet nearest the sun, a phenomenon that had puzzled astronomers for centuries and had not been adequately covered by Newton's law of gravitation. So powerful are the great gravitational fields that they even bend rays of light. In 1919, a few years after the general theory was first announced, photographs taken of a complete eclipse of the sun conclusively demonstrated the validity of Einstein's theory that light rays passing through the sun's gravitational field travel in curves rather than in straight lines.

There followed from this premise a statement by Einstein that space is curved. Revolving planets follow the shortest possible routes, influenced by the sun's presence, just as a river flowing toward the sea follows the contour of the land, along the easiest and most natural course. In our terrestrial scheme of things, a ship or airplane crossing the ocean follows a curved line, that is the arc of a circle, and not a straight line. It is evident, therefore, that the shortest distance between two points is a curve instead of a straight line. An identical rule governs the movements of a planet or light ray.

It is not a logical deduction from Einstein's theory that space is finite. If the universe does not extend forever into space, but has finite limitations, no definite boundaries can be established. There are many cosmological models presently being considered with all sorts of different geometrical properties.

Of all the great scientific discoveries and findings coming from Einstein, his contributions to atomic theory have had the most direct and profound effect on the present-day world. Shortly after his first paper on relativity was published in 1905, in the *Annalen der Physik*, the same journal carried a short article by Einstein projecting his theory further. It was entitled "Does the Inertia of a Body Depend on Its Energy?" The mass-energy relation is a corollary of the special theory of relativity. At the time, he did not state that the use of atomic energy was possible. Later, he pointed out that the release of this tremendous force could be achieved according to a formula he offered, the most celebrated equation in history: $E = mc^2$. To interpret, energy equals mass multiplied by the speed of light and again by the speed of light. If all the energy in a half pound of any matter could be utilized, Einstein held, enough power would be released to equal the explosive force of seven million tons of TNT. Without Einstein's equation, as one commentator pointed out, "experimenters might still have stumbled upon the fission of uranium, but it is doubtful if they would have realized its significance in terms of energy, or of bombs."

In the famous equation $E = mc^2$, Einstein demonstrated that energy and mass are proportional to each other, differing only in state. Mass is actually concentrated energy. The formula, wrote Lincoln Barnett in a brilliant evaluation, "provides the answer to many of the long-standing mysteries of physics. It explains how radioactive substances like radium and uranium are able to eject particles at enormous velocities and to go on doing so for millions of years. It explains how the sun and all the stars can go on radiating light and heat for billions of years, for if our sun were being consumed by ordinary processes of combustion the earth would have died in frozen darkness eons ago. It reveals the magnitude of the energy that slumbers in the nuclei of atoms, and forecasts how many grams of uranium must go into a bomb in order to destroy a city."

Einstein's equation remained a theory until 1939. By that time, its author had become a resident, and was shortly to become a citizen, of the United States, for he had been driven out of Europe by the Nazis. Learning that the Germans were engaged in importing uranium and were carrying on research on an atomic bomb, Einstein wrote President Roosevelt a highly confidential letter:

Some recent work by E. Fermi and L. Szilard, which has been communicated to me in manuscript, leads me to expect that the element uranium may be turned into a new and important source of energy in the immediate future. . . . This new phenomenon would also lead to the construction of bombs, and it is conceivable . . . that . . . a single bomb of this type, carried by boat and exploded in a port, might very well destroy the whole port together with some of the surrounding territory.

As an immediate result of Einstein's letter to Roosevelt, construction of the Manhattan atom-bomb project was started. About five years later, the first bomb was exploded at the Alamogordo reservation in New Mexico, and shortly thereafter the dreadful destruction caused by a bomb dropped on Hiroshima was instrumental in bringing the war with Japan to a quick end.

Though the atomic bomb was the most spectacular of all practical applications of the theories of Einstein, his fame was also established by another remarkable accomplishment. Almost simultaneously with his special theory of relativity in 1905, there was developed Einstein's photoelectric law, explaining the mysterious photoelectric effect. Einstein's finding was extremely important, as being one of the fundamental particles of nature—the "light-quantum" or photon—and it was also extremely important as a step toward the discovery of quantum mechanics several decades later. It was for the discovery of the photoelectric law that Einstein was awarded the Nobel Prize in physics in 1922.

In his later years, Einstein labored indefatigably on what is known as the unified field theory, attempting to demonstrate the harmony and uniformity of nature. According to his view, physical laws for the minute atom should be equally applicable to immense celestial bodies. The unified field theory would unite all physical phenomena into a single scheme. Gravitation, electricity, magnetism, and atomic energy are all forces that would be covered by the one theory. In 1950, after more than a generation of research, Einstein presented such a theory to the world. He expressed the belief that the theory holds the key to the universe, unifying in one concept the infinitesimal, whirling world of the atom and the vast reaches of star-filled space. Because of mathematical difficulties, the theory has not yet been fully checked against established facts in physics. Einstein had unshaken faith, however, that his unified field theory would in time produce an explanation of the "atomic character of energy," and demonstrate the existence of a well-ordered universe. He did not regard the theory as anything that could be tested experimentally, however, and present-day physicists are not inclined to believe that the theory will prove fruitful.

The philosophy which inspired and guided Einstein through decades of intense intellectual effort, and the rewards therefrom, were described by him in a lecture on the origins of the general theory of relativity, at the University of Glasgow in 1933.

The final results appear almost simple; any intelligent undergraduate can understand them without much trouble. But the years of searching in the dark for a truth that one feels, but cannot express; the intense desire and the alternations of confidence and misgiving, until one breaks through to clarity and understanding, are only known to him who has himself experienced them.

On another occasion, Einstein gave evidence of the deeply spiritual side of his nature by this statement:

The most beautiful and most profound emotion we can experience is the sensation of the mystical. It is the sower of all true science. He to whom this emotion is a stranger, who can no longer wonder and stand rapt in awe, is as good as dead. To know that what is impenetrable to us really exists, manifesting itself as the highest wisdom and the most radiant beauty which our dull faculties can comprehend only in their most primitive forms—this knowledge, this feeling is at the center of true religiousness.

Innumerable scientists have paid tribute to Einstein. Quotations from two recent reviews of his career will illustrate his unique hold on the scientific world. Paul Oehser wrote:

Influence is a weak word for the work of Albert Einstein. The theories he advanced were revolutionary. In them was born the Atomic Age, and where it leads mankind we know not. But we do know that here is the greatest scientist and philosopher of our century, who has become almost a saint in our eyes and whose achievement is a justification of our faith in the human mind, a symbol of man's eternal quest, his reaching for the stars.

Another scientist, Banesh Hoffman, concluded:

The importance of Einstein's scientific ideas does not reside merely in their great success. Equally powerful has been their psychological effect. At a crucial epoch in the history of science Einstein demonstrated that long-accepted ideas were not in any way sacred. And it was this more than anything else that freed the imaginations of men like Bohr and de Broglie and inspired their daring triumphs in the realm of the quantum. Wherever we look, the physics of the 20th century bears the indelible imprint of Einstein's genius.

Concerning the present status of relativity, an international conference of theoretical physicists, at Berne, Switzerland, recently agreed that the foundations of the special and general theory have been universally accepted. Experiments have conclusively confirmed the special theory and are convincing for the general theory. The special theory has been incorporated into general physics and is used continually in atomic and nuclear physics.

For a number of years, the general theory was applied mainly to cosmology and cosmogony, but lately relativity is being applied to microphysical problems. The relationship to the quantum theory is still quite undetermined. It is apparent that general relativity provides a new approach to the ultimate properties of space and time. If true, the theory may have as much bearing on the physics of the very small as of the very large. The increasing worldwide interest in general relativity indicates that scientists believe the theory may add further to our understanding of the universe as an organic whole.

29

UPSETTING THE BALANCE OF NATURE

Rachel Carson: Silent Spring

In its impact on public consciousness and demand for instant action, *Silent Spring* (1962) was comparable to Tom Paine's *Common Sense,* Harriet Beecher Stowe's *Uncle Tom's Cabin,* and Upton Sinclair's *The Jungle.* In it Rachel Carson described the disastrous effects on the balance of nature caused by the irresponsible use of insecticides and other pest controls.

Actually, the dark picture painted by Rachel Carson, an eminent marine biologist, was part of a larger canvas—the overwhelming problem of pollution of the air, water, and land which was increasingly disturbing the conscience of the American people. Public-spirited citizens everywhere were realizing with alarm that man was ruining his environment by fouling the air he breathed, the water he drank, the soil that produced his food, and the food itself. Automobiles were filling the cities with lethal fumes; smog was settling down in choking volume on virtually all large urban centers; human and industrial wastes were being dumped into lakes, rivers, and streams, killing fish and steadily reducing potable water resources; oil wastes dumped into the sea were killing millions of seabirds and ruining beaches, and further pollution of the ocean was resulting from the dumping of industrial atomic wastes. Beginning with World War II, the dangerous fallout from nuclear bomb explosions had posed an even more serious dilemma for the world at large.

This was the background against which Rachel Carson wrote. She begins her shocking story with a fable, in which she tells of a small American town, set in the heart of prosperous farmland, with its wild flowers, numerous songbirds, and well-stocked trout streams. "Then a strange blight crept over the area and everything began to change. Some evil spell had settled on the community: mysterious maladies swept the flocks of chickens; the cattle and sheep sickened and died. Everywhere was a shadow of death." Doctors discovered new kinds of sickness appearing among their patients. "There was a strange stillness. The birds, for example—where had they gone? . . . On the mornings that had once throbbed with the dawn chorus of robins, catbirds, doves, jays, wrens, and scores of other bird voices there was now no sound; only silence lay over the fields and woods and marsh."

The town described does not actually exist. "I know of no community that has experienced all the misfortunes," writes Carson, "yet every one of these disasters has actually happened somewhere, and many real communities have already suffered a substantial number of them." What has silenced the voice of spring in countless places, she contends, is indiscriminate blanket spraying of vast areas from airplanes with potent chemicals, and similar misuses of insecticides and herbicides.

The beginnings of the devastation so graphically condemned by Carson were mainly a by-product of World War II. In experiments with agents for chemical warfare, it was found that some of the compounds were deadly to insects. After the war, chemical manufacturers, drug companies, agricultural schools, and government agencies started actively to develop and to promote the use of killers designed to exterminate various types of insects and undesirable plant growths. Handed these new weapons, the forester sprayed to protect his trees, the cranberry picker to protect his bogs, the cotton planter to save his cotton from the boll weevil, and so on down a long procession of farmers and gardeners—with little or no understanding of or concern for the consequences.

For centuries, man had fought to control pests—insects, rodents, weeds, bacteria, and other forms. Until World War II, the chief pesticides were Paris green, arsenic, nicotine, and vegetable derivatives lethal to cold-blooded animals. The chemicals added to the plant-growers' arsenal in the postwar period included the chlorinated hydrocarbons, such as DDT, and the organo-phosphorus substances, of which parathon is a common example. As a direct result of their use, Carson states:

For the first time in the history of the world, every human being is now subjected to contact with dangerous chemicals, from the moment of conception until death. In the less than two decades of their use, the synthetic pesticides have been so thoroughly distributed through-out the animate and inanimate world that they occur virtually every-where. They have been recovered from most of the major river sys-tems and even from streams of groundwater flowing unseen through the earth. Residues of these chemicals linger in soil to which they may have been applied a dozen years before. They have entered and lodged in the bodies of fish, birds, reptiles, and domestic and wild animals so universally that scientists carrying on animal experiments find it al-most impossible to locate subjects free from such contamination. They have been found in fish in remote mountain lakes, in earthworms bur-rowing in soil, in the eggs of birds—and in man himself. For these chemicals are now stored in the bodies of the vast majority of human beings, regardless of age. They occur in the mother's milk, and prob-ably in the tissues of the unborn child.

The sprays, dusts, and aerosols have the power to kill all insects, good and bad, Carson points out, as well as the birds and the fish, and to poison the soil, perhaps permanently—all to get rid of a few weeds and insects. The poisons are insoluble in water and therefore pollute the surfaces of fruits, vegetables, grasses, and grains. Aiming at a troublesome beetle, the chem-ists have wiped out the bird life of whole regions; aiming at a weevil, they have exterminated the race of bald eagles; aiming to save man from malaria, they have put several known cancer-causing agents into permanent circulation; aiming at an insect which was destroying commercial spruce plantations, the Ca-nadians killed off all the salmon of three generations in four large rivers.

Carson builds a damning and persuasive case with innumer-able other specific instances of the destruction being wrought by pesticides. In the mid-nineteen-fifties, the city of East Lansing, Michigan, began a massive spraying of the Michigan State Uni-versity campus to kill beetles which carry Dutch elm disease. The sprayed leaves fell to the ground in the autumn, and were eaten by worms. In the spring, robins ate the worms and within a week nearly all the robins were dead. In eastern Canada, where budworms were gradually killing off the balsams, there was ex-tensive spraying of the forests. "Soon after the spraying had ended," reports Carson, "there were unmistakable signs that all was not well. Within two days dead and dying fish, including many young salmon, were found along the banks of the stream. Brook trout also appeared among the dead fish, and along the roads and in the woods birds were dying. All the life of the stream was stilled."

As a result of the spraying of Clear Lake, California, with DDT, to rid it of gnats for the comfort of fishermen, the swan-like western grebes began dying, until they had dwindled from 1,000 to 30 pairs. In the National Wildlife Refuges at Tule Lake and the Lower Namath, also in California, herons, pelicans, grebes, and gulls died in great numbers—the victims of insecticide residue which had been building up to lethal strength in the water flowing from heavily sprayed agricultural lands. In the Midwest, indiscriminate spraying for the Japanese beetle virtually annihilated robins, meadowlarks, brown thrashers, and pheasants in Blue Island and Sheldon, Illinois.

In "A Postscript to Rachel Carson," Clark C. Van Fleet, California sportsman, author, and conservationist, commented on the increasing use of sodium fluoroacetate, known as "1080." "Used in conjunction with grain as a rodent bait," he observed, "a single kernel will immediately kill a mouse, a rat, a squirrel or a rabbit. . . . Over a hundred deer carcasses were found within a small compass where state agents had carelessly scattered poison grain. . . . Some three thousand ducks and geese in Siskiyou County, California, died as the result of improper spread of grain containing 1080 as a poison for ground squirrels. Hawks and eagles were also found dead."

Two years after the publication of *Silent Spring* the United States Public Health Service had positive proof that the pesticide Endrin was responsible for the deaths of ten million fish in the lower Mississippi River and the Gulf of Mexico; the poison had reached the river through runoff from farms. In July 1968, *Newsweek* reported, "In Borneo, health officials recently launched a campaign to rid rural villages of flies. DDT did the job quickly, but the cure turned out to be worse than the disease. Lizards who ate the flies accumulated the poison in their bodies. Cats ate the lizards and died. Soon the rat population started to proliferate, and plague threatened the entire region."

Rachel Carson continually stressed the perils to man himself from the widespread use or misuse of pesticides. If the chemicals are deadly to animal and plant life, can man eat contaminated meats and vegetables with impunity? A few human victims had already died in convulsions from exposure to certain highly concentrated pesticides, the author points out, and she fears that many others will eventually die of cancer, leukemia, hepatitis, or other dread diseases possibly caused by pesticides. Lethal poisons spread across the land, are blown into farm homes, settle on food, and pollute tanks and ponds. Emphysema, a serious lung disorder, unheard of until recent years, is becoming common in country areas, and respiratory illnesses are increasing by leaps and bounds in orchard and berry country. Because of birth-to-death exposure to dangerous chemicals, there is a progressive buildup of poison in our bodies, and the cumulative effect may well be disastrous. And too, many common insecticides for household use are highly toxic.

The basic fallacy overlooked by those who make extensive use of pesticides, Rachel Carson holds, is that they are upsetting the balance of nature. A vital fact which they ignore is that all life is one life, that the countless species of animals and plants and the soil, water, and air they live on are all intimately interconnected and interdependent. The ancient network of living things, in which each animal and plant depended upon every other one, has been upset by man, who is continually engaged in molding the environment to his own advantage. He must be supreme in nature, the human egotist believes, and the changes he makes are often sudden and profound—and frequently irreversible. Too often, man has looked upon himself as opposed to nature, not as a part of her, and in his efforts to subdue, he has ravished and destroyed.

One of the frightening ways in which nature fights back is to produce new and more dangerous pests. Chemicals have quickly killed off the weak and feeble among the creatures attacked, but permanent control over the survivors is not gained. A thorough spraying may kill 90 per cent of a particular species. The hardier members, however, are resistant to the spray and survive; when they reproduce, most of their offspring inherit the immunity. Furthermore, the survivors often reproduce in fantastic numbers. To combat the new superpests, the chemists develop ever more poisonous sprays, thereby increasing the danger to all living things, including man. Thus, Carson concludes, in upsetting the balance of nature, we are fighting a losing battle: "As crude a weapon as the cave man's club, the chemical barrage has been hurled against the fabric of life—a fabric on one hand delicate and destructible, on the other miraculously tough and resilient, and capable of striking back in unexpected ways."

As the author of two best-sellers, *The Sea Around Us* and *The Edge of the Sea*, Carson was already famous before *Silent*

Spring was published. Readers had a foretaste of her newest book through its partial serialization in *The New Yorker*. When *Silent Spring* came off the press, it was an instant best-seller; it remained on the *New York Times* list for thirty-one weeks, and sold 500,000 copies in hard cover before being brought out in paperback. The book had an immediate and profound effect on American opinion. The potential dangers of pesticides became known to all, and popular pressure speeded up research in industry and government.

After *Silent Spring* was published, the federal government began an investigation of its pesticide control programs to find an answer to how to use chemical pesticides more safely. A world conference, called by the United Nations Food and Agriculture Organization, met in Rome in 1965 to study how pesticides can be used effectively without harming people. The British Ministry of Agriculture, Fisheries, and Food in March 1964 placed severe restrictions on the use of three widely used insecticides related to DDT—aldrin, dieldrin, and heptachlor. The United States Congress in April 1964 closed a a loophole in the machinery for control by ending the "protest registration" system under which a manufacturer whose product was disapproved by the Department of Agriculture could continue to make and sell it. Legislatures in a number of states also tightened controls.

As could have been anticipated, the multi-million-dollar chemical industry, so vigorously attacked by Carson, reacted violently. She had claimed that the industry's introduction of more and more chemicals was often based on profit rather than need. The Carson book was characterized by one commentator as "the most massive indictment of an entire industrial complex since the days of Ida Tarbell." The great corporations involved (mainly the major oil companies and their affiliates, the petrochemical companies), the economic entomologists, officials of the United States Department of Agriculture, and agricultural research workers generally did not submit tamely to the scathing criticisms aimed at them.

A spokesman for the chemical industry, Dr. Robert White-Stevens of the American Cyanamid Company, issued a blast stating that "the book's major claims . . . are gross distortions of the actual facts, completely unsupported by scientific, experimental evidence, and general practical experience in the field." Carson was accused of unfairness, prejudice, and hysteria, and the image of a crackpot was built up by her enemies, who chose to ignore her long career as a professional biologist, her sixteen years' experience with the Fish and Wildlife Service, and other accomplishments.

Departing from personalities, the critics asserted that chemical herbicides and insecticides have become necessary to man's survival. Without them, in a short time there would be no more marketable fruits or vegetables. If chemical pesticides were discontinued, they added, the agricultural areas of the world would soon be ravaged by hordes of grasshoppers, weevils, and other insect invaders. Chemical sprays make possible the huge food crops that farmers can now grow. Lacking them, surplus food stores would vanish, whole populations would starve, rivers and fields would be choked with weeds, and certain diseases would get out of control. Thus, the commercial interests and their spokesmen among the scientists presented a picture as one-sided and scary as anything in *Silent Spring*.

A telling argument used by pesticide supporters is that such chemicals have virtually eradicated many diseases. Mosquitoes, lice, ticks, fleas, and other insects are carriers of malaria, yellow fever, sleeping sickness, typhus, and other scourges. Malaria, which was formerly widely prevalent, has been practically stamped out in the United States and a number of other countries through the use of insecticides. In short, maintain the proponents of pesticides, man has no choice except to upset the balance of nature. Otherwise, the insects will eventually inherit the earth.

Propaganda is not expected to give both sides of an argument, and *Silent Spring* is a fiercely passionate tract—emotional, dramatic, sensational in many respects. Nevertheless, Carson concedes that farm chemicals have a place. "It is not my contention," she writes, "that chemical insecticides must never be used. I do contend that we have put poisonous and biologically potent chemicals indiscriminately into the hands of persons largely or wholly ignorant of their potentials for harm."

Carson offers various constructive alternatives to the use of chemical pesticides. She affirms that in many cases biological controls would be safer than chemical controls. The use of such natural controls has been limited; only about one hundred insect predators have been successfully introduced into the United States. Other alternatives to insecticides are parasites, resistant crop varieties, sterilization of male insects by radiation, chemical sterilants, sex lures and physical attractants, such as light, to draw insects into traps. The potentialities of these approaches were pointed out by an English science writer, Edward Hyams, in an article for the *New Statesman* (February 15, 1963):

Where biologists, and not commercially-interested chemists, have been in charge, methods used to control troublesome insects, and even weeds, have been ecologically sound: there have been some astonishing successes, for example, in inoculating communities of troublesome creatures with the parasites natural to them, often brought from overseas, and in establishing these parasites permanently so that the control is stable and continuous. It is also and invariably enormously cheaper than the chemical methods. Very little work has been done in this field; but there is no doubt at all that if it can be done by biologists and naturalists who understand the whole picture—and not, like the entomologists, only one small piece of it—biological control of most and perhaps all "pests" can be achieved.

This is Carson's vital solution: that insects, pests, and undesirable growths may be controlled by encouraging their enemies —a proposal offered at the beginning of the nineteenth century by Charles Darwin's grandfather, Erasmus Darwin. Ragweed causing hay fever can be fought, writes Carson, by maintaining the dense shrubs and ferns that help to crowd it out; fight crabgrass by providing better soil for high-quality lawn grass; "fight insects by seeking to turn the strength of the species against itself," instead of by the careless, unrestrained use of chemicals. "As matters stand now," asserts Carson, "we are in little better position than the guests of the Borgias."

The chief problem in applying biological controls appears to be a lack of research. According to a recent report, only about one hundred biologists are actively engaged in such research, a majority of them in California. The reason is financial: the universities depend upon industry for research grants and the chemical industry provides 98 percent of the funds for pest-control research. Moreover, the lucrative positions are in chemical research, while biologists must be satisfied with lower-paid jobs as teachers, government workers, or with growers' associations.

Objective appraisals of the situation by scientists with no particular axes to grind have concluded that there is a middle ground where chemistry, biology, wildlife, and mankind can coexist. The complex problems, they say, must be attacked by ecologists and biologists, qualified to assess all factors in the environment; specialists in the medical profession must evaluate and control dangers to public health; and more federal and state funds must be provided for basic research.

An exclamation point was added to Carson's dire warnings when, two years after the appearance of *Silent Spring*, she herself died of cancer. In a front-page obituary, the *New York Times* called Rachel Carson "one of the most influential women of her time." Senator Abraham Ribicoff, former United States Secretary of Health, Education, and Welfare, summed up her career by stating: "This gentle lady, more than any other person of her time, aroused people everywhere to be concerned with one of the most significant problems of mid-20th century life—man's contamination of his environment." Stewart L. Udall, Secretary of the Interior, one of Carson's warmest admirers and supporters, added: "In the success of *Silent Spring* was the hope that those who truly care about the land have a fighting chance to 'inherit' the earth. That the pen of one so unassuming should have such an impact on national events was remarkable, and a heartening sign to conservationists everywhere."

BIBLIOGRAPHICAL NOTES

AESCHYLUS (525–456 B.C.)

Tragoediae Sex [Greek]. Venice: Aldus Manutius, 1518.

AESOPUS (c. 620–560 B.C.)

Fabulae. Utrecht (?): Printer of the *Speculum*, c. 1472. First Greek edition, Venice: Bartholomaeus Justinopolitanus, c. 1498.

ARCHIMEDES (287?–212 B.C.)

Opera Omnia [Greek]. Basle: Joannes Hervagius, 1544.

ARISTOPHANES (c. 448–380 B.C.)

Comoediae Novem [Greek]. Venice: Aldus Manutius, 1498.

ARISTOTLE (384–322 B.C.)

Opera. Augsburg: Ambrosius Keller, 1479. First Greek edition; Venice: Aldus Manutius, 1495–98.

AUGUSTINUS, AURELIUS (354–430)

Confessiones. Strassburg: Johann Mentelin, c. 1470; *De Civitate Dei.* [Subiaco: Conradus Sweynheym and Arnoldus Pannartz] 1467.

BIBLE (c. 1000 B.C.–A.D. 150)

Biblia Latina. Mainz: Printer of the 42-line Bible (Johann Gutenberg), c. 1454–55. English translations: Douai (Roman Catholic Version), New Testament: Rheims: John Fogny, 1582; Old Testament: Doway: Laurence Kellam, 1609–10, 2 vols.; King James (Authorized Version): London: Robert Barker, 1611.

CARSON, RACHEL (1907–1964)

Silent Spring. Boston: Houghton Mifflin, 1962. 368 pp.

393

COPERNICUS, NICOLAUS (1473–1543)
De Revolutionibus Orbium Coelestium. Nuremberg: Johann Petrus, 1543. 196 ff. The first accurate and complete edition was published in 1873, at Thorn (Torun), Poland, by the Copernicus-Verein für Wissenschaft und Kunst.

The first written account of his theories, entitled *Commentariolus,* "Little Commentary," was circulated by Copernicus among students of astronomy perhaps as early as 1510, but was not published in the author's lifetime. The first printed account, *Narratio Prima,* written by a fervent admirer, George Joachim Rheticus, appeared in 1540.

DARWIN, CHARLES ROBERT (1809–1882)
On the Origin of Species by Means of Natural Selection, or the Preservation of Favoured Races in the Struggle for Life. London: J. Murray, 1859. 502 pp.

Darwin's *Journal of a Naturalist* (1839), later expanded into *A Naturalist's Voyage Round the World in H.M.S. Beagle* (1860), describes the beginning of his life work. The theme of the *Origin of Species* was subsequently developed in detail in *The Descent of Man, and Selection in Relation to Sex* (1871), *The Variation of Animals and Plants Under Domestication* (1868), *Expression of the Emotions* (1872), *The Effects of Cross- and Self-Fertilization in the Vegetable Kingdom* (1876), *The Power of Movement in Plants* (1880), and other specialized works.

EINSTEIN, ALBERT (1879–1955)
Relativity, the Special and General Theory. New York: Holt, 1920. 168 pp. Translated from the original German edition of 1916. The 15th edition, incorporating Einstein's more recent thought, was published in 1954.

EURIPIDES (c. 480–406 B.C.)
Tragoediae Quattour. Medea, Hippolytus, Alcestis, and Andromache [Greek]. [Florence: Laurentius de Alopa, 1495] First collected edition, Venice: Aldus Manutius, 1503.

FREUD, SIGMUND (1856–1939)
Die Traumdeutung. Leipzig: F. Deuticke, 1900. 375 pp. Translated by A. A. Brill as *The Interpretation of Dreams.* New York: Macmillan, 1913.

Freud advanced and developed his theories in a long series of publications, of which the most important are *Three Contributions to the Theory of Sex* (1905), *Introductory Lectures on Psychoanalysis* (1916), and *The Ego and the Id* (1923). He was indebted to the *Lessons on the Maladies of the Nervous System* (1880) by the French neurologist, Jean Martin Charcot; to the writings of Pierre Janet, French physician and psychologist; and to James Braid, nineteenth-century English writer on hypnotism and magic.

HARVEY, WILLIAM (1578–1657)

Exercitatio Anatomica de Motu Cordis et Sanguinis in Animalibus. Frankfort: William Fitzer, 1628. 72 pp.

Harvey had predecessors: Vesalius in *De Humani Corporis Fabrica* (1543) noted that the septum between the right and left ventricles is complete; Servetus, in his *Christianismi Restitutio* (1553), stated his belief that the blood circulates through the lungs, but he did not recognize the heart as the pumping organ; Realdo Colombo, author of *De Re Anatomica* (1559), anatomy professor at Rome, correctly taught that blood passes from the right to the left ventricle through the lungs; Fabricius of Padua, Harvey's teacher, author of *De Venarum Ostiolis* (1603), discovered and described the valves of the veins.

HERODOTUS (c. 484–425 B.C.)

Historiae. Venice: Jacobus Rubeus, 1474. First Greek edition, Venice: Aldus Manutius, 1502.

HIPPOCRATES (c. 460–377 B.C.)

Aphorismi. Venice: [Bartolomaeus de Cremona?], 1473. First Greek edition, *Omnia Opera.* Venice: Aldus Manutius, 1526.

HITLER, ADOLF (1889–1945)

Mein Kampf. Munich: F. Eher, 1925–27. 2 vols.

The principal precursors of the Hitlerian racial theories were Joseph Arthur Gobineau's *Essay on the Inequality of the Human Races* (4 vols., 1853–55) and Houston Stewart Chamberlain's *The Foundations of the Nineteenth Century* (1911), both attributing to Teutonic genius all advances in European civilization and attacking mixed races and Jews.

HOMERUS (c. 850 B.C.)

    Opera. [tr. Carolus Aretinus] Venice: n. pr., c. 1475. First Greek edition, Florence: Bernardus Nerlius and others, 1488.

JENNER, EDWARD (1749–1823)

    An Inquiry into the Causes and Effects of the Variolae Vaccinae, a Disease Discovered in Some of the Western Counties of England, Particularly Gloucestershire, and Known by the Name of the Cow Pox. London: S. Low, 1798. 75 pp.

LIVIUS, TITUS (59 B.C.–A.D. 17)

    Historiae Romanae Decades. Rome: Conradus Sweynheym and Arnoldus Pannartz [1469].

LUCRETIUS CARUS, TITUS (99–55 B.C.)

    De Rerum Natura. Brescia: Fernandus [c. 1473].

MACHIAVELLI, NICCOLÒ (1469–1527)

    Il Principe. First edition, Rome: Antonio Blado, 1532. 53 ff.

    Machiavelli's *Discourses on the First Ten Books of Titus Livius* (1521) gives a better rounded and more complete statement of his views on political organization than does *The Prince*. His *The Art of War* (1521) and *History of Florence* (1532) are also primarily concerned with politics, ancient and contemporary.

MACKINDER, SIR HALFORD JOHN (1861–1947)

    "The Geographical Pivot of History." Royal Geographical Society, *Proceedings*, January 25, 1904 (London). *Geographical Journal*, XXIII (1904), p. 431–37. Definitive edition: *Democratic Ideals and Reality*. London: Constable, 1919. 272 pp.

    Karl Haushofer, German geographer and political adviser to Hitler, wrote voluminously on geopolitics, directly inspired by Mackinder's theories. Among his widely circulated works are: *Bausteine zur Geopolitik* (1928), *Weltpolitik von Heute* (1934), *Geopolitik des Pazifischen Ozeans* (1924), *Wehr-Geopolitik* (1932), and *Weltmeere und Weltmächte* (1937).

MAHAN, ALFRED THAYER (1840–1914)

    The Influence of Sea Power upon History, 1660–1783. Boston: Little, Brown, 1890. 557 pp.

Mahan continued his writings on sea power in a series of specialized works, notably *The Influence of Sea Power upon the French Revolution and Empire, 1793–1812; Sea Power in its Relations to the War of 1812;* and biographies of Farragut and Nelson.

MALTHUS, THOMAS ROBERT (1766–1834)

An Essay on the Principle of Population. London: J. Johnson, 1798. 396 pp. Five revised and enlarged editions were printed during the author's lifetime, 1803–26.

MARX, KARL (1818–1883)

Das Kapital; Kritik der Politischen Oekonomie. Hamburg: O. Meissner, 1867. Vol. I, 784 pp. The second and third volumes were published 1885–94, and a fourth was issued 1905–10.

MENANDER (c. 342–292 B.C.)

Ex Comoediis Menandri quae Supersunt. In: Morelius, Gulielmus, *Ex Veterum Comicorum Fabulis.* Paris: G. Morelius, 1553.

NEWTON, SIR ISAAC (1642–1727)

Philosophiae Naturalis Principia Mathematica. London: Printed by Joseph Streater for the Royal Society, 1687. 510 pp.

Newton's researches on light—the composition of light, the nature of color and of white light—which occupied his early years, were summed up in his *Opticks* (1704).

PAINE, THOMAS (1737–1809)

Common Sense, Addressed to the Inhabitants of America. Philadelphia: R. Bell, 1776. 79 pp.

Paine's political ideas were developed further in his *Rights of Man* (1791), written in defense of the French Revolution and answering Edmund Burke's hostile *Reflections on the Revolution in France.* His *Age of Reason* (1794–96), a deistic work sometimes unfairly described as the "atheist's Bible," was written, Paine maintained, to counteract the trend toward atheism among the French Revolutionary leaders.

PLATO (427–347 B.C.)
    Opera. Florence: Laurentius de Alopa [1484]. First Greek
    edition, Venice: Aldus Manutius, 1513.

PLINIUS SECUNDUS, GAIUS (23–79)
    Historia Naturalis. Venice: Johannes de Spira, 1469.

PLUTARCHUS (c. 45–120)
    Vitae Illustrium Virorum. [Rome]: Ulrich Han [1470–71].
    First Greek edition, [Florence, Philippus Giunta, 1517].

POLYBIUS (c. 204–122 B.C.)
    Historiae. Rome: Conradus Sweynheym and Arnoldus Pan-
    nartz, 1473. First Greek edition, Haguenau: Johannes Se-
    cerius, 1530.

SMITH, ADAM (1723–1790)
    *An Inquiry into the Nature and Causes of the Wealth of
    Nations.* London: W. Strahan and T. Cadell, 1776. 2 vols.

SOPHOCLES (495–406 B.C.)
    Tragoediae [Greek]. Venice: Aldus Manutius, 1502.

STOWE, HARRIET BEECHER (1811–1896)
    Uncle Tom's Cabin; or Life among the Lowly. Boston: J. P.
    Jewett, 1852. 2 vols. First published serially in the *National
    Era,* June 5, 1851–April 1, 1852.
        Two other works on slavery came from Mrs. Stowe's pen:
    A Key to Uncle Tom's Cabin (1853), written to prove that
    the original work was not exaggerated or "a tissue of lies,"
    as some detractors charged; and *Dred, A Tale of the Great
    Dismal Swamp* (1856), picturing the evil effects of the slave
    system upon the white man.

TACITUS, CORNELIUS (c. 55–120)
    Opera. [Venice]: Vindelinus de Spira [c. 1473].

THEOPHRASTUS (c. 370–287 B.C.)
    De Historia et Causis Plantarum. Treviso: Bartholomaeus
    Confalonerius, 1483. First Greek edition, Venice: Aldus
    Manutius, 1495–98.

THOMAS AQUINAS (c. 1225–1274)
Summa Theologicae. Basle: [Michael Wenssler], 1485. Part I, Cologne: Ulrich Zel, c. 1470.

THOREAU, HENRY DAVID (1817–1862)
"Resistance to Civil Government." *Aesthetic Papers,* edited by Elizabeth P. Peabody (Boston, 1849), pp. 189–211.

In his most famous book, *Walden, or Life in the Woods* (1854), which has been called the "spiritual autobiography of a rebel wearied by the machine age," Thoreau makes an appealing case for the simple life, for nonconformity and extreme individualism, and demonstrates the unimportance of material things.

THUCYDIDES (c. 455–399 B.C.)
Historia Belli Peloponnesiaci. [Treviso: Johannes Vercellensis, c. 1483.] First Greek edition, Venice: Aldus Manutius, 1502.

VESALIUS, ANDREAS (1514–1564)
De Humani Corporis Fabrica. Basle: Johannis Oporinus, 1543. 664 pp.

The universal genius Leonardo da Vinci (1452–1519) preceded Vesalius in scientific studies of human and animal anatomy and muscular movement, but Leonardo's notebooks containing his anatomical, physiological, and embryological drawings were not published until modern times and therefore may be presumed to have had little contemporary influence.

WOLLSTONECRAFT, MARY (1759–1797)
Vindication of the Rights of Woman. London: J. Johnson, 1792. 452 pp.

The few defenders in print of the rights of women before, and for some time after, Mary Wollstonecraft were men. There are enlightened passages in the writings of Swift, Defoe, and Holberg. Condorcet, and Holbach, among the philosophers of the French Revolution, urged equal citizenship and educational rights for women. William Thomson, socialist disciple of Robert Owen, wrote an *Appeal of One Half the Human Race, Women, Against the Pretensions of the Other Half, Men* (London, 1825). More influential was John Stuart Mill's *The Subjection of Women* (1869), which served as a text for the movement for women's rights throughout the world.

XENOPHON (c. 430–350 B.C.)
Opera [Greek]. Florence: P. Giuñta, 1516.